THESE THREE ARE ONE

Challenges in Contemporary Theology

Series Editors: Lewis Ayres and Gareth Jones

Challenges in Contemporary Theology is a series of co-ordinated books which will engage traditional theological concerns with the main challenges to those concerns. The intention of the series is to promote prospective, critical and contentious positions as well as providing summaries of current debates to situate the arguments of particular books. The series is aimed at advanced undergraduates, graduate students and scholars in appropriate fields.

Volumes will cover key areas of theological debate, fields that have not yet received sufficient theological discussion and will include books in the major themes of Christian theology, the engagement between modernity, postmodernism and theology, culture and media, Christian ethics and Christian self-definition.

Published Works

These Three Are One
The Practice of Trinitarian Theology
David S. Cunningham

After Writing
On The Liturgical Consummation of Philosophy
Catherine Pickstock

Forthcoming

Mystical Theology
The Integrity of Spirituality and Theology
Mark McIntosh

The Practice of Christian Doctrine
Lewis Ayres

Engaging Scripture
Stephen E. Fowl

Theology and Mass Communication
Robert Dodaro and John Paul Szura

THESE THREE ARE ONE

The Practice of Trinitarian Theology

David S. Cunningham

BLACKWELL
Publishers

First published 1998

2 4 6 8 10 9 7 5 3 1

Blackwell Publishers Inc.
350 Main Street
Malden, Massachusetts 02148
USA

Blackwell Publishers Ltd
108 Cowley Road
Oxford OX4 1JF
UK

Library of Congress Cataloging-in-Publication Data has been applied for.

ISBN 1-557-86962-6 (Hbk.)   1-557-86963-4 (Pbk.)

British Library Cataloguing in Publication Data

A CIP catalogue record for this book is available from the British Library.

Typeset in 10½ on 12 pt Bembo by Ace Filmsetting Ltd, Frome
Printed and bound in Great Britain by MPG Books Ltd, Bodmin, Cornwall

This book is printed on acid-free paper

To my wife
Teresa Anne Hittner

and to our daughters
Monica Claire and Emily Ruth
Hittner-Cunningham

who together have taught me
to listen to the music
to give thanks for communion
and to rejoice in difference

CONTENTS

PREFACE

This book is an attempt to think through Christian beliefs about God. Classically, this is called a "doctrine of God" – the word *doctrine* being understood through its Latin cognate, *doctrina*. One possible English translation of this word (and one that captures my purposes in writing) is *teaching*. To write a Christian doctrine of God is to attempt to describe what Christianity should teach – or, better, what Christians should learn – about God. Throughout much of the history of the Church it was widely assumed that, of all the various and sundry things Christians probably ought to learn, one of the most important was that God is *Trinity*: we believe in *the triune God*.

At some point, this widespread assumption lost its centrality; indeed, in some theological systems, it vanished altogether. Contemporary commentators have spilled a great deal of ink trying to sort out precisely when this marginalization of trinitarian doctrine occurred, and who was responsible for it. Fortunately, however, we need not resolve these questions here; wherever we may choose to lay the blame, the outcome is not in dispute. By the late eighteenth century it was possible to write theological accounts of the Christian faith in general, and of its understanding of God in particular, with little or no reference to the doctrine of the Trinity.

Yet despite the shifting sands of theological system-building, a good deal of Christian worship, devotional writing, and popular piety continued to be trinitarian. It would be misleading to suggest that, simply because of its rare appearance in academic theology, the doctrine of the Trinity was somehow "lost." Nevertheless, without occasional attempts to devote some sustained thought to the meaning and significance of a particular Christian belief, the practices that embody that belief can become hollow, insignificant, and ultimately unpersuasive – even to those who undertake such practices with diligence and love.

Fortunately, in the twentieth century, systematic accounts of Christian belief have begun to catch up with trinitarian practice. Theologians such as Karl Barth, Vladimir Lossky, Karl Rahner, and Hans Urs von Balthasar reaffirmed the centrality of the doctrine of the Trinity. In their wake, a number of contemporary thinkers – including Eberhard Jüngel, Walter Kasper, Jürgen Moltmann, and John Zizioulas – have helped put trinitarian categories back into active circulation. More recently, the cultural, ethical, and ecumenical significance of the doctrine has been explored by Leonardo Boff, Elizabeth Johnson, and Catherine Mowry LaCugna – among many, many others.

This "renaissance" of trinitarian theology is, in my view, a very good thing; and I say this despite my disagreements with some of the particulars in the work of the aforementioned theologians. Whatever refinements one might want to offer to a particular approach, we ought to give credit to those theologians who have been willing to attend to trinitarian questions. All the same, a significant theological challenge still lies ahead. To many people, including both Christians and non-Christians, this doctrine (at least as it has traditionally been elaborated) remains esoteric and irrelevant. Too often it is expressed in cryptic formulas, or described in densely compressed philosophical prose; this does little to set the doctrine in a bright and convincing light. Furthermore, the key terms of trinitarian theology continue to be translated with little appreciation for the contemporary context of their reception. Nor is the doctrine very often shown to be of great significance for the day-to-day lives of Christian believers.

In my view, the "next wave" of trinitarian theology should have three goals: (1) to release the doctrine from its imprisonment within the dusty confines of the history of dogma, translating it into our present context; (2) to render it more intelligible, to both Christians and non-Christians (while recognizing the differences between these two audiences); and (3) to testify to its profound significance for the shape of the Christian life. These goals have been foremost in my mind as I have attempted to offer a few reflections on "the practice of trinitarian theology." My use of the word *practice* is an attempt to express my conviction that the doctrine of the Trinity – despite the abstract language which it often must employ – is not just something that Christians *think*; it is also something that they *do*. It should thus be more than just a device for arranging the Tables of Contents in volume after volume of systematic theology. Our belief in the triune God shapes us in profound ways – affecting what we believe, what we say, how we think, and how we live.

Partly as a result of this conviction, I have attempted to make this book reasonably accessible to students and other non-specialists (a brief note, addressed to such readers, follows this preface). I have also engaged other disciplines (classical rhetoric, literature, and communication theory), and have proposed some significant changes – in the traditional translations and formulations of the doctrine, in the practice of trinitarian worship, and in the living of the Christian life. Some of these features may annoy those readers who consider them inappropriate in a work of trinitarian theology; other readers will be disappointed that some of the traditional elements of a "doctrine of God" are nowhere to be found in these pages. To such readers, I apologize in advance. Whatever its flaws, this book is an attempt to practice trinitarian theology, and to make it an interesting enough enterprise that others might be encouraged to do so as well. This approach to the theological task has an ancient pedigree; St Augustine, adopting a commonplace from classical rhetoric, believed that theology's goal was not only to teach, but also to delight and to move.

This book addresses methodological, historical, philosophical, and ethical questions, as well as strictly "doctrinal" ones. It thus reflects the wide-ranging interests of my own teachers – especially Nicholas Lash, Geoffrey Wainwright, and Rowan Williams – in whose debt I continue to stand. In fact, the first seeds for this book were planted when I read, in Professor Lash's book *Easter in Ordinary*, a chapter entitled "Newman and Some Triangles." I had often been told that the doctrine of the Trinity didn't really have anything to do with the numbers one and three; thus, Professor Lash's suggestion that it might, in fact, have a great deal to do with those numbers was intriguing and thought-provoking.

Today, my more immediate teachers are the ever-resourceful members of The Ψ Group – more informally known as "the Pigs" (don't ask why). This is an amorphous collection of former-fellow-graduate-students and their families, many of whom meet every summer to talk about Christian theology and its profound implications for belief, worship, and the practice of everyday life. Our conversations are never restricted to "esoteric" theological subjects; we also talk about how we think and how we live, about the challenges of parenting and the trials faced by our various ecclesial communities. My thanks, first, to those within the group who have probably taught me the most: Andrew, Brendan, Emily, Katie, Liam, Monica, Nate, Peter, Pippa, and Si. And thanks also to their parents, who read an earlier version of this manuscript and offered their usual spirited critiques at our 1995 gathering: A. K. M. Adam, Margaret Adam, Melinda Fowl, Steve Fowl, Teresa Hittner, and Phil Kenneson. As a result of our extended conversations, the entire project was reconceived, mercifully nipping in the bud its (wholly unachievable) pretensions to grandeur. Several group members continued to read drafts, providing comments and correcting errors, right through to the end. Together, these friends have shown me – through their own "practice of trinitarian theology" – a more integral vision of the Christian life.

Many others have offered sustained responses to earlier drafts of the entire book, or at least to substantial portions of it: Wes Avram, Jim Buckley, Robert Cathey, Bill Cavanaugh, Don Compier, Brad Hinze, Randy Maddox, and Steve Webb. Lewis Ayres even managed to read *two* drafts of the whole! Thanks to him and to Gareth Jones, editors of the Challenges series, who caught me in the middle of a family bicycle trip several years back to bring me in on the project.

I would also like to thank the members of two other groups with whom I have met regularly for theological discussion: the Dogmatics Colloquium of the Center for Catholic and Evangelical Theology, and the Lilly Foundation group on the Bible in Theological Education. Thanks to the University of St. Thomas for several internal grants (as well as the usual institutional support); and special thanks to the students in my seminars on the Doctrine of the Trinity during the spring terms of 1993 and 1995, since many of the ideas in this book were distilled in that most rigorous of laboratories – the classroom. Among these students, three deserve special mention: Elizabeth Pratt and Pamela Steiner, who worked as research assistants, and Heidi Kalenberg, whose paper on the trinitarian significance of the stained glass at her church first brought to my attention the image that graces the cover of this book. Thanks to Pam Fickenscher and Susan Windley for long-distance bibliographical assistance, and to Anthony Grahame for accurate and expeditious copy-editing. Finally, thanks to Michael Root and to the Institute for Ecumenical Research in Strasbourg, France, for support rendered when the completion of this book carried well over into a sabbatical year that had been intended for other projects.

In the writing of this book, and in my vocation as a theologian, I have received a tremendous amount of support from many sources, human and divine, known and unknown. To all of them I can only say, "thanks, and thanks, and ever thanks." My greatest debt – not only with respect to "professional" matters, but also for whatever capacity I may have for the authentic practice of trinitarian theology – is acknowledged on its dedication page.

Feast of the Annunciation
of our Lord Jesus Christ
to the Blessed Virgin Mary
Anno Domini 1997

A NOTE TO STUDENTS
AND NON-SPECIALISTS

I have tried to make much of this book accessible to non-specialists, including students (especially upper-level undergraduates and postgraduate students). However, it is not an "introduction" to trinitarian thought; it assumes some background in the history of the doctrine, including its roots in the biblical texts and in the early Church. If you lack this background, you may want to begin elsewhere and come back to this book afterwards. I provide a long list of recent texts, along with some comments about the particular "angle" of each, in Appendix I at the end of this book.

I'm assuming, then, that you have some background in trinitarian theology, and are simply interested in thinking about it further (or that you have been assigned to read this book!). I want to offer a few words of encouragement, since I know that much of what is written under the general heading of "theology" is *painfully* boring. My own students are often surprised when I acknowledge this; they assume that, since I'm a theologian, I must not find it boring or I wouldn't read it. Unfortunately, I too have to study material that I'd rather not even read. In fact, I've spent much of my scholarly life wading through great, thick tomes of dense prose – only to be reassured that, indeed, Christians ought to keep on believing precisely the same things they have always believed, in precisely the same way, and that their lives need not be much altered as a result. While reading such books, I vowed that I would never write one.

So although you will undoubtedly find some sections of this book to be a bit dry, I've also tried to make it interesting. You'll find material here relating trinitarian doctrine to other fields of study, including literature, literary theory, rhetoric, political science, and economics. As you'll see from the text, I think that Christian beliefs about God really do make a difference, and that some of the classical formulations of these beliefs are inadequate and need to be re-thought. I've tried to focus on issues that really matter, to talk about the practical and ethical ramifications of the doctrine, and to throw in a few surprises.

On the other hand, this book is not written "just" for students. Sometimes you'll find me engaging questions and issues that seem to be relevant only to professional theologians. I apologize for that; it's one of the inherent dangers in trying to write for a wide audience. But don't worry – even if you find certain sections to be unnecessarily esoteric, there will probably be scholars who will tell me (in their published reviews of this book) that those same sections weren't nearly esoteric *enough*.

In partial compensation for asking you to wade through these sections, I've added a few devices to make the book easier to use. Headings and subheadings appear often and are designed so that, when a section gets too turgid, readers can find a logical point of re-entry. (Students, beware – these are probably the sections that will come up in examinations . . .) I've also tried to confine most of the "scholarly infighting" to the footnotes – except in chapter 1, which examines what's been going on in the contemporary debate. I've also tried not to use the footnotes for anything I thought would be extraordinarily significant for students and general readers. In other words, you have my permission to skip the footnotes (unless your instructor tells you to read them – but then you'll have to blame her or him, not me!).

I also need to warn you that the book includes quite a few foreign words and phrases – mostly Greek, but also some Hebrew and a bit of Latin. I use these words because there is often something seriously misleading about a straightforward English translation of the word(s). When I first use these words, I usually try to offer a brief comment on how they might be rendered into English (or why they can't be); sometimes, though, it's not possible to provide such an explanation within the text, or to do so at sufficient length. Thus, I've added a glossary at the back of the book (Appendix II); all the foreign words and phrases appear there (indexed by page number, so that you can always find what you're looking for, even if you are unfamiliar with the particular alphabet). In each case I've offered a transliteration of the word (for the Greek and Hebrew) and a description of some of the issues and problems surrounding the word's translation into English.

Finally, for those who are interested in how some of the new trinitarian language that I propose in this book might find its way into the liturgy, I offer some worship-related resources in Appendix III.

I would never claim that trinitarian theology is an easy practice; writing this book was certainly a difficult enough endeavor. But I do think it is an important practice, and a rewarding one.

And now to business.

Quoniam tres sunt, qui testimonium dant in coelo
Pater, Verbum et Spiritus Sanctus,
et hi tres unum sunt.

Et tres sunt, qui testimonium dant in terra
Spiritus et aqua et sanguis,
et hi tres unum sunt.

For there are three who bear witness in heaven,
the Source, the Word, and the Holy Spirit,
and these three are one.

And there are three who bear witness on earth,
the Spirit and the water and the blood,
and these three are one.

                    1 John 5:7, the "Johannine Comma"

ABBREVIATIONS

CD   Karl Barth, *Church Dogmatics*, 4 parts in 14 vols, trans. and ed. G. W. Bromiley, T. F. Torrance, and others (Edinburgh: T. & T. Clark, 1958–77).

Denz   Heinrich Denzinger, *Enchiridion Symbolorum*, 37. Aufl., hrsg. Peter Hünermann und Helmut Hoping (Freiburg: Herder, 1991).

KD   Karl Barth, *Die Kirchliche Dogmatik*, 4 parts in 14 vols (Zollikon–Zürich: Evangelischer Verlag, 1932–70).

ST   St Thomas Aquinas, *Summa Theologiae*, cited by part, article, and question, followed by a reference to the Blackfriars edition, 60 vols (New York: McGraw-Hill; London: Eyre and Spottiswoode, 1963–70).

T-D '   Hans Urs von Balthasar, *Theo-Drama: Theological Dramatic Theory*, 5 vols, trans. Graham Harrison (San Francisco: Ignatius Press, 1988–).

TD   Hans Urs von Balthasar, *Theodramatik*, 4 parts in 5 vols (Einsiedeln: Johannes Verlag, 1973–83).

Classical sources are cited according to the abbreviations in *The Oxford Classical Dictionary*, ed. N. G. L. Hammond and H. H. Scullard, 2nd edn (Oxford: Clarendon, 1970).

Complete bibliographical information is listed at the first citation of a work, except in the case of recent studies of trinitarian theology; these are listed in an annotated bibliography (Appendix I). Information on the original-language edition of works, when available, appears in square brackets after the citation of the English translation.

Biblical quotations, unless otherwise noted, follow the translation of the New Revised Standard Version, sometimes slightly altered.

Introduction

PRACTICE

. . . the words *you utter or what you think as you utter them are not what matters, so much as the difference they make at various points in your life. How do I know that two people mean the same when each says he believes in God? And just the same goes for belief in the Trinity. A theology which insists on the use of* certain particular *words and phrases, and outlaws others, does not make anything clearer (Karl Barth). It gesticulates with words, as one might say, because it wants to say something and does not know how to express it.* Practice *gives the words their sense.*

Ludwig Wittgenstein[1]

"The words you utter" and "what you think as you utter them" would seem, at first glance, to be of great significance for Christian theology. Over the past two thousand years, theologians have expended an enormous amount of energy in arguments about the use of one set of words over another. These debates have sometimes gone on for centuries, and have profoundly shaped the course of Christian history. The word *theology* itself includes the suffix *-logy*, which appears in the names of many academic disciplines; this suffix derives from a Greek word that means (among other things) *word*. Given the monumental theological significance of *words*, Wittgenstein's claim that they are "not what matters" would seem to be, at the very least, inapplicable to theology.

Surprisingly, however, it is precisely to theology that Wittgenstein turns in order to provide a specific example of his more general point. He focuses first

---

[1] *Culture and Value*, ed. G. H. von Wright and Heikki Nyman, trans. Peter Winch (Chicago: University of Chicago Press, 1980) [ET of: *Vermischte Bemerkungen* (Frankfurt am Main: Suhrkamp Verlag, 1977)], 85.

on the word *God* – noting that its invocation by two different people does nothing to guarantee that they are talking about the same thing. The word *God* has become such a standard piece of linguistic furniture for us that we often forget how many different references it can have. For example, in one of the courses that I teach, I ask my students to read Descartes's *Meditations* and Pascal's *Pensées*. Both writers make much use of the word *God*, and students naturally assume that their uses have a common point of reference. Before long, however, it becomes obvious that they are using the same word to mean two profoundly different things. Pascal is referring to a portrait of God gleaned from reading the Bible and the creeds, and Descartes is referring to a portrait which specifically excludes any attention to these sources (so that it may be accessed by "reason alone").

The case of Descartes and Pascal is only a particularly clear example of a much more common occurrence. Wittgenstein's point, which I think we must grant, is that the use of the same word by two people says very little about whether they agree or disagree. "And just the same goes for belief in the Trinity" – despite the fact that, here again, *very specific words* would seem to be of utmost importance. Indeed, one could say that the entire course of trinitarian theology, and indeed a great deal of European history, was quite profoundly shaped by a *single* word – the Latin word *filioque*, which some people thought belonged in a place where others thought it had no business. From the earliest Christian believers to the headline-writers of today, many people have advocated a theology that "insists on the use of particular words and phrases, and outlaws others," thinking that this will somehow make things clearer or more unified.

Of course, insisting and outlawing does little to help. In support of this point, Wittgenstein places a name that may surprise some readers, since many regard Karl Barth as having insisted on a great many particular words and phrases. On closer inspection, however, Barth's theology does not match his stereotype as a linguistic tyrant. When Wittgenstein wrote this parenthesis, he might have had in mind a passage of Barth's such as this one:

> In the raw material of dogmatics, the first object is a series of expressions which, more or less constantly and emphatically, usually make up the spoken matter of proclamation in the whole Church ... But here, as everywhere, these expressions acquire their meaning from the associations and contexts in which they are used.[2]

[2] *CD* I/1, 86, cited from the first English translation (to which Wittgenstein would have had access) in Fergus Kerr, *Theology After Wittgenstein* (Oxford: Basil Blackwell, 1986), 152; the passage appears in a revised form in the second English edition at 77-78 [*KD* I/1, 79].

In fact, one could point to a wide variety of passages in Barth's work to echo Wittgenstein's point. For example, Barth claims that dogmatic statements "should never stand in the air (perhaps as statements constructed for the sake of logical or philosophical or moral completeness) in such a way as to be unintelligible as a preparation for Church proclamation."[3] For Barth, it is never a matter of simply repeating the same words that have always been used. Dogmatics "does not ask what the apostles and prophets said, but what we ought to say on the basis of the apostles and prophets."[4]

And we discover "what we ought to say" only by attending to how our words will be heard in the particular contexts in which they are used. Otherwise we merely "gesticulate with words," or perhaps hurl them at one another as though they were weapons of war. Simply insisting upon (or outlawing) particular words does nothing to insure that our conversation-partners will "see the light." Indeed, they may be *unable* to see the light – or, better, unable to see the same light that *we* see – because this "same" set of words has, for them, become associated with an entirely different set of practices. Hence there may be a considerable gap between "the difference [the words] make at various points" in the lives of others, and the difference they make in our own lives.

So, for instance, Pascal's use of the word *God* in the *Pensées* is associated with practices such as devotional prayer, participating in the liturgy, reading the Scripture, and debating with the Jesuits about moral theology. Descartes' use of the word *God* in the *Meditations* is bound up with searching for philosophi-cal bedrock, contemplating sense-experience, and debating with other philosophers about the existence of God. Descartes, too, may have read the Scriptures and participated in the liturgy, but there are no obvious signs of this in his text; he has deliberately excluded such practices, so they are not formative for his argument. "*Practice* gives the words their sense."

"And just the same goes for belief in the Trinity." No matter how many words we may agree upon, and no matter how arduously we may work to understand, explicate, and promulgate this central doctrine of the Christian faith, our efforts will be fruitless unless the words are "given sense" by particular forms of Christian practice. Theologians should be concerned not merely with the words that are uttered with respect to this doctrine, nor merely with what we think while we are uttering them, but with the difference they make at various points in our lives. The doctrine of the Trinity becomes meaningful

---

[3] *CD* I/1, 280 [*KD* I/1, 297].
[4] *CD* I/1, 16; the translation has "must," but the German is *was . . . wir selbst sagen sollen* [*KD* I/1, 15].

only in the context of Christian practices; and thus we must be attentive not just to the theory, but also to the *practice*, of trinitarian theology.

This does not mean that trinitarian theology need not employ words, nor that all discussions of theory are relegated to second-class status. For one thing, much of our source-material for the doctrine of the Trinity consists of *words* – words set down in an attempt to describe the one God who is revealed, through the Spirit, in the history of Israel and in the person of Christ. In order to "practice" trinitarian theology, we must depend heavily upon texts – scriptural texts, credal statements, and writings of theologians through the ages. A trinitarian theology must certainly attend to the *words* in these texts; but it must also attend to the practices which give those words their sense. After all, the textual sources of trinitarian theology are derived from widely varying contexts; they employ a wide range of styles and approaches to the use of language, from the propositional to the poetic; they quote from other texts, often translating and interpreting them in the process; and they are related in complex ways to various practices of worship, teaching, and everyday life. In Wittgenstein's idiom, these texts belong to a wide variety of "language games" – including Jewish and Christian worship, Greek and Roman philosophy and rhetoric, and the political, economic, and sociological assumptions of the cultures in which they were written.

Given these complexities, we might be tempted simply to *avoid* words whenever possible. We could take Wittgenstein at face value when he says that the words are "not what matters," and jump ahead to a lengthy list of practices that give sense to the Christian belief in the triune God. Perhaps this would even be the most reverent course; in the face of mystery, we often feel called to respect its depths. Wittgenstein knew that too: "Concerning anything about which we cannot speak, we must remain silent."[5] Yet he also realized that this was not the end of the story; for even though words are only given their sense by practices, there can be no practices without words. Even a practice performed in silence is meaningful only because it is already part of a larger context in which language plays an important role. For example, Christians who make the sign of the cross may use no words in the process; nevertheless, what makes this a practice (and not merely a random gesture) is its relation to the central narratives of the faith, which tell of a crucified Jew who was raised up from death by God and made Lord of all. And so we are brought back, once again, to words.

The human being is, as the Greeks taught, a ζῷον λόγον ἔχων – not

---

[5] Final sentence of the *Logisch-Philosophische Abhandlung*, my trans. from the German text in *Tractatus Logico-Philosophicus*, ed. C. K. Ogden (London: Routledge & Kegan Paul, 1922), 188.

merely "a rational animal," as the phrase is often translated, but "a living being
who has language." This use of language seems quite natural to us; and if we
more guardedly admit that it is a learned phenomenon, we must also admit that
we have learned it for so long, and so well, that its very conventionality is often
obscured from our sight. We turn to it in an effort to get others to understand
– to think as we think, to act as we act. We often seek to communicate, and in
order to do so we use signs (words, usually). Words are a necessary vehicle for
communication; but because they derive their sense from the contexts in which
they are used, they can also become an obstacle to communication. When
divorced from the practices from which they take their meaning, they can
become an elaborate coded message to which there is no key. Language can
obliterate distinction, as when a single word is used to describe widely varying
beliefs and practices; conversely, when diverse words are used to describe one
thing, they can create confusion where there need be none.

   In its more reflective moments, theology has been aware of the importance
and the limits of language – and especially language about God. Christians
believe that God has been revealed to us, and that this has been accomplished
by God's own act. Nevertheless, we also believe that we have not fully
comprehended, nor can we hope to express, the fullness of God. A central
biblical description of God as "revealed mystery" is found in Exodus 33, in
which Moses asks to be shown the glory of God. Yet even the very name of
God is a testimony to this mystery (which is why I prefer to leave the four
famous Hebrew letters untranslated):

> And [יהוה] said, "I will make all my goodness pass before you, and will proclaim
> before you the name, 'יהוה'"; and I will be gracious to whom I will be gracious,
> and will show mercy on whom I will show mercy. But," [יהוה] said, "you
> cannot see my face; for no one shall see me and live." And יהוה continued, "See,
> there is a place by me where you shall stand on the rock; and while my glory
> passes by I will put you in a cleft of the rock, and I will cover you with my hand
> until I have passed by; then I will take away my hand, and you shall see my back;
> but my face shall not be seen." (Exod. 33:19–23)

Must we be denied the *face* of God? In order to identify one another, to
differentiate among individuals, we usually need to see a *face*; but this is
precisely what remains hidden. And even though the New Testament
revelation in Jesus Christ is complete, it is still revealed *as mystery*. The God
of whom Christ is "the image" nevertheless remains "the invisible God" (Col.
1:15); similarly, the writer of the fourth Gospel insists that "no one has ever
seen God" (John 1:18) – even though the Word has made God known to us.
Not only on Sinai, but also at Bethlehem, we are shown no definitive "face";

witness the striking variety of portraits of Mary and of Jesus that have been produced by various cultures around the world.

God, although revealed, remains a mystery. This should not be taken to mean (as it often has been) that it does not really matter what is said of God, since "it's all a mystery anyway," or that the word *mystery* is primarily a "retreat" into the sublime, in order to cover over confusion, inconsistency, or sloppy thinking.[6] On the other hand, an awareness of this mystery is necessary as a reminder that we ought to exercise some degree of caution when speaking about God. We need to be aware of the fallibility of all our discourse, and of the difficulties inherent in the task we have set for ourselves.

Indeed, reflection on the doctrine of the Trinity seems beset with nearly insuperable obstacles: the impenetrability of divine mystery, the inherent ambiguities of language-use, and the difficulties of attending to the practices that give language its meaning. Undertaking this reflection seems hazardous, perhaps foolish. One is reminded of the opening of Shakespeare's *Henry V*, which expresses some doubt about the very idea of attempting to recreate the Battle of Agincourt on a tiny theatre stage: "Can this cockpit hold the vasty fields of France?" The very first lines of the play sound something like a prayer:

> O for a Muse of fire, that would ascend
> The brightest heaven of invention.

Only with the help of something beyond ourselves can we hope to narrate and enact a story of epic proportions – such as, for example, the story of the triune God. "Nowhere," says St Augustine, is "erring more perilous, nor seeking more laborious, nor gleaning more bounteous."[7]

Yet the peril and the labor are justified by the bounty of the harvest; for the doctrine of the Trinity is the highest achievement of Christian theology. It is the central claim of the faith, in which all other elements find their center. Like the keystone at the top of a gothic arch, it could only be put in place after lengthy and painstaking labor; yet without it, the entire vault would eventually collapse. Many of the difficulties that Christian theologians have faced, as they have attempted to shore up various structures of the faith over the past several centuries, can be traced in part to the faulty construction (or

---

[6] An unfortunate example of this use of the term can be seen in Peters, *GOD as Trinity* (16–17, 113–14, and elsewhere). Although Peters attempts to distinguish *God* (who remains a mystery) from the *doctrine* of God (which does not), his overall assessment of "mystery" is a negative one. (Complete bibliographical data for this and other recent studies of trinitarian theology may be found in Appendix I.)

[7] *De Trin.* I.1.5, my translation.

in some cases, the complete absence) of this all-important keystone. And it retains its paramount importance, regardless of whether one thinks of the theological enterprise as primarily a speculative, or grammatical, or ethical endeavor. These three approaches are not actually distinct from one another; but they do say something about the varying emphases of particular theologies, so it may be worthwhile to say a word about each.

At the speculative level, the doctrine of the Trinity is an example of *theology* in its most basic etymological sense: words about God, an account of God, or the contemplation of the reality of God. Whatever Christians have to say about God, they are saying about the Trinity; for, "to put the matter as baldly, and hence as contentiously, as possible, the doctrine of the Trinity simply *is* the Christian doctrine of God."[8] So an exploration of trinitarian doctrine needs to seek to describe, however inadequately, "what is the case" with respect to God. Secondly, on the level of grammar, the doctrine of the Trinity creates a structure for our talk about God. It serves as a summary of the biblical narratives, and thus identifies the Christian faith and differentiates it from other confessions. Trinitarian doctrine thus helps to prevent talk about God from degenerating into a mere projection of our own greatest aspirations onto something outside ourselves. It also helps tie together the various elements of the Christian faith, including the doctrines of creation, redemption, and sanctification. Finally, on the level of ethics, the doctrine helps us understand the kind of lives we are called to live. The way we understand God affects the way we understand our relation to God and our relations to one another; thus, the articulation of a doctrine of the Trinity has concrete ethical implications. However, matters of concrete practice are a concern, not just for the *last* of these three perspectives, but for the others as well: the grammatical and speculative aspects of trinitarian theology are meaningful only through attention to "the differences they make at various points in [one's] life."

In this book, I make claims about each of these levels or aspects of theological discourse. First, at the level of speculative theology, I want to defend the thesis that the Christian doctrine of God, in positing the concept of *Triunity*, asks us to affirm the rather counterintuitive thesis that something can be *three* and *one* simultaneously – a claim that would appear to be foolishness to mathematicians and a stumbling-block to the rationalists.

[8] Nicholas Lash, "Considering the Trinity," *Modern Theology* 2, no. 3 (April 1986): 183. Ingolf Dalferth endorses this point, and offers additional reasons why it must be so, in "The Eschatological Roots of the Doctrine of the Trinity," in Schwöbel, ed., *Trinitarian Theology Today*, 147–70.

Usually, the threeness and oneness of God are treated as separate conceptual categories, as in the common tag-line "one being, three persons." While I accept the value of such conceptualizations, I also believe that, in God, "these three are one" in a stronger, more paradoxical sense – a sense that defies our standard logical and mathematical descriptions of "one" and "three." The doctrine of the Trinity calls into question our assumption that the categories of oneness and difference are incommensurable, incompatible, or even necessarily in tension with one another. The doctrine is thus an implicit critique of the dominant philosophical tradition of the West, in which "otherness" is associated primarily with fragmentation or revolt.

My second goal, at the level of theological grammar, is to inquire into the relationship between God's Triunity and a similar simultaneity of threeness and oneness in the created order. I want to ask: to what extent is it theologically legitimate to develop accounts of triunity within creation as a whole – and, in particular, in human beings (who are "created in the image of God")? Is the claim that "these three are one" unique to God, or can we also describe the world (or at least of some elements of the world) using such language? Any such analogical movement from God to the created order is fraught with difficulties, so we will have to tread carefully. But I believe that there is some such movement to be made – with the result that the doctrine of the Trinity will affect how we understand creation in general (and humanity in particular). Trinitarian theology is not *only* a speculative endeavor about the life of God (though such speculation must continue to play a role); it is also an exploration of the joys and hopes, the sorrows and the griefs of the whole creation.

And this, in turn, leads to the third level or aspect of theology described above – the ethical. If the claim that "these three are one" applies not only to God but, *mutatis mutandis*, to the created order as well, then it has dramatic implications for the kinds of lives we are called to live. Discipleship has something to do with a willingness to allow God to take us up into the divine life, fulfilling the destiny for which we were created. Clearly, though, many of our common cultural practices push us precisely in the opposite direction: they assume, and reinforce, a stark separation between the categories of oneness and difference. We may describe ourselves as members of various "communities" (family, workplace, church, city, nation), but we typically work very hard to prevent these structures from interfering with our "individual" lives. The doctrine of the Trinity is a challenge to the modern cult of the individual; it teaches us to think in terms of complex webs of mutuality and participation. The practice of trinitarian theology thus calls us into newness of life – a life that bears a very different shape from what we have come to regard as "ordinary" existence.

These three concerns – the simultaneous oneness and threeness of God, the link between this "heavenly" Triunity and the earthly triunity of the created order, and the implications of these claims for Christian life and worship – come together in a passage of text to which the title of this book refers. It appears in the First Epistle of John, and is a much-disputed text. The first part of it appears in no early Greek manuscript; it is almost certainly a late addition to the Latin text of the Vulgate. My interest in the passage, however, concerns neither its canonicity nor its provenance, but rather the way it summarizes the three goals of my project. The passage – quoted in full as the epigram to this book – refers to three who bear witness in heaven (for which it offers the three Latin substantives *Pater*, *Verbum*, and *Spiritus Sanctus*), and to three who bear witness on earth ("the Spirit and the water and the blood"). In each case, according to the text, "these three are one." Many commentators have been eager to discount the first half of this text, citing the usual source-critical criteria;[9] but they cannot wholly avoid the strange quasi-mathematical equation of three and one, since it appears again in the second half of the text (which *is* in the early Greek manuscripts). Obviously, one can take the easy way out, interpreting "are one" to mean "in agreement" or "cohering"; the NRSV translates "and these three agree." But I would propose that we opt for the more difficult translation – the "obviously false" claim that three can be one. And I would further propose that we take this claim seriously – as a call to reconcile oneness and difference, and to allow this reconciliation to affect our understanding of God, of the created order, and of our proper response to God's gracious self-revelation.

The "three earthly witnesses" mentioned in the text – the Spirit, the water, and the blood – have sometimes been read as referring to particular Christian practices, such as baptism and the eucharist.[10] These practices are indeed central aspects of the Christian witness to the triune God; I will return to them often in this book. On the other hand, there is no need to confine these three words to these practices alone; to do so would be to lose the figurative richness of the language. The words *spirit*, *water*, and *blood* evoke a wide range of biblical and theological motifs, both triumphant and tragic: the creation of the world, the birth of children, the sacrifice of animals, the murder of human

---

[9] See, e.g., Rudolf Bultmann, *The Johannine Epistles*, trans. Philip O'Hara (Philadelphia: Fortress Press, 1973), 81 [ET of: *Die drei Johannesbriefe*, 2e. Aufl. (Göttingen: Vandenhoeck und Ruprecht, 1967), 84].

[10] See, e.g., C. H. Dodd, *The Johannine Epistles* (London: Hodder & Stoughton, 1946), 128–31; Rudolf Schnackenburg, *Die Johannesbriefe*, 2e. Aufl. (Freiburg: Herder, 1963), 261–2; Stephen F. Smalley, *1, 2, 3 John*, Word Biblical Commentary, vol. 51 (Waco: Word Books, 1984), 281–3.

beings, the freeing of slaves, the conquest of lands, and the warnings of prophets. And these words also call us to be attentive to the Christological focus of trinitarian theology, through their invocation of two central Christian images of love – images in which Spirit, water, and blood issue forth, simultaneously, from a human being: the images of Mary giving birth, and of Jesus dying on the cross.

Clearly, the practice of trinitarian theology touches on a wide range of concerns – thus rendering yet more salient the "nearly insuperable obstacles" that I have already acknowledged. Overcoming them will require us to recognize the provisionality of our claims, even while we attend to the practices that give those claims meaning. The relationship between language (however provisionally formulated) and matters of concrete practice was the primary focus of the classical rhetorical tradition; thus, rhetorical assumptions will be at work in various parts of this book. In the contemporary setting, *rhetoric* is a much-disputed term; my own appropriation of the word follows that of Aristotle, who defined it as "the faculty of discovering, in the particular case, the available means of persuasion."[11] On this definition, rhetoric is concerned with the interaction of words and practices – with the ways in which people can be moved to action by the written or spoken word. It is concerned not only with the words themselves, but with the persuasive *effects* of words – how they will be read or heard in particular contexts (and what audiences might be likely to do as a result). A "rhetorical" approach is needed to examine the uses of language in circumstances which, although very contentious and difficult to resolve in an absolute manner, are nevertheless of enormous practical significance.[12]

Rhetoric is concerned with arguments of monumental importance – the guilt or innocence of a defendant, for example, or the course of action needed to insure a particular institution's future survival. No one would deny the importance of speaking and arguing about such matters; yet none of these matters can be adjudicated by means of a rigid formula or reduced to a statistical analysis. In fact, whatever decisions are made could turn out to be all wrong; the jury might ignore a decisive piece of evidence, or future events

---

[11] *Rh.* 1355b26.

[12] According to Aristotle, rhetoric begins with the "common opinions" (ἔνδοξα) about any problem presented (*Rh.* 1355a14–18; *cf. Top.* 100a18–21; *Soph. El.* 183a37–183b1). Because these opinions are malleable and highly specific to place and time, they cannot be universalized or abstracted from their context; rhetoric calls for attention to the idiosyncrasies of concrete, historical reality. Consequently, rhetorical argument cannot guarantee tautological finality. What would be the use of deliberating about something which could never be otherwise? "Nothing would be gained by it" (*Rh.* 1357a7).

might render an institutional process useless. Nevertheless, there is no alternative; we must do *what we can* with *what we have*. Some matters are simply too important for us to be silent about them, even if we can only speak tentatively and provisionally. Indeed, the most urgent matters, it seems to me, are those upon which there exist no "automatic" solutions, no universally-accepted criteria of judgment. Only the most banal matters generate wide-spread agreement; we undertake the time-consuming and often painful process of disagreement and defense – and thus of *persuasion* – only concerning matters of great urgency.

Christian theology is one such matter. Because it does not operate within a wholly closed system of assumptions (as do, for example, formal logic or lower-order mathematics), its claims have a necessarily provisional character. In this sense, good theology recognizes its own limitations, especially with respect to the knowledge of God. Nevertheless, despite the provisional and tentative nature of our knowledge, we must continue to speak, write, make claims, and assess arguments – and indeed, to do so with a firmness and a confidence that logicians might consider reckless. The rhetorical tradition provides us with warrants for speaking with conviction, even in the midst of the incomplete character of our knowledge. Perhaps it is thus not entirely accidental that the Christian thinkers who were most influential in the development of trinitarian theology – from St Paul the Apostle to St Gregory of Nazianzus, from St Athanasius to St Augustine – were all well-schooled in rhetoric.

In an earlier work, I offered a detailed methodological justification for the theological appropriation of rhetoric.[13] I will not attempt to condense that account here; in any case, the elaboration of what counts as "rhetorical theology"[14] has now been taken up by others, both in the study of particular theologians[15] and with respect to theological method in general.[16] Nor will I

---

[13] *Faithful Persuasion: In Aid of a Rhetoric of Christian Theology* (Notre Dame, Ind.: University of Notre Dame Press, 1991).

[14] For reviews of the recent literature, see Don H. Compier, "The Incomplete Recovery of Rhetorical Theology," *dialog* (Summer 1995): 187-192; and Bradford F. Hinze, "Reclaiming Rhetoric in the Christian Tradition," *Theological Studies* 57, no. 3 (September 1996): 481–99.

[15] E.g., Serene Jones, *Calvin and the Rhetoric of Piety*, Columbia Series in Reformed Theology (Louisville: Westminster/John Knox Press, 1995); Michael J. Scanlon, O.S.A., "Augustine and Theology as Rhetoric," *Augustinian Studies* 25 (1994): 37–50; Stephen H. Webb, *Re-Figuring Theology: The Rhetoric of Karl Barth*, SUNY Series in Rhetoric and Theology, ed. David Tracy and Stephen H. Webb (Albany: State University of New York Press, 1991).

[16] E.g., Rebecca S. Chopp, *The Power to Speak: Feminism, Language, God* (New York:

offer a history of the rhetorical tradition, since a number of excellent synopses are available.[17] In this book, the proof of the method will need to be in the doing; the uses and disadvantages of rhetoric for theology will be judged according to the successes and failures of the arguments contained herein. Perhaps I can best prepare readers to render those judgments by describing, very briefly, three of the features of the rhetorical tradition that have guided my own practice of trinitarian theology.

Contextuality

Doctrines are "official formulations of the faith which have become classical but which are conceivably not the only ways of stating the faith."[18] Doctrines are discursive structures, and as such are meaningful only within their larger contexts. This context comprises three primary elements: a source (someone writes them or speaks them); an audience (people read or listen); and some kind of content. All three of these features of linguistic expression can change: a variety of speakers or writers can employ the same doctrinal statements (perhaps with similar purposes in mind, but perhaps not); different audiences may impute varying meanings to a single doctrine; and of course, the language itself may change.[19] This means that Christian theology cannot simply repeat the formulas that it has proclaimed in the past; in attempting thus to create

---

Crossroad, 1989); Gareth Jones, *Critical Theology: Questions of Truth and Method* (Cambridge: Polity Press; New York: Paragon House, 1995); David Tracy, *Dialogue with the Other: The Inter-Religious Dialogue*, Louvain Theological and Pastoral Monographs, vol. 1 (Leuven: Peeters Uitgeverij, 1990; reprint, Grand Rapids, Mich.: William B. Eerdmans, 1991).

[17] For example: George A. Kennedy, *Classical Rhetoric and Its Christian and Secular Tradition from Ancient to Modern Times* (Chapel Hill: University of North Carolina Press, 1980); James J. Murphy, ed., *A Synoptic History of Classical Rhetoric* (New York: Random House, 1972; reprint, Davis, Calif.: Hermagoras Press, 1983); and, still the definitive work in this field, George A. Kennedy, *A History of Rhetoric*, 3 vols (Princeton: Princeton University Press, 1963–83). The constituent volumes of this set are: 1. *The Art of Persuasion in Greece* (1963); 2. *The Art of Rhetoric in the Roman World, 300 B.C.–A.D. 300* (1972), and 3. *Greek Rhetoric Under Christian Emperors* (1983).

[18] Geoffrey Wainwright, *Doxology: The Praise of God in Worship, Doctrine, and Life* (Oxford and New York: Oxford University Press, 1980), 9.

[19] The fact that doctrine is widely recognized as being able to *develop* would seem to underscore this point. The most important work on the subject remains John Henry Newman, *An Essay on the Development of Christian Doctrine*, 6th edn (London, 1878; reprint, with a Foreword by Ian Ker, Notre Dame, Ind.: University of Notre Dame Press, 1989). See also Avery Dulles, *The Survival of Dogma: Faith, Authority, and Dogma in a Changing World* (1971; reprint, New York: Crossroad, 1987).

continuity, it would in fact insure *discontinuity*. Audiences change; hence, the associations evoked by particular forms of language will also change. Any discourse that hopes to maintain some degree of continuity over time must, paradoxically, *change* in order to do so.[20]

For example, theologians cannot maintain continuity with respect to the words used in baptism by simply repeating a phrase that appears in the New Testament (for example, in Matthew 28:19). For one thing, this would mean reciting it in Greek, in which case most contemporary Christians would not understand it. One can attempt a translation, but this does not really address the problem; all translation is heavily mediated by the assumptions of the translator and the interpretive communities that are involved in the use of the language. And even if a translation has been largely agreed upon (at least within a particular linguistic community), the words that are chosen will continue to pick up a variety of associative references over time.[21] Thus, my arguments in this book pay attention to how certain forms of language are likely to be heard and read by audiences in the contemporary context, and to offer alternative formulations where necessary.

Holism

Long before the word *postmodern* entered the lexicon, Cardinal Newman recognized the ways in which Enlightenment rationalism had disfigured our understanding of what it means to inhabit a world. For Newman, theology was not simply about changing minds, but about changing hearts and souls; thus, it should not be aimed only at the intellect. "After all, man is *not* a reasoning animal; he is a seeing, feeling, contemplating, acting animal."[22] Indeed, says Newman, "the whole man moves";[23] and thus theology should not be done as though the members of its audience were disembodied brains that needed only to *think* rightly in order for a theological argument to have done its work. Nothing will come of a theology that fails to affect the emotions, the imagination, and ultimately, the will – for only then can it "make a difference" at various points of the lives of those whom it addresses.

Newman drew much of his inspiration for these views from the rhetorical

---

[20] For further commentary on this problem, see the work of Nicholas Lash, e.g. *Change in Focus: A Study of Doctrinal Change and Continuity* (London: Sheed and Ward, 1973).

[21] I develop some of these points in detail in "On Translating the Divine Name," *Theological Studies* 56, no. 3 (September 1995): 415–40.

[22] John Henry Newman, "The Tamworth Reading Room," in *Discussions and Arguments* (London: Longmans, Green, and Co., 1872), 294.

[23] John Henry Newman, *Apologia Pro Vita Sua* (1864; reprint, Garden City, NY: Doubleday, Image Books, 1956), 264.

tradition.[24] The art of rhetoric developed in ancient Greece precisely in order to compete with the persuasive power of the prevailing mode of discourse, which was epic poetry. In order for it to do so, it could not simply "state the facts"; rather, it had to be "capable of rivaling poetic performances in its power to satisfy the curiosity, engage the sympathies, and fire the imagination of the audience, whether hearers or readers."[25] These same goals were applied to Christian theology by St Augustine, who argued that, like rhetoric, theology should seek "to teach, to delight, and to move."[26] Achieving these goals requires that the theologian employ a variety of styles and attend to the assumptions of the audience. Doctrines may be presented in propositional form, in an attempt to insure the soundness of the teaching (or at least to make things clearer); however, as Wittgenstein's comment reminds us, rigid adherence to a certain form of words does not necessarily insure clarity. Moreover, such an approach rarely brings about any degree of "delight" (often just the opposite, in fact), and almost always fails to "move" the members of the audience – except perhaps to drive them as far away from theology as possible.

Thus, one possible approach to a "rhetorical theology" is to make use of narratives, poetry, and art as a means of exploring the shape of doctrine and attending to the practices that give it meaning.[27] Artists and poets often recognize the importance of cultivating new ways of speaking in ever-changing rhetorical contexts. They may thus occasionally provide us with some useful interpretations of Christian doctrine – even when it was not their conscious intention to do so. Recent efforts to employ such works in the service of Christian theology have been, I think, quite successful.[28]

---

[24] See Walter Jost, *Rhetorical Thought in John Henry Newman* (Columbia: University of South Carolina Press, 1989); he discusses Newman's "holism" at 2–3 and 76–84.

[25] Thomas Cole, *The Origins of Rhetoric in Ancient Greece* (Baltimore: Johns Hopkins University Press, 1991), 28–9.

[26] *De doct. Chr.* IV.27(74).

[27] To those who consider the use of novels, art, or poetry too "fuzzy" or "philosophically imprecise" to count as Christian theology, I would offer two responses: first, the distinction between "fuzzy" and "precise" forms of inquiry is dubious in itself, and has lately been brought under significant critique; secondly, all the philosophical precision that one can muster will not matter a trice if readers do not read (because doing so is drudgery), or if those who do read are unmoved to form their minds and their lives according to the claims of the argument.

[28] Consider, for example, the use of *Watership Down* in Stanley Hauerwas, *A Community of Character: Toward a Constructive Christian Social Ethic* (Notre Dame, Ind.: University of Notre Dame Press, 1981); the use of Gerard Manley Hopkins, George Herbert, and others

Practice

Here we return to the claim with which this Introduction began. Doctrines are not formulated as an end in themselves; they draw their meaning from, and are ultimately intended to have some effect on, the practices of the believing community. Doctrines are "communally authoritative teachings regarding beliefs and practices that are considered essential to the identity or welfare of the group";[29] consequently, they always have immediate (though not necessarily obvious) practical import. They should not be treated as mere intellectual abstractions; rather, they should be examined in relation to the practices of the community they address.

By being attentive to the ways that an audience is persuaded or "moved," a rhetorical theology necessarily attends to the practical implications of doctrine. It thus does not inquire into the "truth" of a doctrine in a purely abstract sense, as though the doctrine were a proposition that could be verified or falsified regardless of the circumstances in which it is used. Instead, attention is directed to contexts and outcomes. A rhetorical theology asks questions such as: Given the practices that are already in place, how will this particular formulation of doctrine be "heard"? If this doctrine is taught in this form, what is likely to result among Christians? What will they believe, and how will they live? Will Christian identity be clarified, and will believers be strengthened in their desire to become disciples of Christ? Questions such as these, rather than abstract claims about meaning and reference, will be at the forefront as we attempt to evaluate the adequacy of particular doctrinal formulations.

The foregoing comments certainly do not exhaust the ways in which a theology can be "rhetorical"; but they do summarize the methodological assumptions with which I operate. They also serve as a reminder that this book, too, is an exercise in persuasive argument, and that its success will depend not merely on what it teaches, but also on whether readers are sufficiently delighted by it to be moved to undertake the practice of trinitarian theology themselves.

---

in Nicholas Lash, *Easter in Ordinary: Reflections on Human Experience and the Knowledge of God* (Charlottesville: University Press of Virginia, 1988); and the use of a variety of novels, short stories, and films in L. Gregory Jones, *Embodying Forgiveness: A Theological Analysis* (Grand Rapids, Mich.: William B. Eerdmans, 1995). These works provide good examples of *rhetorical* theology (even if not always self-consciously so), in that they are able to delight and to move, as well as to teach.

[29] Lindbeck, *The Nature of Doctrine: Religion and Theology in a Postliberal Age* (Philadelphia: Westminster; London: SPCK, 1984), 74.

This book is divided into three parts. (Readers must ultimately judge whether these three parts are, in any strong sense, "one.") Part One, *Source: Trinitarian Beliefs*, comprises three chapters. Chapter 1 places this book in the context of contemporary trinitarian theology, and seeks to appropriate some of the most promising insights of the current discussion while avoiding its most significant pitfalls. In chapter 2, I offer a capsule account of the Christian doctrine of God, focusing primarily on the classical accounts of God's processions, relations, and missions; this chapter also provides a justification for some of the terminology that I employ throughout the book. In chapter 3, I present an argument for construing the created order as bearing certain "triune marks" that echo the Triunity of God. Here I examine the traditional teaching of the *vestigia trinitatis*, taking into account the strenuous objections raised against this approach. I then offer a detailed account of one such triune mark, and assess its value in explicating a number of complex trinitarian claims.

Part Two, *Wellspring: Trinitarian Virtues*, describes three aspects or characteristics of God that seem to be implied by the doctrine of the Trinity – dispositions to which human beings are also called by grace. We come to recognize the form of these virtues through our encounter with Christ, the Word made flesh; thus, these chapters have a Christological focus, supplemented by rhetorical and literary analysis. Then, in Part Three, *Living Water: Trinitarian Practices*, I examine the implications of my approach for three particular aspects of the Christian life. Here the focus is on the Holy Spirit as the vehicle of God's continuing action in the Church and in the world. More detailed introductions to these two sections of the book appear at the beginning of each.

In writing this book, I have sought to persuade my readers to believe in the triune God, and to recognize the profound implications of this belief for the Christian life. In order to see this project through to its end, I have had to call more than once upon a certain "Muse of Fire" – though I cannot say whether it is the same one to whom Shakespeare appealed. To the extent this book succeeds in its goals, therefore, it will have done so by an act of grace: from the One who spoke from the fire of the bush that was not consumed; the One who came to earth to baptize with the Holy Spirit and with fire; the One who was poured out on the Church in the tongues of fire at Pentecost. Three gifts of fire, in heaven *and* on earth: and these Three are One. For such a gift, thanks be to God, the holy and undivided Trinity.

Part One

SOURCE:
TRINITARIAN BELIEFS

Chapter 1

POSITIONING

In 1986, the journal *Modern Theology* published a special issue focused on the doctrine of the Trinity. The introductory article, written by Catherine Mowry LaCugna, spoke of a renaissance of the doctrine, and cited nine books on the Trinity that had been published during the 1980s.[1] Today, one can cite an even longer list of constructive trinitarian theologies, all of which have appeared since LaCugna's survey;[2] several more are forthcoming. Indeed, so prevalent have such studies become that the phenomenon begins to look not so much like a renaissance as a bandwagon. Once threatened by its relative scarcity in modern theology, the doctrine of the Trinity now seems more likely to be obscured by an overabundance of theologians clustered around it.

In the light of such theological enthusiasm, readers could certainly be forgiven for wondering whether we need yet one more book about the Trinity. Their doubts deserve a response, and this chapter is an attempt to provide one. It also sets the context for my own approach to the doctrine by offering a thematic sampling of recent work on the subject. I begin by exploring what I see as the positive contributions of contemporary trinitarian theology; I then turn to a critique of what I see as having gone seriously awry. In the third section, I point to some new issues, which – despite their importance – have not yet been recognized as essential concerns for contemporary trinitarian theology. This chapter makes no attempt to offer a "review of the current literature"; such accounts are available elsewhere for those

[1] "Philosophers and Theologians on the Trinity," *Modern Theology* 2, no. 3 (April 1986): 169–81; here, 179n1. After this book had already been copy-edited, I learned of Dr LaCugna's tragic death. Although I disagreed with her on some issues, I am grateful for her willingness to grapple with the complexities of trinitarian doctrine. *Requiescat in pace.*

[2] I provide a partial listing in Appendix I.

seeking a more general overview.[3] This chapter's highly selective comments constitute not a survey, but rather an attempt to position my own perspective within the contemporary conversation.

Readers may also be able to glean from this chapter a preliminary picture of what it might mean to talk about trinitarian theology as a *practice*. In the Introduction, I emphasized the importance of focusing on concrete particulars, of attending to the reception (and not just the intention) of doctrine, and of exploring practical ramifications (that is, how doctrine leads to action, and not only to thought). Many of my assessments here are bound up with the degree to which recent contributions in trinitarian theology have (or have not) attended, at least implicitly, to these concerns.

Some Positive Developments

In the Preface of this book I suggested that the contemporary trinitarian theology should aim to render the doctrine less abstract, more intelligible, and more relevant to the Christian life. These goals are already being pursued by a number of recent contributors. These theologians have emphasized, first, that the doctrine of the Trinity was not merely an invention of certain third- and fourth-century thinkers who had imbibed too much Plato and Plotinus; it developed out of careful reflection on the narratives of God and God's action in the world. Second, recent trinitarian theology has emphasized the relational focus of the doctrine. God is not simply a solitary entity, nor three individual "somethings," but a complex network of relations. And third, theologians have begun to explore the practical ramifications of trinitarian doctrine in a much more self-conscious way. Each of these "movements" in contemporary trinitarian theology deserves a brief summary.

---

[3] In addition to LaCugna's essay cited in note 1 above, see also her discussion of the contributions during the 1970s and early 1980s, "Current Trends in Trinitarian Theology," *Religious Studies Review* 13, no. 2 (April 1987): 141–7. An author-by-author portrayal appears in Ted Peters, *GOD as Trinity*, 81–145. For a (perhaps overly) sympathetic portrait of the contribution of Barth, Pannenberg, and Jüngel, see John Thompson, *Modern Trinitarian Perspectives* (Oxford: Oxford University Press, 1994). My own assessments of several recent works appear in "Trinitarian Theology since 1990" and "What's [Not] New in Trinitarian Theology," both in *Reviews in Religion and Theology* – 1995, no. 4 (November): 8–16, and 1997, no. 1 (February): 14–20, respectively.

Concrete narratives of יהוה, *Christ, and the Spirit*

Despite its reputation for being a highly abstract teaching, the doctrine of the Trinity actually arose from a very concrete historical problem. The earliest followers of Jesus were Jews; throughout their lives, they had been taught that there is only one God. "Hear O Israel, יהוה your God, יהוה alone," announces the best-known of all Hebrew prayers (Deut. 6:4).[4] Nevertheless, the earliest Christian narratives describe the followers of Jesus as eventually becoming convinced that they had, in some very real sense, beheld the presence of God in their midst. It thus became necessary to explain how Jesus could be God, yet without exhausting the full reality of the One who transcends all specificity. Only יהוה is God; and yet, somehow, יהוה was made manifest in a human being, even while continuing to dwell in light inaccessible.

A further complication arose – again according to the earliest Christian narratives – after Jesus was no longer physically present to those who had followed "the Way." Jesus had promised them the gift of the Spirit, who would continue to offer divine guidance, yet would be present differently than he had been. According to the narrative of Acts and the letters of St Paul, these followers increasingly came to understand themselves as having experienced this guidance. This divine presence was more concrete and specific than some general pantheistic speculation (i.e., a claim that "God is present every-where"); and yet God's specific presence among the believing community was not understood as denying God's absolute transcendence.

So the narratives depict three historical encounters with God: with יהוה, the sole God of Israel; with Christ, incarnate and dwelling among us; and with the Spirit – not incarnate, yet still concretely present. These elements of Christianity's founding narrative forced the earliest Christian thinkers to grapple with simultaneous oneness and difference in God. They did not want

---

[4] My translation of the *Shema* here, and throughout the book, follows the decision, in the 1962 English translation of the Hebrew Bible by the Jewish Publication Society, to render the last word of the verse as "alone," rather than "one" (compare RSV, NRSV, and most modern translations). While either translation is certainly possible, I think the case has been made very well that the language of "one" here is largely due to a desire to make the text cohere with a Greek metaphysical view of the unity of God. See Michael Wyschogrod's essays, "The 'Shema Israel' in Judaism and the New Testament," in *The Roots of Our Common Faith: Faith in the Scriptures and in the Early Church*, ed. Hans-Georg Link, Faith and Order Paper 119 (Geneva: World Council of Churches, 1983), 23-32, and "The One God of Abraham and the Unity of the God of Jewish Philosophy," unpublished paper, delivered at the Society for Scriptural Reasoning, New Orleans, 1996.

to claim that there were three Gods; and yet "these three" were far too concrete to be understood as mere accidental properties or "masks" of God.

Thus, the active formulation of trinitarian doctrine began as an attempt to account for God's definitive self-revelation in the coming of the Messiah, and in the gift of the Holy Spirit to the Church. However, none of this occurred in a cultural and philosophical vacuum. When Christian theologians sought to make sense of this narrative, they (quite naturally and appropriately) turned to the philosophical categories that were available to them. But this fact should not be allowed to eclipse the concrete reality of the particular narratives that gave rise to trinitarian thought.

Nor were these narratives restricted to a description of God's encounter with the world. God was understood as *having* a history, as well as interacting with human history. And God's history does not begin at the moment of creation; rather, the creation is a continuation of an "eternal story" that can be told about God. As Catherine LaCugna puts it, the acts of God in history "were the original subject matter of trinitarian theology. As it comes to be understood, of course, God's relations to us in history are taken to be what is characteristic of the very being of God."[5] Thus, God has both an "external" history (to the world) and an "internal" history (the inner life of God). The biblical narratives encouraged theologians to think through the concrete details of both of these aspects of the "history of God."

Throughout most of the Christian era, the significance of God's "internal and external" history was taken for granted; it was assumed into Christian consciousness as part of the realistic reading of the biblical narratives. In the eighteenth and nineteenth centuries, however, it began to be neglected.[6] This was due, at least in part, to what Hans Frei has called "the eclipse of the biblical narrative": a reluctance to accept that narrative and its concrete implications at face value, coupled with a tendency to search for a "reality" that was thought to lie "behind" the text.[7] The theological damage caused by this process would be difficult to overestimate. One example of its fallout was that, due to the shift in focus away from the narratives themselves, doctrines such as those of the Trinity and of the person of Christ began to *appear* to be little more than the product of speculative philosophers with too much time on their hands, rather than a natural and altogether appropriate inquiry into the implications of the

---

[5] LaCugna, "Philosophers and Theologians," 173.

[6] Some commentators date this neglect much earlier; this claim will be critically examined in the second section of this chapter.

[7] Hans W. Frei, *The Eclipse of the Biblical Narrative: A Study in Eighteenth and Nineteenth Century Hermeneutics* (New Haven: Yale University Press, 1974).

narratives. Fortunately, the biblical narrative seems to be emerging from its eclipse – in contemporary theology in general,[8] and in discussions of trinitarian doctrine in particular.

Here, as often, Karl Barth and Hans Urs von Balthasar stand as figures of extraordinary importance. Barth's *Church Dogmatics* can be read as a thorough-going attempt to reassert the centrality of the doctrine of the Trinity by grounding it in the narrative of God's relationship with Israel and the Church, both of which find their ultimate center in Christ.[9] And Balthasar's various works develop a theology of the Trinity focused on the claim that God gives away all that God is, such that Jesus becomes cursed for our sake and experiences the condemnation of godforsakenness.[10] In both cases, the narratives of God, including God's encounter with the vicissitudes of the created order, are central for trinitarian theology. More recent writers have followed suit. Walter Kasper, even by the very title of his book (*The God of Jesus Christ*), indicates that trinitarian reflection is never merely abstract speculation, but must remain firmly grounded in the life, death, and resurrection of Jesus. Perhaps the most widely-read contemporary exponent of this emphasis is Jürgen Moltmann; his most sustained reflections appear in *The Trinity and the Kingdom*, but their origins may be found in his earlier works, and their further implications in later ones as well.[11]

Moltmann sought to free trinitarian theologians from their commitment to interiorized, abstract speculation about a distant being, and to allow them to consider the intersection of God with history. This move had three major ramifications. (1) It helped theology to suspend its fascination with the solitary individual as the primary locus of trinitarian analogies (a position often attributed – wrongly, as I have argued[12] – to St Augustine). Moltmann

---

[8] See especially Lindbeck, *The Nature of Doctrine*; William C. Placher, *Unapologetic Theology: A Christian Voice in a Pluralistic Conversation* (Louisville: Westminster/John Knox, 1989); Hauerwas, *A Community of Character*; and the essays collected in Stanley Hauerwas and L. Gregory Jones, eds, *Why Narrative? Readings in Narrative Theology* (Grand Rapids, Mich.: William B. Eerdmans, 1989).

[9] For some valuable insights on Barth as a "narrative theologian," see David Ford, *Barth and God's Story* (Frankfurt am Main: Verlag Peter Lang, 1985). And of course, Frei's work in *Eclipse* drew on his encounter with Barth's thought.

[10] See the useful commentary in Edward T. Oakes, S.J., *Pattern of Redemption: The Theology of Hans Urs von Balthasar* (New York: Continuum, 1995), e.g., 282.

[11] His most significant early reflections appear in sections of *The Crucified God: The Cross of Christ as the Foundation and Criticism of Christian Theology*, trans. R. A. Wilson and John Bowden (New York: Harper and Row, 1974) [ET of: *Der gekreuzigte Gott*, 2e. Aufl. (München: Christian Kaiser Verlag, 1973)]; recent essays are collected in *History and the Triune God*.

[12] "Trinitarian Theology since 1990", 13–14.

explicates trinitarian doctrine through categories that are primarily social rather than psychological. (2) It emphasized that God, being active in history, is also revealed in history; and so, like Barth, Moltmann helps to reunite the doctrine of the Trinity with the doctrine of revelation. (3) This new attention to revelation has helped to free Christian theology from an excessive devotion to the standard theistic claims about God that had circulated since long before the Christian era. Themes such as divine simplicity and impassibility, which had been taken for granted in some theological speculation, now had to be re-thought – since they had sometimes been allowed to eclipse the concrete story of God's encounter with the world.

This last point is especially important. Many Enlightenment thinkers were fond of creating generic portraits of God that could be justified (so they believed) by the use of "reason alone." The historical sojourn of these portraits is well known; their ostensible ability to "prove" the existence of God was eventually undermined. As a result, the Christian doctrine of God – no longer considered a discourse to which many of the canons of high rationalism were essentially foreign – was instead seen as something which *ought* to have been proved by reason alone, but which was not. And the ascendancy of these rationalist categories in the later Enlightenment insured a permanent place for modern atheism.[13]

The root cause of this problem was – once again – a neglect of the concrete narratives of the Christian faith. This point is made especially clear in the work of Eberhard Jüngel, who argues that the attempt to secure the "rational certainty" of God (in, for example, the work of Descartes) actually destroyed the "metaphysically grounded certainty of God."[14] Claims about the certainty of God's existence were made to rest on the bedrock of the self-authenticating claim of the human being ("I think, therefore I am"), thereby making God dependent on humanity, rather than the other way around. Jüngel traces this development through Fichte, Feuerbach, and Nietzsche. All three, he notes, "share the understanding of God derived from the metaphysical tradition. All three thinkers are, however, also thinking in terms of the modern self-grounding of thought in 'I think.'"[15] Modern atheism was thus born of a

---

[13] Perhaps the fullest account of this process is that of Michael J. Buckley, S.J., *At the Origins of Modern Atheism* (New Haven: Yale University Press, 1987). Many have taken up and extended Buckley's thesis; one recent example is William C. Placher, *The Domestication of Transcendence: How Modern Thinking About God Went Wrong* (Louisville: Westminster/John Knox Press, 1996).

[14] Eberhard Jüngel, *God as the Mystery of the World*, 111; developed at greater length at 122–6 [*Gott als Geheimnis der Welt*, 146, 161–7].

[15] Ibid., 150 [200].

wholesale neglect of the concrete narratives of the Christian faith. God's self-contained difference, the gospel of Christ crucified, and the active presence of God in the world were deemed largely irrelevant, having been replaced by questions about the existence of a generic "god."

The renewed emphasis on the narratives of God's history has re-invigorated trinitarian theology by emphasizing the concrete grounding of its claims – even its most abstract claims, which are themselves ultimately dependent on the biblical narratives of God's encounter with the world. These narratives need to be read, not according to the supposedly context-independent assumptions of rationalism, but in the context of Christian participation in concrete practices of worship, education, and discipleship.[16] This further implies that the claims of trinitarian doctrine need to be under constant critical assessment; we need to respect the philosophical precision that they supply, but also to ask whether they continue to convey the truth of the narratives to ever-changing audiences. I will return to this question again, both in this chapter and throughout the book.

Relationality

If we had to name a single issue on which recent trinitarian theologians have achieved the greatest degree of consensus, we might well point to their collective enthusiasm for the category of "relationality." This category is seen as providing an alternative to the metaphysics of substance, which has so significantly shaped theological reflection on the Trinity. Admittedly, the ambiguous phrase "metaphysics of substance" denotes a variety of assumptions held in various eras of the history of Christian thought; as such it probably blurs too many distinctions.[17] In general, however, most recent trinitarian theology has expressed some discontent with the traditional emphasis on an abstract property, an "essence," that "stands under" God (Latin *substantia*, from *sub* + *standere*). The traditional claim that God was "a single divine substance" tended to evoke an image of an isolated, passionless monad – thus obscuring both God's internal relationality and God's loving relationship with the world. This image came to dominate most Western theology – whether in its original metaphysical form, or in its transformation in German Idealism into the idea of the "absolute subject." In either case, it was used in the service of all sorts of mischief, from

[16] See especially Stephen E. Fowl and L. Gregory Jones, *Reading in Communion: Scripture and Ethics in Christian Life,* Biblical Foundations in Theology (London: SPCK; Grand Rapids, Mich.: William B. Eerdmans, 1991).

[17] Even in the ancient world, for example, words like οὐσία and *substantia* had wide ranges of reference; see G. Christopher Stead, *Divine Substance* (Oxford: Clarendon Press, 1977).

starkly monarchical accounts of ecclesiastical, political, and familial hierarchies, to caricatures of God as distant, disengaged, and incapable of suffering.

Although contemporary trinitarian theologians vary enormously in the degree to which they are willing to renounce their allegiance to a metaphysics of substance, they seem to agree that more stress should be placed on the claim that God is *relational*. Jürgen Moltmann offers a typical formulation: "The concept of God's unity cannot in the trinitarian sense be fitted into the homogeneity of the one divine substance, or into the identity of the absolute subject either;"[18] instead, "their common divine nature" bears "the character of relation with respect to the other Persons."[19] Similarly, Catherine LaCugna argues that "person, not substance, is the ultimate onto-logical category. . . . the ultimate source of all reality is not a 'by-itself' or an 'in-itself' but a person, a toward-another. . . . God is self-communicating, existing from all eternity in relation to another."[20] Elizabeth Johnson com-ments that the "priority of relation in the idea of the triune God . . . challenges classical theism's typical concentration on singleness in God. . . . Since the persons are constituted by their relationships to each other, each is unintel-ligible except as connected with the others. Relation is the very principle of their being."[21] And Robert Jenson, with characteristic precision, elaborates a similar claim: "The original point of trinitarian dogma and analysis was that God's relations to us are internal to him, and it is in carrying out this insight that the 'relation' concept was introduced to define the distinction of identities. If God is 'one substance,' this is a 'substance' with internal relations to other substances."[22] The breadth of consensus on this point is underscored by the fact that the last two authors mentioned here – Elizabeth Johnson and Robert Jenson – are not usually noted for being in close agreement with one another. Further corroboration of this consensus may be found in the work of Leonardo Boff, Colin Gunton, Ted Peters, and Alan Torrance.[23]

The contemporary focus on relationality can be traced to two primary influences. First and foremost has been the reintroduction into Western Christianity of certain strands of Greek Patristic thought. This "turn to the

---

[18] Moltmann, *Trinity and the Kingdom*, 150, trans. slightly altered [*Trinität und Reich Gottes*, 168].

[19] Ibid., 171–2 [188].

[20] LaCugna, *God For Us*, 14–15.

[21] Elizabeth Johnson, *She Who Is*, 216.

[22] Jenson, *The Triune Identity*, 120. Jenson's use of the term *identities* in this quotation refers (as it does throughout his book) to that of which there are three in God.

[23] Boff, *Trinity and Society*, 134–48; Gunton, *The One, the Three and the Many*, 164; Peters, *GOD as Trinity*, 30–4; Torrance, *Persons in Communion*, ch. 4.

East" was prompted by Théodor de Régnon at the turn of the century, who focused primarily on the role of the Cappadocians in emphasizing relation over substance.[24] His description of this process (which he did not necessarily see as a positive one) was embraced by Orthodox writers such as Vladimir Lossky and John Zizioulas.[25] The focus on relationality has also been shaped in part by various postmodern influences that have urged a rethinking of the concept of *personhood*. The Enlightenment idea of *person* as an isolated individual consciousness, theoretically detachable from the rest of the world, has been called into question. Personhood cannot be divorced from relation – a claim that seems to be substantiated in a wide variety of humanistic disciplines, from sociology and psychology to history and literature.

However, despite this general agreement concerning God's relationality, theologians differ widely on the terminology that should be used to express it. There seems to be no consensus, for example, on how to translate the word ὑπόστασις, which was used to identify that of which there are three in God.[26] As long as trinitarian theology had concentrated on the idea of a unitary divine substance, the question of "three what?" did not seem particularly pressing. But the current emphasis on relationality has forced the issue back on to the theological agenda. The traditional English translation, "person," is hazardous; to most listeners "three persons" means "three people," however closely "related" they might be.[27] (Despite the postmodern critique, the pull of the Enlightenment – which identifies a "person" with an individual center of consciousness – has not been overcome.)

Barth used τρόπος ὑπάρξεως, a phrase that had been employed in the early Church but which sounded strangely modalist when translated into English (usually as "mode of being").[28] Rahner, agreeing with Barth but also drawing

---

[24] Théodor de Régnon, S.J., *Études de théologie positive sur la Sainte Trinité*, 4 vols (Paris: Victor Retaux, 1892-98), e.g. I:335-65. De Régnon's influence is explored in Michel René Barnes, "De Régnon Reconsidered," *Augustinian Studies* 26, no. 2 (1995): 51–79.

[25] Vladimir Lossky, *The Mystical Theology of the Eastern Church*, trans. Fellowship of St. Alban and St. Sergius (Cambridge: James Clark & Co., Ltd, 1957; reprint, Crestwood, NY: St. Vladimir's Seminary Press, 1976), [ET of: *Essai sur la Théologie Mystique de l'Église d'Orient* (Paris: Aubier, 1944)], especially ch. 3; John D. Zizioulas, *Being as Communion: Studies in Personhood and the Church* (Crestwood, NY: St. Vladimir's Seminary Press, 1985), 83–9.

[26] Etymologically, the word is closely related to the Latin *substantia* – both words being derived from a prefix suggesting "under" and a verb meaning "to stand." But any such translation is ruled out by the fact that this same Latin term was often used to translate οὐσία, which designated that of which there was only *one* in God.

[27] As noted by Nicholas Lash, *Believing Three Ways in One God*, 31–2.

[28] Barth, *CD* I/1, 359-68 [*KD* I/1, 379-88]; see also Jüngel, *Doctrine of the Trinity*, 25–9 [*Gottes sein ist im Werden*, 36-41].

heavily on St Thomas, suggested "distinct manners of subsisting."[29] Robert Jenson speaks of three "identities."[30] A few writers are quite happy with the word *person*; some have even offered positive arguments toward its rehabilitation.[31] Most, however, seem to continue to use the word simply for lack of an alternative.

There is nothing sacred about the term *person*; even Augustine admitted that he finally chose the Latin word *persona* only in order not to be reduced to silence when asked "Three whats?"[32] One answer might be "three relations"; Augustine himself develops this notion at length,[33] and I will often refer to claim that there are three relations in God. Yet this too can be misleading, since we ordinarily assume that relations exist among (potentially independent) entities. The consistent use of the term "relation" to designate that of which there are three in God would probably have the same rhetorical effect as does the language of "three persons": it would call to mind, above all else, three people. As Nicholas Lash has observed:

> We call God "one". We call God "three". One what? Three whats? We might, in either case, say simply "thing" or "things" (for this is, after all, what the ancient terms amounted to). This would, admittedly, be inelegant but, if we insist on having an answer to the question "three whats?", then there is something to be said for choosing an expression which does not misleadingly appear (as "person" does) to be informative.[34]

I want to push this point yet further, and suggest that we do not have to answer the question, "Three whats?" In my own writing, I have intentionally opted out of the quest for the perfect substantive; instead, I simply use the phrase "the Three."

My decision is based on a rhetorical observation concerning the question of what audiences are likely to think when they read or hear the claim that God is "three persons." As I noted above, in the present rhetorical context (at least), what they are most likely to hear is "three people." And one of the things that

---

[29] Rahner, *The Trinity*, 103–15 [*Der dreifaltige Gott*, 385–93].

[30] Jenson, *Triune Identity*, 118–20.

[31] Most thoroughly Alan Torrance, *Persons in Communion*; my own reservations about Torrance's position will become clear in later chapters. A less nuanced attempt to rehabilitate the usage of *person* appears in Weinandy, *The Father's Spirit of Sonship*, 111–21, where the author seems almost willing to embrace the idea that God is three people (see esp. 119–20).

[32] Augustine *De Trin*. V.10.

[33] In *De Trin*. V–VII and elsewhere; see the commentary and citations in J. N. D. Kelly, *Early Christian Creeds*, revised edn (San Francisco: Harper and Row, 1978), 274–5.

[34] Lash, *Believing Three Ways in One God*, 31–2.

they are *least* likely to hear is that "in God there are two processions and thus three relations" – and yet this (as I will emphasize in chapter 2, and repeat often in this book) is what we are called to believe. Thus, without seeking to cast aspersions on those who have argued valiantly for one term over another, I suggest that, whenever possible, we use no term at all – speaking simply of "the Three," and capitalizing the nominalization to minimize its ambiguous reference. I am certainly not the first to take this path; it is employed, for example, in the theological orations of St Gregory of Nazianzus.[35] Gregory also employs a wide variety of analogies to describe the Three; and when he does identify them by means of a common conceptual term, it is not always the same term.[36] He thus reminds us that doctrinal formulation is not simply a philosophical endeavor, but a poetic one as well. He knew that the best way to answer the question "Three whats?" is *to tell the story of God* – both through the language of the biblical narrative, and through conceptual language as well.

Practical ramifications

A third praiseworthy element in recent trinitarian thought will receive only a brief mention here. Theologians seem increasingly convinced that the doctrine is not merely an abstract theological affirmation, but that it should have real, concrete implications for how Christians are called to live their lives. Here again, one can cite a broad consensus among a wide variety of thinkers. Indeed, it seems to have become something of a rhetorical commonplace that writers begin their books with a claim that the doctrine has too often been treated on a merely theoretical plane, and that it should be something that really *matters* in concrete ways. (Readers may recall something of that sort in the Introduction to this book as well.) Karl Rahner's description of the problem has been often cited:

> Despite their orthodox confession of the Trinity, Christians are, in their practical life, almost mere 'monotheists'. . . . It is as though this mystery has been revealed for its own sake, and that even after it has been made known to us, it remains, as a reality, locked up within itself. We make statements about it, but as a reality it has nothing to do with us at all.[37]

---

[35] τὰ Τρία: e.g., *Or.* 6.11; 6.22; 31.9.

[36] On Gregory's happy embrace of this "inconsistency," see the fine account by Frederick W. Norris in his introduction to *Faith Gives Fullness to Reasoning: The Five Theological Orations of Gregory Nazianzen*, trans. Lionel Wickham and Frederick Williams, Supplements to Vigiliae Christianae, vol. 13 (Leiden: E. J. Brill, 1991), esp. 17–53.

[37] *The Trinity*, 10–14 [Der dreifaltige Gott, 319–22].

Catherine LaCugna puts the point more positively, using it to give shape to her own study: "The doctrine of the Trinity, properly understood, is the affirmation of God's intimate communion with us through Jesus Christ in the Holy Spirit. As such, it is an eminently practical doctrine with far-reaching consequences for the Christian life."[38] Similarly Boff: "The mystery of the Trinity should be the deepest source, closest inspiration and brightest illumination of the meaning of life that we can imagine."[39]

Much of the increasing attention to concrete practice can be traced to the work of Jürgen Moltmann, who made this a central focus of his entire theological approach. Its specifically trinitarian applications began to appear in *The Crucified God*, where he argued that

> the doctrine of the Trinity is no longer an exorbitant and impractical speculation about God, but is nothing other than a shorter version of the passion narrative of Christ in its significance for the eschatological freedom of faith and the life of oppressed nature.[40]

For Moltmann, the practical implications of trinitarian doctrine flow directly from God's salvific activity through the cross of Christ. Other elements of trinitarian doctrine have also been cited as warrants for this claim; LaCugna points toward the God–world relationship in general terms, whereas Boff finds the internal communion of the Three to be the most compelling aspect of the doctrine for questions of concrete practice. Appeals to all of these aspects can be found in the work of Elizabeth Johnson.

In short, contemporary trinitarian theologians seem to agree that the doctrine has not had much effect on the Christian life, but that it should have. Most of them seem to express some hope that their own treatises will help to address this deficiency. Whether they actually do so is another matter, and one which I will take up later in this chapter. For the present, however, I want to offer a positive acknowledgment of those authors who have demonstrated, at the very least, an *awareness* of this need.

Some Troublesome Tendencies

I now turn to a more critical appraisal of the current conversation. I believe that the practice of trinitarian theology would be significantly advanced if it

[38] LaCugna, *God For Us*, ix.
[39] Boff, *Trinity and Society*, 111.
[40] Moltmann, *The Crucified God*, 246 [*Der gekreuzigte Gott*, 232].

were to dispense with three tendencies that have recently become prevalent. These three concerns are related to the three concerns of the previous section; indeed, in some ways, they are the opposite sides of the three "coins" described above.

Historical scapegoating

One of the most troubling features of current trinitarian theology seems of small importance at first glance, but actually turns out to be quite significant. This feature, which I shall call "historical scapegoating," represents the apparent necessity felt by many theologians to explain the decline of trinitarian theology by casting aspersions on a particular theologian or theological movement. In some cases the blame is assigned to St Thomas Aquinas; this claim has roots in the work of Karl Rahner, and has been frequently repeated.[41] For others, St Augustine is the culprit; Colin Gunton and Robert Jenson assert this explicitly in their respective works.[42] There even seems to be something of a contest in progress, seeing just how far back into Christian history a theologian can locate the beginnings of "the decline of trinitarian theology." Catherine LaCugna, for example, finds fault not only with Gregory Palamas, Thomas Aquinas, and Augustine, but also with the Cappadocian fathers, Athanasius, and even the Council of Nicaea. And Jürgen Moltmann employs historical-critical methods in order to suggest that certain problematic tendencies in trinitarian theology are really the fault of one or more of the Evangelists.[43]

As I noted in the Preface, I think very little is to be gained by quarreling over who took the first wrong turn (or the largest, or the most damaging one). What concerns me here is that the most common suspects seem to be those ancient writers who were among the doctrine's most powerful exponents. Whatever their failings, these ancient writers at least acknowledged the importance of grappling with the simultaneous oneness and threeness of God. This does not mean, of course, that everything these authors wrote has to be taken at face value, nor that one cannot criticize their work. (Indeed, any study that purports to be a wholly neutral recapitulation of an ancient author thereby provides, in that very assertion, a strong argument for reading the ancient author, rather than the "transparent" study!) Nevertheless, specific criticisms

[41] Rahner, *The Trinity*, 15–17 [323–5]; the claim is willingly accepted in, e.g., LaCugna, *God For Us*, 145.

[42] Gunton, *Promise*, ch. 3; Gunton, *The One, the Three, and the Many*, 54, 72, 82, and *passim*; Jenson, *Triune Identity*, 114–38.

[43] For example, in *History and the Triune God*, ch. 1.

about an ancient author's particular claims do not invalidate that author's entire contribution. Some contemporary commentators seem so perturbed by one or more strands in the tradition that they become blind to the important resources that it can provide. This in turn creates several larger problems, which I here describe in increasing order of significance.

First, the wholesale invalidation of a particular theologian's approach to trinitarian theology tends to cast doubt on the subsequent tradition – whether or not this claim is made explicitly. For example, if one claims, as does Karl Rahner, that St. Thomas's approach was methodologically suspect, much of the tradition that flows from Thomas is thereby brought into question. The resulting historical portrait of trinitarian doctrine is then colored primarily by the contemporary author's judgment about "where everything went wrong." And of course, the shape of the whole becomes more idiosyncratic, the further back the writer is willing to go to find a scapegoat. Rahner's anxieties about the medieval approach at least provides him with a broad range of pre-scholastic writers upon whom he can draw. But for writers such as Gunton and Jenson, who stake a great deal on the claim that everything went wrong with Augustine, the range of "uninfected" sources becomes much smaller. Catherine LaCugna sees a decisive wrong turn at the Council of Nicaea, and thus critiques (implicitly or explicitly) almost all post-Nicene theologians. In each of these cases, historical judgments about the tradition come to dominate the work of the modern commentator, such that whatever contributions might otherwise have been made to contemporary trinitarian theology get lost in the historical minutiae.[44]

Second, and more troublesome, is the contemporary tendency to assess and vilify one's chosen historical scapegoats with instruments that are primarily the creation of some later period of intellectual history. Ancient authors are accused of theoretical imprecisions, historical-critical inaccuracies, and assumptions about human personhood that would have been totally foreign to the thought-world in which they lived and operated. I would describe this as a failure to read these theologians *rhetorically* – a failure to recognize the context in which they wrote, the audiences they addressed, and the particular range of argumentative structures that they likely had in their toolboxes.

So, for example, Karl Rahner worries that Thomas Aquinas, by turning first

---

[44] This problem was especially evident in the case of Catherine LaCugna. Reviews of her book tended to focus on (what reviewers regarded as) problems with her appraisal of the tradition, and to ignore or discount her discussion of the practical implications of trinitarian doctrine for worship and ethics – even though these latter concerns chiefly motivate the book. See for example the review by J. A. DiNoia in *Modern Theology* 9, no. 2 (April 1993): 214–16.

to the doctrine of the one God (*de Deo uno*), and only later to the doctrine of the triune God (*de Deo trino*), sets in motion the process of decline away from a fully-articulated doctrine of the Trinity.[45] But Thomas knew that, among the members of the audience to which *he* was speaking (in the *Summa Theologiae*, at any rate), it *would not even have crossed their minds* to imagine God in anything *other* than trinitarian categories. Centuries later, audiences may no longer operate with this assumption; we need to take this into account, but it can hardly be blamed on Thomas.[46] Similar complaints have been lodged with respect to Gunton's treatment of Augustine and LaCugna's treatment of the post-Nicene Greek fathers.[47]

The most serious flaw of this process of "historical scapegoating" is that it tends to saddle ancient Christian authors with positions that were not their own, but that were created by later interpretations. In Rahner, the focus is less on Thomas than on the neo-Thomist recasting of Thomas; in Gunton, we get not Augustine but a paraphrase of Augustinian thought into categories developed much later.[48] Thus, recent writers remain captive (perhaps unwittingly) to the methodological and metaphysical framework of a later age. Moreover, this captivity is masked by shifting the blame onto a Christian thinker of an earlier age. Under such circumstances, one can hardly hope for a real reinvigoration of the doctrine of the Trinity.

Now, one might acknowledge the force of these criticisms and yet remain unpersuaded that such "historical scapegoating" can be avoided by any trinitarian theology (including the one being read at this moment). One might ask: Isn't that precisely what modern theology is all about? Must we not point to the fault-lines in the tradition so that it can be reshaped in fairly fundamental ways? Isn't this the only alternative to a wholesale subservience to the

---

[45] Rahner, *The Trinity*, 16–17 [324–5].

[46] This is not to say that Thomas's appropriation of Aristotle was philosophically innocent, of course; on this point see Buckley, *At the Origins*, 341–3. I simply want to suggest that contemporary critics have not always taken Thomas's rhetorical context into account. Among exceptions to this rule, see David B. Burrell, C.S.C., *Aquinas: God and Action* (Notre Dame, Ind.: University of Notre Dame Press, 1979), and Eugene F. Rogers, Jr., *Thomas Aquinas and Karl Barth: Sacred Doctrine and the Natural Knowledge of God* (Notre Dame, Ind.: University of Notre Dame Press, 1995).

[47] See Lewis Ayres, "Augustine, the Trinity and Modernity," *Augustinian Studies* 26, no. 2 (1995): 127–33, and my comments in "Trinitarian Theology Since 1990."

[48] Gunton seems to rely on certain commentators who were themselves highly critical of Augustine. For further comments on Gunton's approach, see Lewis Ayres, "Augustine, the Trinity and Modernity"; for a more general critique of this tendency, see Michel René Barnes, "Augustine in Contemporary Trinitarian Theology," *Theological Studies* 56, no. 2 (June 1995): 237–50.

tradition, which would merely perpetuate the problems and conflicts of the past, and ignore the new circumstances that we face?

I do not believe that we are faced with the "either/or" of historical scapegoating versus passive traditionalism. I propose that we read the history of the tradition with "critical respect" – a process that involves acknowledging the peculiarities of the perspective that we bring to the process of interpretation, giving ancient authors a reasonably charitable reading, and remaining vigilant about the ways in which their apparent flaws may be due to the ways in which they have been read and interpreted. The rhetorical tradition provides some useful tools for this process. We need to ask ourselves about the writer's original audience; about the range of arguments that were available at that historical moment ("in the particular case," as Aristotle says); and about the rhetorical goals of the work in question (what "persuasive" work it was doing). Only through some such process of recontextualization will we be able to sort out how much of a particular criticism applies to the ancient author, and how much of it applies to particular schools of translation, reception, and interpretation of that author's work. We may still need to criticize the ancient authors, but we should do so only after exploring how strongly our own understanding of their works is influenced by the assumptions of those who stand on their shoulders.

The strategy of "critical respect" is, I think, of special importance when the author in question has been "officially" received or canonized (as in the case of the biblical authors, or the saints of the Church). I say this not out of some idolatrous deference to the Bible and/or the Church, but rather on the basis of the rather "postmodern" claim that no interpretation is wholly innocent – that all readings are influenced by the interpretive community in which one stands. This means that *every* reading of a theologian is, in some sense, an ecclesial reading: with every reading, one positions oneself in relation to certain claims of (some instantiation of) the Church. Of course, we may eventually decide that certain texts do nothing to build up the Body of Christ, but only fragment and distort it. But as Rowan Williams has noted (in a different context, commenting on descriptions of holy lives), our

> awareness of this distortion or fragmentation can also encourage us to look with anachronistic severity at some past styles of Christian sanctity; a commitment to the unity of God's action should at least give us reason to spend time asking what points of "analogy" may exist with what we take for granted as the pattern of holiness now – and how our present accounts of it may be questionable and partial.[49]

[49] Rowan Williams, "The Unity of Christian Truth," *New Blackfriars* 70 (February 1989): 85–95; here, 91.

It seems to me that this is good advice for approaching past styles of Christian doctrine as well. Those of us who write trinitarian theology today and those who wrote it a thousand years ago – for all our differences – are involved in an identifiably similar practice. We will not carry it out in exactly the same way, but our tasks are ultimately very similar: we seek to formulate trinitarian doctrine so that it speaks to the present context.

Dichotomous structures

A second problem in the current conversation is its tendency to erect polar oppositions – to focus on two mutually-exclusive alternatives. This tendency is due, at least in part, to the triumph of analytic forms of thought in the modern age. By "analytic forms of thought," I am referring to those that, according to Aristotle, begin with certain "first principles" from which one may deduce a variety of propositions that can be classified as either true or false. Undeniably, certain forms of analytic thought have been highly influential (and altogether appropriate) in certain fields, such as the natural sciences and mathematics – though even here, questions have been raised about the degree to which these disciplines are wholly dependent on "unalterable first principles."[50] Even more questionable is the overwhelming influence that these analytic forms have had on the humanities and social sciences – and especially, for my purposes here, on theology.[51]

Aristotle argued that analytic forms of thought were simply not appropriate in certain kinds of discourse – especially those that did not proceed from generally-accepted first principles (including politics, poetics, law, and ethics). Unfortunately, this point has been largely overlooked, both in the modern interpretation of Aristotle[52] and in the widespread desire to apply analytic

[50] Classically, in works such as Michael Polanyi, *Personal Knowledge: Towards a Post-Critical Philosophy* (1958; reprint, London: Routledge and Kegan Paul, 1973) and Thomas S. Kuhn, *The Structure of Scientific Revolutions*, 2nd edn (Chicago: University of Chicago Press, 1970); more recently, see Paul Feyerabend, *Against Method: Outline of an Anarchistic Theory of Knowledge*, revised edn (London: Verso, 1988); Lawrence J. Prelli, *A Rhetoric of Science: Inventing Scientific Discourse*, Studies in Rhetoric/Communication, ed. Carroll C. Arnold (Columbia: University of South Carolina Press, 1989); and the flurry of new works appearing under the general heading "science studies."

[51] The deleterious effects of theology's appropriation of certain forms of social science are due, in part, to their excessive embrace of analytical structures. See especially John Milbank, *Theology and Social Theory: Beyond Secular Reason*, Signposts in Theology (Oxford: Basil Blackwell, 1990).

[52] The point has been made most clearly and persuasively in William M. A. Grimaldi, S.J., *Aristotle, Rhetoric I: A Commentary* (New York: Fordham University Press, 1980).

forms of thought to the human sciences. As a result, many people have attempted to reduce, to a series of "either/or," "true/false" propositions, fields of discourse that cannot possibly be so reduced. To put the matter simply, and therefore somewhat simplistically, we have become excessively fond of thinking in dichotomous terms – assuming that there are always exactly two alternatives, and that the choice of one excludes the other.[53]

This is not to say, of course, that division into two mutually-exclusive categories is not sometimes very useful. The problem is not dichotomous division itself, but its widespread employment in realms where it had formerly been assumed to be inapplicable, or of only marginal utility. While it makes sense to classify certain logical propositions into the categories of "true" or "false," and the counting numbers into "odd" or "even," it makes little sense to ask – in the field of politics for example – "democracy or monarchy?" Clearly, this is not an absolute disjunction, since other alternatives obviously exist – not to mention hybrids that are formed by combining certain features of each. Our tendency to assume the appropriateness of dichotomous structures across a broad range of endeavors has had the effect of depleting the rich complexity of some of these endeavors, under the misguided assumption (especially manifest under the influence of the natural sciences) that this would insure their soundness and their rigor. A good example of this "either/or" thinking can be witnessed clearly in the work of René Descartes; today we continue to speak both of "Cartesian dualism" and of the "Cartesian anxiety" which prompted it.[54]

Theological discourse as a whole should not be drawn into that realm of enterprises that must conform to the true/false dichotomies of Boolean logic. Most theologians are already aware of the debilitating effects of attempting to classify the entire universe into dichotomous categories: human or divine? history or myth? body or soul? – these are all misleading polarities (at least in many contexts). They are (most typically) attempts to apply the analytic process of disjunction to realms of discourse that cannot be easily divided into two mutually exclusive categories. Of course, realms of discourse that do not rely on disjunction are much messier and more complicated (thus provoking

---

[53] "There is a penchant among systematic theologians for categories of polar opposition, grounded in the belief that ideas 'out there' in the past really existed in polarities, and that polar oppositions accurately describe the contents and relations of these ideas." Barnes, "Augustine," 239.

[54] For a useful account of how Descartes's enthusiasm for dualistic structures was motivated by his fear of uncertainty, see Richard J. Bernstein, *Beyond Objectivism and Relativism* (Oxford: Basil Blackwell, 1983). See also Stephen Toulmin, *Cosmopolis: The Hidden Agenda of Modernity* (New York: Macmillan, Free Press, 1990).

Descartes's anxiety). On the other hand, they also tend to be more interesting.

One example of the problem of disjunction is Catherine LaCugna's focus on the opposition between the inner life of God (the immanent Trinity), and the ways in which God is revealed in the world (the economic Trinity). She acknowledges from the start that these two realms are in fact inseparable, and returns several times to Karl Rahner's famous dictum that "the 'economic Trinity' *is* the 'immanent' Trinity, and *vice versa*."[55] She even admits that the writers of the Nicene era made very little use of the distinction between *theologia* and *oikonomia*.[56] Nevertheless, the primary thrust of her book is to read these two categories as mutually exclusive, and to argue for the latter over the former.

This dichotomy leads to some odd historical claims. For example, LaCugna posits the Nicene Council as the turning point between an early concern for the economic Trinity and a later fascination with the immanent Trinity. She thus makes no mention of the strong affirmations about the inner life of God in a wide variety of pre-Nicene sources – from Colossians and the Fourth Gospel to Tertullian and Origen. Nor does she account for the thoroughgoing attention to the economy of salvation that one finds in later accounts – e.g., in the first seven books of Augustine's *De Trinitate*. Indeed, the disjunction upon which she bases her account leads her to make sweeping claims that seem very difficult to justify – e.g., that "for a millennium and a half the doctrine of the Trinity as a matter of fact has been restricted to a consideration of the immanent Trinity."[57]

LaCugna's economic/immanent dichotomy tends to encourage disjunctive thinking about other realms of theological discourse as well. For example, she speaks of subordinationism as though it were a simple matter of "who's in charge," rather than a complex dialectic of mastery and servitude. From the beginning, Christians claimed to believe in one "who, though he was in the form of God, did not regard equality with God as something to be exploited, but emptied himself, taking the form of a slave, being born in human likeness" (Phil. 2:6–7). To name this a "subordinate" role is to beg the question. The Christian faith confounds the dichotomy of master and slave, asking: Is the servant *merely* subordinate? Or is the servant, in fact, the Lord of all?

Dichotomous thinking tends to feed upon itself, so that an absolute disjunction leads to excessively absolute claims. For example, LaCugna seems to deny that we can have *any* knowledge of the inner life of God: "The

[55] Rahner, *The Trinity*, 22 [328].
[56] LaCugna, *God For Us*, 42.
[57] Ibid., 217.

existence of such an intradivine realm is precisely what cannot be established on the basis of the economy, despite the fact that it has functioned within speculative theology ever since the late fourth century."[58] She is even willing to move beyond this strong agnosticism to an implicit denial of the very *existence* of an intradivine realm: "the language of 'in' God creates the impression first of all that God has an 'inner life,'" she says.[59] Indeed, LaCugna suggests that any (even hypothetical) discussion of the immanent Trinity, if it does not actively affirm the crucial role of *the world*, is "a fantasy about a God who does not exist."[60] This would seem to imply that, if there were no created order, no human beings to experience redemption, the triune God might simply vanish into oblivion. The most charitable reading of this claim is that LaCugna has so allowed the immanent/economic dichotomy to drive the argument that she has not carefully attended to where it has led. The underlying assumption seems to be that, unless God exists wholly for the sake of humanity, then God must be nothing at all.

The difficulties of LaCugna's project may raise serious questions about the use of the terms *immanent* and *economic*, precisely because of the dichotomous division they imply.[61] To whatever degree such a distinction is necessary, it should be possible to speak of the immanent and economic Trinity without falling into such manifestly disjunctive modes of thought. For example, Rahner's claim about the mutual indwelling of the immanent and economic trinity seems to avoid the sharp disjunctions that LaCugna imposes; for Rahner, ultimately, the two cannot be completely distinguished.[62] Similarly, Balthasar comments that "the absolute image of God is necessarily cosignified in the image of the economy of salvation which emerges," and goes on to stress that *oikonomia* and *theologia* are mutually interdependent realms of discourse.[63] Henri de Lubac is even more explicit in his recognition of a certain mutuality of the economic and immanent realms. Speaking of Paul and of the writers of the early Church, he comments that

---

[58] Ibid., 223.

[59] Ibid., 224.

[60] Ibid., 230.

[61] Barnes ("Augustine," 240n17) suggests that this terminology is largely an invention of nineteenth-century historiography.

[62] The Trinity, 24 [329].

[63] Hans Urs von Balthasar, *Glaubhaft ist nur Liebe: Christ heute 5* (Einsiedeln: Johannes-Verlag, 1963), cited in Henri de Lubac, S.J., *The Christian Faith: An Essay on the Structure of the Apostles' Creed*, trans. Richard Arnandez, F.S.C. (San Francisco: Ignatius Press, 1986), 105 [ET of: *La Foi chrétienne. Essai sur la structure du Symbole des Apôtres* (Paris: Aubier-Montaigne, 1969), 120–1].

the 'economic' aspect of *theologia* led them to inquire into the 'theological' depths of the *oikonomia*. Knowledge of God's works cannot fail to throw some indirect light on God himself, a light which eliminates many unworthy or insufficient ideas rather than providing us with positive enlightenment.[64]

Surprisingly, though, LaCugna cites *this very passage* of de Lubac's text as justification for her claim that "theologians began to reflect on *theologia* itself, in some cases before or without considering the economy of salvation."[65] Once again, it seems, the dichotomy has encouraged an error in judgment by requiring the classification of everything on one side or the other of a great divide.

A different sort of dichotomy is constructed by Colin Gunton, whose Bampton Lectures depict a battle between Heraclitus and Parmenides, between the "many" and the "one." At first, Gunton appears to be very circumspect about the distinction, questioning its absolute nature; nevertheless, he says, "for the moment we shall remain within their framework, and use the expression of alternatives by Heraclitus and Parmenides as a heuristic device."[66] Unfortunately, this "heuristic device" becomes a basic dichotomy that Gunton is never really able to escape.

On the side of "the one," Gunton enlists Plato and most of the Western philosophical and theological tradition, including St Augustine, St Thomas, and Kant. Then, a shift occurs: "the modern world makes its choice for Heraclitus against the Parmenidean past."[67] Although roots of this shift are sought in William of Ockham and even in Augustine, the main troublemakers are Feuerbach, Marx, and Nietzsche. Soon, everything else is drawn into the dichotomy: for example, the ancient devotees of the One are described as enthusiastic about the soul, whereas the modern cult of the Many focuses on human embodiedness.[68] The varieties of postmodern discourse are collapsed into a single category and classified as a celebration of Heraclitean flux. Conversely, the whole of Western Christianity is described as embracing the unity of Parmenides, thus rendering it incapable of entering into relation.

Not only does this account blur important distinctions within these overly-broad categories; it also reads the history of thought through a Hegelian scheme of thesis and antithesis. Once the entire intellectual tradition of the West has been read in such a dichotomous fashion, the much-anticipated

---

[64] *The Christian Faith*, 107 [*La Foi chrétienne*, 123–4].
[65] LaCugna, *God For Us*, 43, and the accompanying footnote at 52n107.
[66] Gunton, *The One, the Three, and the Many*, 18.
[67] Ibid., 27.
[68] Ibid., 48–50.

synthesis will necessarily break down. This is not to say that Gunton does not attempt to overcome the disjunction: "Parmenides and Heraclitus have called the tune and so have obliterated the trinitarian categories which enable us to think of the world – and therefore also culture and society – as both one and many, unified and diverse, particular and in relation."[69] But Gunton's attempt to read the doctrine of the Trinity as a grand compromise ultimately fails; his account ends up being drawn in to the very dichotomy he has constructed.

Gunton begins his attempted synthesis by arguing that the theologian's concern is properly "with the universal dimensions of meaning suggested by the concept of God."[70] Moreover, he seeks a conception of truth that "is in its own way universal and objective" (whatever it may mean for something to be universal "in its own way").[71] Such claims about universality, objectivity, and truth provide clear evidence that, having spent the first part of the book aligning Christian thought with the Parmenidean option (the One), Gunton cannot now find a way to break free from it. He thus dismisses major contemporary alternatives (such as nonfoundationalism and narrative theology) with little argument, assuming that anything other than an objective foundation must be wholly relativistic.[72] Little attention is paid to the creative ways that this false dichotomy has been criticized by authors ranging from Stanley Fish and Cornel West to Hans Frei and Stanley Hauerwas.

Gunton's own program is built on a theory of "open transcendentals," which he hopes will draw together the universality of the One with the flexibility and potentiality of the Many.[73] Whatever one may think about wedding the idea of a "transcendental" (with its associations of universality and certainty) to limitedness, disagreement, provisionality, and finiteness, one must admit that Gunton's own dichotomy will make this a difficult marriage. For one thing, he has already categorized all the past Christian thinkers who have employed transcendentals as Parmenidean devotees of the One, so he

[69] Ibid., 124.

[70] Ibid., 129.

[71] Ibid., 131; see the review of Gunton's book by Philip D. Kenneson in *Modern Theology* 11, no. 2 (April 1995), 270–2.

[72] Ibid., 134: "When anything goes, then with it goes any notion of the overall unity and coherence of being and thought." Such easy dismissals of serious alternatives as a naïve form of relativism evade the questions at stake. See Philip D. Kenneson, "There's No Such Thing as Objective Truth, and It's a Good Thing, Too," in *Christian Apologetics in a Postmodern World*, ed. Timothy R. Phillips and Dennis L. Okholm (Downers Grove: InterVarsity Press, 1995), 155–70.

[73] Gunton, *The One, the Three, and the Many*, 142–3.

will be unable to draw significantly on any of them as sources for developing his new notion (thus providing another good example of the hazards of "historical scapegoating"!). Moreover, Gunton fails to give adequate attention to those fields of discourse that questioned the dichotomy of "the many" and "the one" in the first place – including rhetoric, literary theory, and (at least some forms of) postmodern thought.[74]

In my view, a discussion of oneness and difference need not surrender to an "either/or" mentality. But this is where it will likely end up if one begins with a large-scale historical construction of the eternal opposition of two forces, and then expects to effect a grand compromise between the two. Instead, we need to begin again from the beginning – with an entirely different, and non-dichotomous, conceptuality.

Practical ramifications revisited

The attempt to envision theology as an "analytic" endeavor has also had an impact on its approach to concrete practices. The individual case, as Aristotle pointed out, cannot always be grasped by a universal analytical principle. In concrete matters, we often find formal logic to be relatively useless, even if its truths seem clear enough in the abstract. This seems to be one of the primary claims of Newman's *Grammar of Assent*:

> It is plain that formal logical sequence is not in fact the method by which we are enabled to become certain of what is concrete; and it is equally plain, from what has been already suggested, what the real and necessary method is. It is the cumulation of probabilities, independent of each other, arising out of the nature and circumstances of the particular case which is under review; probabilities too fine to avail separately, too subtle and circuitous to be convertible into syllogisms, too numerous and various for such conversion, even were they convertible.[75]

---

[74] For example, Gunton too quickly dismisses John Milbank's creative claim that, "as for the finite world, creation *ex nihilo* radically *rules out* all realism in its regard. There are no things, no substances, only shifting relations and generations in time" (*Theology and Social Theory*, 426, cited in *The One, the Three and the Many*, 193n16). Because Milbank's approach calls into question the dichotomy of the "one" and the "many," it provides a better starting-point for trinitarian reflection. See further Milbank's "Theology Without Substance: Christianity, Signs, Origins," *Literature and Theology* 2 (in two parts): no. 1 (March 1988): 1–17 and no. 2 (September 1988): 131–52.

[75] John Henry Newman, *An Essay in Aid of a Grammar of Assent* (1870; reprint, Notre Dame, Ind.: University of Notre Dame Press, 1979), 230.

We sometimes avoid questions of concrete practice because they necessarily imply a lack of complete control over every possible outcome – something that an analytical approach seems to provide.[76] Abstract theoretical claims can be made universally; but concrete claims require attention to the particulars, which may vary widely. Thus, our teachings tend to sound a good deal less magisterial when we actually address concrete instances.

And this is why, for all their valuable comments about the practical consequences of trinitarian doctrine, very few writers in the contemporary conversation have actually provided a specific account of precisely what we ought to do differently in order to "enact" or "perform" the Christian doctrine of God. Too often, writers merely offer some general recommendation of both diversity and unity, phrased so abstractly that the partisans of almost any social, political, or ecclesial position could probably understand themselves as favoring it. How will the generic slogan of "diversity within unity" help us to address issues of identity and difference in matters of gender, sexual orientation, or criminal punishment? What are the specific implications of this claim for the political order? How does it help us to think about the justification of military action, for example? Or, more locally: how should a local congregation resolve the problems created by its declining numbers – problems that are tearing it asunder? What does the doctrine of the Trinity have to say about these matters? Even if it can give us no hard and fast rules, does it not at least point us toward particular assumptions and practices that should shape our lives?

Everyone seems to agree that it *should*, but few seem willing to *specify* these assumptions and practices. To offer one example, Catherine LaCugna devotes a chapter to "Living Trinitarian Faith," so one might reasonably expect it to address questions with some concrete specificity. Unfortunately, however, such specifics are generally avoided. With respect to questions of human sexuality, for example, LaCugna claims that

> alienated or alienating expressions of sexuality, practices that are truly "unnat-ural" in the sense of being contrary to personhood, contravene the very life of God. In contrast, fruitful, healthy, creative, integrated sexuality enables persons to live from and for others.[77]

---

[76] This provision of "absolute certainty" is illusory, or at best banal, since it is guaranteed only by prior agreement about first principles. This is easily illustrated with respect to simple arithmetic, where specific equations (e.g. $7 + 9 = 16$) appear to be timeless truths, until it is recognized that they depend upon agreement about a decimal-based system of numerals (in a hexadecimal system, common in computer programming, $7 + 9 = 10$).

[77] LaCugna, *God For Us*, 407.

About this passage, I would make three observations: (1) The doctrine of God that has been developed throughout the previous nine chapters of the book would appear to have little if any connection to this statement – neither warranting it nor being warranted by it. In what way does God's Triunity relate to this claim? (2) Christians who hold widely divergent views about sexuality could probably all embrace this statement, since the author makes no attempt to define or illustrate what might constitute alienation, contrariety to personhood, fruitfulness, health, or creativity. (3) The statement thus does nothing to help us think through the concrete questions about sexuality that the Church faces today, and which threaten to rend it asunder: Should the Church bless monogamous same-sex relationships? How should it deal with the widespread cultural acceptance of divorce, and the merely "serial" forms of monogamy that often result from it? Should it ordain married persons? gay and lesbian persons? How should the Church respond to advertising, much of which is based on sexual allure and outrageous stereotypes?

It may seem a bit churlish to lift one sentence out of a book and to note how obviously it fails to address these concrete issues. I am not suggesting that LaCugna needed to have addressed these issues in particular; I certainly will not be able to address all of them in this book. But the widespread failure to address *any* of these issues concretely – a failure that is certainly not unique to LaCugna – is illustrative of a monumental problem in contemporary trinitarian thought: no one wants to get down to cases. (The widespread tendency, in theological curricula, to divide doctrine from ethics is probably both a symptom, and a perpetuating cause, of this problem.)

Even Jürgen Moltmann – who is sometimes accused of being too "political," too willing to draw out the specific implications of his theological reflections – tends to do so at a fairly high level of abstraction. His recent essays on the problem of patriarchy in the doctrine of God, for example, offer some quite laudable claims about the need to re-think this question (I discuss some of his comments in the next section). But he rarely offers suggestions as to how the theoretical changes that he advocates might be brought about in practice. He offers few concrete suggestions as to how (for example) Christian worship or the practices of families might help to mitigate the effects of patriarchy, as he believes the doctrine of the Trinity calls us to do.

The tendency to avoid concrete cases is aided and abetted by an anxiety among some theologians about making any positive ethical claims whatsoever, for fear that it might compromise claims about "Christian freedom." For example, in the work of Alan Torrance, even LaCugna's mild and abstract ethical suggestions are thought to border on legalism. Similarly, Torrance criticizes Leonardo Boff for suggesting that trinitarian doctrine might actually lend some support to socialist forms of economic organization.[78] In general, Torrance seems to believe that a trinitarian understanding of persons in communion is "neither a form of 'praxis' nor a mode of *doing*, but a dynamic in which we find ourselves" – from which no ethical description can be derived.[79]

This, surely, is a failure of nerve. If all the hard work required to untangle the complexities of trinitarian doctrine led to nothing more than banal observations about the "dynamic in which we find ourselves," then Christians would be quite justified in dismissing it as irrelevant. Perhaps this is not quite what Torrance means, because he elsewhere claims that the doctrine of the Trinity has "very substantial socio-political implications."[80] Unfortunately, however, he never says what they might be.

The concrete case is rarely given adequate attention in doctrinal theology, because it upsets the smoothness (and thus, it seems to be assumed, the persuasiveness) of the system. One can enunciate a theoretical formula and perhaps win for it widespread agreement, since every reader's application of the formula to the concrete case will differ. (LaCugna's comment on sexuality is again a good example of this problem.) Once one makes a concrete claim, one is immediately exposed to critique by those who believe in the doctrine but do not want to abide by the concrete practices that the author claims that the doctrine implies. For example, if one were to make the claim that the doctrine of the Trinity provides no warrant for treating same-sex relationships any differently than the way in which we treat opposite-sex relationships, then one has to expect some fallout; many people are bound to disagree. (I discuss this matter in chapter 8. No peeking ahead!) By and large, systematic theology has tended to avoid the fallout, sticking with theoretical or abstract positions, since they are so much "safer" to hold. Of course, they are also much less relevant.

I think that a trinitarian theology *ought* to address questions about gay and lesbian relationships, as well as questions about violence, about hierarchy, about consumerism, and about the other issues that confront us, in concrete ways, every day of our lives. This is not to say that a single trinitarian theology has to address all of them. But in the current setting, very few works in trinitarian

---

[78] Torrance, *Persons in Communion*, 249n94. Actually, Boff makes only a mild claim in this regard; for a more explicit argument, see M. Douglas Meeks, *God the Economist: The Doctrine of God and Political Economy* (Minneapolis: Fortress Press, 1989). A more recent work takes up these questions in detail: Joachim Ackva, *An den dreieinen Gott glauben*, Frankfurter Theologische Studien (Frankfurt am Main: Josef Knecht, 1994).

[79] Torrance, *Persons in Communion*, 320.

[80] Ibid., 249n94.

theology address any of them.[81] I make some initial (and, admittedly, all too tentative) efforts to address this deficiency in parts two and three of this book.

Some New Concerns

Thus far, I have offered my assessment of positive and negative features of some of the broad tendencies in recent discussions of trinitarian theology. But what about issues that have not yet become central to the conversation? These are issues that may have been raised only at the periphery, or only by a few authors – or issues that have become very important in other realms of Christian theological discourse, but not (yet) with respect to the doctrine of God.

It is here, I think, that we have the most to gain by re-envisioning trinitarian theology as a *practice*. Too often, we have assumed that the issues faced in a previous era are the only issues that we need to face in our own, and that previous ways of framing those issues are the only ways they can be framed. Debates thus often devolve into an unsettled and often unsettlable argument about whether a particular form of words can or cannot be altered, or whether contemporary description "means" the same thing as an ancient author "meant." As Wittgenstein reminds us, what matters is not so much the words as the difference they make in our lives. And this requires us to face new concerns – because certain trinitarian claims will make a difference for our lives in ways that ancient authors could not have imagined.

In seeking to address these new issues in the present, it will help us to recognize that – as I will argue in greater detail in chapters 2 and 3 – meaning is formed *rhetorically*: language is not permanently imbued with certain properties, nor can identical forms of language be assumed to cause, in all times and in all places, identical effects. Meaning and effect are a product of the relationships among the writer (or speaker), the text (or speech), and the reading (or listening) audience. As these elements change, the entire equation is altered; words take on new shades of meaning, and authors become more (or less) credible with the passage of time.[82]

---

[81] There are exceptions, of course. In addition to works mentioned in the preceding notes (Boff, Meeks, Moltmann, and Ackva), see John Dear, *The God of Peace: Toward a Theology of Nonviolence* (Maryknoll, NY: Orbis Books, 1994), esp. ch. 4.

[82] A good guide here is Nicholas Lash, who speaks of "container" theories of meaning to describe what I would call "non-rhetorical" approaches. See, among other works, "What Might Martyrdom Mean?" in *Suffering* and *Martyrdom in the New Testament*, ed. William Horbury and B. McNeil (Cambridge: Cambridge University Press, 1981), 183–98; reprinted in *Theology on the Way to Emmaus* (London: SCM Press, 1986), 75–92.

In this section, I identify two sets of concerns, both of which have arisen primarily in the modern era, and which should, in my view, be taken into account by a contemporary exploration of the Christian doctrine of God. These issues certainly have been addressed in *some* recent trinitarian thought, and sometimes quite passionately; but they have also been just as passionately *ignored* by other contributors to the contemporary discussion. By discussing them here (and returning to them at various points in this study), I hope to encourage others to move them off the periphery, and into the center, of the practice of trinitarian theology.

Gender

On those occasions when Christian theologians have found a need to do so, most have emphatically denied that the category of gender could be applicable to God. St Gregory of Nazianzus, for example, scoffed at those among his opponents who claimed that, because God is referred to as grammatically masculine, this implied some kind of sexual differentiation in the Godhead.[83] Many writers in the history of the tradition never had occasion to comment on this matter, but those who did usually followed a similar line of thought.

And yet, in language, art, poetry, liturgy, hymnody, and so many other realms of Christian signification, masculinity and divinity have been inextricably linked. In most languages that assign grammatical gender, the referential parallels to the word *God* are masculine. Grammatically masculine pronouns are used to refer to God. Jesus was male, and all the canonical accounts of the twelve disciples list twelve (apparently) male names. Roman Catholic and Orthodox Christians have exclusively male clergy. Artistic representations of God – not only of Jesus, but also of "God the Father" – have been almost exclusively masculine. Despite the formal denials of the appropriateness of assigning gender to God, we have in fact assigned gender to God where it matters most: in our *practices*. Any contemporary trinitarian theology must face this problem squarely, and not brush it off as an irrelevance that has somehow been wrongly "imported" into theology.

Now it is of course possible to understand the masculine language and imagery of God as a *critique* of patriarchy, rather than an enforcement thereof. This claim appears in the recent work of Jürgen Moltmann, who believes that Jesus' message points us away from the structures of patriarchy and toward a renewed messianic future. The patriarchal mode of fatherhood will be replaced by "a fatherliness without claim to domination and rights to property,

---

[83] *Or.* 31.7; cf. Athanasius *De synod.* 42; Hilary *De Trin.* 1.18.

in communicative and participatory love, love which is merciful and ready for responsibility."[84] According to this interpretation, rather than carrying the notion of fatherhood across to God, we are asked to carry the message of compassion across to fathers. But does this really address the problem, or simply shift it into new territory? The overall effect, even if construed in the rather less offensive way that Moltmann (and others) recommend, remains a message chiefly *for fathers*. As long as this aspect of God's character is described exclusively in terms of *fatherhood*, without even an occasional alternative formulation, it will often be read as addressing only fathers – whether to reinforce their authority or to call them to be more compassionate (or perhaps both at once).

Admittedly, Moltmann goes on to emphasize what he calls the "feminine aspects" of God's fatherhood. The Father is the one who "gives birth" to the Son; the Son is born from the Father's womb, as the Council of Toledo insisted.[85] In this metaphor, the "maleness" of God's fatherhood is radically questioned by assigning it an exclusively female physiological function. The emphasis on the womb allowed the tradition to stress "that passionately painful feeling of mercy (rach[a]mim) located in the feminine body which is capable of giving birth."[86] The translation of this language into the Latin *misericordia* meant that the seat of mercy shifted from the womb to the heart, which was of course just as possible in a male body as in a female body; consequently, the masculinity naturally assigned to the word *father* was given free reign. In Moltmann's view, had the notion of mercy remained firmly attached to the *womb*, we would not be so tempted to associate God's fatherhood with maleness.

But would this have actually been the case? Moltmann seems to assume that, if we simply apply female qualities to a word (*father*) normally associated exclusively with the male, we get a more feminine reference. But that is only one of the ways in which figurative language can work. A metaphor such as "the father's womb" is certainly jarring; it makes us stop and rethink the relationship between two seemingly irreconcilable ideas (the womb and maleness). It opens up new possibilities of meaning. "The interesting thing

---

[84] *History and the Triune God*, 17 [43]. Ellen Charry has proposed a similar construal of *father* language: "Is Christianity Good for Us?," in *Reclaiming Faith: Essays on Orthodoxy in the Episcopal Church and the Baltimore Declaration*, ed. Ephraim Radner and George R. Sumner (Grand Rapids, Mich.: Eerdmans, 1993), 225–46.

[85] A number of other authors have noted this interesting phrase (*de Patris utero*) in the text of the Eleventh Council of Toledo (*Denz* 526); see, for example, Boff, *Trinity and Society*, 170.

[86] *History and the Triune God*, 22 [49].

about metaphor, or at least about some metaphors, is that they are used not to redescribe but to disclose for the first time. The metaphor has to be used because something new is being talked about."[87]

What "new thing" is here being described? Is it a God beyond gender? Or is it a male God — the pull of *father* is, after all, very strong — who has simply absorbed certain qualities that we had previously considered the exclusive domain of the female? Admittedly, when the focus shifted to two terms which did not create this tension (the *heart* and maleness), the jarring effect was lost and Christians were less likely to think about God in terms which transcended gender. But no form of language controls the ways it is read; a phrase such as "the father's womb" *might* be read as a critique of the maleness of God, but it might also be read as yet another effort — on the part of a largely male cadre of theologians — to "reduce all others to the economy of the Same."[88] The male simply absorbs and ingests the "otherness" of the female, reinforcing the dominance of the male and continuing to exclude feminine language for the divine.

While Moltmann's "solutions" to this problem have certain flaws, he can at least be commended for wrestling with the issue; unfortunately, however, not many contemporary trinitarian theologians have done so. Of course, a few writers have defended exclusively masculine language of God, and wear it as a sort of badge of honor;[89] indeed, some have staked out a position yet more patriarchal than that of much of the tradition, implying some essential connection between the masculine, or at least masculine language, and the divine.[90] And, on the other side, entire books have been written focusing only or primarily on the issue of gender and the Trinity.[91] But my concern here is not so much with those contributions that make this issue their focal point;

[87] Janet Martin Soskice, *Metaphor and Religious Language* (Oxford: Clarendon Press, 1985), 89.

[88] Luce Irigaray, *This Sex Which Is Not One*, trans. Catherine Porter and Carolyn Burke (Ithaca: Cornell University Press, 1985), 74, entire phrase italicized [*Ce sexe qui n'en est pas un* (Paris: Les Éditions de Minuit, 1977), 72].

[89] This is true, for example, of most of the essays in Alvin F. Kimel, Jr., ed., *Speaking the Christian God: The Holy Trinity and the Challenge of Feminism* (Grand Rapids, Mich.: William B. Eerdmans, 1992).

[90] This seems to be the position of some of the essays in *Speaking the Christian God*, e.g. those by Elizabeth Achtemeier, Roland M. Frye, and Alvin F. Kimel.

[91] Particularly important is Johnson, *She Who Is*; see also Ruth C. Duck, *Gender and the Name of God: The Trinitarian Baptismal Formula* (New York: Pilgrim Press, 1991) and Elizabeth Rankin Geitz, *Gender and the Nicene Creed* (Harrisburg, Pa.: Morehouse Publishing, 1995).

I am concerned instead with the absence of attention to this issue in broader, more general accounts of trinitarian doctrine. Here, the typical tendency has been to acknowledge the problem only begrudgingly, to express distress over most of the proposed solutions, and then to retreat into the same troubled language. Catherine LaCugna, for example, prints a long footnote of apology.[92] Ted Peters addresses the question at greater length and demonstrates some sympathy for the critique of the traditional language; nevertheless, he continues to employ it.[93] One of the most sympathetic recent accounts is that of Leonardo Boff, who offers a very clear description of the problem, both recognizing the lack of any *necessary* connection between masculine language and patriarchy, and yet acknowledging how easy it is for the two to become linked. He argues that, in technical terms, "God the Father" transcends sexuality; however, he also admits that

> this reality can be presented only in symbols and images. These are produced by particular cultures, and in ours have been controlled by the dominant group, which is made up of men. The image of God the Father, in its prevailing cultural significance, can hardly indicate what lies beyond it. . . . It is normally identified with a human father-figure, and therefore runs the risk of becoming an idol and legitimizing the domination of fathers and bosses over their children, women, and anything seen as feminine in nature.[94]

Boff also realizes that these idolatrous assumptions will not be changed simply by substituting feminine figurative language for masculine figuration. Nevertheless, he does argue briefly for the acceptability of the word *Mother* for God, and offers a number of instances in scripture and tradition in which God is referred to in feminine terms.[95] Unfortunately, however – having inserted this very laudable two-page caveat – Boff resorts to the traditional terminology, employing the word *Father* almost exclusively.

The problem here, as often, is that when a writer or speaker thinks about what language "means," the focus is primarily on the intention with which it is used, rather than on its reception. Certainly, Boff realizes that *father* is very likely to be received in gender-specific ways, as the above quotation indicates. But he still claims that "calling God 'Father' is not using sexist language"[96] – implying only, of course, that it need not be done with sexist *intent*. But as I

[92] LaCugna, *God For Us*, 18n7.
[93] Peters, *GOD as Trinity*, 46–55.
[94] Boff, *Trinity and Society*, 121.
[95] Ibid., 170–1.
[96] Ibid., 170.

have already argued, a word's "meaning" is most emphatically *not* determined by the intention of the speaker or writer; it is a rhetorical construct, and its content is, at least in part, in the hands of its hearers and readers. It is therefore dependent upon the shape of their lives and the practices in which they are engaged. When we use words that have a great many "male" associations (and in the case of *father* and *son*, these associations are almost exclusively male), it seems likely that these associations will be carried over to the reality to which the word is attempting to refer.[97]

In this book, I will employ a variety of strategies to attempt to overcome this particular "language disease." For example, I will sometimes use alternative translations to name the Three; moreover, I will suggest that the problem arises in part from *the very need we feel* to name the Three (that is, to use nouns to identify them). This tends to demarcate them as distinct individuals, thus working against many of the claims that the triune God would make on our lives. Thus, I believe that my attempt to ameliorate some of the problems generated by our gender-specific language for God will converge with a more satisfactory account of the doctrine of the Trinity in general – both of which are important goals of the practice of trinitarian theology.

Politics and the nation-state

A second issue that has not yet taken center stage in recent trinitarian theology is the relationship between the Christian doctrine of God and the rise of the modern nation-state. Certainly, there is a rather significant theoretical literature on the question of theology's general relationship to the state,[98] and a few commentators have taken it up with respect to trinitarian theology in particular. But, like the issue of gender, it has not yet become a theme that all contributors feel compelled to consider.

Among those writers who *have* addressed this question, the primary focus has been the idea that particular doctrines of God help to underwrite particular political structures. Jürgen Moltmann provides a starting point:

> Monotheistic monarchianism was, and is, an uncommonly seductive religious-political ideology. It is the fundamental notion behind the universal and

---

[97] I have explored this issue in greater depth in "On Translating the Divine Name," esp. in the subsections labelled "Words," "Meanings," and "Audiences," 427–36.

[98] See the bibliographies in Moltmann, *The Trinity and the Kingdom*, and in Michael J. Hollerich, "Retrieving a Neglected Critique of Church, Theology and Secularization in Weimar Germany," *Pro Ecclesia: A Journal of Catholic and Evangelical Theology* 2, no. 3 (Summer 1993): 305–32.

uniform religion: One God – one Logos – one humanity; and in the Roman empire it was bound to seem a persuasive solution for many problems of a multinational and multi-religious society. The universal ruler in Rome simply needed to be the image and correspondence of the universal ruler in heaven.[99]

The point is taken up more explicitly in the work of Leonardo Boff, who suggests that there are "dangerous consequences, in the political and religious spheres, of a monotheism detached from a trinitarian concept of God." He continues: "Strict monotheism can justify totalitarianism and the concentration of power in one person's hands, in politics and religion."[100] He cites examples in ancient Israel, the Roman empire, and the modern age.

Yet it is extraordinarily difficult to make this argument broadly persuasive. While one can certainly cite cases in which monotheism accompanied monarchy, one can also cite cases where *polytheism* accompanied monarchy (e.g., most of ancient Israel's enemies), or where monotheism accompanied democracy (e.g., the modern state of Israel). Even if one could show a general correlation, this would not settle matters of causation: does monotheism lead to monarchy, or do monarchical cultures just tend to evolve a religious monotheism? Or are both political and religious orientations the product of larger cultural tendencies?

I want to suggest that Moltmann and Boff have drawn our attention to an important issue, but that they have misstated the problem. They have taken for granted the authority of the state, and have suggested that monotheism promotes a particularly bad sort of state (an absolutist one), whereas a trinitarian conception of God promotes a better form of the state (Boff focuses on democracy, Moltmann on a fusion of socialism and "personalism"). Both positions fall into a typically modern trap – namely, the claim that Christians ultimately owe some form of allegiance to the nation-state (and therefore have an abiding interest in the improvement of its structure). But it is *this* claim – about the allegiance owed to the nation-state, *whatever* its form – that the doctrine of the Trinity most clearly calls into question.[101]

---

[99] Moltmann, *The Trinity and the Kingdom*, 131, altered. The last sentence is difficult to construe; Moltmann writes "Dem Weltenherrscher im Himmel mußte nur der Weltherrscher in Rom abbildlich entsprechen" (*Trinität und Reich Gottes*, 146).

[100] Leonardo Boff, *Trinity and Society*, 20.

[101] The neglect of this question is especially striking in Boff's *Trinity and Society*, since, in the Latin American context at least, the Base Christian Communities provide exactly the sort of alternative politics described here. The connection is clearer in some of Boff's other works, as well as in more general studies of the BCCs, e.g., Margaret Hebblethwaite, *Base Communities: An Introduction* (New York: Paulist Press, 1993).

The rise of the modern nation-state required the invention of the concept of *religion* as separable from the Church – as William Cavanaugh has demonstrated in a recent essay.[102] In order for the state to reign supreme, Christians had to be convinced that their beliefs were a merely private affair, and that their public allegiance was owed to the temporal sovereign. Indeed, for writers such as Thomas Hobbes, the sovereign displaces the Church altogether, with the capacity to take over all priestly and prophetic activity.[103] In order for this to occur, all public claims about the nature of one's belief – even claims about the specific attributes of the God whom one worshipped – were marginalized. This allowed for broad toleration of the interiorized religious conscience, since only public declarations of theological truth could threaten the rule of the sovereign.

Thus, as the portrait of God becomes more "generic" – as specifically trinitarian features are erased or minimized – its concrete ramifications for the nation-state become fuzzy and indeterminate. A generic portrait of God need not stress the Jewish origins of Christianity, nor its advocacy on behalf of those dispossessed groups that the nation-state might prefer to ignore, nor the act of political subversion that stands at the very heart of its narrative: namely, that its central figure was executed by the "state." Moreover, such specific portraits of God require public debate and defense, and this is hazardous to the well-being of the state. Cavanaugh refers to the sixteenth-century political theorist Jean Bodin, who indicates that he is unconcerned about what particular religion a people chooses; "what is important is that once a form of religion has been embraced by a people, the sovereign must forbid any public dispute over religious matters to break out and thereby threaten his authority."[104] Thus, the generic portraits of God that became so commonplace during the Enlightenment are indeed supportive of the nation-state – but *not* because their monotheism supports monarchy. Rather, the *generic* nature of their portraits support the state *in general*. These portraits employ broad philosophical attributes such as omnipotence and dispassion, rather than the specifically *theological* attributes that might give rise to political strife.

So Moltmann and Boff turn out to be right in their fundamental insight that

---

[102] William T. Cavanaugh, "'A Fire Strong Enough to Consume the House': The Wars of Religion and the Rise of the State," *Modern Theology* 11, no. 4 (October 1995): 397–420.

[103] Thomas Hobbes, *Leviathan, or the Matter, Forme and Power of a Commonwealth Ecclesiastical and Civil*, ed. Michael Oakeshott, with an Introduction by Richard S. Peters (1651; reprint, New York: Macmillan, Collier Books, 1962), ch. 42, *passim*. I owe the reference to Bill Cavanaugh.

[104] Cavanaugh, "A Fire Strong Enough," 405.

the evacuation of trinitarian theology has consequences for the state. What they miss is that this evacuation supports not merely absolutist states, but *all states in general*, to the detriment of the allegiance that Christians owe to God and to the Church. One of the important consequences of a rebirth of trinitarian theology, then, should be a radical questioning of the allegiance that Christians owe, not just to those nation-states that they find distasteful, but to *all* nation-states. A generic portrait of God can easily be absorbed by the state, because – as the Enlightenment thinkers testified – it can be accepted by "all rational people" (though of course they left the concept of *rationality* quite uninterrogated). But the triune God forms Christians into the Body of Christ, which is the only real rival to the dominant social body of the modern age – the state.[105] A specifically trinitarian account of God, with all kinds of practical ramifications following in its wake, cannot be brought into the nation-state's embrace; it thus poses a genuine threat to the state's idolatrous demand that it receive our highest allegiance.

The Practice of Trinitarian Theology

In this chapter, I have attempted to locate my own approach in the context of the contemporary revival of trinitarian theology. I hope that I have said enough about what I find to be laudable, dubious, and absent to give readers some sense of where I stand (and where I may be heading). Part of what it means to *practice* trinitarian theology is to enter into conversation with others who are similarly engaged. Whether readers will be persuaded by my own practice of it, or by that of other theologians, can only be determined in the course of the book as a whole – and quite appropriately so, since we can really only understand and evaluate those practices in which we *participate*.

In this book, I am attempting to articulate the relationship between the triune God and the lives of Christian believers. Thus, although these opening chapters describe the assumptions from which I begin, they are not mere "prolegomena"; rather, I understand them to be the "source" of the entire project. A trinitarian theology is necessarily a circular endeavor, in this sense at least: the doctrine of the Trinity should be not only the *goal* of the investigation, but also its starting point, and the chief influence on its method.

---

[105] I owe this formulation of the matter to Bill Cavanaugh (personal conversation). For some striking examples of how the Body of Christ can act as a rival to idolatrous and murderous state practices, see Cavanaugh's *Torture and Eucharist in Pinochet's Chile* (Ph.D. dissertation, Duke University, 1996).

We should seek not simply to promulgate a trinitarian theology, but to think and to live in trinitarian ways. In the practice of trinitarian theology, we learn not to be conformed to this world, which is passing away, but to be transformed by the renewing of our minds, so that we might discern the will of the triune God – what is good and acceptable and perfect.

Chapter 2

PRODUCING

As I observed in chapter 1, the biblical narratives describe how the earliest Christians came to the belief that they had beheld God in their midst. They had seen Jesus' works of power; they had seen him crucified by the authorities of the day; and they were witnesses to his resurrection. He had ascended into heaven; but God's presence had not thereby departed from those who believed in him. Instead, Jesus had breathed the Spirit upon them, giving them "another advocate" (John 14:16) in his place. The entire narrative is well summarized in Acts, where Peter proclaims that the one God of Israel, ever transcendent and all-powerful, had nevertheless come to dwell among the people – twice. First, in Jesus of Nazareth, God had worked "deeds of power, wonders, and signs" (Acts 2:22) and eventually worked the greatest sign of all – raising him from the dead, making him Lord and Christ. Then, the Spirit of God had been poured out on all flesh, fulfilling the prophecy of Joel and empowering the disciples to proclaim Christ's resurrection and saving power (Acts 2:16–21).

The doctrine of the Trinity is, at the most fundamental level, an attempt to account for these phenomena. Christians believed that (1) God remained all-powerful and transcendent, and yet (2) Jesus, who died and was raised by God, was somehow also God; moreover, (3) the Spirit, poured out on the Church, is also God, and yet (4) there is only one God. To an outsider, this could make no more sense than a mathematical problem that ended with the equation 3 = 1. How can these Three be One?

To answer this question, Christian theologians speculated on what would need to be the case with respect to God, in order to hold together all four of the aforementioned claims. This was not an *abstract* speculation; the circumstances that engendered it were the very concrete events to which the biblical narratives bore witness. The concrete basis for these speculations often goes unnoticed, especially since they resulted in a rather complex description of the inner life of God. This account included the rather arcane-sounding claims that there are *processions* in God, and that these imply certain internal divine *relations*. These processions and relations were, in turn, the basis for two divine *missions*: the incarnation of the Word in Christ and the pouring out of the Spirit upon the Church (both described in Peter's speech in Acts). Thus, the traditional account of the inner life of God – what some theologians have referred to as the "immanent Trinity" – is already firmly rooted in the economy of salvation.[1] However abstract it may seem, the speculative account of God's inner life is "simply the biblical account in drastic summary, construed as an account of God's own reality."[2]

Some recent theologians have discounted such speculative descriptions of God, as part of a well-intentioned effort to make trinitarian doctrine easier to understand. Unfortunately, this effort has driven a wedge between God and the world, thus actually making it *more* difficult to understand the character of the triune God. Without attention to an account of God's inner life, we are left only with our own experiences of the acts of God; we thus remain wholly passive partners in this relationship, accepting the gifts that we are given but never inquiring into the character of the giver. Our own human relationships would look rather odd if we followed this model – "I don't care who you are or what you're like, but I will gladly take what you give me." Of course, we can never experience another person's perspective in any absolute sense; but our relationships would seem rather shallow if we were never moved to inquire into the character of others, nor to try to see things as others see them. Indeed, failing to inquire into the perspective of the other is likely to provide a distorted picture of one's relationship with that person; and this applies to one's relationship with God as well.

Consider, for example, the standard description of God's acts toward the world in the Christian accounts of creation, redemption, and sanctification. Because of the ways that these divine acts are narrated in the story of salvation, they seem to take place in a clear temporal sequence. Most Christians would see very little wrong with such an account: first, God creates the world; later, having noticed that things have gone awry, God redeems it; and then, God spends the rest of history trying to maintain its rather precarious state by means of sanctification. But a moment's reflection should alert us to the inadequacy of this picture. It makes God into a sort of cosmic air-traffic controller, who – having given out too many licenses to fly – must now manage the confusion

---

[1] See the comments by Balthasar and de Lubac, cited above in chapter 1, notes 64–5.

[2] Robert W. Jenson, "What is the Point of Trinitarian Theology?" in Schwöbel, ed., *Trinitarian Theology Today*, 36; see also Williams, "Unity," 89.

and prevent collisions. We can obtain a clearer picture if we attempt to think about God's acts from *God's* perspective. This helps us to recognize that they cannot be a series of events that transpire in a certain order (whether temporal, logical, or otherwise). They are all wholly, equally, and eternally constitutive of God's loving relationship with the world.

The doctrine of the Trinity postulates an integral connection between God's own character and God's relationship to the world. Thus, for example, if we are to understand the claim that we are created by God, we must also think about what it means for God to "generate" or "give birth" to the eternal Word.[3] And as we investigate both these aspects of divine action – internal and external – we need to remain aware that our knowledge of these actions is itself dependent on God's own act of self-revelation. We thus need to hold together three strands that are always threatening to unravel: the character of God's inner life, the nature of God's relationship with the world, and God's role as the ultimate source of our knowledge of God. In this chapter, I attempt to braid these strands together, by offering an account of the divine activity of *producing*.[4]

The verb *produce* shares with all transitive verbs a threefold grammar, implying a subject and object as well as an action. There can be no producing without a *producer* and a *product*. Moreover, this verb is particularly useful when seeking to emphasize a close relationship between its subject and its object. Especially when the verb is predicated of persons, we tend to infer that the very existence of its object is due to the action of its subject; the product owes its existence to the producer, and the producer is responsible for the product. In this sense, producing is an *engaged* activity – one in which the (grammatical) subject and object are bound together in a close mutual relationship.

Moreover, this term (as I am construing it here) implies more than simply

---

[3] John Milbank argues that the "disassociation of the act of creation *ad extra* from the generation *ad intra* . . . sealed the displacing of the Trinity from the centre of Christian dogmatics" ("The Second Difference: For a Trinitarianism Without Reserve," *Modern Theology* 2, no. 3 [April 1986]: 213–34; here, 219).

[4] For a similar use of the language of producing, as well as the image of "gardening" that I will mention shortly, see Nicholas Lash, *Believing Three Ways in One God*, chs 4 and 7. One could also make a case for the word *gifting*, as does Stephen H. Webb in *The Gifting God: A Trinitarian Ethics of Excess* (Oxford: Oxford University Press, 1996). This word perhaps more clearly evokes God's gracious and loving character; but it also requires rather more extensive philosophical groundclearing, given the current discussion of gift and exchange in the work of Jean-Luc Marion, Jacques Derrida, and others. For a thorough discussion of the trinitarian implications of this conversation, see John Milbank, "Can a Gift Be Given? Prolegomena to a Future Trinitarian Metaphysic," *Modern Theology* 11, no. 1 (January 1995): 119–61.

creating an object and leaving it to its own devices. "Producing" describes the activity of (for example) a gardener – who must not only sow good seed, but must take care that the plants are not choked by weeds or allowed to go too long without water. Or, consider a different analogy: our use of the word *produce* to describe the process of putting on a play or making a film. The creation and assembly of the raw materials – script, space, equipment, money – is a necessary, but not sufficient, condition for the production of the play. Scripts need abridgement and emendation; actors' disputes need to be settled; equipment needs to be repaired and maintained. Producing is never a matter of simply beginning something and then abandoning it to take care of itself.

These analogies, of the garden and the play, may shed some light on our interrelated descriptions of God, of God's acts, and of God's role as the source of our knowledge of God. In all three cases, we can employ the language of "producing" – a complex, fully-engaged process of superabundant love and willing donation. First, *God produces God*; more specifically, God (the source and origin of divinity) gives birth to the Word and issues the Spirit. In addition, *God produces the world* – not merely creating it, but caring for it, redeeming and sustaining it. Finally, *God produces our knowledge of God* – through the definitive revelation in Christ, but also in empowering us to receive this revelation (through the practices of the Church), and in providing us with the tools and materials to make this knowledge clear and persuasive to others.

By examining these diverse theological claims under the single term of *producing*, I hope to show their dependence on one another – and thereby to underscore the importance of all three for the practice of trinitarian theology. This is the first step in the process of articulating a fully trinitarian way of thinking – not only about God, but also about the world, and about the relationship between them.

God Produces God

Of the three activities of "producing" that I will examine in this chapter, this one will require the longest and most complex description. As I have already indicated, speculative accounts of the inner life of God are not mere abstract juggling-acts, but are attempts to describe God in ways that are true to the biblical narratives of יהוה, Christ, and the Spirit. I begin with a systematic account of the process by which "God produces God"; I then turn to my own reinterpretation of this process and the formulation of some alternative trinitarian language.

A systematic account of the divine processions

One of the clearest systematic statements of the way in which "God produces God" may be found in the *Summa Theologiae* of St Thomas Aquinas. Thomas is clearly drawing on the tradition he has inherited; many of his claims could be just as easily illustrated from the work of St Gregory of Nazianzus or St Augustine (though in those cases certain details would vary). But Thomas has already put this account together for us in a rather tidy package, so we can make a start by listening to the story as he tells it. I will also offer a number of interpretive comments of my own.

Thomas begins by considering what we may know of God on the basis of what has been revealed to us. He answers that we may know that there are two processions in God: the procession of the Word, which he calls generation or begetting (*generatio*), and the procession of Love, which – because it is the procession of the Spirit – is called "spiration" (*spiratio*; Boff translates, more helpfully, "breathing out"[5]). Despite the fact that Thomas employs abstract terms, the processions are fundamentally based on the biblical account of God's revelation through Christ and the Spirit.[6] Indeed, Thomas's first argument for the whole idea of "processions in God" is a quotation of John 8:42 – the words of Jesus, "I came forth from God."[7]

God, then, is an internally self-differentiated being. At first, this seems similar to the neo-Platonic descriptions of "emanations" that flow forth from God, forming a great chain of Being in which all beings participate to a greater or lesser degree (depending on their distance from God). But that picture is decisively altered in the Christian tradition, in that the divine emanations do not flow forth and animate the created order; rather, they are described as wholly *internal* to God.[8] Moreover, this is not merely an act of self-duplication on God's part; it is an act of self-abandonment, a giving up of oneself in order that there might be an Other to oneself.[9]

The idea of an "internally self-differentiated being" is a difficult one; in the created order, there are no perfect analogies to describe it. Yet because Thomas's discussion of this matter is highly technical, a concrete example will be needed, however imperfect it may be. The best example, in my view, is

---

[5] Boff, *Trinity and Society*, 90–1.

[6] This challenges the contemporary commonplace, noted above (pp. 32–3), that the ordering of the *Summa* divorces trinitarian theology from the economy of salvation.

[7] *ST* Ia.27.1, trans. Velecky, VI:3.

[8] Milbank, *Theology and Social Theory*, 428.

[9] See Balthasar, *T-D* III:518,526 [*TD* II/2:475,481].

one that wasn't available to Thomas: it is the example of pregnancy.[10] The formation of a child in a woman's womb is a good example of "going forth from oneself," which is the notion behind the divine processions: the mother gives her own self to the "other" within her, becomes "other" to herself, yet does not thereby diminish herself. Again, the analogy is not perfect; she does not do this as a pure act of her own will, and the production of the "other" is not entirely internal, since it requires at least one sperm. Nevertheless, despite its imperfections, this analogy will help us think about the concept of internal, self-differentiating processions. We will return to it again as Thomas develops his argument.

The processions within God would seem to imply relations within God; and in question 28, Thomas examines the idea of "real relations."[11] A "real" relation is not merely logical or external; it belongs to the very nature of an act (as in the relations of giving a gift and receiving it), and is not merely accidental (as in the relations among the books scattered across my desk). Real relations also arise when something has the same nature as that from which it comes; in that case, "both that which issues and that from which it issues belong to the same order; and so must have real relationships with each other."[12] Since the divine processions are of the same nature as the source from which they come, they give rise to real relations in God.

Note that Thomas has not yet spoken of divine "persons"; indeed, in these questions he mentions the traditional terms *Pater*, *Filius*, and *Spiritus Sanctus* only rarely. The real relations described here are not relations *among* individuals; rather, they are deduced from the internal divine processions. If there are two processions, there must be four real relations; each procession implies two relations, signifying the two perspectives from which each procession can be viewed (for example, the bestowal of a gift can be characterized as a relation of giving or a relation of receiving). Thomas names these relations *paternitas*, *filiatio*, *spiratio*, *et processio*,[13] which I translate: initiation, fruition, issuance, and emergence.[14]

To explicate Thomas's claim, the example of pregnancy will again be useful; but we will need to make it a bit more complicated. Since Thomas speaks of *two* divine processions, we need to ask whether pregnancy can also

---

[10] Not available, because of the biology of his era, which claimed that the woman was a merely passive vessel in matters of reproduction, and therefore gave nothing of significance to the child.

[11] *relationes reales*, Ia.28.1.

[12] *ST* Ia.28.1, trans. Velecky, VI:25.

[13] *ST* Ia.28.4.

[14] An *apologia* for these idiosyncratic translations will appear in the next subsection.

have this feature. One way to develop this analogy would be to speak of a woman carrying twins; this approach would in fact be very useful in describing the account that developed in Eastern Christianity, in which the two processions are described as identically related to that from which they come.[15] However, Thomas is operating according to the Western view, in which the two processions are more clearly differentiated. So we will need to venture further, and remember that, in a pregnancy, a mother must "go forth from herself" and "become other to herself" *twice*: first in conception, and again in the production of an organ of mediation between mother and child (the placenta).[16] We can therefore say that, in pregnancy, there are four real relations as well. The process of conception creates the relations of "motherhood" and "childhood"; and the production of the placenta creates the relations of (let us say) "mediating" and "being mediated."

I want to underscore the active way in which these relations are here described – both in our example of pregnancy and in the language that Thomas offers. This is not static language of fixed and isolated entities; the processions and relations tend to imply one another, and thus to evoke movement and flux. These active forms are primary for Thomas, and are solidly in place when he turns to discuss the Three.[17] After some definitional groundclearing, he asks a very specific question about the Latin word *persona* (which traditionally designated that of which there were three in God). His question is whether it signifies a relation; and his answer is that it does, and specifically, a *subsistent relation*.[18]

To "subsist" is to be self-grounded, to exist in and of oneself, and not to be dependent on some other thing. A "subsistent relation" is thus not an easy

---

[15] In Eastern Orthodoxy the "Father" is described as the principle of unity in God, the fount from which both processions flow in equal measure; the Western *filioque* describes the procession of the Spirit differently. My own sympathies are mainly with the East, but I will follow the Western view here in order to explicate Thomas. On the Eastern view, see Zizioulas, *Being as Communion*, 83–9. More on the *filioque* below.

[16] The importance of the placenta in summarizing the role of the "necessary third" in reciprocal relationships is developed in the work of Luce Irigaray. See, inter alia "Body against Body: In relation to the mother," in *Sexes and Genealogies*, trans. Gillian C. Gill (New York: Columbia University Press, 1993), 9–21 [ET of: "Le corps-à-corps avec la mère," *Sexes et parentés* (Paris: Éditions de Minuit, 1987)], and the interview with Hélène Rouch in "On the Maternal Order," ch. 4 in *je, tu, nous: Toward a Culture of Difference*, trans. Alison Martin (New York: Routledge, 1993), 37–44 [ET of: "A propos de l'ordre maternel," *Je, Tu, Nous: Pour une culture de la différence* (Paris: Bernard Grasset, 1990), 45–54].

[17] *ST* Ia.29.

[18] *significat relationem ut subsistentem* (*ST* Ia.29.4).

concept to grasp, since we are generally accustomed to thinking about individual entities who *have* relations, or who *enter into* relations, rather than about relations that just "are." Relations, to us, seem to be dependent upon the presupposed "beings" that are "in relation"; yet the applicability of this assumption to God is here expressly denied. The Three are derived from the divine processions. They are not individuals who come into relation; they are not endpoints, between whom there are relations; they are, simply, relations.[19]

As I noted above, Thomas is building on the insights of St Augustine, the Cappadocians, and an entire tradition of trinitarian thought; his claims here are not particularly new.[20] But they are (as I have just noted) somewhat counterintuitive. As Robert Jenson comments, "our inherited ways of thinking suppose that – obviously! – there must first be *things* that in the second place may be variously related. But there is nothing intrinsically obvious about it; in fact, by biblical insight it is the other way round."[21] In the biblical narratives (as in most narratives), individuals are not defined in the abstract and then shown to be related to one another; the character of persons becomes apparent only through their relatedness to others. This biblical insight was the starting-point for the speculative formulation which developed over the centuries (and which Thomas systematizes here).

But given Thomas's claim that the Three are "subsistent relations," diligent readers will have noticed a problem: our discussion of the two divine processions led to a claim that there are *four* real relations in God. Why are there only *three subsistent* relations? Thomas answers that, in God, a real relation is only subsistent if it is distinct from the other relations; and this distinction requires a relative contrast. As it turns out, one of the relations does not manifest this contrast, and so is not distinct.

Thomas's discussion here is extremely technical,[22] so let us return to our analogy. Motherhood and childhood are clearly contrasting with one

---

[19] Many standard treatments of the tradition get this point backwards. See, for example, Boff, *Trinity and Society*, 85–92, where the discussion of nature and persons precedes the discussion of processions and relations.

[20] Cf. Gregory of Nazianzus *Or.* 29.16; Augustine *De Trin.* V–VII; for a summary of Augustine's views, with bibliography, see Kelly, *Early Christian Doctrines*, 274–5; on their importance, see Milbank, "Can a Gift," 150–4.

[21] Jenson, *The Triune Identity*, 123.

[22] "The several persons are subsisting relations which in reality are distinct from one another. Now real distinction between divine relations can come only because of relative contrast. Hence two contrasting relations must belong to two persons. If any relations are not contrasting then they must needs belong to the same person." *ST* Ia.30.2, trans. Velecky, VI:69.

another, and can thus be clearly distinguished; they are both subsistent relations. And one of the other two relations ("mediating") manifests this difference as well; it can be contrasted with both motherhood and childhood, neither of which bears this actively "mediating" character. But the fourth real relation – "being mediated" – cannot be fully distinguished from the first two relations (motherhood and childhood). To understand why, we need only ask: what exactly is "being mediated" in the complex, self-differentiated reality of pregnancy? The answer is that motherhood and childhood are "being mediated"; thus, the relation of "being mediated" duplicates relations that have already been described. So although it is a *real* relation within pregnancy, it is not a *subsistent* relation; it is not self-grounded, but is dependent upon another pair of relations. There remain only three subsistent relations: motherhood, childhood, and mediating.

Thomas offers a similar description of the divine relations. The relations of "initiation" and "fruition" are clearly contrasting; thus, they mark two of the Three. Similarly, the relation of "emergence" can be contrasted with both of these; so it is also subsistent.[23] But the fourth real relation, "issuance," cannot be contrasted with either initiation or fruition; indeed, in Thomas's view, it duplicates *both* of these relations.[24] Since it cannot be fully distinguished from the other relations, it is not subsistent.

But Thomas does not use the same words to describe the subsistent relations as he used to describe their corresponding real relations. For the latter he used *paternitas, filiatio*, and *processio*; but for the former he uses the substantives *Pater, Filius*, and *Spiritus sanctus*. This move is understandable, because (a) Thomas wants to provide a mark of difference between the real relations and the subsistent ones; (b) he wants to provide a reminder that the subsistent relations are self-grounded, that they have at least a temporary stability, allowing us to refer to them as entities (which is easier to do with substantive names than with verbal, relational forms); and (c) he wants to describe them by using names for the Three that are woven into the biblical narratives and that have therefore dominated the history of the tradition. Unfortunately, however, in the process, he dispenses with any need to continue to employ the strongly verbal (and thus, very active and relational) terms that he first used to describe them (I translated them initiation, fruition, and emergence). These verbal terms are

---

[23] Thomas points out that *processio* cannot mark either *Pater* or *Filius* (or both), as this would imply that *Pater* "emerged" from something (and thus was not the ultimate source), or that there was a procession prior to that of *Filius*. Thus, he concludes, the relation of *processio* must marks a third person, *Spiritus Sanctus*.

[24] This claim is related to Thomas's defense of the *filioque* clause; *spiratio* marks both *Pater* and *Filius* because the Spirit proceeds from the Father "and the Son."

replaced with relatively static substantives. These terms still imply relation at some level, but the hearers of these terms rarely bring those relational elements to mind.

When we hear the words offered as ordinary translations of his substantive terms – *Father*, *Son*, and *Holy Spirit* – we do not normally call to mind the real relations from which these names are derived.[25] Instead, we think of them as separate entities, as distinct centers of consciousness – in short, as isolated individuals. And as a result, one of the most important claims of trinitarian theology – that the Three are most fundamentally *relations* – is lost from our view.[26] (We could note a similar problem with the use of substantives to designate the relations in pregnancy: once we begin to speak of "mother" and "child," we tend to assume that they can be defined in isolation from one another – a tendency that is evident on all sides in the current politics of pregnancy. I will return to this point in part two.)

I do not mean to blame St Thomas for our tendency to "miss" the notion of relationality with which he hoped to invest the words *Pater, Filius,* and *Spiritus Sanctus*. In Thomas's context their relational qualities may have been clearer, and we may (by means of thoughtful translation) help to repristinate those qualities. On the other hand, it may simply be the case that *any* naming of the divine persons by static substantives will make it difficult to remember that the Three are *relations*. As readers and listeners, when we hear three nouns, we think of three entities; any relations, we assume, would need to be *among* these entities. But when we hear three verbal forms – such as "initiation, fruition, and emergence" – we are probably less likely to think in terms of stasis and potential isolation, and more likely to think in terms of motion and relation. These verbal forms are probably too abstract for consistent liturgical use (which is why I will eventually attempt to offer some substantives); however, in technical theological reflection, the relational terms would probably be less misleading.

In any case, we have now followed the rather arduous path that was cleared by a wide variety of trinitarian theologians in the early and medieval eras. We began with the processions in God; from them we derived the real relations; and we noted that three of these are subsistent relations. Having traced this process, we are in a better position to resist the tendency to think of the Three

[25] As I will note at several places in this book, the words *Father* and *Son* retain a faint trace of their relational origin, but the individualizing tendencies of our culture have all but obliterated them.

[26] The significance of this claim is underscored by Robert Jenson, who describes it as "the main place at which the metaphysically revolutionary power of the gospel breaks out in Western theology" (*Triune Identity*, 123).

as isolated individuals who *have* relations, or who make a decision to *come into* relation. Instead, we can begin to understand the Three as "relation without remainder," constituted by the two processions that are internal to God.

Reinterpreting the processions and relations

In the previous section, I used the analogy of pregnancy to explicate Thomas's understanding of processions and relations in God. This analogy has roots in the tradition (though in a very different form), since one of the two processions – that of the Word – is named *generatio* (usually translated "begetting," but contemporary biological assumptions make "conceiving" just as adequate a term). This, in turn, implies two relations; or, we might say that it can be seen from two perspectives (conceiving, and being conceived). Thomas's terms, *paternitas* and *filiatio*, have typically been rendered "fatherhood" and "sonship"; but I used different translations ("initiation" and "fruition"). Why?

One problem, of course, is the masculine language. It is true that Jesus was male; it is also true that the narratives describe him as using, to address God, a word that Greek-speaking readers of the Gospels would have used to identify a male parent. But Thomas is not here addressing Jesus' sex or his address to God; he is discussing the divine processions, the internal self- differentiation of God. Thus, if we prescind from Thomas's biological assumptions, there is no need to translate his terms into contemporary English as masculine terms. I have already noted that the Christian tradition has, in its more philosophically reflective moments, avoided the attribution of gender to God (though given its production of language and symbol, one could hardly tell it!). Of course, Thomas had an additional reason for using masculine language for the procession of begetting: he believed that only males could do it. In his biological world, the male provided the true seed, reason and intelligence; the female provided only matter.

> In a scheme where only males are truly generative then, in a sense, only males can truly give birth. The only true parent is the father, source of seed which it is the female task to nurture. Lest we think this all just 'mere metaphor' we can note that one reason given by Aquinas in the *Contra Gentiles* why we ought not speak of the first person of the Trinity as *Mother*, is because God begets actively, and the role of the mother in procreation is, on the other hand, passive.[27]

---

[27] Janet Martin Soskice, "Trinity and 'the Feminine Other'," *New Blackfriars* 75 (January 1994): 2–17; here, 8, citing St Thomas Aquinas, *cont. Gent.* IV.11.

St Thomas, perhaps, could not have thought otherwise; but we can. In fact, our contemporary perspectives on biology, sexuality, and gender make it very difficult to retain his assumptions about the wholly active role of the man and the wholly passive role of the woman.[28]

So why not simply use the language of "motherhood" and "daughterhood," or perhaps (since we believe that male and female both contribute to the process) "parenthood" and "childhood"? These questions are understandable, especially given the significant use of a parent–child analogy in the previous section. Note, however, that it was not just *any* parent–child analogy, but specifically an analogy to *pregnancy*; and the problem with all such analogies, to put it bluntly, is that pregnancies eventually come to an end.

My wife would want me to emphasize that, in general terms, this is most certainly *not* a problem! My point, however, is that *because* pregnancies end, the analogy is disrupted. Children are born, they grow up, they leave home; in general, and perhaps especially in our culture, we tend to think of parents and their children as separate people. (This in itself is a problem, to which I will return in chapter 8.) And my analogy in particular, which described the mediating role of the placenta as a subsistent relation, completely falls away in the process of giving birth. Any language that draws heavily on parent–child imagery will thus probably contribute to our tendency to think of the Three as distinct individuals – in spite of the fact that parents share with their children a "common substance" at the genetic level. To describe the notion of a *wholly internal procession* by means of a human analogy, pregnancy is probably our best choice, and I will return to the analogy frequently in this book; but it too has flaws. If I were forced to choose, I would say that mother–child imagery is probably a better way to convey the reality of the divine processions than is father–child imagery, due to the biological realities of pregnancy and breastfeeding.[29] But as long as our

---

[28] My translations are thus attempts to describe what might have been lying behind Thomas's terms, if we could somehow abstract them from his biological assumptions. This is always a risky endeavor, and can be criticized not only by advocates of the *status quo* but also from a feminist perspective (Irigaray). I do not seek to excuse Thomas, nor to deny the sexuate character of language, but rather to "use what can be used" in a contemporary elaboration of trinitarian theology. I think my guesses are reasonable ones, given the assumptions of his era; I will offer more specific arguments in this respect as I discuss the relations, below. Of course, Thomas's language would allow him to move naturally into the dominant trinitarian liturgical formula of his time; mine does not. More on that point shortly.

[29] I strongly object to the claim that "father" language is somehow more literal or less metaphorical than "mother" language. Despite the predominance of the former, it too is analogical, as are the biblical terms (usually translated into English as *Father*, *Son*, and *Spirit*) which helped to provide the narrative warrant for the processions and relations. Karl Barth

culture sees parents and children as fundamentally separate entities, any such language will contribute to difficulties in maintaining the simultaneity of oneness and difference in God.[30]

Thus, whatever one may think about the "masculinity" of this language as traditionally translated, it has another (and in my view, just as serious) problem – and one that is not solved by transforming it into its feminine or non-gender-specific "equivalent." Namely, it encourages us to think of the divine processions as a process of separation and division, and to think of the divine relations as occurring *among* quasi-independent *entities*. The Nicene Creed sought to mitigate the temporal and dividing aspects of parent–child language by describing the "Son" as "eternally begotten"; but this in turn lessened the impact of the analogy – what would it mean, in our experience, for a child to be "eternally begotten"? A never-ending pregnancy? Or perhaps a never-ending labor?[31]

Perhaps the idea of internal divine relations would be easier to understand if we were to employ a different analogy altogether. Imagine a spring of water,[32] coming up out of the ground: here we have movement, procession, a going-out-from-itself-to-itself. Such a procession implies two relations; or, put another way, we can describe this upward movement from two different perspectives. To do this we may have to imagine ourselves as immersed in the spring itself (which means we will need to imagine a very big one). We can

---

makes this point very clearly at *CD* I/1, 340: "the analogies adduced by the Fathers are in the long run only further expositions and multiplications of the biblical terms Father, Son, and Spirit, which are already analogical." [*KD* I/1, 359: "der ebenfalls schon analogischen biblischen Begriffe."]

[30] I hope I have made it clear that I do not wish to de-personalize the divine relations, but only to discourage reading them as separate entities that are (or can become) relatively independent of one another.

[31] Actually, there is considerable potential for creative theological reflection here, with respect to the suffering of God; certainly, the language has considerable biblical warrant. See Frances Young, "The Woman in Travail," ch. 3 of *Can These Dry Bones Live? An Introduction to Christian Theology* (New York: Pilgrim Press, 1993), 43–63.

[32] This image already has a rich trinitarian history; Tertullian used it explicitly, and we find the image of a "source" or "fount" (πηγή; *fons*) to describe God, and/or the internal divine origin of the processions, in a wide range of writers – the Cappadocians, pseudo-Dionysius, St Bonaventure, and Calvin, among many others. Its "cardinal importance" for Calvin, and for the Reformers generally, is developed in B. A. Gerrish, *Grace and Gratitude: The Eucharistic Theology of John Calvin* (Minneapolis: Fortress Press, 1993), 31–8. The image also illustrates the complete coincidence of essence and giving in God; in "giving" alone, God "is" (cf. Milbank, "Can a Gift?," 154).

imagine ourselves floating on our backs, facing up, in the same direction as the flow of the water – looking, as it were, from the inside out. Or, we can imagine ourselves face down (bring scuba gear), against the flow – looking from the outside in. In the first case, our perspective is similar to that of the origin of the water – of where it might have come from (even though we are not located at that point and thus cannot actually see where it begins). We can call this relation *initiation*. In the other case, when we are situated "against the flow," we adopt the perspective of the destination of the water's movement, and become aware of its moving out beyond itself; this relation can be called *fruition*.[33]

Trinitarian doctrine posits another procession in God as well; the procession of Love. Since it is described as the procession of the Spirit, it has traditionally been associated with language that calls to mind the image of wind or breath. Thomas's terms, *spiratio* and *processio*, have always posed a significant challenge for translators; the standard English attempts have little to recommend them. ("Spiration" is virtually meaningless; "procession" is easily confused with the use of the term to describe *both* divine processions.) "Breathing out" and "being breathed out" are better;[34] they make an analogical reference to the process of respiration and thus connect back to the Spirit (via its Hebrew and Greek roots). But this analogy faces some difficulties too. It lacks the intimacy and reciprocity of a parent–child relationship; and while parents share "the same substance" with their children, it is less easy to see how this is the case with respect to breath (though perhaps more clearly so with "spirit"). Moreover, just as we find it difficult to imagine an "eternal begetting," so it is difficult to imagine an "eternal breathing out." And finally, like the image of childbirth, the language tends to suggest two quasi-independent (or at least separable) entities: the breather and the breath. But the idea of a "procession in God" posits *not* a separation into two independent entities, but rather two relations; and thus, again, a different analogy may help.

Consider again the image of the spring.[35] Upon closer inspection, we realize

[33] I think these translations can be supported on the basis of a recontextualized account of Thomas's language. For him, *paternitas* would have been strongly associated with initiation, since (as noted above) the *pater* was considered the initiating force in procreation. Similarly, *filiatio* would have been associated with fruition; for Thomas, a truly fruitful offspring would have been one who could continue to be fruitful, namely a *filius*.

[34] I first encountered these translations in Leonardo Boff, *Trinity and Society*, where Paul Burns uses them to translate Boff's Portuguese; I do not know whether they have been employed by others writing in (or translating into) English.

[35] The association of water with "the Spirit" has deep biblical roots. Water revives the spirit (Judg. 15:19); the gift of God's Spirit is associated with the gift of water (Neh. 9:20); and

that (of course) the movement of the water does not end in its rising up from its source; it flows out, away from the place of our original focus, providing moisture to the area that surrounds it. We can now think of the spring as "processing" in two ways: "upward" and "outward." The outward-flowing procession can also be understood from two perspectives – again, from the inside looking out, or from the outside looking in. We can call these relations *issuance* and *emergence*, respectively.[36]

Summarizing briefly: the Christian narratives led theologians to speak of God's two processions (of the Word and of Love), and thus four relations: initiation, fruition, issuance, and emergence. While we recognize that these relations are all internal to God (and thereby do not compromise God's oneness), we also recognize that they seem to endow God with internal difference. How can we characterize this difference? At first glance it would appear to be fourfold, but we know from the above exposition of St Thomas that one of these four real relations is, in a certain sense, duplicative; it cannot be distinguished from the others.

We can map this claim onto our analogy of the spring and its two processions. In our discussion of the "upward" procession, we spoke of relations of initiation and fruition; these are clearly distinguishable, so they can be described, using Thomas's term, as "subsistent relations." We now turn to the other procession – that of the water that flows out away from the spring. One of its relations (that of "emergence" – the one suggested by a perspective of "outside looking in") is similarly distinguishable; to speak metaphorically of our "position" within the spring, it requires us to be in a different place, looking in, "horizontally," toward the upward flow of source-to-spring. But how shall we describe the other relation – "issuance" – the one that seeks to describe this "outward" procession from the opposite perspective (that of the inside looking out)? The problem here is that any attempt to describe this relation as "subsistent" – acknowledging it as self-grounded – would duplicate

---

the Spirit is described as being "poured out" (Isa. 32:15, Ezek. 39:29; Joel 2:28–9, Acts 2:17–18), sometimes with an explicit parallel to water (Is. 44:3, Rev. 22:17). And of course, the Spirit is closely associated with the water of baptism (John 3:5; Acts 10:47; Tit. 3:5, 1 John 5:6–8).

[36] Again, I think these terms find some support in Thomas's relational categories, as well as in other ancient traditions. They describe the two "perspectives" on this procession; yet their range of reference is not so tightly restricted to breath-oriented imagery. They thus create space for the relations to be described with a wider range of language, drawing on other entities that can be understood in terms of procession, of which *water* is an obvious instance.

the relations that we have already named. It would have to be understood either as doing the same work as the relation of initiation (described above as the perspective of origin), or that of fruition (the water's upward movement), or perhaps of both. In any case, it would duplicate a relation that has already been named. Thus, only three of the relations are subsistent: initiation, fruition, and emergence.

The question we must now ask is: Will we stay with these purely relational terms, using them to name the Three? Or will we do as Thomas did, employing more substantive, static nouns? The first option would underscore the dynamic, reciprocal structure that we discovered in our analysis of processions and relations. Indeed, this approach may be the only way to describe the Three as wholly internal relations (and thus to describe God as "relation without remainder"). Nevertheless, this would also be a hazardous course of action, since Christian theology has almost always named the Three with substantive terms. We will create great difficulties farther down the line, when we attempt to compare this language with other translations and other explications of the divine processions and relations. We will also create problems for the translation of the creeds and for liturgical language. Somehow, the relational language must remain primary, and the use of substantives to name these relations will obscure this point. Nevertheless, concrete specificity is often essential in Christian practice; we speak to God, we invoke God, we baptize in God's name. We sometimes need substantives. But the ones that we have traditionally used present us with some obvious inadequacies.

The traditional English-language substantives for the Three employ triads such as "Father, Son, and Holy Ghost," "Father, Son, and Holy Spirit," "God, Word, and Spirit," or even "Mother, Child, and Spirit" – or some hybrid of these. Some of these obviously have a very long history. Despite their predominance, however, in the contemporary context they tend to minimize the classical trinitarian claims as we have traced them here. They do very little, indeed almost nothing, to evoke the divine processions and relations. But if it is true (as Thomas claims) that the processions and relations provide nothing more than a philosophically rigorous account of the same information that we are given in the biblical narratives, then something has gone wrong. As useful as these traditional formulations may be in their use of biblical vocabulary (or at least our prevailing translations thereof), they have, in our contemporary context at any rate, lost most of their power to evoke the central claims upon which trinitarian doctrine is based.

The result is that, by and large, very few Christians can make sense of trinitarian theology. It is already difficult enough to imagine that anything could be exhaustively defined by processions and relations (since we tend to think of relations as something that occurs "between" two entities). The task of explication is rendered yet more difficult under the influence of the traditional English formulations, which seem – certainly at first glance, and perhaps at second and third glance as well – to posit three individuals who are theoretically separable from one another. This is not what trinitarian doctrine proposes with respect to God; it posits not three persons who "have" relations, but rather, *three subsistent relations*. As Nicholas Lash has put the matter, we tend to speak of human beings as *having* relations; God, on the other hand, *is* the relations that God has.[37]

Certainly, it is easy enough to account for the dominance of the traditional formulations. They were taken to be relatively "natural" translations of terms that were employed very early on by Christians as a shorthand for referring to the God whose story they were attempting to tell. These terms were employed very early in Christian history – long before the accounts of the divine processions and relations were worked out in any detail. To return to the architectural metaphor that I employed in the Introduction, the "vaults" of Christian doctrine were being built, but the keystone was not yet in place. Moreover, the various builders had not all imagined an identical location and shape for that keystone. The vaults soared upward, but they were not all headed in the same direction.

Indeed, the biblical language for God is something of an architectural patchwork; it is greatly varied and highly unsystematic. Christians believed in one God, but the stories they were trying to tell about this God were diverse. This was the God to whom Jesus referred as πατήρ, the God who became flesh and dwelt among us, and the God who indwelt the community of believers at Pentecost. Thus, a variety of names were employed to describe God, depending upon what particular aspect of the story was being told at the time. I will explore this variety in more detail in chapter 6; meanwhile, suffice it to say that, from very early on, a variety of words were used to name what would later come to be understood as God's internal, subsistent relations.

Developing alternate formulations

Given that a wide variety of terms were in use from the beginning, and given that we still need to translate these terms from their Greek and Hebrew contexts, I think it is very appropriate that we attempt to develop alternative formulations, *not to replace, but to be used alongside* the traditional forms of

---

[37] *Believing Three Ways*, 32.

naming the Three. At their best, these new formulations would call to mind the divine processions and relations, and yet also make it possible to hold fast to the oneness of God. They should thus name the Three in ways that might discourage us from thinking of them as independent entities.

In this book, I continue to use the traditional language in some places, pointing out how we might extract some of its residually relational character. I also employ the analogy of pregnancy with some frequency. Typically, however, I will use language that again draws on the analogy of the spring, and offer the following substantives for the Three: *Source, Wellspring, and Living Water*.[38] I do not offer this as a singular substitute for the prevailing English-language substantives; it is simply part of an ongoing experiment in the practice of trinitarian theology.[39] In the first instance, at least, I am not proposing it as liturgical language, but as technical theological language; it seeks to emphasize the claim that the Three are fundamentally *relations*. On the other hand, this language may come to have certain liturgical, catechetical, and ethical advantages; but the only proof of that will come in the practices. Some early local experimentation has been attempted, and has led me to be optimistic that, if employed in a variety of contexts (dogmatic, homiletical, and liturgical), and with due attention to the need for ongoing catechesis, this formulation can have a variety of positive effects (some of which I will explore in later chapters). I also offer some very preliminary liturgical suggestions in Appendix III.

I do not propose that this language be used for a wholesale retranslation of the biblical text. Many of the narratives would be incomprehensible if this were done in a mechanistic fashion. On the other hand, biblical texts can often shed new light when translated anew. In this book, I have used both traditional and new translations, depending on the context of the passage.

Needless to say, my alternative translations do not address all the problems faced by the use of substantives to name the Three. The words that I have offered are certainly still nouns, and thus are not completely resistant to being

---

[38] I have already noted the biblical and patristic roots of water imagery for God. Whether this formula can be called a "translation" of the traditional trinitarian formula will depend upon a number of issues, including one's theory of translation; see my comments (and attendant bibliography) in "On Translating the Divine Name." In any case, before quickly dismissing this formula as "unbiblical," critics should recall that God is explicitly called "a fountain of living water" (Jer. 2:13, 17:13), and that the "living water" is the gift that Christ gives to the world (John 4:10–14); this living water is explicitly associated with the Spirit at John 7:38–9.

[39] For this formula, and for some of the discussion that follows, I owe particular thanks to the Ψ Group – and especially to Margaret Adam, who not only played a pivotal role in developing the language, but also took the lead in incorporating it into liturgical practice.

perceived in very static ways. On the other hand, to most audiences, these words may imply at least some degree of motion. Perhaps their very novelty will remind us to attend to the relations that they attempt to name (relations of initiation, fruition, and emergence). In this respect they are an improvement, for the present context of English-language theology, over the traditional terms, which are no longer so clearly connected with the subsistent relations.

I realize that this language will be found by some readers to be odd, and perhaps even off-putting. I can only ask that such readers be patient; my rationale for the use of these terms in particular will become clearer over the course of the book as a whole. But I also hope I have made it abundantly clear that I am *not* advocating the widely-held view that one can simply invent such language at whim, seeking to satisfy perceived "needs," without attention to the claims of the tradition.[40] The practice of trinitarian theology is an attempt to make important claims about the nature of God and of God's relationship to the world; it has far-reaching implications, and should not be lightly dismissed. New language cannot be accepted simply because it "speaks to us today"; it must be tested in both theory and practice. We thus need to develop language that not only addresses the contemporary rhetorical context, but also remains attentive to the central claims of trinitarian doctrine. I hope that others will join in this process; I also hope that theologians will neither simply dismiss *nor simply accept* such alternatives, but will offer thoughtful assessments of their theological, pastoral, liturgical, and ethical ramifications.[41]

[40] Sallie McFague's proposal, "Mother, Lover, and Friend," is described as an attempt to dethrone the language of "Father, Son, and Holy Spirit"; but she also indicates that she has no interest whatsoever in attending to the traditional claims of trinitarian doctrine, whether formulated by St Thomas or anyone else. Indeed, she is quite willing to dispense with the Trinity altogether, claiming that its only purpose is to express the transcendence and immanence of God, and that in any case it must be subordinated to the "independent, communal, reciprocal" God–world relationship that is "needed today." *Models of God: Theology for an Ecological, Nuclear Age* (Philadelphia: Fortress Press, 1987), 183-4 and the notes on 223-4. If theology is nothing more than the *ex nihilo* creation of gods that are "needed today," I must confess that I do not see the point.

[41] For example, the formulation "Creator, Redeemer, Sanctifier" was briefly popular, but was brought under fairly careful and nuanced criticism, e.g., in Wainwright, *Doxology*, 353 and 555n866. (It would seem to be either modalist or tritheistic, depending on whether the three activities are attributed to one agent or three; it also encourages us to think of the external works of God as divided.) As a result, the early enthusiasm expressed for it seems to have waned significantly (as noted by Ted Peters, "The Battle over Trinitarian Language," *dialog* 30 (1991): 44–9; here, 48n13). Unfortunately, it now serves as a straw figure, used by critics in an attempt to undermine the entire enterprise of seeking such alternative formulations by suggesting that all such attempts suffer from an utter lack of theological sophistication (see e.g. the comments in Torrance, *Persons in Communion*, 237).

One test of new language such as this is to see whether it can be used to translate some of the traditional claims about the relations. We can say, for example, that the Source is the Source of the Wellspring, and the Wellspring is brought forth (or given birth) by the Source. Attending to the Creed of Constantinople, we can say that the Living Water flows forth from the Source. The addition of the word *filioque* to the Latin version of the Creed heavily influenced the subsequent Roman tradition; those who continue this tradition could say that the Living Water flows forth from the Source *and the Wellspring*.[42] Those interested in pursuing the yet-more-technical claims of trinitarian theology will also discover that this language can be used to map the standard elements of the pseudo-Athanasian Creed,[43] as well as rendering the five trinitarian "notions" (those characteristics that enable us to know each of the Three as different from the others).[44]

This lengthy discussion of how "God produces God" has provided us with a new vocabulary that will help clarify a number of other claims about God and God's relation to the world. It has also reminded us that, despite the apparently abstract nature of these claims, they are meant to be faithful to the biblical narratives on which they are based. Those narratives also tell us about God's actions *toward the world* – and, here, their claims are more straightforward. Thus, our next section will be considerably shorter and simpler.

God Produces the World

As noted in the previous section, God's processions bear some resemblance to the neo-Platonic concept of "emanations." They differ, however, in that God's processions are wholly contained within God; they do not flow forth and animate the created order. From the Christian perspective, the world is

[42] Interestingly, the language I have offered helps explain why each side of this debate thought it was providing the more adequate description of the relations. What is the origin of the Living Water? Clearly, its origin is the Source. But it cannot flow directly from the source without somehow involving the Wellspring. Does it simply "pass through" the Wellspring, or can we think of it flowing forth from both? Thus the *filioque* debate.

[43] For example: The Source is God, the Wellspring is God, and the Living Water is God, but the Source is not the Wellspring, nor the Wellspring the Living Water, nor the Living Water the Source. The Source is not made, nor created, nor brought forth. The Wellspring is not made nor created, but is brought forth by the Source alone. The Living Water is not made nor created nor brought forth, but emerges from the Source and the Wellspring.

[44] The Source is uninitiated and initiating; the Wellspring is bearing (as in the phrase "bearing fruit"); the Source (together, according to the Western view, with the Wellspring) is issuing; and the Living Water is emerging.

not created out of God; it is created out of nothing (*ex nihilo*). God and creation are thus separated by what Kierkegaard called an "infinite qualitative difference."

Yet this *difference* does not necessarily imply *distance*; and even less does it imply a lack of concern, care, or involvement. God creates the world as something wholly other-than-God, gives to it the gift of life, in order that the world might return the gift to God – and to do so of its own accord, not as a result of the divine pulling of various strings. And it does so; the created order glorifies God – it "returns the gift" – simply by being what it most fully is, and thereby testifying to God's loving act of donation. But one particular group of the creatures in this creation have been given even more – and of them, more is required. Human beings are given not only their life and breath; they are also given a rather extravagant degree of freedom. Created in the image of God, they possess even the power to turn away from God. They – and perhaps they alone – are capable of choosing not to return the gift.

And because such creatures are part of the divine plan from the outset, God's relationship to the world is not exhaustively defined by the notion of "creation"; in other words, God does not simply leave the creation to its own devices. Creatures who have the power to say "no" can be expected to act on that power at some time or another. God creates us in order that we might come into communion with God; God awaits our response, our "yes," our return of the gift. Having thus created us, God does not abandon us; even when we fail to fulfill our purpose (to glorify and enjoy God forever), God provides a way for us to turn and be converted – a way for those who have said "no" to God to say "yes" instead. Of course, even those who do eventually say "yes" are still free, and they may turn away again. Thus, God sustains them in their willingness to return the gift, taking them up into the divine life and giving them a foretaste of its glory.

God creates, redeems, and sanctifies the world: as I noted at the beginning of this chapter, this is not a series of rearguard actions, in which God attempts to rectify the mistakes of the past. They are all necessarily bound up with the creation of an "other." If this other is truly *other* – and is thus endowed with the freedom and power to turn away – then we should perhaps not be completely surprised when it chooses to exercise that power. If its creator wants it to turn back and be reconciled, then such a creator must also be willing to expend the energy – and, if necessary, to pay the price – to call the other, again and again, into communion.

Here again, an analogy of parents and children may help. Despite its flaws in describing God's inner life, it provides a rather good analogy for God's relationship to the world. It is, of course, an imperfect analogy; we do not "create" children in the strong sense that God creates the world. Nevertheless, it is useful in that good parents recognize that bringing a child into the world involves more than a mere act of "creation," a pleasurable sexual event that "initiates" the child's life. Children are not fully under the control of their "creators"; they have the freedom to turn away. Parents who wish to remain in communion with their children know that they must do more than simply "make a baby." They must also provide a means whereby children can turn a defiant "no" into a willing "yes" – and they must find ways of sustaining that decision by means of a long, fully-engaged process of reconciliation. At its best, parenthood is not simply a series of emergency measures, each under-taken as a way of coping with the willful otherness of the child. Good parents know from the outset that children cannot simply be "made" and left to their own devices.

And God is the best of all possible parents. Having created the world, and having created human beings (whose freedom is so extensive that they are able even to turn away from God), God redeems them from their isolation and alienation, providing a means by which they can be taken up, once again, into the divine life. And God also endows them with the power to sustain this return by sanctifying them, setting them apart from those elements of the world that militate against this process of reconciliation, giving them strength and courage to do God's work in the world.

Before all time, God made a decision to *produce* the world. This decision may be compared to that of a gardener who will stay with the project through thick and thin – "through hell and high water" as my grandfather used to say (a Kansas wheat-farmer is, after all, a gardener of sorts). Before the seeds are planted, before the garden is even laid out, a decision is made to do whatever it takes to bring these frequently obstinate creatures into full flower. Some may eventually refuse to bloom; but the good gardener does everything possible to get them to do so. The biblical parable of the vineyard plays on this image explicitly: God is the owner of the vineyard, who continues to care for it despite being out of sight; in the end he even sends his beloved son, handing him over to the wicked tenants, and all for the sake of the vineyard (Matt. 21:33–46 // Mark 12:1–12 // Luke 20:9–19).

The redemption and sanctification of the world is accomplished through two divine "missions": we can describe them as missions of incarnation and inspiration, or as the "sending" of the Son and the Spirit, or perhaps as the birthing of the Wellspring and the pouring out of the Living Water. The two missions (like all of God's external actions) are singular actions of God, and are in no way divided among the Three; the agent of each of them is the triune God. (That they each seem to focus on only one of the Three is a result of our limited perspective; of this, more in a moment.) The two missions, though differentiated, are both eternal; they are decisions that God has made from all eternity, though from our temporal perspective they only come to pass in the fullness of time.[45] Their "right time" is the moment of the Annunciation to Mary, or more precisely, the moment when she actively accepts God's initiative: "Let it be with me according to your word" (Luke 1:38). At this point, the Word of God becomes incarnate in the flesh of Mary, through the power of the Holy Spirit. Thus, the mission of the Word and the mission of the Spirit begin, from our perspective, at the same time – even though the Spirit's mission is at first focused only on the person of Christ.[46] After the Resurrection, and most clearly on the day of Pentecost, the mission of the Spirit reaches its full breadth, as the Living Water is poured out on the whole world. Here, I want to describe each of the missions briefly.

The birthing of the Wellspring is the means by which God brings about the redemption of the world. The term "birthing" refers not only to the precise moment of birth, though that moment is certainly significant; it refers to everything that is involved in God's decision to send God into the world. It includes a number of actions on the part of Mary – her acceptance of her role as God-bearer, her giving of herself in pregnancy and breastfeeding, and the love and care required to raise a child. And it involves actions on the part of Jesus as well: his acceptance of baptism and of his mission; his teachings, healings, and signs of wonder; and of course, his willingness to suffer and die. These actions, which can sometimes appear disjointed or disconnected, are all part of the mission of incarnation. God thus carries out the redemption of the world, not by an external imposition, but through free human acts – the willingness on the part of Mary and Jesus to return to God the gift that we have all been given.[47] And this willingness must also be shared by God: a willingness to be born into the world, to speak to it and to suffer it, and indeed, to be killed by the world. "To be 'sent into the world' is tantamount to being 'given up to death.' "[48] Again, this is not a temporal decision on God's part, made at some point after things had gone awry; rather, "God chose us, in Christ, before the

---

[45] As emphasized by, e.g., Balthasar, *T-D* III:513 [*TD* II/2:470–1].

[46] See Moltmann, *Trinity and the Kingdom*, 122, and the bibliography at 238n38 [*Trinität und Reich Gottes*, 137].

[47] See Milbank, "Can a Gift," 136: "Mary's praise already cancels sin since it is able to speak *the logos* into being. Of course this is all under grace, and Mary's *fiat* is from that perspective inexorable, but nevertheless creation is restored, given back to us, in the same manner that it was first given to us in a gift that is (inexorably) our free reception and infinite return of the gift."

[48] Jüngel, *God as Mystery*, 364 [*Gott als Geheimnis*, 499].

foundation of the world" (Eph. 1:4). God's decision to stay with us – to "produce" us, in spite of our (inevitable?) waywardness – was part of the plan from the beginning.

The mission of "inspiration" – the pouring out of the Living Water – is the means by which God brings about the sanctification of the world. Until the resurrection, its focus is on the person of Jesus; described in the New Testament with the word πνεῦμα and its cognates (usually translated with reference to spirit or breath), it describes that which animates and empowers Jesus to carry out the will of God. It rests on Jesus at his baptism (most clearly in Matthew's account, where it is described as "descending like a dove and alighting on him," Matt. 3:16); it drives him into the wilderness at the outset of his ministry (Mark 1:12 par.); it empowers his teaching in Galilee (Luke 4:14); and he commends it back to his Father as he dies (Luke 23:46). But after his resurrection, Jesus breathes it out on the disciples (John 20:22), and in Acts it is described as being poured out on all flesh on the day of Pentecost (Acts 2:17). As such, it empowers those who have been incorporated into Christ to keep their hearts and minds focused on God, to whom they have been reunited through God's act of redemption.

The divine missions link the internal divine processions (which constitute God's Triunity) to our experience of God in history.[49] In other words, our salvation can be carried out as it is (through the birthing of the Wellspring and the pouring out of the Living Water) only because God is already self-differentiated. Imagine, for a moment, that there were no internal processions in God: this would make it very difficult to speak of God "becoming" flesh, and dying, and being raised up by God. Similarly, we could make little sense of the claim that God is both the one who "pours" the Living Water (or "breathes" the Spirit) upon the world, and yet that God is also that which is being poured (or breathed). In God's act of producing the world, God is simultaneously agent, action, and act; and this requires some notion of divine self-differentiation.

The divine missions, and their close alignment with the divine processions, are explicated by means of a helpful analogy in Hans Urs von Balthasar's *Theo-Drama*.[50] Balthasar describes our salvation as the production

[49] "The concept of 'mission' creates an inner bond between the doctrine of the immanent Trinity and the Three Persons revealed in revelation and in the economy of salvation." Leo Scheffczyk, *Der Eine und Dreifaltige Gott* (Mainz: Grünewald, 1968), 122, cited in Balthasar, *T-D* III:515n1 [*TD* II/2:472n8].

[50] Although the analogy pervades the work, its component parts are explicated at *T-D* I:268–305 [*TD* I:247–83] and given specifically trinitarian application at *T-D* III:515–35 [*TD* II/2:463–89].

of a play that takes place upon the world stage, in which God is simultaneously the author, the primary actor, and the director. God has written the
script, and so is the ultimate source of the action; God performs the play,
entering the world to enact the script that has been written; and God directs
the play, bringing the other actors into a proper relationship with the central
actor, and providing the necessary promptings to insure the successful
enactment of the drama.

The analogy is a rich one, and Balthasar uses it to make a number of
important points about the Trinity. It helps us to understand God's external
actions as undivided; the missions are not a "division of labor" among
the Three, but a single endeavor to which each of the Three contributes.
The author always writes with some ideas about how the actor and director
might work with the script; indeed, many authors may imagine how
they themselves would undertake these tasks, and write accordingly.
Authors thus have something of a continuing effect upon their works, an
effect which "extends to the sphere of the actor and director – not
tyrannizing them but providing them with an area for creativity."[51] Similarly, the director has to take account of both the author and the actor(s), but
has a particular responsibility for the drama's enactment, such that it will
eventually have its effect upon the audience. And yet, in the actual
performance of the play, the director will not be seen (nor will the author);
only the actor(s) can "incarnate" the action to which all three have
contributed.[52]

As Balthasar is well aware, the analogy is of course not a perfect one; we will
misunderstand its point if we try to make God into three separate people (who
quarrel and rebel and try to assert their individual egos). Nor will it do to think
of those playwrights who have also starred in and directed their own plays; for
here, the three activities become merely separate tasks or modes, taken up at
different times for different purposes.[53] The point of the analogy is not to
provide one-to-one resemblance with the triune God, but to give us a sense
of why the divine missions are integrally related to the internal self-
differentiation in God. It reminds us that the missions and the processions are
bound to one another, and that we *cannot even separate out* the categories of the
"immanent" and the "economic" Trinity – let alone privilege one over the
other.

---

[51] Ibid., I:279 [I:258].
[52] Ibid., I:301–2 [I:279–80].
[53] In trinitarian terminology, the first assumption makes the analogy tritheistic, whereas the
second one makes it modalist.

Indeed, the notion of distinct or divided realms of God's activity of producing (what I have sometimes called "internal" and "external" acts) is a relatively late one; it does not play a major role in the early formulation of trinitarian doctrine. God's processions and God's missions are understood as a single reality; their linkage is evident, for example, in the Nicene Creed. An examination of some of the features of that Creed, with special attention to its explication of God's "producing" activity, will conclude the present section.

We believe in the producing God

As described in the Nicene Creed, God is a producing God, a God of abundance and willing donation. God produces God, by an act of eternal self-differentiation – the processions of the Wellspring and the Living Water. God also brings the world into existence, creating it out of nothing. These aspects of God's activity of producing are woven together in the Creed.[54] The first article is a confession of belief in:

one God,	ἕνα Θεόν,
the Source, the all-powerful,	πατέρα, παντοκράτορα,
creator of heaven and earth.	ποιητὴν οὐρανοῦ καὶ γῆς.

In these lines, two elements in particular evoke the notion of producing: πατέρα, which I translate *Source*, is the origin of something, strongly implying the existence of an Other (a source is always the source of something). The Source is the origin of an Other; it brings this Other into existence. Secondly, the verb ποιέω, usually translated by *make* or *create*, reminds us that God is the creator of heaven and earth (which, as the Creed goes on to elaborate, constitutes "all that is, seen and unseen"). Thus, the activity of producing is constitutive of both the inner life of God and God's role as the creator of the world.

The second article of the Creed continues to shape our understanding of God's activity of producing. We confess a belief in:

---

[54] The Greek text from which I am working here is actually that of the Council of Constantinople, which came to be known in the seventeenth century as the "Nicene–Constantinopolitan Creed" (*Denz* 150). I provide a new translation of the whole Creed, with attention to the issues raised in this chapter and with suggestions for its liturgical use, in Appendix III.

one Lord, Jesus Christ,	ἕνα κύριον Ἰησοῦν Χριστόν
sole Wellspring of God,	τὸν υἱὸν τοῦ Θεοῦ τὸν μονογενῆ
eternally brought forth by the Source,	τὸν ἐκ τοῦ πατρὸς γεννηθέντα
	πρὸ πάντων τῶν αἰώνων, . . .
. . . of one being with the Source,	ὁμοούσιον τῷ πατρί,
through whom all things were made.	δι᾽οὗ τὰ πάντα ἐγένετο·
Who, for us	τὸν δι᾽ἡμᾶς τοὺς ἀνθρώπους
and for our salvation	καὶ διὰ τὴν ἡμετέραν σωτηρίαν
Came down from heaven,	κατελθόντα ἐκ τῶν οὐρανῶν
And became incarnate	καὶ σαρκωθέντα
by the Holy Spirit	ἐκ πνεύματος ἁγίου
and the virgin Mary	καὶ Μαρίας τῆς παρθένου
and was born a human being.	καὶ ἐνανθρωπήσαντα

Here we make further claims about the character of God's producing, on two levels. First, we learn the identity of the Other who is brought forth by the Source. The Greek word υἱός, here translated *Wellspring*, is closely bound to the Source; it is brought into existence by the Source, but in such a profoundly self-giving sense that the essential properties that belong to one belong also to the other (they are "of one being," as the Creed says). And on a second level, we learn that the world that God created is not merely left to its own devices; rather, in order to bring about our salvation, God *becomes* the world, becomes flesh – in the womb of Mary, in the body of Jesus.

The Wellspring is "eternally brought forth" by the Source. Like an ever-flowing spring, the Source is *always* producing the Wellspring; this is not a process that only takes place during a certain moment of time. This is, I think, a more intelligible image than that of an "eternal begetting"; yet it still describes the divine procession not as a separation or division, but as an eternal act of self-differentiation. On the other hand, when we proclaim the incarnation of the Wellspring, the imagery of birth is entirely appropriate; God, having created the world, is so deeply committed to it as to be *born* into it, to live and die in it. We thus proclaim that the Wellspring "was born a human being"; the imagery of birth emphasizes the true humanity of Jesus much more clearly than did the traditional translations ("and was made man" or even "and became truly human").

Finally, when we recite the Creed's third article, we testify again to God as a producing God. We confess a belief in:

| the Living Water, | τὸ πνεῦμα τὸ ἅγιον, |
| the Lord and Giver of Life, | τὸ κύριον καὶ ζωοποιόν, |

emerging from the Source, . . .	τὸ ἐκ τοῦ πατρὸς ἐκπορευόμενον,
who has spoken through the	. . .τὸ λαλῆσαν διὰ τῶν προφητῶν.
prophets.	

The Living Water emerges from the Source; this divine procession completes and perfects the relationality of God, helping us to see that God's internal self-differentiation does not remain closed in on itself;[55] rather, it opens out so that the whole creation may be drawn back to God. The mission of the Living Water is the sanctification of the world; it is our sustainer and advocate, providing a constant reminder that the world, created and redeemed by God, will never be abandoned. It will be sustained by this "giver of life," who brooded over the face of the deep before the foundation of the world.

What we discover throughout the Creed is a *producing* God, with respect both to God's own self and to the world. God's producing involves not only creation (God as the source of God and of the world) but also redemption and sanctification, signifying God's eternal love and care. Traditionally, God's long-term "involvement" with and care for the world has been emphasized through the theological category of *grace*. In creating the world, God wills into existence something radically other-than-God; but the world's "otherness" is not something that cuts it off from God. There is thus no "pure nature"; nature is always graced. And it is graced not just because it was created by God long ago, but because God is *always* actively redeeming and sustaining it. Our clearest indicators of God's willingness to care for the world are the birthing of the Wellspring and the pouring out of the Living Water. God becomes flesh, suffers the world, for our sake; and God becomes active within the world, moving us to a more profound faith and a more faithful life.

God Produces the Knowledge of God

We now turn to the final element in God's "production" of the world: God's active role in providing us with knowledge about God, a process usually described under the rubric of "the doctrine of revelation." Nothing so

---

[55] The Living Water is a "second difference" that prevents "the very perfection of the relation" of the Source and the Wellspring from collapsing into an undifferentiated unity (Milbank, "The Second Difference," 230). See also Dumitru Staniloae, "The Holy Trinity: Structure of Supreme Love," in *Theology and the Church*, trans. Robert Barringer (Crestwood, NY: St. Vladimir's Seminary Press, 1980), 73–108 and notes, 231–34; here, 93–5.

grandiose as that will be presented in the few paragraphs that remain in this chapter. Nevertheless, a few comments are needed, because "God's production of the knowledge of God" bears a similar structure to the two acts of producing that we have discussed so far. In other words, God's production of the knowledge of God is a trinitarian event, just as are God's production of God and of the world.[56]

The definitive focal-point for God's revelation is the person of Christ. God's willingness to enter the world provides us with the most complete and definitive knowledge of God that we can hope to have. At the same time, however, it should be noted that this "complete and definitive" form of revelation comes not as a statement, nor as a set of propositions, but as a human being. Hence, this knowledge is marked by all the beauty and the ambiguity inherent in any knowledge that we gain from another human being. In order to "come to know" something through the life of another, we have to interpret that person's words and actions, to ask for clarification (when it is possible to do so), and to rely on the testimony of others. In Christ, God is revealed to us – but this is obviously not the end of the story. We must still *interpret* what the apostles saw with their eyes, what they looked at and touched with their hands.

Fortunately, we are not left to our own devices in doing so. As in the case of God's production of the world, God recognizes that an act of initiation is not sufficient. We are free and fallible beings, and adequate knowledge of God cannot be assured by one definitive act of unveiling, just as an adequate attitude toward God cannot be assured by one definitive act of creation. Instead, God provides us with ongoing interpretive guidance; this is part of the mission of "inspiration," in which the Church is enlivened by the Living Water to proclaim the word and administer the sacraments. These ongoing practices help to give shape to our encounter with Christ, such that we learn to read the biblical narratives as God would have us read them – and such that they testify to Christ as the one point of contact, the definitive revelation of God. The production of the knowledge of God begins with the mission of incarnation, but it does not end there; for many have read those narratives in wholly privatized ways, and have then barricaded themselves away in the company of their "own personal Jesus." True knowledge of God is only possible through a communally-normed reading of the biblical narratives that is made possible by the Spirit-filled Church.

[56] Karl Barth speaks of a threefold structure of revelation, which he sees as the central biblical foundation for the doctrine of the Trinity (*CD* I/1, 295–333; *KD* I/1, 311–52). My own account is different from Barth's; I address his approach to the grammar of the word *reveal* in chapter 3.

But this is not quite all. The knowledge of God, given to us in the incarnation of the Word and interpreted to us through the pouring out of the Living Water, must still be rendered intelligible, concrete, and persuasive. This task requires us to draw on the widest possible range of resources and tools, to "take every thought captive to obey Christ" (2 Cor. 10:5). We believe that God produces the world, and does so for the sake of the incarnate Word ("all things have been created for him," Col. 1:16); thus, there is a certain sense in which the world expresses, and thereby resembles, God.[57] This should not be confused with "natural" theology as it is sometimes understood, i.e., knowledge that human beings can have of God without God's prior action. There can be no purely natural knowledge of God, for there is no pure nature; the world is not a "naturally-occurring phenomenon." It is created, redeemed, and sustained by God – in short, it is *produced* by God. So any knowledge of God that we can glean from the world must also be produced by God.

The difficulty, of course, is that with each successive description of revelation that I have offered here (Christ, Church, world), the focus becomes less sharp. We do not have a perfect picture of Christ – we do not have a definitive "face" – but we have enough narrative material and a clear enough story to have a sense of the whole. The Church is animated by the Spirit, but its work is carried out through human beings; thus, the knowledge of God that comes through word and sacrament requires careful discernment if we are to determine what is true knowledge and what is simply the highest hope of the individual interpreter. When we turn to the world at large, the focus becomes still less clear. If *everything* can give us knowledge of God, then this knowledge loses its particularity and becomes banal. In other words, if God can be seen in everything, then God loses any specific identity.

We may be able to make better sense of "God's production of our knowledge of God" if we tie it more closely to God's production of the world. That activity can be likened to the work of the master of a craft, or to the work of an artist. God is free to act or not to act; the production of the world is thus a loving act of donation – a "gift." The artist, too, freely "produces" the work of art – not only bringing something new into existence, but continuing to look after that creation in the desire that it be treated well, enjoyed, and used for its intended purpose. We often say that the artist "puts something of herself" into the work that she produces. By this we do not mean that the work

---

[57] This point is made at length and with great clarity by Bruce Marshall in his forthcoming *Trinity and Truth* (Cambridge: Cambridge University Press), ch. 5. My thanks to him for access to the manuscript.

of art is itself a human being, nor that it contains some small spark of the essence of humanity. We mean, rather, that the production of the work of art involves sacrifice and gift. The artist gives up something of who she is (or who she otherwise might be) in order to create the work of art. And often (though not always), the artist uses the work of art as a medium through which to communicate something to others. For all these reasons, the work of art "bears the mark" of the artist; it reflects her character.

Of course, this does not mean that we can learn everything there is to know about the artist by examining her work. We might be able to piece together a few details; for example, if the artist has painted a crucifixion scene, we might reasonably assume that she had some acquaintance with the story of Jesus. We might even be able to make some educated guesses about the artist's religious belief, psychological makeup, economic class, and so on. But none of these conclusions would follow necessarily from our observations of the work of art. The tortured body on the cross, for example, might just as easily have been undertaken out of historical interest in a (once common) means of capital punishment, or out of aesthetic interest in the anatomical structure of the human body, or some combination of these and other motives.

In general, then, we can gain little definitive information about the creator of a work of art by examining the work itself. But let us invert the example and suppose that, before we see the work of art at all, we have learned a great deal about the life of the artist. We know something about her social history, family background, psychological makeup, religious affect, and many other details of her life. Now, when we come to examine her work of art, we will be able to make considerably better sense of the relationship between creator and creation. If we know, for example, that her own family was desperately poor, then the delineation of wealth and poverty in her art may become more salient for us.

This relationship between the artist and the work of art is closely analogous to the relationship between God and the created order. If we knew nothing at all about God – if God had not been revealed to us in the missions of incarnation and inspiration – we would be unable to learn anything simply by looking around at the world. Doing so might lead us assume that, given the depth of suffering within the world, God must have something of a cruel streak. Those who dwell in warmer climes would assume that God loved balmy temperatures and the color green, whereas arctic inhabitants would assume a divine passion for frigid temperatures and infinite whiteness. Or consider the example of the scientist who had spent most of his life classifying living creatures into discrete categories. When asked what feature of the Creator was most obvious to him through his study of the creation, he replied:

"an inordinate fondness for beetles"! Any portrait of God that we might derive from the world would depend largely on *our own perspective* on the world, and thus would depend largely on ourselves. Such portraits of God typically do a much better job of describing their human creators than they do portraying the nature of God.

But again, let us reverse the image: if we already know something about God, then we are in a much better position to think about how certain features of God's character are made salient in the world that God has created. If we believe, for example, that God values human freedom above all else (and even above human safety and predictable outcomes), then we may be able to make some marginal degree of sense out of the evil that we see in the world around us — at least to the extent that it can be traced to the free operation of the human will. Note how poorly the example works in reverse: by observing the evil around us, we could hypothesize a God who is simply apathetic, or cruel, or a gambler, or one who delights in the ways of the wicked, or any of a number of other possible hypotheses. But if we begin with certain beliefs about the One who produces the world, we can go on to draw inferences about the world as God's "production" — which may in turn help us better understand our beliefs about its producer.

The triune God is very much like the artist who "puts something of herself" into the work of art, and thereby "leaves her mark" on it.[58] And if we know something about this particular artist (because this knowledge has been revealed to us), we will be able to discern the reflections and echoes of the artist's life in the work that she has created. Doing so produces no "new" knowledge per se; everything that we can learn about God by studying the world is *already* known to us through God's act of revelation. Nevertheless, this process can give our knowledge a different *shape*; it can help us find new language to express what we have already heard, allowing us to explain it more clearly and present it more persuasively. This process can thus lead us toward a more integral vision of the theological task by encouraging us to put the knowledge into practice — so that it may (as Wittgenstein says) make a difference at various points in our lives.

By thinking about the ways that the world bears the mark of its maker, we force ourselves out of the habit of simply repeating the standard affirmations of the doctrine of God over and over again, until our minds become numb

---

[58] Colin Gunton makes a similar point, but uses language that is (to my mind) far too heavily dependent upon an essentialist metaphysics: "If the triune God is the source of all being, meaning and truth, we must suppose that all being will in some way reflect the being of the one who made it and holds it in being." *The One, The Three and the Many*, 145.

PRODUCING 87

from the process. Consider, for example, the standard scholastic claim about God's Triunity, which I discussed above: "There are two processions in God: the begetting of the Word and the breathing-out of the Spirit." It is easy enough to memorize and repeat this formula, as many students can attest; thousands of times, the standard claims of trinitarian doctrine have been repeated, in speech or in writing, and thousands of times, instructors have marked them "right" or "wrong." But in how many of these cases does the student have the slightest notion of the significance of the statements, or of what their claim might be upon the Christian life?

However, after affirming the above-mentioned scholastic claim, we might go on to note that this very God, in whom "there are two processions," has created and redeemed and sustained the world. We might then ask: what it is about the world – the world that God has produced and continues to produce – that shows it to be the production of one "in whom there are two processions"? What elements, in the created order, can be described as bearing the marks of such a maker? How can the process of thinking about these elements give a new shape to our knowledge, such that we can better understand what we mean when we say that "there are two processions in God"? And how might these elements be employed, in the Christian practices of dogmatics, proclamation, and catechesis, to educate the faithful and to show hospitality to the stranger? These questions are urgent ones, because *practice* gives the words of trinitarian theology their sense.

Because the world is produced by God, it can give new shape to our knowledge of God – making it clearer and more persuasive – even though that knowledge has already been revealed to us. This claim is hardly new; it dates back to the early Christian apologists, and finds its high point in the Cappadocians and in Augustine. It seems to be assumed by many of the biblical writers, including St Paul: "What can be known about God is plain to them, because God has shown it to them. Ever since the creation of the world God's eternal power and divine nature, invisible though they are, have been understood and seen through the things God has made" (Romans 1:19–20). Elsewhere, Paul makes it abundantly clear that Christ is a necessary condition of our knowledge of God; nevertheless, the created order still tells us something – even if perhaps nothing "new" – about God's power and nature. Without wishing to ignore the intense exegetical and theological battles that have been fought over these verses,[59] I would simply observe that St Paul seems to have believed that, at least in some circumstances, a careful

---

[59] A useful contribution to this discussion is Eugene F. Rogers, Jr., "Thomas and Barth in Convergence on Romans 1?" *Modern Theology* 12, no. 1 (January 1996): 57–84.

consideration of "the things God has made" would not be a wholly useless endeavor.

Similarly, St Augustine believed that the created order, like the work of art, bore the marks of its maker – that even here, God had sought to produce the knowledge of God. Augustine was under no illusion that one might be able to deduce the precise nature of God from an examination of the material world. Moreover, he embarked upon the theological task with certain beliefs, practices, and knowledge that had already shaped his understanding of the created order. Nevertheless, he believed that his theological knowledge could be given new shape – that it could become more educative for the faithful, more intelligible to outsiders, and more persuasive to everyone – if he undertook the task of probing the created order for the marks of its maker. He thereby helped to form a theological tradition that has exercised the hearts and minds of some of the most notable theologians of the Christian era – though they have not all reached the same verdict concerning its value. This embattled theological tradition provides the framework for the constructive theological task that I call "parallelling" – which is the subject of the next chapter. This task is an attempt to "return the gift" of producing – a gift bestowed on us by the Triune God: who created the heavens and the earth, whose Spirit moved over the waters of the deep, and without whose Word was not anything made that was made.

Chapter 3

PARALLELLING

In this chapter, I argue that Christians should construe the created order as bearing certain "triune marks." As I attempted to make clear at the end of the previous chapter, the world does not provide us with any wholly independent knowledge of God, nor can we derive from it an account of God's Triunity. Precisely the reverse: *because* God's Triunity has already been revealed to us through the divine missions (as narrated in the story of our salvation), we can offer accounts that describe the created order as reflecting this Triunity in significant (though imperfect) ways. In other words, we can construct certain parallels between the (often very technical) claims of the Christian doctrine of God, on the one hand, and certain elements of the created order on the other.

For the purposes of my argument, these triune marks need not be understood as being somehow "embedded" in creation. A case may be made for such a claim, especially in the case of human beings (since they are created in the image of God); and perhaps also for other creatures, even though some of them may bear the marks of God with "immeasurable vestigial remoteness."[1] But the idea of a "triune mark" does not necessitate that it be immanent in the created order. In my view, triune marks are constructions, construals, illustrations; they are developed *by human beings* as interpretations of the world. They are thus always dependent on what we already know about the triune God by means of God's own self-revelation. We construct these triune marks, not in the hope of providing wholly independent knowledge of God, but rather to render the traditional claims of trinitarian doctrine more intelligible and more persuasive. I have sought to emphasize the "human, all-too-

---

[1] I owe the phrase to Bruce Marshall, who uses it in a slightly different context in "'We Shall Bear the Image of the Man of Heaven': Theology and the Concept of Truth," *Modern Theology* 11, no. 1 (January 1995): 93–118; here, 113.

human" nature of this process by means of the name I have given it: "parallelling." The triune marks need not be understood as something that God "imprints" upon creation so that we can discern the character of God; rather, they are construals that we develop on the basis of the character of God (which has already been revealed to us). In short: *God* does the producing; *we* do the parallelling.

I make the case for parallelling in two stages. First, I offer an account of the theological tradition of the *vestigia trinitatis*, from which my description of "triune marks" is derived. Then, I offer an example of the practice of parallelling: I examine the process of "rhetorical invention" (the production of persuasive discourse), construing it as bearing certain triune marks. I conclude by assessing this example, showing how it helps to clarify several technical claims of trinitarian theology – claims that will, in turn, be of considerable importance for my argument in parts two and three of this book.

Vestigia Trinitatis: Triune Marks

My phrase "triune marks" is drawn from a theological tradition that is most commonly known by its Latin name: *vestigia trinitatis*. Translating this term into English will prove to be difficult – as I will note in the first part of this section, which explores the concept as it appears in the work of St Augustine. Augustine certainly was not the first to employ the *vestigia*, but he was certainly prolific in developing them, and he also undertook a theoretical examination of their usefulness. His work will thus provide us with a convenient point of entry. I will then turn to the critical assessment of this tradition, especially in the work of Karl Barth. After offering an analysis of Barth's argument, I will provide my own evaluation of the significance of this tradition for today.

Augustine's approach[2]

In Book 13 of the *Confessions*, Augustine complains briefly about the endless debates and quarrels in which Christians seem to be engaged concerning their various speculations on the Trinity. He suggests an alternative:

---

[2] An analysis of Augustine's approach, accompanied by a surplus of citations, appears in Étienne Gilson, *The Christian Philosophy of St. Augustine*, trans. L. E. M. Lynch (New York: Random House, 1960), 210–24 and the notes at 348–59 [ET of: *Introduction à l'étude de Saint Augustin*, 3. éd., Études de philosophie médiévale (Paris: Vrin, 1949), 275–98].

I wish that human disputants would reflect upon the triad within their own selves. These three aspects of the self are very different from the Trinity, but I may make the observation that on this triad they could well exercise their minds and examine the problem, thereby becoming aware how far distant they are from it.[3]

Here Augustine sounds a theme that he will take up again, in much greater detail, in *De Trinitate*. There, he draws on Romans 1:20 in particular as an invitation to offer a triadic reading of structures in the created order – but one that refers back, constantly, to the Triunity of God: "So then, as we direct our gaze at the creator by understanding the things that are made, we should recognize the Trinity, whose mark appears in creation in a way that is fitting."[4]

The word that I have here translated as *mark* is the Latin *vestigium*, from which we also derive the English word *vestige*. In Latin, the word typically referred to a *footprint* or *track* – a meaning which also survives in English dictionary definitions (albeit with the notation "archaic"). The word *vestige* has developed the more general meaning of a visible sign of something that is no longer physically present. The word also carries a second meaning – referring to a very slight amount of one entity that is present in another (the English word *trace* brings out this meaning: traces of a mineral in water, for example). From this definition, it has also developed into a technical term (in biology) for an organ or part of a body that remains only as a remnant of what was once, perhaps, a fully-functioning part of the organism.

As a rendering of Augustine's concept, this second definition would be wholly inadequate. It would suggest either (a) that God places little bits of divinity into the created order, thereby implying some version of pantheism; or (b) that humanity was originally created divine, but now only contains a trace of its original divinity. Augustine is elsewhere very clear that God is not a part of the created order – nor are human beings divine (not even before the Fall). Thus, the idea that some residual divinity might be found in creation must be ruled out from the start. On the other hand, neither can we be wholly

---

[3] Augustine, *Confessions* XIII.xi; trans. Henry Chadwick (Oxford: Oxford University Press, 1992), 279.

[4] Augustine *De Trin.* VI.10(12): *Oportet igitur, ut creatorem per ea quae facta sunt intellectum conspicientes, trinitatem intelligamus, cuius in creatura, quomodo dignum est, apparet vestigium.* Translation (slightly altered) from *The Trinity*, ed. and trans. with an Introduction by Edmund Hill, O.P., The Works of Saint Augustine: A Translation for the 21st Century, vol. 5 (Brooklyn, NY: New City Press, 1991), 213.

satisfied with the first definition of the English word *vestige* mentioned above – that is, a mark or a sign of something that is no longer present. This definition suggests that God creates the world and then abandons it (leaving us the task of deciphering the divine fingerprints).

Thus, I have not used the English word *vestige*; neither of the typical clusters of meaning surrounding it can adequately describe Augustine's project. Indeed, these two definitional choices create a false dichotomy: they suggest that God must either be "in" creation in some sort of quasi-pantheistic sense, or else God must be wholly absent from creation, like a divine watchmaker who now has better things to do. Neither story is the Christian story; for we believe that the God who created the world (as something radically other-than-God) is the same God who became flesh in order to redeem the world, and is the same God who is poured out on all flesh in order to sanctify the world. God *produces* the world; recalling the analogies of the play and the garden, this is an activity that requires full-scale engagement with the other. This understanding of producing cannot allow for a dichotomy of identity-or-absence; to produce something is neither to create a duplicate copy of oneself, nor to create something and then simply to abandon it. The *producing* God is wholly other than the world, yet remains constantly involved with it.

This is why the divine "missions" – incarnation of the Word and the sending of the Spirit – are such important prerequisites to Augustine's investigation into the *vestigia trinitatis*. The word *mission* itself tends to evoke a simultaneous otherness and involvement; "going on a mission" requires us to care enough about a task to leave our comfortable surroundings and venture into a foreign land. Similarly, God – though not collapsed into the world – still remains involved with the world. Augustine recognizes that all our theological speculations would be worthless if God had not already shown a willingness to continue to care for the created order. And only because of God's revelation to us (through Israel and through the missions of incarnation and inspiration) do we have the slightest notion of how we might begin to "read" the created order in such a way that it could help give shape to our knowledge of the triune God.

In an attempt to avoid the "presence-or-absence" dichotomy posed by the typical uses of the English word *vestige*, I have instead employed the word *mark*. This word is not normally used to refer to a small quantity of something within a larger whole; for example, one would not usually speak of "a mark of copper in water." It thus allows us to avoid the most problematic cluster of meanings surrounding the word *vestige*. Moreover, unlike footprints and tracks, a mark need not be left accidentally; this is also important, since God does nothing accidentally. And even though a person who "made a mark" or "left a mark" is no longer physically present, the very decision to "leave one's mark" implies both an interest in the other (a mark can be left *for* someone) and a degree of personal involvement (one typically has some purpose in leaving a mark). These latter aspects of the word's usage suggest that the source of the mark, though invisible, nevertheless continues to have an influence – precisely by means of this mark.

This sense of "presence-in-absence" is emphasized when the word *mark* is attached to a possessive structure – when I speak, for example, of having "left my mark" on something. This strengthens the word's evocation of active interest and personal involvement. We use this structure, for example, to speak of one's overall impact on a particular sphere of influence ("she really made her mark on that institution"); and something similar is at work in the phrase "the mark of the maker" that I discussed in the previous chapter. In order to make it clear that this mark is God's own, I use the phrase "triune marks" to translate Augustine's *vestigia trinitatis*. This phrase may not evoke all the resonances that Augustine hoped to call to his readers' minds with his language, but it seems an improvement over the more common English translations.

As is well known, Augustine goes on in the later books of *De Trinitate* to offer a large number of threefold *vestigia*: the lover, the beloved, and love; the mind, its knowledge, and its love; memory, understanding, and will; man, woman, and child; and many others (twenty different ones are listed in the index to a recent translation of *De Trinitate*[5]). Some of these Augustine mentions only briefly, then quickly discards; others he develops at great length. In every case, though, he eventually observes that the particular *vestigium* fails to mirror the Trinity perfectly, and that each one has specific inadequacies in addition to the more general point (which I have already emphasized) that no *vestigium* can provide a complete and unmistaken account of that which produced it. "There are not a number of such trinities, experience of some of which could enable us . . . to believe that the divine Trinity is similar."[6]

Augustine picks up the same theme, in a more condensed form, in *The City of God*. Here, he suggests that *the doctrine of creation itself* grounds the expectation that the *vestigia* will appear in creation.

---

[5] Joseph Sprug, indexer, in Hill, ed., *The Trinity*, s.v. *trinities*, 469.

[6] *quasi multae sint tales trinitates, quarum aliquas experti sumus, ut . . . illam quoque talem esse credamus . . . Quod utique non ita est. De Trin.* VIII.8, trans. from *Augustine: Later Works*, ed. John Burnaby, Library of Christian Classics, vol. 8 (Philadelphia: Westminster Press, 1955), 46.

> If the divine goodness is nothing else than the divine holiness, then certainly we are being reasonably diligent, and not excessively presumptuous, in inquiring whether, in the works of God, this same Trinity is not suggested to us (in an enigmatic form of speech, intended to catch our attention) whenever we ask of each creature: Who made it? And by what means? And why?'[7]

Augustine then discusses the role of the whole Trinity in creation, suggesting that the Three correspond, respectively, to the three questions that he raises at the end of the above passage: they are the maker, the means, and the purpose. Consequently, says Augustine, "the whole Trinity is revealed to us in its works."[8] He goes on to note echoes of this revelation in the division of philosophy into three parts, and especially in human beings as the image of God.

In this passage, the word *vestigium* does not appear at all; however, the word translated by "suggested" – *insinuata* – may help us further refine our understanding of Augustine's approach. The English cognate *insinuate* suggests an unstated or understated claim made by someone. But we usually use the English word to refer to claims made about others (rather than about ourselves); and often these are negative, judgmental claims (we rarely speak of "insinuating" something positive about someone). Nevertheless, the word does evoke resonances of intentionality and personal involvement. Whether or not we accept what the insinuation implies about *someone else*, it often gives us a clearer perspective on the character of the person who does the insinuating. And this, I think, is part of what Augustine may be suggesting here. When we inquire about the maker, the means, and the purpose of creation, we discover that God seems to be "insinuating something"; as a result, God's triune character is enigmatically suggested to us. Clearly, Augustine is arguing neither that God is immanent in creation nor that God is simply absent; rather, God's activity in creation has certain effects on us, such that one might reasonably speculate on the relationship between the created effects and the One who produces them.

Yet despite the positive use to which Augustine and many others have employed the tradition of the *vestigia trinitatis*, it has not been a central feature of recent trinitarian theology. A typical assessment is offered by Colin Gunton, who speaks of the "famous and futile quest for analogies of the Trinity in the created world." Their "weakness," he claims, "is their employment as

---

[7] . . . *ut in operibus Dei secreto quodam loquendi modo, quo nostra exerceatur intentio, eadem nobis insinuata intellegatur trinitas, unamquamque creaturam quis fecerit, per quid fecerit, propter quid fecerit.* Augustine *De civ. Dei* XI.24; my translation.

[8] *universa nobis trinitas in suis operibus intimatur.* Ibid.; trans., altered, from that of Marcus Dods in *The City of God* (New York: The Modern Library, 1950), 369.

attempts to illustrate the divine Trinity: the world is used to throw light on God, rather than the other way round."[9] The assumption here seems to be that all theological knowledge has its origins *either* in God alone, *or* in the world (and that the former is legitimate while the latter is illegitimate). In order to explore at greater length this commonly-held negative assessment of the *vestigia*, I turn to its detailed presentation in the work of Karl Barth.

Barth's objection

Barth argues that the root of the doctrine of the Trinity is the threefold form of revelation. God is, as it were, the subject, verb, and object of the word *reveal*. Barth does not seek to deduce the entire doctrine of the Trinity from this threefold form; rather, he believes that the biblical witness alone allows us to move from a recognition of the threefold nature of revelation to the doctrine of the Trinity itself.[10] Before going on to discuss the doctrine, however, Barth pauses to consider the tradition of the *vestigia trinitatis*, wondering whether we might here have a second "root" of the doctrine of the Trinity placed alongside that of the biblical witness, accessible to human reason without the aid of revelation.[11]

Barth worries that this may be a slippery slope: if we can find God's Triunity in the created order, then our knowledge of the triune God might come not only through divine revelation, but also through *reason*; and if also through reason then perhaps through reason *primarily*; and if primarily, perhaps *only* so. Or again, revelation might be merely a confirmation of something that can be adequately known through the natural order; and if so, what is known might be merely a human projection rather than the "wholly other" creator God. Thus, for Barth, the very idea of a *vestigium trinitatis* raises the specter of the reduction of theology to mere anthropology.

But since the *vestigia* have played so large a role in the tradition, Barth cannot simply dismiss the idea without comment. He examines a variety of *vestigia*, grouping them into five categories: phenomena from nature, from culture,

---

[9] Colin Gunton "Trinity, Ontology, and Anthropology: Towards a Renewal of the Doctrine of the *Imago Dei*," in *Persons, Divine and Human*, ed. Christoph Schwöbel and Colin Gunton (Edinburgh: T. & T. Clark, 1991), 55n18; see also *The One, The Three and the Many*, 144n23.

[10] *CD* I/1, section 8.2 ("The Root of the Doctrine of the Trinity").

[11] "The concern here was with an essential trinitarian disposition supposedly immanent in some created realities quite apart from their possible conscription by God's revelation. It was with a genuine *analogia entis*, with traces of the trinitarian Creator God in being as such, in its pure createdness" (*CD* I/1, 334 [*KD* I/1, 353–4]).

from history, from religion, and from the life of the soul. Barth seems open to the employment of the *vestigia* tradition within particular constraints, that is,

> as an interesting, edifying, instructive and helpful hint toward understanding the Christian doctrine, not to be overrated, not to be used as a proof in the strict sense, because we need to know and believe the Trinity already if we are really to perceive its *vestigia* as such in the microcosm and the macrocosm, but still to be valued as supplementary and non-obligatory illustrations of the Christian Credo which are to be received with gratitude.[12]

This passage, I think, is an excellent description of the benefits afforded by the *vestigia* tradition. Barth cites Irenaeus, Augustine, Peter Lombard, and Thomas Aquinas as all having recognized the importance, both of the construction of *vestigia*, and of keeping this caveat firmly in mind.

Thus, Barth's initial treatment of the *vestigia* seems to be a positive one. When theologians sought to talk about specific aspects of the Trinity, he says,

> they opened their eyes and ears and found they could and should venture to refer, with this end in view, to spring, stream, and lake, or weight, number, and measure, or *mens*, *notitia*, and *amor*, not because these things were in and of themselves suitable for the purpose but because they were adapted to be appropriated or, as it were, commandeered as images of the Trinity, because those who knew God's revelation in Scripture thought they might be given the power to say what in and of themselves they naturally do not say and cannot say.[13]

Barth's words *appropriated* and *commandeered* provide something of the flavor that I am attempting to suggest in my use of the word *parallelling*. It is clearly something that *we* do – a construal or construction, a way of "narrating" the created order. In the same paragraph, Barth goes on to suggest that most of those who employed this tradition

> did not believe that the Trinity is immanent in things and that things have the capability of reflecting the Trinity. On this side everything is admittedly incomplete and questionable and dependent on preceding revelation. But they did have confidence that the Trinity can reflect itself in things, and all the more or less felicitous discoveries of *vestigia* were an expression of this confidence, not of confidence in the capacity of reason for revelation but of confidence in the power of revelation over reason.[14]

---

[12] Ibid., 338 [357–8].
[13] Ibid., 340, trans. slightly altered [*KD* I/1, 359–60].
[14] Ibid., 341 [360].

In these comments, Barth seems to be building up the possibility of a wholly appropriate and carefully safeguarded function for the *vestigia*.

And yet, in his own rhetorical context, Barth had witnessed something very much like the *vestigia* tradition being used as a second (or first, or only) root of the Christian doctrine of God, and (thereby) had witnessed the reduction of theology to anthropology. He thus worried that the caveats – inserted, almost unanimously, by the theologians who have employed this approach – would fail, and that the *vestigia* would be used to reason from the created order back to the nature of God – perhaps even to the complete exclusion of God's revelation in Israel and in the Church.[15] Too often, Barth believes, the *vestigia* have been treated as an independent proof; and what they proved, ultimately, was another god, "an epitome, a supreme principle of the world and ultimately of human beings."[16] Thus, if there is to be a *vestigium trinitatis*, it can only be "the form which God Himself in His revelation has assumed in our language, world, and humanity."[17] This is, according to Barth, the only way to insure that we move from God's revelation to our knowledge, rather than the other way around. Barth thus eventually comes to denounce the *vestigia* tradition – and (as we will see in the next section) to do so in extraordinarily vehement terms.

Barth's condemnation of the *vestigia* has been overwhelmingly influential. For example, Colin Gunton's quick dismissal of the tradition, noted above, is made much easier by Barth's influence. Barth's notion that there can only be one true *vestigium trinitatis* was taken up explicitly by Eberhard Jüngel, who argued that only in this way can our discussions of trinitarian doctrine be prevented from lapsing into groundless speculation.[18] As Walter Kasper observes, Roman Catholic theologians have been generally less willing to follow Barth here, given their differing views on analogy.[19] Yet Kasper himself implicitly accepts Barth's recasting of the *vestigia* by agreeing that "the real *vestigium trinitatis* is therefore not the human being but the God–human Jesus Christ."[20]

---

[15] Ibid., 341–2 [360–1].

[16] Ibid., 342, trans. slightly altered [*KD* has "Menschen," 361].

[17] Ibid., 347 [367]; earlier (334 [353]), the locus of this true *vestigium* is specified as "the form that God assumes in His unveiling as the Son or Word."

[18] Jüngel, *God as the Mystery of the World*, section 22, 343–68 [*Gott als Geheimnis der Welt* 470–505].

[19] Kasper, *The God of Jesus Christ*, 273 [*Der Gott Jesu Christi*, 332].

[20] Ibid., 273, trans. altered [*Mensch, Gott-Mensch*: 333]. See also Balthasar's surprising anxiety on this issue at *T-D* III:508 [*TD* II/2:466] – though his worries concern content (the importance of avoiding modalism and tritheism) rather than form. A more positive evaluation appears at III:525*ff.* [II/2:480*ff.*] and elsewhere.

Given Barth's own theological context, his concern was understandable. He had witnessed, first in the endorsement of the Weimar war effort by the leading exponents of liberal theology, and then in the Nazi-sympathizing theology of the "German Christian" movement, a relatively successful effort to disconnect the doctrine of God from its grounding in the biblical narratives of salvation history. Eventually, under the Nazi influence, God was transformed from the God of Israel (whose Jewish messiah was executed for proclaiming the good news of salvation to all people) to the Aryan God (whose antimessiah executed Jews and anyone else whom he believed obstructed his absolute power). To the extent that the tradition of the *vestigia* provided any degree of aid and comfort to this murderous and idolatrous process, it certainly deserved the full force of Barth's critique.

And yet, one has to wonder whether Barth – in his wholly laudable attempt to block every possible theological route travelled by the Nazification of Christianity – did not occasionally tend to eliminate the good along with the bad. We can accept that, in Barth's own era, the *vestigia* tradition had been put to such evil purposes that it was perhaps best to forgo it altogether. Yet this acceptance does not entail that it must be forgone in all times and all places – nor that its careful employment necessarily leads to the kinds of consequences to which it led in Nazi Germany. As the ancient Sophists knew, *any* argument can be put to evil use by a person of bad character; this does not necessarily speak against the argument itself.

Assessing Barth's critique

Barth is certainly right to suggest that the development of "triune marks" is a risky business, in that there will always be some potential for reading them the wrong way around. But theology must always take risks, and if we are to accept Barth's condemnation of this rather significant practice of the theological tradition, we could reasonably expect to be shown that the risk is real and significant, and that it extends beyond the particularities of his own context. Yet Barth never really explains when or how the classical tradition "crossed the line" and sought to use the *vestigia* as an independent proof. He certainly cites a number of Christian theologians who have described various *vestigia*; but as noted above, he also admits that they seem to have gladly accepted the caveat that one must always move from God to the *vestigia*, not the reverse. None of them seem to use the idea as any kind of independent proof of the doctrine. Where shall we look in order to find the abuse of the *vestigia*, over which Barth has shown such great anxiety?

Interestingly, Barth does not cite many of the arguments of the German

Christians as evidence of this move.[21] Undoubtedly, he believed that his objection would carry more weight if it were understood as a broader critique of the tradition, rather than a charge aimed specifically at his own *particular* theological enemies. But this leaves him few specific cases to cite as the downfall of the tradition, since most Christian theologians (as Barth himself notes) employed it with such care. Instead, Barth makes reference to "the development of anthropological speculation by way of Descartes and Kant to Schelling and Hegel and finally and logically Feuerbach"[22] – though one would hardly expect the standard safeguards on the use of the *vestigia* to be in place for these thinkers. The only direct reference to a Christian theologian who "went too far" is one B. Keckermann, whose 1611 systematic theology is quoted as moving from an observation about the nature of humanity to a claim about the necessity of God's triune nature.[23]

Undoubtedly, Barth was not basing his entire case against the *vestigia* tradition on the error of one relatively obscure seventeenth-century writer; he believed that it has had much more profound and wide-reaching negative consequences. Otherwise he could not have gone on to minimize, and even to trivialize, this longstanding theological tradition – describing it as "trifling," "a game that cannot yield serious results," and speaking of "the feeling of frivolity that we can hardly avoid in its presence."[24] He believes that, even when undertaken with the best intentions, it is likely to lead us astray. At the heart of his objection is the claim that, since everything that can be known of God can be known through revelation, there is no reason to look for enigmatic hints about God in the created order. It is a case, he believes, of nothing to be gained and everything to be lost.

This account, in my view, has both rhetorical and theological flaws. Rhetorically, it does not consider the degree to which both the speaker and the audience must contribute (in different ways, to be sure) to the production of knowledge. Only some such admission can account for the differing ways that a single text can be read by varying audiences. Moreover, from a theological perspective, Barth's account understands revelation as a zero-sum game, in which it is assumed that the control of the whole process is *either* entirely in God's hands *or* entirely in our own. In my view, this is an

---

[21] Of course, this was only 1932. At *CD* I/1, 337 [*KD* I/1, 356], Barth does mention (among various *vestigia trinitatis*) Moeller van der Bruck's application of the idea of a "third kingdom" to the political sphere in *Das dritte Reich* (2nd edition, 1926, p. 13).

[22] *CD* I/1, 343 [*KD* I/1, 362].

[23] Barth quotes the Latin text at ibid., 343 [362]: *quam est necessarium, hominem esse rationalem, . . . tam est necessarium in Dei essentia tres esse personas.*

[24] Ibid., 344 [363].

inadequately *incarnational* account of knowledge.[25] God's willingness to "take the world into the bosom of God" by becoming flesh serves as both a warrant and an interpretive key for offering an adequate account of triune marks within the created order. In the remainder of this section, I will attempt to unpack these claims a bit.

Barth admits that our understanding of revelation is an equivocal matter, and that one must use the tools available within the created order to witness to God's revelation. Yet Barth draws a sharp distinction between revelation itself (which is always God's alone) and the human responses to revelation – namely proclamation and dogmatics.

> Theology and the Church, and even the Bible itself, speak no other language than that of this world which is shaped in form and content by the creaturely nature of the world and also conditioned by the limitations of humanity: the language in which human beings as we are, as sinful and corrupt human beings, wrestle with the world as it encounters us and as we see and try to understand it. The Bible, the Church and theology undoubtedly speak this language on the presupposition that there might be something in it, namely, that in this language God's revelation might be referred to, witness might be given, God's Word might be proclaimed, dogma might be formulated and declared.[26]

Here, Barth certainly attends to the human necessity to use fallen language to witness to God. What is missing, however, is any clear sense of the human role in *receiving* revelation – hearing it, understanding it, coming into conversation with it.[27] Barth's minimization of the human role in this process is clear even from the language that he sometimes uses to arrange the biblical concept of revelation – the language of "veiling, unveiling, and impartation." All three of these activities minimize the role of the audience; its members can only "watch" as the mystery of God is veiled or unveiled.

---

[25] George Hunsinger has argued quite convincingly that Barth's account of double agency bears a "Chalcedonian" character. But I think this tendency develops over time in the *Dogmatics*; it does not seem to be especially evident in I/1, and especially not in Barth's treatment of the *vestigia*, to which my remarks here are directed. At the very least, I would argue that the necessarily "asymmetrical" nature of double agency is, in I/1, so heavily balanced in God's direction that human agency is eclipsed. See *How to Read Karl Barth: The Shape of His Theology* (New York: Oxford University Press, 1991), 185–224.

[26] *CD* I/1, 339, trans. altered [*KD* I/1, 358].

[27] Many commentators have criticized passive accounts of the reception of revelation, in Barth and in others; see, e.g., Milbank, "Can a Gift," 141–2; Kathryn Tanner, *God and Creation in Christian Theology: Tyranny or Empowerment?* (Oxford: Basil Blackwell, 1988), 90–104; Webb, *Gifting God*, 98–104 and 177–80.

Indeed, in the case of "impartation," the audience wouldn't even have to be watching.[28]

Again, I do not want to deny that, in Barth's own rhetorical and theological context, he had good reason to minimize the human role in the reception of revelation. I simply want to ask whether the specificity of his context should be used to put a stop to the productive theological conversations that the *vestigia* tradition has generated across the centuries. I would certainly insist, with Barth, that the source of revelation must be God, not a projected set of human aspirations. Nevertheless, I would argue that not only proclamation and dogmatics, *but also the human reception of God's revelation*, must occur within the "creaturely nature of the world" and be "conditioned by the limitations of humanity." Revelation is not revelation unless it is revealed *to* someone; this, in turn, requires active reception on the part of the recipient. Revelation cannot bypass the human will, as though it were medicine injected with a syringe.

To put the matter differently: the verb *to reveal* does indeed share the threefold structure of other transitive verbs (revealer, act of revealing, and that which is revealed: subject, verb, and object) – just as Barth describes it. But unlike many such verbs, it also requires a fourth element: the one *to whom* the revealer reveals (indirect object – dative case). Thus, the grammar of "revealing" does not in fact bear a threefold character (as Barth argues), but rather a fourfold character; it is incomplete without the active participation of those who *receive* revelation.

Barth is not oblivious to this aspect of revelation; it comes out more clearly when he uses the language of "hearing" to speak of our reception of it (a metaphor that suggests a more active role for the audience than does the language of "unveiling" or "imparting"). Consider, for example, the passages with which I opened the Introduction of this book – as well as Barth's assessment of his own active role as a *hearer* of revelation: "If I understand what I am trying to do in the *Church Dogmatics*, it is to listen to what the Bible is saying, and tell you what I hear."[29] Despite these admissions, however, in his discussion of the *vestigia trinitatis*, Barth argues very strongly that the human role should be minimized. In the process of revelation, our "hearing" is (according to Barth) not really integral to the event, but is always something like "overhearing." While his own context may have given Barth some good reasons to think in these terms, it may have also prevented him from

---

[28] Compare the more active role assigned to the audience (in this case, the audience of a dramatic event) in Balthasar, *T-D* I:308–313 [*TD* I:286–91].

[29] Robert C. Johnson, "The Legacy of Karl Barth," *Reflection* 66, no. 4 (May 1969): 4. I owe the quotation to David Ford, *Barth and God's Story*, 11.

recognizing the real value of a careful and nuanced employment of the *vestigia* tradition in the process of the human reception of revelation.

Just how thoroughly Barth works to remove human beings from the process of reception can be seen in a discussion with which he ends his section on the tradition of the *vestigia*. Here Barth sets up a distinction between the activities of *interpretation* and *illustration* – the first being a legitimate enterprise, and the second, an illegitimate one. The difference between them, says Barth, is that "Interpretation means saying *the same thing* in other words," whereas "Illustration means saying the same thing *in other words*." He admits that "where the line is to be drawn between the two cannot be stated generally," but nevertheless insists that "there is a line."[30]

And in fact, this unspecifiable line becomes urgently important as the paragraph continues and gathers steam. Eventually "illustration" is aligned with the process of "proof" – precisely what the contributors to the *vestigia* tradition emphasized they were *not* doing. (Of course, Barth wisely does not offer an outright accusation in this respect; he simply raises the possibility in the minds of his audience, mentioning "the power to illustrate revelation" and then adding a casual-sounding "and who knows but what we should say at once its power to prove it."[31]) Indeed, by the time the paragraph is over, Barth will have aligned interpretation with everything that is right and good (theology, faith, and right worship), whereas illustration will have been successfully associated with – among other things – mere anthropology, unbelief, and idolatry![32] The rhetorical brilliance of Barth's moves throughout this paragraph should not be denied; what began as a simple difference in emphasis (on *the same thing* or on *other words*) has now become the difference between truth and falsehood.[33]

But the distinction does not have this absolute character.[34] As Barth's own

---

[30] *CD* I/1, 345 [*KD* I/1, 364].

[31] Ibid.

[32] Ibid., 345 [364–5].

[33] Passages like this brilliantly exemplify Barth's rhetorical skill, as explored in Stephen Webb's *Refiguring Theology*. They also provide a source of amusement when reading Barthians who complain about those theologians who use "emotive terms" applied in "pejorative ways" or whose writing has "a journalistic gloss" that "risks taking the place of careful argumentation" (all comments about Moltmann by Alan Torrance, *Persons in Communion*, 243n76). Reading Barth's work should have been the surest cure for such rhetorically spurious distinctions.

[34] One could differentiate the two categories formally, noting that interpretation appears to make a stronger claim for the adequacy of its articulation of reality; but in this case one would expect Barth to be more cautious about interpretations, since even though they are created by human beings, they still make a strong claim to be the "same" as what is revealed.

definition indicates, it is a matter of judgment; the two sentences that he uses to describe interpretation and illustration are, of course, grammatically and syntactically identical. They differ in the location of the emphasis; and emphasis (as all good rhetoricians know) is not a property of words, or meanings, or any other momentarily stable feature of language. Rather, emphasis is placed by writers and speakers, who make judgments about the persuasive power of various forms of emphasis, and implement them accordingly. Ultimately, Barth's distinction between interpretation and illustration is simply an assessment of a theological claim's legitimacy. If Barth considers it an adequate account of revelation, it is an interpretation (and thus it is theology, leading to faith and right worship); if inadequate, it is an illustration (and thus it is anthropology, leading to unbelief and idolatry).

Needless to say, Barth did not want this distinction to be reduced to a simple matter of judgment. He knew that a distinction of the sort that he constructed would be far more persuasive than a simple claim that "in my view, some approaches are adequate and some are not." The success of his approach is well demonstrated by the lengths to which some have gone to defend his distinction as naming an objective difference among theological statements. Alan Torrance, for example, begins by quoting Barth's definition of the distinction, and then attempts to magnify it:

> "Interpretation means saying *the same thing* in other words. Illustration means saying the same thing *in other words*." Clearly, what is intended in this slightly abstruse expression of the distinction is that the latter involves conceptual parallelisms (thus reducing theological affirmation to conceptual expression) whereas the former is testimony to one reality with which there are no parallelisms but which may be articulated (or, rather, which may articulate itself) in a whole variety of different ways.[35]

This exegesis – from its very first word ("Clearly"?!) – suggests more a desire to plead Barth's case than an attempt to recognize what is (and is not) at stake in the distinction. One might well wonder: what, in Barth's two-sentence definition, could possibly warrant this description? Why *must* one approach be conceptual – and how can the other fail to be? Why *must* only one involve parallelisms – and how can the other avoid doing so? And why is God suddenly described as the agent of interpretation, as the "one reality" that "articulates itself," as though human interpreters played no role?

Nor can Barth's own claims about the dangers of "illustration" serve to warrant the distinction, because each of them is also true for interpretation.

---

[35] Torrance, *Persons in Communion*, 204.

Consider three examples:[36] (1) If we illustrate revelation, says Barth, "we set a second thing alongside it and focus our attention on this." But the same is true, of course, for the *interpretation* of revelation: here too, we set a second thing (the interpretation) alongside the revelation, and focus our attention on it. It is possible, of course, to remain focused on the revelation itself as well; but this is also possible with illustration. (2) "We no longer trust revelation in respect of its self-evidential force." Again, also true for interpretation: if the revelation had truly been self-evident, no interpretation would have been necessary. (3) "What we say about [revelation] must be buttressed and strengthened and confirmed by something other than itself." Again, also true for interpretation: it uses (as Barth admits) "other words," and thus is something "other than" revelation. Again, if the theologian believed that revelation does not need to be "buttressed and strengthened and confirmed," why would an interpretation be offered?

Ultimately, illustration and interpretation both require a *human* agent – and this is precisely the feature of "interpretation" that Barth would like to minimize. He wants to describe interpretation as the *appropriate* human response to revelation, in which God is allowed to speak and human beings do not get in the way. Barth does not make this claim explicitly; in fact, one senses that he recognizes the problem here, especially when he admits that his own discussion of the threefold character of revelation failed to protect itself against the suspicion that it "might be using an illustration and playing a little game with a supposed *vestigium trinitatis*."[37] But Eberhard Jüngel seems much more confident that the human factor can be removed completely from the process of revelation:

> It is clearly a problem of the *sameness* of revelation. Interpretation protects the sameness of revelation in that it brings revelation (and only this) *as* revelation to speech. Illustration endangers the sameness of revelation in that it brings *with* revelation *also* language (*nomina*) as revelation to speech. But where also language (*nomina*) as revelation is brought to speech along with revelation, revelation is no longer protected as revelation *and* language no longer as language.[38]

Jüngel here attempts to drive a wedge between revelation and language, as though revelation could be "brought to speech" without language; this, at any rate, would seem to be the force of the parenthesis "(and only this)" in the

---

[36] All are from *CD* I/1, 345 [*KD* I/1, 364].

[37] Ibid., 345 [365].

[38] Jüngel, *Doctrine of the Trinity*, 13–14 [*Gottes sein*, 24–5].

second sentence of the above quotation. Such a claim, surely, is sheer mystification. That the source of revelation is divine, we need not doubt; but it cannot be brought to speech without the very *human* structures of language. Interpretation is not something that revelation "does" – it is, manifestly, something that human beings do – in the power of the Spirit to be sure, yet without eclipsing human agency.[39]

In a lengthy footnote, Jüngel attempts to clarify the distinction further through a discussion of the way that revelation "captures" language. The goal of interpretation, it would seem, is to reiterate the process of revelation capturing language, rather than to focus exclusively on the text itself as a static residue of the event of capture. Although Jüngel does not say so explicitly, he seems to align Barth's positive evaluation of "interpretation" with the hermeneutical interest in "the *capture* of the language by revelation as it becomes perceptible in the captures (texts!). Hermeneutics attempts so to preserve revelation as revelation and language as language precisely where revelation takes place, i.e. where God comes to speech."[40]

It is hard to know what to make of all this.[41] Clearly Jüngel (like Barth) would like to get around the thorny problem of language, and to claim that revelation uses language in such a way that all human linguistic activity is excluded. If it were possible to achieve this end, it would serve the very useful function of eliminating the Feuerbachian critique of revelation as the height of human striving, since it would take the agency of bringing revelation to language completely out of the hands of human beings. This, however, would be inadequate as a Christian doctrine of revelation; for in Christianity, the incarnational focus of the faith demands that the all-too-human use of language must always have a significant role to play.

This is not to suggest, of course, that Barth and Jüngel ignore the incarnation. However, rather than understanding it as a warrant for the

---

[39] On the human activity essential to the process of interpretation, see Nicholas Lash's essays "What Might Martyrdom Mean?" and "Performing the Scriptures," both of which are reprinted in *Theology on the Way to Emmaus*.

[40] Jüngel, *Doctrine of the Trinity*, 14n43 [*Gottes sein*, 25n43].

[41] Indeed, it needs to be said that the language in this passage is extraordinarily opaque, even by Jüngel's own standards, both in translation and in the original. I have never read anyone who has made a bit of sense out of this passage, in which revelation seems to be personified and given a will of its own that allows it somehow to operate without the help of language, and to "capture" language in ways that evade the wills of the human beings who use this language. For example, Alan Torrance quotes the passage (in *Persons in Communion*, 206), offering little comment other than to say that Jüngel here argues "with great profundity" – which means, I assume, that Dr Torrance has no more of a clue about what it means than do any of the rest of us!

necessity of the human reception of revelation (and therefore supportive of the *vestigia* tradition generally), they limit the significance of the incarnation to the person of Jesus, describing him as the one true *vestigium trinitatis*. But for the ancient authors, far from limiting the search for *vestigia*, the incarnation actually *warrants* that search – and indeed, reduces the likelihood that it will be converted into the kind of vain speculation that Barth and Jüngel seem to fear. Christ teaches us to "read" the triune marks of the created order, by providing us with a keynote and example. Through the incarnation, we learn something about the *character* of God's "producing" of words (and of the Word). Secure in this knowledge, we can explore the created order widely, developing triune marks as they seem appropriate – since the nature of God's involvement with the world has been revealed to us.

Saving the vestigia

We are now in a better position to appropriate the valuable features of the *vestigia* tradition while avoiding its dangers. At the outset, we need to grant Barth's concern that the tradition can be and has occasionally been abused as a warrant for allowing human conceptions of God to eclipse the concrete narratives of God's "production" of the world though Israel, Christ, and the Church. Thus, the positive lesson to be learned from Barth's critique is that these concrete narratives cannot be allowed to fade into the background. They must always be the starting-point and the touchstone of any Christian doctrine of God.

On the other hand, there seems to be no reason to accept Barth's conclusion that there is nothing to be gained from the search for *vestigia*. By way of summary, three points can be offered here. (1) The knowledge of God is not an all-or-nothing affair. Even if we agree with Barth that the revelation of God in Christ is the ultimate source of our knowledge of God, it does not necessarily follow that this knowledge is made clear to us, nor that we understand it, nor that we are persuaded of its truth and its relevance. Even if the *vestigia* produce no wholly new knowledge, they can help to give shape and clarity to what has already been made known to us. In this sense they can be an aid to dogmatics and proclamation. (2) The reception of revelation, like the hearing of any word, requires human thought and action. Consequently, the search for *vestigia*, when done with adequate attention to the concrete narratives of the Christian faith, is not fundamentally different from (for example) reading the Bible as preparation for preaching a sermon. In each case, the theologian seeks to be attentive to the revealed word of God – but also to be attentive to the created order, and to employ human language to interpret and/or illustrate divine revelation. (3) We believe in a "producing" God, who does not abandon the world; having created us, God remains active, gracing us with the power to respond by faith to the redemptive and sustaining love that God freely gives us. This belief has implications for our understanding of revelation. Having revealed to us something of the divine life, God does not abandon us to "figure it all out for ourselves," but remains at work in the created order, providing a context within which we may hear, understand, and be persuaded by God's self-revelation.

In my view, these three points are at the heart of the *vestigia* tradition as it has been practiced by Augustine, Bonaventure, Luther, and many others throughout the history of Christianity. Augustine, for example, does not begin his *De Trinitate* with a discussion of *vestigia*. Only after seven full books – in which he begins with the biblical narratives and develops an account of the divine relations, the trinitarian missions, appropriated and proper actions, and similar elements of the doctrine of God – does he turn to the created order and construe it as marked by God. And as he does so, he constantly refers the reader back to the missions of incarnation and inspiration as touchstones of theological adequacy, so that the *vestigia* never drift off into abstract speculation. And while he admits that none of his analogies is perfect, he hopes that at least some of them will provide his readers with greater clarity and understanding about the triune God. They are no substitute for the concrete narratives of יהוה, Christ, and the Spirit; but they help make those narratives clearer, more relevant, and more persuasive.

Because God is ever about the business of producing the world, everything in the world reflects the glory of God; the mark of the maker can thus be discerned, by those who "know how to look," in everything that is made. This does not provide us with new knowledge of God, but it does help us to understand that we too live in the midst of triunity – precisely because the whole world is produced by one who is Triune. This is why I believe we should once again take up the tradition of the *vestigia trinitatis*. Ever mindful of the need to ground our work in the biblical narratives and the creeds, and especially attentive to the incarnation of the Word as our touchstone, we should construe the created order as bearing triune marks.

The Practice of Parallelling

A rehabilitation of the *vestigia* tradition would, I think, help to ameliorate some of the problems in the current conversation, as discussed in chapter 1 – including its anxieties about attending to concrete practices and its evasion of matters such as gender and politics. More broadly: increased attention to the relationship between God and the world would help to re-establish the profound significance of the doctrine of the Trinity, on all three of the levels of theological inquiry that I described in the Introduction: the speculative, the grammatical, and the ethical. Thus the practice of parallelling – the construal of God's "triune marks" – is an important component of the *practice* of trinitarian theology. The Christian doctrine of God should not only be accurate in the abstract; it must also be effective, which is to say that the practices that it engenders should cohere with the claims that it makes.

Rhetorical invention as a triune mark

As an example of the practice of parallelling, I here describe the process of rhetorical invention as bearing certain triune marks. By "rhetorical invention," I mean that preparatory process, prior to the presentation of a persuasive appeal, in which a person attempts to "discover" all the means of persuasion that might be available in a particular case. In Roman rhetoric, this process was called *inventio* – the "invention" or "creation" of an argument (as opposed to the processes of memorization, delivery, and so on). One might think of an attorney planning a summarizing statement, or a politician getting ready to deliver a campaign speech, or a pastor preparing a sermon. I want to suggest that this process can be understood in parallel to the description of the divine processions and relations that we explored in the previous chapter.

My focus here is not on the "empirical" process of persuasion that takes place when someone stands at (for example) the bar in a courtroom, the podium at a political rally, or the pulpit in a church. Rather, I want to attend to the activity of those who are *preparing* to persuade a particular audience of a certain course of action. This process includes two activities in which such persons must "go forth from themselves" and become "other" to themselves. These two "processions" concern (1) the formulation of the words that will be written or spoken; and (2) the process of "stepping outside oneself" into the position of the audience, so that one can imagine how the language will be received. We can refer to these two processions as the "production of language" and the "construction of the audience."

Persuasion takes place through some form of communication. Its goal is to move the audience to take particular actions – such as returning a certain verdict, voting for a certain candidate, or living a certain kind of life. In these instances, at least, communication requires the use of language – though we would probably want to define language in the broadest possible way. It could be any system of symbols; a gesture, such as a hand waved in the air, could be language in this respect. Often it is a combination of words and gestures; but the gestures are often meaningful only because of a certain form of words that has accompanied or preceded them. In any case, persuasion involves the production of language.

We can consider this production from two perspectives – depending on whether we are thinking about the process from the "inside looking out" or from the "outside looking in." This gives rise to two relations, which we could name as "speaking" and "being spoken." Note that these two relations are wholly dependent on each other; we can imagine an event of "speaking" only if something is "being spoken," and something is spoken only if someone speaks.

Of course, in our ordinary discussion of this activity – as we noted in chapter 2 – we tend to move immediately from these verbal, relational forms to specific names; thus, we usually describe the process of the production of persuasive language *not* as "two relations" of speaking and being spoken, but as something that requires a speaker and a speech. Notice, however, what happens as a result: we quickly forget that these two are dependent on one another. We assume that we can abstract the speech from its context, reprint it, circulate it, ask someone else to deliver it, and so on. And we assume that the speaker can walk away from this process, going on about her daily business, most of which has nothing to do with her relation to this particular speech. But this picture is faulty, because (as was more clear when we were using verbal terms), the speaker and the speech depend upon each other for their very definition. Once the speech is reprinted, circulated, and so on, it is no longer what it originally was – that is, a discourse of words spoken by *this* person in *this* particular context. And once the speech has ended, the speaker is no longer a speaker. She may continue to be many other things (a human being, a worker, a daughter, a mother), but she is no longer the "speaker" in terms of the relational language we are using here.

The production of language is a necessary condition for persuasion, but not a sufficient one. By itself, without an "other" to whom it is directed, this language cannot persuade (nor even communicate); the relations of "speaking" and "being spoken" remain enclosed within a solipsistic world in which no one is "moved" to a change of will (the goal that persuasion seeks). The speaker may be speaking, but this language need not be intended for anyone in particular. Perhaps the speaker speaks a language of his own invention, that no one else understands; others might not even recognize it as language. What is lacking in this scenario is an externality or difference – something that can bring the production of language out of its self-contained world and allow it to encounter that which is truly *other* to itself. In order for persuasion to occur, there must be more than a begetting of words. This event of language-production must go beyond itself – must "process," to use the theological term – so that it can be received and witnessed.

This other procession that takes place in rhetorical invention also requires a "going-forth-from-oneself" – an act of stepping outside oneself, postulating oneself as an other. In this case, one must step into the position of the audience who will hear the speech. This is always a somewhat speculative endeavor, since the audience can never be known perfectly, and especially not ahead of time, when the various means of persuasion are being developed and discovered. One must ask oneself a number of very important questions about how the audience will receive the speech. Will they understand the language I am using? Will they recognize my references to literature, to current events, to popular culture? Will they remain interested enough in my speech to listen to it until the end? Will they ultimately be persuaded? In some cases, answering these questions may be mere guesswork; but one's success in answering them depends also on the ability to move outside oneself, to become "other" to oneself, so that one hears the speech from the other's point of view, and not merely from one's own.

Of course, the audience being "constructed" here is obviously not the empirical audience that actually hears the speech. That group may be very different than that which has been speculatively "constructed" ahead of time – which helps us to understand why some efforts at persuasion fail, even if the form of language that they use is well-reasoned and insightful. Here, we are focusing on the construction of the audience as a procession *within* the process of rhetorical invention, in which a person "becomes" other to him- or herself, in order to "hear" the speech from the audience's perspective and make judgments about its persuasiveness. In this procession, we can again speak of two relations: constructing and being constructed. As was the case with the first pair of relations, the very grammar of the words make them clearly dependent on one another (the same verb is used, in active and passive moods). They require each other, and cannot exist in isolation from one another.

Again, however, observe what happens when we move from these verbal terms to substantives: we usually speak simply of "the speaker" and "the audience." As in the previous case, this obscures the close mutual relationship between the two; we tend to assume that they could exist in isolation from one another. In addition, in this second case, something even more trouble-some occurs: we forget that the audience is, at least in the first instance, an imaginative construction of the speaker; we tend to jump ahead to the empirical entity that actually hears the speech – an entity that is wholly external to the process of rhetorical invention. This further exacerbates the tendency to think of these two entities as wholly separable, rather than the mutually dependent realities named by the relations of "constructing" and "being constructed."

Summarizing, then: in rhetorical invention there are two processions, the production of language and the construction of the audience. We can in turn think of these as four relations: speaking and being spoken, and constructing and being constructed. These relations differentiate the process of persuasion, such that we can understand certain activities as taking place within it, "internally" as it were. Our substantive terms for these relations – words such as *speaker*, *argument*, and *audience* – are less cumbersome, and are therefore useful (as we noted in the previous chapter, with reference to names for God) in providing some "temporarily stability" to discussions of a complex, differentiated, relational whole. Nevertheless, these nouns are less clearly interdependent (implicated by and implicating one another) than are the verbal forms from which they are derived. These substantives tempt us to abstract one or another of the three from its context and treat it as an isolated entity. This, however, is an artificial separation; all three are necessary, and if any one is missing the entire process of persuasion vanishes. This point will, I think, become clearer when I turn to some of the specific implications of the rhetorical analogy in the following section.

Some initial implications

I now want to suggest what might be gained, theologically, through this development of "the process of rhetorical invention" as a triune mark. I thereby hope to provide some corroboration for my general comments concerning the value of the *vestigia* tradition, as well as clarifying what I take to be the particular significance of rhetoric for the practice of trinitarian theology. Here, I offer only a few initial observations concerning the light that this analogy sheds on the doctrine of the Trinity; these insights will be taken up and explored in greater depth in parts two and three of this book. My comments in this chapter are restricted to three of the more difficult (and, some might say, arcane) aspects of trinitarian doctrine. In each case, I begin with a brief synopsis of (what I take to be) the most important trinitarian claims about the issue at hand; I then show how a rhetorical parallel can help us make each of these teachings clearer, more relevant, and more persuasive.

Radical equality
One of the central claims of classical trinitarianism is that the Three are radically equal to one another; none is in a position of superiority over the

others. In order to rule out Arianism and other forms of subordinationism, the Nicene Council rejected a whole variety of attempts to place the Three in an hierarchical order – logical, causal, temporal, or otherwise. The Council's clarity on this point is especially visible in the Nicene anathemas, which claim that there was no time when the Word "was not." And in order to make it clear that the "begetting of the Son" need not imply temporal order, the Creed states that this begetting takes place "eternally." Nor is there a logical hierarchy among the Three; they all imply one another and are dependent on one another, so that no one of them can be understood in a position of primacy over the others. In the language that I developed in chapter 2, we can say that, without the Source, neither the Wellspring nor the Living Water could be; they would have no "source." But then again, without the Wellspring and the Living Water, the Source would not be Source – that is, there would not be anything of which it could be "source." The Source cannot be Source unless it is the source *of* something.

This is a difficult concept to grasp, not least because most things in our experience *can* be expressed in causal or temporal order. But the Three are not "entities" in the normal sense of our experience; they are *relations*. Relations are not independent entities that can be arranged in temporal or logical sequence; they implicate one another and are dependent upon one another. Two of the three relations are commonly given names that attempt to preserve this mutual dependence – the two that we usually translate "Father" and "Son." At first, we might assume that a father precedes his son, both logically and temporally; but this is an illusion. Certainly, the older man precedes the younger man; but the older man does not become a *father* until he has a *child*. Without a child, no parent – and without a parent, no child; "the advent of the child, in a sense 'gives birth' to the father."[42] This aspect of divine relationality was emphasized in later Greek trinitarian theology, where the parental–filial language was thought to provide an especially clear description of two entities whose very existences were wholly dependent upon one another.[43] Similarly with respect to causal sequence: while there is a certain sense in which a parent is a *cause* of a child, there is an equally valid sense in which the child is the cause of the parent – for unless there is a child, the parent is not a parent! Such other-constituting relations are "retroactively causative."[44]

Unfortunately, the traditional translations failed to make this mutuality

---

[42] Soskice, "Trinity and 'the Feminine Other'," 11.

[43] "For the Cappadocians the idea of an original that only *is* through its imaged presentation is a necessary further spelling out of 'essential fatherhood'" (Milbank, "The Second Difference," 220).

[44] Ibid., 219.

clear with respect to the Holy Spirit. If "Spirit" and "Father" imply one another, they do so in a much less obvious sense than do "Father" and "Son." (Perhaps this is why the Spirit is sometimes seems to be the "forgotten member" of the Trinity.) The alternative translations that I have offered attempt to preserve the relational focus of "Father and Son," as well as extending it to cover "Spirit" as well. The Source is the cause of the Wellspring and the Living Water; but the Wellspring is also the cause of the Source (which must be source of something) *and* the cause of the Living Water (causing it to flow forth). Finally, the Living Water is the cause of the Source and of the Wellspring, bringing them into full life and providing a vehicle through which they can act upon the world.

Even in some of the most important trinitarian speculation of the early period of Christian history (for example, that of the Cappadocians), this radical equality was not always made completely clear. While emphasizing the lack of any temporal sequence in God, they still spoke of an "order" [τάξις], and sometimes spoke of only one of the Three as the cause [αἰτία].[45] They are not always completely consistent in these matters; nevertheless, such language tends to diminish the full equality of the Three, so that (for example) in later Orthodox theology, one of the Three (namely the Source) gets raised to the status of "the principle of unity" in God, or the ultimate ground and origin of the Godhead. This in turn has been taken over by a number of Western theologians; Walter Kasper, for example, goes out of his way to establish God as, fundamentally, a single transcendent person (the Father).[46] As John Milbank has noted, this tendency "obscures the really interesting and rigorous notion of an absolute origin that is 'always already' difference and succession."[47]

Finally, the radical co-equality of the Three has also been obscured by the common practice of describing them with ordinal numerals as the "first," "second," and "third" persons of the Trinity. As useful as this language may be, it very strongly suggests a logical or temporal sequence, and students of trinitarian doctrine can thus be forgiven for assuming that the "first person" is, in some way or another, "first." (For this reason, I have tended to avoid such language altogether in the present work.)

The trinitarian notion of a radical, relational co-equality can be illustrated, and perhaps made clearer, with reference to the process of persuasion. Here, we also speak of three: the rhetor, the argument, and the audience. Here too, there appears at first glance to be a temporal or logical sequence; we assume

---

[45] See, e.g., the discussion in Norris, *Faith Gives Fullness*, 45–6.

[46] Kasper, *The God of Jesus Christ*, part 1, and especially section 1 of part 2.

[47] Milbank, "The Second Difference," 218.

that the rhetor is "first," and that the argument comes later (and the audience later still). But if we concentrate on the process of rhetorical invention as described above, we may be able to recognize the fully relational, and thus the fully equal, nature of these three elements. The rhetor does not *become* rhetor except through the production of language and the construction of the audience. The audience is not a last-minute addition to the process, but must be constructed even as the argument is being developed. And the argument only exists in having been produced *by* someone and *for* someone.

Thus, the three are fully and mutually dependent on one another; all three must be present in order for any of them to be present. We can *imagine* them as isolated entities, but only by abstracting them from the very process that gives them their names. A person can stand alone in a room and offer an impassioned plea for some cause or another, but if the words are not intended to be heard by anyone, then "rhetorical invention" is not really taking place, and there is no sense in which this person is a *rhetor*; there is no one to be persuaded. Nor is the language employed in such a circumstance an "argument," except in some proleptic sense; it is not intended to move anyone to action.

Thus, the relationship among rhetor, audience, and argument mirrors that among Source, Wellspring, and Living Water: the rhetor becomes a rhetor only when producing an argument for an audience; the argument becomes argument when so produced; the (constructed) audience becomes audience upon being postulated as the target of the argument by the rhetor. Certainly, the human being who is about to take on the role of rhetor pre-exists the rhetorical context; but that person cannot be named by a relational term such as *rhetor* until the other elements of the process of rhetorical invention are also in place. Only then do the relations of "speaking" and "constructing" play a role. Similarly, a group of people assembled in a room, waiting, is not yet an "audience" in any strong sense; and even when they do hear the argument, they are not its "original" audience, for an audience first had to be constructed in the mind of the rhetor in order for the argument to be formed. Each of the three causes the others and is simultaneously caused by the others; there are no logical, temporal, or causal hierarchies among them. And just the same goes for the Trinity; the Three implicate one another, making one another what they are.

The external works of God are undivided
I have repeatedly noted our tendency to treat the Three as separable entities that can be described and understood in isolation from one another. One of the attempts to offset this tendency was the development of the language of

mutual coinherence (περιχώρησις; *circumincessio*), which describes the Three as indwelling and interpenetrating one another so completely that we can never intelligibly speak of one without involving, at least implicitly, the other two as well. The Three exist in a dynamic interrelationship with one another, giving to and receiving from one another what they most properly are.

This implies, in turn, that nothing positive can be said about any one of the Three that cannot be said about all of them. Everything that can be said of the Source can be said also of the Wellspring and the Living Water (except that we cannot say that they are the Source) – and similarly for the other two of the Three. And this further implies that God's external actions (actions toward the created order) are undivided – that is, none of them are accomplished by one of the Three acting alone, but only by all Three acting in concert (though each acts in a way that is appropriate to each).[48] Thus, we do not speak of one of the Three being uniquely responsible for some external divine action. This would misrepresent their character as *relations*; it would make no sense to speak of a relation doing something by itself. Thus, for example, the incarnation – while it is most obviously the work of the Wellspring – is also the work of the Source (who initiates it) and the Living Water (who effects, sustains, and completes it).[49]

Likewise, in the process of persuasion, the three relations of rhetor, argument, and audience are so closely bound to one another that we can speak of their mutual coinherence. This is not to say that the human beings who fulfill the roles of rhetor and audience are somehow grafted on to one another. It does mean, however, that the "external works" of the process of rhetorical invention are undivided; that is, we cannot speak of the persuasive power of speaker or argument or audience alone without speaking of the other two as well. We can say, for example, that the argument persuades, but it does not do so outside the context of particular speakers and particular audiences.

In this respect, the rhetorical context is very different from arguments in formal logic, in which (at least in theory) the argument *can* be separated from the character of the speaker. Logicians consider their syllogisms to be valid irrespective of the particularities of the audience they construct (though it usually needs to consist of "reasonable" persons). The argument can thus be

---

[48] The commonly-cited Latin tag is *opera trinitatis ad extra indivisa sunt*; this is clearly a working assumption for Augustine (*De Trin*. I.4.7, I.5.8, and elsewhere). It also informs the writing of the Cappadocians (e.g. Gregory of Nyssa *ad Ablab.*). It recurs through out the later councils, e.g., the 6th, 11th, and 16th Councils of Toledo (in AD 638, 672–6, and 693), as well as the Council of Venice (796/7); see *Denz* 491, 535, 571, 618.

[49] The Toledo Councils emphasize this point as well, as does the Fourth Lateran Council (1215). See *Denz* 491, 535, 571, 801.

separated from its original context and applied to very different contexts.[50] But such attempted separation of audience from argument does not work in the process of persuasion, since the chances of success in persuading the audience will depend in part on the rhetor's ability to imagine the perspective of its members and develop an argument that will speak to them specifically. Thus, we cannot isolate any one of these three elements of the rhetorical context and claim that it alone has caused persuasion to occur; persuasion always results from the interdependent relationships among rhetor, audience, and argument.

Indeed, the components of the process of persuasion occasionally even fade into one another and are simply not distinguishable. For example, sometimes the (perceived) character of the person making an argument actually *becomes* the argument. If that person is trusted and respected by the members of the audience, the words that are offered as an argument can be filled with logical fallacies and even blatantly false statements; nevertheless, many members of the audience may still be persuaded, because they have come to trust the speaker. This is a very common technique, for example, in television advertising: the spoken or (implicit) visual claims of the advertisement may be outlandish or silly (e.g., "with these shoes you can jump forty feet into the air"); however, because the shoes are being advertised by a well-known basketball star, the audience (which is expected to consist of people who have a very high regard for the star) are likely to be persuaded by the ultimate message ("buy these shoes!"). Audience members thus decide to re-order their own lives (forgoing whatever other purchases they would have made with the money to be spent on shoes) and thus dissolve certain aspects of their own particularity and merge their lives into those of the star and the claim. Speaker, audience, and argument are still all present and active in this process, even though (at least from the perspective of those being persuaded) the whole argument seems to merge into an undifferentiated whole.

The claim that "the external works of God are undivided" may seem arcane at first; ultimately, though, it is a way of emphasizing that the Three are not independent actors, but implicate and depend upon one another. Similarly, the three elements of rhetorical invention are never entirely separable; all contribute to the process of persuasion, even if they do so to different degrees and in different respects. Yet we still need to explore why it seems to us that certain activities *seem* to be primarily the work of only one of the Three – and

---

[50] As I have argued elsewhere (*Faithful Persuasion*, 149–64), logic also employs certain elements of persuasion, though logicians try very hard to deny this. Here, I employ the contrast merely as a heuristic device.

why, in certain forms of persuasive discourse, only one of the three elements seems active.

The doctrine of appropriations
Even though God's external activities are indivisible, certain activities of God can be made more meaningful and intelligible if we focus, at least temporarily, on one of the Three as the primary site of a particular divine activity. We "appropriate" a particular activity to one of the Three, in order that we might better understand its role in the overall divine plan, and thereby grow closer to God. Thus, the activity of creation is commonly appropriated to the Source, because we can understand the significance of the act of creation most clearly when we connect it to the divine relation of *initiation*. Nevertheless, the Wellspring and the Living Water are also at work in creation; to this the scriptures testify, as do the early councils.[51] Similarly, the work of redemption is always the undivided work of God; it is initiated by the Source, carried out by the Wellspring, and perfected by the Living Water. Yet we come to understand our salvation most clearly by appropriating it to the Wellspring, who became incarnate and suffered for our sake. And the work of sanctification, because it is an ongoing process, is most clearly understood in connection to the divine relation of emergence – which we describe as the Living Water, poured out upon the world at Pentecost. But as in the other cases, this is only an appropriation; our sanctification is brought about not by the Spirit alone but by the triune God, acting indivisibly.

A similar process of appropriation can be observed in the realm of rhetoric. We described the three relations of speaking, being spoken, and being constructed, to which we give the names rhetor, argument, and audience. We can think of a number of "works" of the process of persuasion that, while they are (obviously) the result of the whole, can be better understood when associated with one or another of the relations. One such appropriation would be of the three primary "means of persuasion" described by Aristotle: πάθος, which is concerned with emotional appeals; ἦθος, which focuses on appeals to character; and λόγος, a generic heading for all other forms of argument. None of these is possible unless all the relational elements of the process of rhetorical invention (rhetor, audience, and argument) are present. Nevertheless, we can understand these three "means of persuasion" more clearly if we associate them, at least temporarily, with one or another of the elements of the process. For example, ἦθος, which concerns matters of character, is often

---

[51] E.g., the Councils of Rome (382) and Constantinople II (553), *Denz* 171, 421. I examine the scriptural warrants for this claim in chapter 4.

associated with the rhetor, whose character can affect the outcome of the argument. But this is only an appropriation; in order to be persuasive, character must be evaluated (by the audience). And there must also be an argument, in order that there be some specific content to the persuasion that occurs by means of character. Similarly, the effectiveness of an emotional appeal may depend mostly on the kind of audience one hopes to persuade, so it is often appropriated to the audience. Yet an emotional appeal also requires carefully chosen forms of language and a speaker who is capable of carrying out the appeal with sincerity.

Another rhetorical example of appropriations can be seen in the claim that the ends of rhetoric are "to teach, to delight, and to move." Again, all three of these are properly the result of the rhetorical process as a whole. But we may understand its *teaching* role most clearly by examining the content of its argument. Similarly, the degree to which persuasive discourse "delights" may be a function of the rhetor's charisma; and the extent of "movement" that takes place may depend on the dispositions of the audience. Note, however, that none of these appropriations is fixed; one could just as easily say that persuasive discourse only "moves" someone to action when the rhetor is particularly skilled, or that "delight" is a function of the audience's emotional state. The process of appropriation is not a fixed categorization that can be predetermined; it is a judgment made by the commentator who offers the appropriation.

Of course, in both theology and rhetoric, some appropriations have been very widely and repeatedly affirmed, such that they seem to become part of the tradition itself. A theological example would be the appropriations in the Nicene Creed: creation is appropriated to the Source, salvation to the Wellspring, and prophetic inspiration to the Living Water. But even these classical appropriations are not absolute; they are subject to revision, and they are certainly not meant to displace the claim that *all* the external works of God are properly the work of God as a whole, and not just of one of the Three. Creation, salvation, and inspiration are all initiated by the Source, brought to fruition by the Wellspring, and emerge into the world through the work of the Living Water.

On what basis, then, is a particular work appropriated to one of the Three, either in theology or in rhetoric? Interestingly, the criterion for appropriation is a rhetorical one. We know that all the works of God are the work of all Three, acting in concert; nevertheless, by appropriating a particular work to one of the Three, we may be able to understand it better, to believe it more firmly, and to articulate it more persuasively. Thus, (for example) the longstanding appropriation of creation to the Source is undertaken in the belief that Christians will better understand what is at stake in the act of creation if they focus on it as an undertaking of God the Source, that is, the relation of *initiation*. And similarly for other appropriations.

Taking the next step

The practice of parallelling is an attempt to take seriously the claim, made at the end of the previous chapter, that God *produces* our knowledge of God – first and foremost in God's self-revelation through Christ, but also in the power of the Spirit in the Church, and finally (though much less precisely) through the created order generally. If this is true, then we are called to "commandeer" the created order (to use Barth's idiom) in order to help us say what we ourselves find difficult to say, even though it has already been revealed to us in Christ.

I do not know, of course, whether my own audience has been persuaded by means of the example I have offered. Does my description of rhetorical invention as a "triune mark" make these rather arcane claims of trinitarian doctrine any less abstract, any clearer, any more persuasive? If so, this provides at least an initial argument in favor of this approach. If not, I hope readers will bear with me; for I intend to unpack these descriptions, and offer additional (though much less extended) examples of parallelling, in the remainder of this book. By attending to the created order, and by construing its triune marks, we become more aware of the ways that our lives bear the image of God's Triunity – and we may learn to live into that image in ever more faithful ways. As I will argue in part two of this book, we can be formed in certain "trinitarian virtues," which strengthen the relationship between God's triune character and our own. And as I will suggest in part three, we can allow these trinitarian virtues to inform, and even to reshape, our practices – and to do so in ways that make us yet more receptive to God's gift. I will thus speak of "trinitarian practices" and "trinitarian virtues" as bound together in a circle (or, better, an ascending spiral) – mutually reinforcing each other and leading us into ever deeper communion with God.

The close relationship between theory and practice should be a natural outcome of trinitarian theology. The doctrine of the Trinity teaches us that the God whom we worship is not a merely theoretical deity, remote and disengaged, but is rather the Living God who created us, who became incarnate and dwelt among us, and who dwells among us still in the communion of the Church. A God so intimately involved with our lives can never be of purely theoretical importance; for in this God we live, and move, and have our being.

Part Two

WELLSPRING: TRINITARIAN VIRTUES

INTRODUCTION TO
PART TWO

In part one of this book, I discussed the doctrine of the Trinity as having developed out of the Christian narratives of יהוה, Christ, and the Spirit – and as having been formalized in the claim that these narratives imply processions, relations, and missions in God. These narratives, as well as their philosophical formalization, help us to recognize that, in God, "these three are one" – that is, oneness and difference are not in essential conflict. This claim will be given more specific shape in this part of the book, which describes three key elements of God's triune character. These chapters will also continue the practice of parallelling – construing the created order as marked, however faintly, by these same triune elements.

Thus, these chapters offer meditations on the uncreated Trinity of God, as well as explorations of the triune marks of God's creation. In order to keep both aspects of this discussion in play, I will employ the language of *virtue*. This is a highly contested term in the history of philosophy and theology, and I will not be exploring all its nuances here. I construe the word as naming dispositions that *God has by nature*, and in which *we participate by grace*. The "trinitarian virtues" are characteristics of the triune God that are bestowed upon us, freely, as part of God's work of *producing* the world. As gifts, these virtues are not forced upon us; but we can allow them to form us, and thus allow God to take us up into the divine life.

Although the virtues have received renewed attention of late,[1] they have

---

[1] See Alasdair MacIntyre, *After Virtue: A Study in Moral Theory*, 2nd edn (Notre Dame, Ind.: University of Notre Dame Press, 1984); Stanley Hauerwas and Charles Pinches, *Christians Among the Virtues: Theological Conversations with Ancient and Modern Ethics* (Notre Dame, Ind.: University of Notre Dame Press, 1997); L. Gregory Jones, *Transformed Judgment: Toward a Trinitarian Account of the Moral Life* (Notre Dame, Ind.: University of Notre Dame Press, 1990); Jean Porter, *The Recovery of Virtue: The Relevance of Aquinas for Christian Ethics* (Lousiville: Westminster/John Knox Press, 1990); and Paul Wadell, *Friends of God: Virtues and Gifts in Aquinas* (New York: Peter Lang, 1991).

not generally been the primary focus for descriptions of the moral life in the modern era. Until quite recently, ethical theory has been dominated by the investigation of

> character-properties which attach to a moral subject. These character-proper-ties, defined as "values," were viewed as having their origin in a valuing subject. This valuing subject, posited as the center in a moral theory of the self, had conferred upon it a position and function similar to the knowing subject. . . . Value and knowledge became viewed as properties possessed by a subject.[2]

This "value-centered" approach to moral theory has been tremendously (and, in my view, disastrously) influential. One of its most unfortunate side-effects has been to encourage us to think of a virtue as a moral position that one adopts wholly by oneself, under one's own power. In common parlance, a "virtuous" person is thought to be someone who has made an autonomous and well-disciplined decision to conform steadfastly to certain moral norms. This usage obscures the longstanding Christian claim that the virtues are primarily gifts of God.

On the other hand – at the opposite end of the spectrum – the virtues have sometimes been characterized as a divine work in which human beings play a wholly passive role. This tendency is perhaps reinforced by the description of certain virtues as "infused"; this metaphor is sometimes read as suggesting wholly active impartation and wholly passive reception (a sort of "lightning bolt" experience in which one is overcome by an irresistible external force). On such an account, the free will of human beings is minimized – sometimes leading to a moral quietism that obscures the role of human beings as moral agents.

Somewhere between these two extremes is a view of virtue that does not understand the relationship between divine action and human action as a zero-sum game. God is certainly active in gracing human lives with virtues; but human beings are also active in allowing this grace to be formative in their cultivation of particular habits. These two activities, divine and human, are not separate and sequential; that is, one of them does not need to have been

---

[2] Calvin O. Schrag, *Communicative Praxis and the Space of Subjectivity* (Bloomington: Indiana University Press, 1986), 201. Cf. also the discussions of "value" in Sabina Lovibond, *Realism and Imagination in Ethics* (Minneapolis: University of Minnesota Press, 1983), 1–23; Alasdair MacIntyre, *After Virtue*, 11–35; and Eberhard Jüngel, "Value-Free Truth: The Christian Experience of Truth in the Struggle Against the 'Tyranny of Values,'" *Theological Essays II*, ed. John Webster, trans. Arnold Neufeldt-Fast and John Webster (Edinburgh: T. & T. Clark, 1994), 191–215 [ET of "Wertlose Wahrheit. Christliche Wahrheitserfahrung im Streit gegen die «Tyrannei der Werte»", in *Wertlose Wahrheit. Zur Identität und Relevanz des christlichen Glaubens. Theologische Erörterungen III* (München: Christian Kaiser Verlag, 1990), 90–109].

completed in order for the other one to take place. Instead, they are relational, and are thus inseparable. This is how many Christian thinkers understood the virtues. St Thomas, for example, makes it clear that human agency is relevant in the formation of virtue; it "is caused in us by God without our action, but not without our consent."[3] Moreover, a virtue bears fruit only when *we* are active as well: "As to those things which are done by us, God causes them in us, yet not without action on our part, since God works in every will and in every nature."[4] The virtues emphasize both God's activity and our own; we can thus define them as "the presence of God's grace in the development of good habits."[5]

In these three chapters, then, I am attempting to describe aspects of God's character that are present, by grace, in the development of human habits. More specifically, they are elements of the *triune* character of God, and they are present in our development of specifically *trinitarian* habits. In this way, our lives can come to take on a triune character as well, conforming more closely to the image of God in which we were created. This involves narrating the trinitarian character of both God and the created order, thus encouraging us to think about what it might mean to claim (with respect to both God and ourselves) that "these three are one."

Because this part of the book attends "stereoscopically" to the human and the divine, its keynote will be *incarnation*. This event provides Christianity with its clearest perspective on the link between God and humanity. In the life, death, and resurrection of Mary's son, Jesus of Nazareth, Christians learn something of the form and content of divine Triunity.[6] Throughout these

---

[3] *ST* I–II.55.4 ad 6; trans. W. D. Hughes, O.P. (slightly altered), XXIII:17.

[4] Ibid.

[5] I owe this formulation to Bill Cavanaugh, who employs it in an unpublished paper entitled "Human Habit and Divine Action in Aquinas' Account of the Virtues." See also Wadell, *Friends of God*.

[6] Some readers will have noted that, when I have mentioned the name of Jesus, I have often included, nearby, the name of Mary as well. I am trying to take seriously Mary's role in the incarnation – something that I think much contemporary theology has failed to do (especially outside Roman Catholic and Orthodox circles). I have not worked out the Christological implications of my usage, nor have I attended to the ecumenical hazards it may raise; I am certainly no expert in Mariology. Nevertheless, greater theological attention to Mary seems necessitated by the trinitarian virtues that I describe in these chapters. I frequently employ the images of *pregnancy* and *parenting* in the explanation and description of these virtues; and since the keynote of these chapters is Christological, it seems necessary to take into account the role of Mary as well as that of Jesus. Much of what we know about mothers and children would seem to raise questions about independence and individuality as they are commonly constructed in post/modern culture. (Special thanks to Margaret Adam for urging me to think about these issues.)

chapters, I will turn to this narrative of "God with us" in order to develop my account of trinitarian virtues. This narrative, which I read in the light of specific Christian practices, will help give concrete content to these virtues – helping us trace the shape that our lives might take, if we accept God's grace in the cultivation of a trinitarian way of life.

These three chapters have a common structure. Each begins by defining the trinitarian virtue with which it is concerned, and developing it in light of its role in recent theology. I then show how that virtue is embodied in a particular Christian practice, making use of the Johannine reference to the three earthly witnesses, "the Spirit and the water and the blood." The central section of each chapter is a theological analysis of the virtue, focusing on the incarnation and the biblical texts that witness to it. I then conclude each chapter with a construal of some elements in the created order as bearing certain "triune marks," thereby helping to place these trinitarian virtues in a brighter and more convincing light.

Chapter 4

POLYPHONY

The claim that "these three are one" asks us to call into question the common assumption that oneness and difference are mutually exclusive categories. The rigid separation of these categories is, however, a common feature of many of the conceptual worlds in which we operate – conceptual worlds such as arithmetic, formal logic, and analytic philosophy. These interpretive frameworks can make little room for the claim that "three" can in any sense be equated with "one." If we are to take that claim seriously, we will need an alternative space for thinking. I suggest a concert hall.

Making Music Together

Music often requires that more than one thing happen at a time. One may, of course, produce or listen to music in which one person plays or sings a consecutive series of notes, alone, without accompaniment. But often, music consists of multiple notes being played or sung at the same time – perhaps by one person (as is possible on a keyboard instrument, for example), or by a group. In fact, this rather more complex form of music is so common that one of the words for a musical performance (*concert*) actually reflects this multiplicity (from *con* + *certare*, "to act together").

When we attend a concert, and hear more than one note being played at once, we do not usually react negatively. We do not consider the simultaneous sounding of two notes to be contradictory, meaningless, or against reason. Neither do we believe that this has somehow violated a principle of music (or of reason); indeed, we often *enjoy* hearing a number of different sounds at once. In music, such simultaneous multiplicity seems not only to be allowed, but to be encouraged and rewarded.

Not all enterprises allow this – at least not in the relatively unconstrained way that music does. For example, we would think it odd if someone claimed that a wall was to be built entirely out of bricks and that the same wall was to be built entirely out of wood. We recognize that two wholly different building materials cannot coexist in precisely the same space and time. Music is different: the musical notes $F\#$ and A can easily co-exist within the same time and space. And we would not be at all surprised if a pianist played the two notes simultaneously.

In a concert hall, we often hear many notes played simultaneously, and are the richer for doing so. In fact, we often hear more than one melody played simultaneously; thus, we hear not only multiple tones (as in a chord), but also entirely different sequences overlapping one another. Music theory has a technical term for this – *polyphony*. We can apply the same term to other contexts: any time we understand two or more different (even, possibly, "opposing") ideas being performed or enacted simultaneously, we have located an example of polyphony.

Sometimes the word *polyphony* is taken to be a synonym of *harmony*; and in music theory the two terms are closely related. Etymologically, polyphony (from *poly*, many + *phonē*, voice or sound) would seem to refer to *any* simultaneous sounding of different notes. *Harmony*, on the other hand, implies the existence of certain audiological standards about the frequency of musical tones, certain aesthetic standards about what constitutes a well-tempered scale, and so on. Polyphony could theoretically be either "harmonious" or "dissonant." Its chief attribute is simultaneous, non-excluding difference: that is, more than one note is played at a time, and none of these notes is so dominant that it renders another mute.

A theological perspective informed by *polyphony* would seek to examine, in a critical way, any claim that two categories must necessarily work against one another. Too often, theology has operated with false dichotomies, in which it is assumed that increased attention to one element necessarily decreases the significance of the other. For example, I have already referred to the tendency of some theologians to think of revelation, or of the virtues, as a "zero-sum game" – in which, the more active God is understood to be in the process, the less active human beings can be. Such approaches have been helpfully described by Kathryn Tanner as "contrastive" descriptions of the God–world relationship.[1] One can see such positions at work in, for example, the claim that any increase in emphasis on the humanity of Christ necessarily diminishes the divinity of the incarnate

---

[1] Tanner, God and Creation, 46–7.

Word, or the argument that God's transcendence is subverted by any attention to God's immanence.[2]

Of course, such contrastive approaches may be perfectly legitimate in some cases. Too often, however, we have simply *assumed* that two elements operate in a zero-sum relationship to one another, without asking ourselves whether they might be better understood as bearing a "musical" character. In music, multiple themes are not necessarily contrastive; music is not a zero-sum game. The addition of a new contrapuntal theme does not obliterate (or even necessarily diminish) the significance of the theme(s) already in place; nor does a symphony's brilliant cello part, for example, eliminate the need for trombones. The category of *polyphony* provides us with a critical perspective from which to examine all contrastive claims about God and the world.

Christianity proclaims a polyphonic understanding of God – one in which *difference* provides an alternative to a monolithic homogeneity, yet without becoming a source of exclusion. Attention to any one of the Three does not imply a diminished role for the others; all three have their distinctive melodies, and all are "played" and "heard" simultaneously without damage to God's unity. Moreover, we can come to understand the created order as marked by the polyphonic character of its Maker. In this section, these claims will be given more concrete content, as we explore the application of *polyphony* to trinitarian theology.

Theology as a musical endeavor

A number of theologians have turned to music to express something that they considered central to the Christian perspective. While this is not the place for an extended treatment of the theme (let alone for the development of a theology of music), it may be helpful to consider a few examples of the use of the analogy. The concept has an ancient pedigree, having been taken up by St Augustine in numerous sermons and pastoral writings, and in a systematic way in his *De musica*.[3] Here, I will examine the analogy in the work of three twentieth-century theologians.[4]

---

[2] For a fine critique of "contrastive" views, especially with respect to transcendence and immanence, see Placher, *The Domestication of Transcendence*, esp. ch. 7.

[3] On this treatise, see (in addition to John Milbank, whose work I will discuss below) Catherine Pickstock, "Ascending Numbers: Augustine's *De musica*" in Lewis Ayres, ed., *Studies in Christian Origins: Theology, Rhetoric and Community* (London and New York: Routledge, 1998).

[4] The analogy has been frequently employed, though I know of no study analyzing or

Dietrich Bonhoeffer's letter to Eberhard Bethge, written from Tegel prison on 20 May 1944, offers an interesting meditation on the "musical" relationship between our love of God and our love of the created order.[5] Bonhoeffer suggests that the latter is wholly legitimate, but that it should not be detached from the former. He draws an analogy to the relationship between *cantus firmus* and counterpoint. The *cantus firmus* ("firm song") originally referred to church music that was set by ecclesiastical decree. This led to a derived meaning, namely, any fixed melody to which other parts can be added. Bonhoeffer builds on this theme:

> God wants us to love him eternally with our whole hearts – not in such a way as to injure or weaken our earthly love, but to provide a kind of *cantus firmus* to which the other melodies of life provide the counterpoint. One of these contrapuntal themes (which have their own complete independence but are yet related to the *cantus firmus*) is earthly affection.[6]

The polyphony that Bonhoeffer here describes is not just a random assortment of sounds, but rather a relationship among various melodies (earthly and heavenly).

For Bonhoeffer, the key characteristic of polyphonic music is its ability to maintain difference – even within an apparent unity. He gives some specific shape to this idea by means of a Christological image:

---

comparing its use among modern theologians. Though I have not explicated them here, interesting examples (ranging from brief illustration to full-scale development) include: Karl Barth, *CD* III/3, 297–9 [*KD* III/3, 337–9]; Barth, *Wolfgang Amadeus Mozart*, trans. Clarence K. Pott (Grand Rapids, Mich.: William B. Eerdmans, 1986) [ET of: *Wolfgang Amadeus Mozart, 1756/1956* (Zürich: Theologischer Verlag, 1956)]; James H. Cone, *The Spirituals and the Blues* (New York: Seabury Press, 1972; reprint, Maryknoll, NY: Orbis Books, 1991); Jaroslav Pelikan, *The Melody of Theology: A Philosophical Dictionary* (Cambridge: Harvard University Press, 1988); Paul Ricoeur, *Figuring the Sacred: Religion, Narrative, and Imagination*, ed. Mark I. Wallace, trans. David Pellauer (Minneapolis: Fortress Press, 1995); F. E. D. Schleiermacher, *Christmas Eve: Dialogue on Incarnation*, trans. Terrence N. Tice (Richmond: John Knox Press, 1967) [ET of: *Die Weihnachtsfeier: ein Gesprach*, ed. Hermann Mulert (Leipzig: Dürr'schen, 1908)]; and Frances Young, *Virtuoso Theology: The Bible and Interpretation* (Cleveland: Pilgrim Press, 1993).

[5] My thanks to Stephen Fowl for reminding me of Bonhoeffer's brief but suggestive use of this analogy.

[6] Dietrich Bonhoeffer, *Letters and Papers from Prison*, trans. Reginald Fuller, 3rd edn (London: SCM Press, 1971; reprint, New York: Macmillan, Collier Books, 1972), 303 [ET of: *Widerstand und Ergebung: Briefe und Aufzeichnungen aus der Haft* (München: Christian Kaiser Verlag, 1970), 192].

Where the *cantus firmus* is clear and plain, the counterpoint can be developed
to its limits. The two are "undivided and yet distinct," in the words of the
Chalcedonian Definition, like Christ in his divine and human natures. May not
the attraction and importance of polyphony in music consist in its being a
musical reflection of this Christological fact and therefore of our Christian life?[7]

Bonhoeffer obviously had little opportunity to work out these thoughts in
detail. It is unclear, for example, just how "foundational" he considers the
cantus firmus to be; is it the only "essential" element in a piece of music, while
other themes are "optional extras"? Because he is here describing the
relationship between God and human beings, he (quite understandably)
describes the two aspects as asymmetrical, accenting the priority of the *cantus
firmus* as opposed to the counterpoint (though he does allow the latter some
measure of independence). In any case, the musical paradigm helps him to
show that divine and human love need not be understood as contrastive. They
are not a "zero-sum game" – that is, the increase of one does not necessitate
the diminution of the other.

> I wanted to tell you to have a good, clear *cantus firmus*; that is the only way to
> a full and perfect sound, when the counterpoint has a firm support and can't
> come adrift or get out of tune, while remaining a distinct whole in its own right.
> Only a polyphony of this kind can give life a wholeness and at the same time
> assure us that nothing calamitous can happen as long as the *cantus firmus* is kept
> going.[8]

Although Bonhoeffer does not explore the specifically trinitarian implications
of this analogy, his comments alert us to the significant theological importance
of polyphony: it helps us to think in terms of simultaneous difference that need
not be synthesized into a single, homogeneous unity.

Hans Urs von Balthasar's small book *Truth is Symphonic* touches on many of
these same themes. The book's prologue begins by reminding readers of the
importance of the different voices which "sound together" to create symphonic music. Balthasar then draws an analogy to the created order:

> The world is like a vast orchestra tuning up: the players play to themselves, while
> the audience take their seats and the conductor has not yet arrived. All the same,
> someone has struck an A on the piano, and a certain unity of atmosphere is
> established around it: they are tuning up for some common endeavor. . . . The

---

[7] Ibid., 303, trans. slightly altered [*Widerstand*, 193].
[8] Ibid.

choice of instruments comes from the unity that, for the moment, lies silent in the open score on the conductor's podium.[9]

The conductor – God – provides a pivot-point that allows the analogy to extend to both the Creator and the creature:

> In revelation, God performs a symphony, and it is impossible to say which is richer: the seamless genius of the divine composition or the polyphonous orchestra of Creation that God has prepared to play it. . . . The unity of the composition comes from God. That is why the world was, is and always will be pluralist (and – why not? – will be so increasingly). . . . But the purpose of its pluralism is this: not to refuse to enter into the unity that lies in God and is imparted by God, but symphonically to get in tune with one another and give allegiance to the transcendent unity.[10]

The language of polyphony thus allows Balthasar to emphasize oneness as well as difference.

Moreover, Balthasar recognizes that this image has significant trinitarian implications. In advocating close attention to the narrative description of the person and mission of Christ, for example, he suggests that any "purely historical" portrait of Jesus fails to attend to the polyphony of the whole Trinity.

> It is utter folly to try to "grasp" Christ: he always slipped through the hands of those who wanted to seize him. . . . "Do not hold me, for I have not yet ascended to the Father." We learn his secret by allowing him to return to his origin. And the Spirit who proceeds from Father and Son, since he is neither Father nor Son but their reciprocal love, introduces us into this mystery. Even eternal Truth itself is symphonic.[11]

Balthasar's language stresses both oneness and difference in God, as well as providing a number of pointers as to how these terms might be applied to the created order.

John Milbank provides a final example – and in doing so brings us full circle, in that many of his reflections are developed in conversation with Augustine's *De musica*. He begins by distancing Christian theology from the realm of

[9] Hans Urs von Balthasar, *Truth is Symphonic: Aspects of Christian Pluralism*, trans. Graham Harrison (San Francisco: Ignatius Press, 1987), 7-8 [ET of: *Die Wahrheit ist symphonisch. Aspekte des christlichen Pluralismus* (Einsiedeln: Johannes Verlag, 1972), 7–8].

[10] Ibid, 8–9, translation slightly altered [*Wahrheit*, 8].

[11] Ibid, 11–12 [11].

formal logic and substantialist metaphysics; the claim that God created the
world "out of nothing" is an admission that *becoming* and *emergence* take
precedence over fixed essences or a static notion of *being*. Christian theology
postulates "a reality of flux, a reality without substance, composed only of
relational differences and ceaseless alterations."[12] Milbank then considers how
this construal of the world differs from that offered by postmodernism – a
difference that Augustine's *De musica* helps him to make explicit. Like much
postmodern thought, Christianity remains resolutely open to new insights and
additions; however, it brings all this variety into harmony in the Body of
Christ. And the idea of a unified (yet open and differential) series is the idea
of *music*: "In music there must be continuous endings and displacements, yet
this is no necessary violence, because only in the recall of what has been
displaced does the created product consist."[13]

Milbank then transposes this "musical" conceptuality into concrete practices, suggesting that the Christian conception of community recognizes the
same sort of non-exclusionary difference that is exemplified in polyphonic
music:

> For Christianity, true community means the freedom of people and groups to
> be different, not just to be functions of a fixed consensus, yet at the same time
> it totally refuses *indifference*; a peaceful, united, secure community implies
> *absolute* consensus, and yet, where difference is acknowledged, this is no
> agreement in an idea, or something once and for all achieved, but a consensus
> that is only in and through the inter-relations of community itself, and a
> consensus that moves and "changes": *a concentus musicus*.[14]

Because music can help us imagine the idea of a "moveable" consensus, it is
extraordinarily useful – both for an account of God's Triunity, and for a triune
reading of the created order.

Another aspect of Milbank's approach that seems especially fruitful is his
recognition that Christians are able to recognize the *form* of God's music
because they are engaged in specific common practices that teach them how
to do so – though he does not map out these practices in detail. We can further

---

[12] John Milbank, "'Postmodern Critical Augustinianism': A Short *Summa* in Forty Two
Responses to Unasked Questions," *Modern Theology* 7, no. 3 (April 1991): 225–37; here,
227.
[13] Ibid., 228. He continues: "Perhaps this is partly why, in *De Musica*, Augustine – who
realised that creation *ex nihilo* implied the non-recognition of ontological violence, or of
positive evil – puts forward a 'musical' ontology."
[14] Ibid.

explore his insight by examining how Christian communities embody an image or echo of God's musicality. We can begin this process by thinking about the relationship between communities and practices.

Practices of the interpretive community

The activity of listening to music brings us into contact with other human beings. One person plays, another listens; a group plays, and a group listens; and even the solitary devotee who hears only recorded music is distantly reminded of others (who wrote, performed, recorded, produced, and marketed the recording that is being heard). We develop our conceptions of musical beauty (and ugliness) through contact with others; that is, our assessment of music is always related to others' assessments (both positive and negative). What is taken to be the most beautiful music in one cultural milieu might not even be *recognized* as music in another.

Listening to music thus takes place within the context of an interpretive community.[15] The members of such communities do not make identical evaluations and assessments, but they do operate by means of a mutually understood language, which at least allows them to carry on a conversation about their likes and dislikes, their interpretations, and their newest discoveries. These communities can overlap; a person can be a member of many different ones simultaneously, and to different degrees. In my own case, for example, I could have an intelligent conversation with devotees of most Western "classical" music, with some fans of rock music, and with a small selection of listeners to Celtic and North American folk music. My ability to participate in these communities is dependent upon my sharing common practices with others in the community: we listen to the same recordings, attend the same sorts of concerts, and may also share a number of other practices in ancillary fields (what books we read, what visual arts we enjoy, and so forth).

In a similar way, Christians interact with an interpretive community that is engaged in similar processes of listening and learning. This interpretive community is the Church: the gathering of those who, through the activity of Christ and the Spirit, have been "called out" into a special relationship with God, and who are engaged in common practices, such as worship, education, and care for others. These practices provide a "common language" that allows

[15] My use of the language of "interpretive communities" is adopted from the work of Stanley Fish, e.g., *Is There a Text in This Class? The Authority of Interpretive Communities* (Cambridge: Harvard University Press, 1980).

Christians to engage one another as they "listen to the music" of the triune God.

Of these practices, one of the most important and fundamental is that of *baptism*. Through this practice, people are initiated into the life of the believing community; they become a part of the household of God. Baptism is the sign of a person's entry into the community of the faithful, the Church. It is a widely shared practice among Christians – even though our accounts of it vary greatly across and within Christian communities. It can thus help us to recognize the contours of a specifically *trinitarian* polyphony; it should also begin to *form* us polyphonically, urging us to understand ourselves and others as the various melody-lines that contribute to the symphony of the Church.

A witness to polyphony: the water

The first epistle of John names "the water" as one of "the three who bear witness on earth." The word *water* evokes the practice of baptism; moreover, many other water-related Christian symbols are brought into focus by the language of the baptismal rite. The prayer over the water of baptism, for example, is rich in water imagery:

> We thank you, Almighty God, for the gift of water. Over water the Holy Spirit moved in the beginning of creation. Through water you led the children of Israel out of their bondage in Egypt into the land of promise. In water your Son Jesus received the baptism of John and was anointed by the Holy Spirit as the Messiah, the Christ, to lead us, through his death and resurrection, from the bondage of sin into everlasting life.[16]

This text collects various roles of water in the Christian narrative – from the beginning of creation, through the salvation of Israel, to the baptism of Jesus. The prayer continues beyond what I have quoted here, mentioning water as the site of our burial with Christ in death and our sharing with Christ in resurrection.[17]

All these elements are brought together in the dense sacramentality of the

---

[16] Based on the version in the *Book of Common Prayer* authorized for the United States province at the time of this writing (the 1979 version), but substituting *water* for the word *it* at several points in the text. This minor revision has several liturgical benefits – an insight which I owe chiefly to Margaret Adam.

[17] In Appendix III, I offer a possible revision of the prayer that also takes into account two additional and highly significant aspects: the water that flowed from Mary in the birth of Jesus, and the water that poured from Jesus' side while Mary knelt at the foot of the cross.

moment of baptism. The water signifies a new creation: by its presence we are reminded of birth and death, and we pass through it into new life. The water of baptism is thus a witness to divine polyphony – in at least three ways. First, it reminds us that a single entity (water) can evoke meanings that are many and various, yet still be held together by the centrality of a particular practice (that of baptism). Second, it signifies the drawing together of diverse individuals into a single body, the Church. As Paul describes it,

> just as the body is one and has many members, and all the members of the body, though many, are one body, so it is with Christ. For in the one Spirit we were all baptized into one body – Jews or Greeks, slaves or free – and we were all made to drink of one Spirit (1 Cor. 12:12-13).[18]

And third, the central biblical account of baptism – that of Jesus in the Jordan river – brings together God, Christ, and Spirit in a compact yet rich account of divine polyphony. The voice of God, the human being Jesus, and the descent of the dove provide an account of trinitarian presence that is simultaneously aural, visual, and bodily. From very early in the history of the Church, the baptism of Jesus was understood as a focal point for the revelation of God's Triunity; "the whole triune life is manifested here at the very beginning of the public economy."[19]

Christians are able to recognize trinitarian polyphony – to "see its form," in Balthasar's phrase – only because they have already begun to share in the divine life through the common practice of baptism. Unfortunately, this practice is not always experienced by Christians in ways that make clear its formative character. I will thus close this section by naming three aspects of the practice of baptism that need to be kept in a place of prominence. These elements are necessary – not in order for baptism to have sacramental significance, which is guaranteed by God regardless of our inadequacies – but rather, in order that it become a focal point in which we "see the form" of God's polyphony.

First, baptism requires preparation. The candidates' sponsors (and the candidates themselves, to whatever extent their capacities allow it) should have a clear sense of the meaning of the rite, and especially of its earth-shattering significance – for it is, from a Christian point of view, a matter of

---

[18] I note in passing that the words *Living Water* could be substituted for the words *one Spirit* in this passage to good effect, giving the water of baptism a clearer trinitarian focus and shedding new light on Paul's metaphor of "drinking."

[19] Kilian McDonnell, O.S.B., *The Baptism of Jesus in the Jordan: The Trinitarian and Cosmic Order of Salvation* (Collegeville, Minn.: Liturgical Press, Michael Glazier Books, 1996), 119.

life and death.[20] Although its sacramental effectiveness is not hindered by a deficit in such understanding, its educative role – as a witness to God's triune polyphony – may well be diminished if we fail to emphasize the fundamental change that it brings about in the life of the person who is baptized.

Second, except in emergency circumstances, baptism should *always* be a communal event. A so-called "private" baptism obliterates its function as a sign of the reception of the candidate into the community of the faithful. It also undermines the focus on the forgiveness of sins, since God's forgiveness is enacted and embodied in our forgiveness of one another – an act that clearly calls us into the presence of one another. Unless the newly-baptized person's link to the community is clearly emphasized, these central aspects of the sacrament can be obscured or entirely eclipsed. Moreover, in such circumstances, the event loses its character as a *common* practice, in that most members of the community are excluded from it.

And finally, baptism requires follow-up. Most Christian baptismal ceremonies provide some opportunity for the gathered community to express its willingness to support the newly-baptized person in this new life in Christ. Some of these declarations are very strongly worded: "Will you do everything in your power to see that . . ." – and the congregation responds, in a loud and confident tone, "We will!" Then, as often as not, there is never again any contact between the baptized person and the gathered community. If these solemn declarations are to have any meaning, and if baptism is truly to mark the point at which a person becomes a full member of the community (and thus in a certain way "responsible" to it), then that community must truly do "everything in its power" to bring the newly baptized person into the concrete life of the Church.

When these aspects of baptism are emphasized, it can become a witness to the Christian belief that "these three are one" – by reflecting to the rich textures of God's polyphony in the musical waters of the font and in the harmonic structures of the community. It is the moment in which we all – the newly baptized person and sponsors, and the gathered community as well – acknowledge the *cantus firmus* that draws us together, as well as the various counterpoints that we offer. Those who have been baptized into the life,

[20] See the discussion in Robert W. Jenson, *Visible Words: The Interpretation and Practice of Christian Sacraments* (Philadelphia: Fortress, 1978), 126-73. Perhaps no single text expresses the life-and-death nature of baptism more clearly than Flannery O'Connor's brilliant novel *The Violent Bear It Away*, in *Three By Flannery O'Connor* (New York: New American Library, Signet Classics, 1983), 121–267. O'Connor makes use of the "life and death" language in some of her letters concerning the novel, collected in *The Habit of Being: Letters*, ed. with an Introduction by Sally Fitzgerald (New York: Farrar, Straus, and Giroux, 1979).

death, and resurrection of Christ are given the grace to discern the contours of a specifically trinitarian polyphony.

The Contours of Trinitarian Polyphony

Christians come to "see the form" of divine polyphony by means of their encounter with Christ, which is sustained by the Holy Spirit. By listening to and enacting the narratives of the incarnation of the Word, we learn something of the *character* of God – and thus begin to understand the role of polyphony as part of the grace-filled context in which we can cultivate trinitarian habits. This attention to the incarnation should not be construed as a focus on the Gospels alone; one can read the whole Bible Christologically, such that the entire text bears witness to the enfleshed Word. This section begins by recalling this polyphonic hermeneutic; it then offers some particular readings of the Bible, in the service of an initial description of divine polyphony.

Polyphonic readings of the Bible

Throughout most of Christian history, the Bible has been read in a polyphonic way; that is, varying interpretations of a single text have been allowed to co-exist without being understood as contradictory or necessarily incommensurable. This is visible even in the canonization process; the differing accounts offered by the four evangelists, for example, were not seen as a barrier to the inclusion of all four in the canon. From at least the time of Origen, allegorical readings flourished.[21] A rich tradition of biblical interpretation developed over the centuries, in which multiple interpretations were expected and even desirable. Theologians spoke of a "golden chain" (*catena aurea*) of interpretive wisdom – which linked together the (widely varying) interpretations of writers across the centuries for each verse of the text.[22] Medieval interpreters referred to a "fourfold sense of scripture," in which each text was plumbed for

---

[21] See Henri Crouzel, *Origen: The Life and Thought of the First Great Theologian* (San Francisco: Harper and Row, 1989); David Dawson, *Allegorical Readers and Cultural Revision in Ancient Alexandria* (Berkeley: University of California Press, 1992); Karen Jo Torjeson, *Hermeneutical Procedure and Theological Structure in Origen's Exegesis*, Patristische Texte und Studien, Bd 28 (Berlin and New York: de Gruyter, 1986); and Joseph W. Trigg, *Origen: The Bible and Philosophy in the 3rd-century Church* (Atlanta: John Knox Press, 1983).

[22] St Thomas Aquinas, *Catena Aurea*, 6 vols (Oxford: Parker, 1842).

specific applications to doctrine, moral teaching, and questions about the destiny of the world, as well as its literal sense.[23]

Today, however, the richness of polyphonic reading is often lost – reduced to a wooden hermeneutical absolutism in which there is assumed to be "only one right answer." This has been visible not only in Protestant fundamentalisms and in certain claims of the Roman Catholic *magisterium*, but also in the highly reductive assessments sometimes offered within the guild of modern biblical scholarship, whose historical-critical judgments seem to take on an air of infallibility. This latter tendency has softened somewhat in the last decade or so, as a variety of hermeneutical methods have led commentators to recognize, once again, the rich depths of the text. But the drive toward a single "correct" interpretation has not vanished; witness the "Jesus Seminar," which calls news conferences to announce, *ex cathedra*, its latest teachings. These teachings are determined by forcing each text into one of four mutually exclusive categories – the very antithesis of polyphony.[24]

The quest for "the one right interpretation" has (at least in some cases) been partially motivated by a fear that the only alternative to it would be an endless multiplication of bizarre and incomprehensible interpretations – pure hermeneutical anarchy.[25] This fear, however, is unfounded; it is much like saying that, in music, the only alternative to a single melody line is a pure cacophony of disjoint sounds. Although interpretations are rightly multiple, they are always wedded to the rhetorical contexts within which they are promulgated – that is, to the assumptions of the interpretive community in which they are read. For Christians, interpretation takes place within the context of the *Christian* interpretive community (namely, the Church). As I suggested in the

---

[23] For general descriptions, see Beryl Smalley, *The Study of the Bible in the Middle Ages*, 2nd edn (1951; reprint, Notre Dame, Ind.: University of Notre Dame Press, 1964) and Henri de Lubac, *Exégèse médiévale: les quatre sens de l'écriture*, 4 vols (Paris: Aubier, 1959–63). For a recommendation of this approach in the contemporary era, see David C. Steinmetz, "The Superiority of Pre-Critical Exegesis," *Theology Today* 37, no. 1 (April 1980): 27–38, reprinted in *The Theological Interpretation of Scripture: Classic and Contemporary Readings*, ed. Stephen E. Fowl (Oxford: Basil Blackwell, 1996), 26–38. (Fowl's collection provides additional bibliography on "polyphonic" approaches to biblical interpretation.)

[24] For a thoroughgoing critique, see Luke Timothy Johnson, *The Real Jesus: The Misguided Quest for the Historical Jesus and the Truth of the Traditional Gospels* (San Francisco: Harper/Collins, 1996).

[25] The worry is hardly new; critiques of allegorical readings, such as those of Origen, seem to be based on this concern. See, e.g., R. P. C. Hanson, *Allegory and Event: A Study in the Resources and Significance of Origen's Interpretation of Scripture* (Richmond: John Knox Press, 1959).

previous section, the baptized – those who are "called out" into the Church – share a set of common practices and beliefs which influence their reading of Scripture. This is not to say that they will all read the texts in precisely the same way; it is, however, to say that fears of a complete relativism are unfounded, because these common practices and beliefs give form to the interpretive process.[26] Moreover, Christian interpretations have usually attended to Christ as the "hermeneutical center" of the texts, giving them form and holding them together.

Every reading of the biblical text is an *ecclesial* reading, in which the reader is never a solitary individual but is formed in particular virtues and animated by the life of the reading community. And Christians are confident in such readings precisely to the extent that they believe the Spirit to be at work in the communities that offer the particular interpretation. Even Luther's clarion call to *sola scriptura* was made with this awareness; he recoiled in horror at (what he saw as) "churchless" readings of the Bible among some of the Radical Reformers. Today, we have often uncritically assumed that a solitary individual could, quite apart from communal formation, pick up the biblical text and suddenly be brought into a profound relationship with God. Such hermeneutical isolationism, though sometimes attributed to the Reformation, might be better understood as the product of Enlightenment individualism.

In any case, through most of its history, Christianity has employed a polyphonic and communally-normed hermeneutic – a practice which we very much need to retrieve. In the next section, I offer a series of Christologically-focused readings of a variety of biblical texts. I have chosen themes that illustrate something about the polyphonic character of the triune God, grouping my observations around the three themes of creation, Christ, and the Church.

Creation

Under the influence of Enlightenment Deism, the creator God was often portrayed on the model of a divine watchmaker – a skilled craftsman, working

---

[26] On this point see Fowl and Jones, *Reading in Communion, passim*; Kenneson, "There's No Such Thing," 159–62; and especially a number of works by A. K. M. Adam: "The Sign of Jonah: A Fish-eye View," *Semeia* 51 (1990): 177–91; *What is Postmodern Biblical Criticism?* (Minneapolis: Fortress Press, 1995), 18–23; and "Twisting to Destruction," *Perspectives on New Testament Ethics*, ed. Perry V. Kea and A. K. M. Adam (= *Perspectives in Religious Studies* 23 [1996]): 215–22.

alone in his studio, fashioning the perfect instrument (preferably one that could be wound up and then abandoned to run forever). As I noted in chapter 1, modern theology made a Faustian bargain with this mode of thought, trading away its particular understanding of God for a generic portrait that would fit the spirit of the times. Through most of its history, Christian theologians had offered a very different narrative of the creation of the world – one based on the account in Genesis and read in Christological and trinitarian ways. These readings described God as marked by community rather than by solitude, and by engagement rather than detachment.

In the beginning, in the presence of the Spirit, God speaks (Gen. 1:1-3), and thereby creates. The Hebrew text names God with a plural form (אֱלֹהִים, *Elohim*), sometimes described as the inclusion of a heavenly assembly, or a plural of majesty (the "royal we"). But this word can also be read as implying differentiation within God. Moreover, the designation of this God as speaking (and getting results!) recalls our discussion of the process of persuasion; it implies something spoken, and the construction of an audience as well. What is spoken is the "Word" – who is not mentioned explicitly in this narrative, but without whom "was not anything made that was made" (John 1:3, RSV). The Word is not a mere by-product of this creative activity, but is constitutive of it; thus we are told, not only that the Word was *God's*, but that the Word was *God* (John 1:2). And the audience of this creative speech is the Spirit, the divine witness to the event of creation.

Such a reading of Genesis might have been quite natural to the trinitarian theologians of the early Church, given their Christological hermeneutic and their rhetorical training. In Genesis, God is described as going forth from God – most obviously so in the speaking of the Word, but also in the Spirit's role as a witness to creation. These "processions" are obscured by our tendency to read the narrative as implying a temporal order among the Three – first God (1:1), then the Spirit (1:2),[27] then the Word (1:3). But as I suggested in chapter 3, such temporal ordering is misleading; it implies that one of the Three can exist without the others, whereas the two divine processions – of Word and Spirit – are *eternal* processions. Neither of them is in any way dependent on the event of creation, and their corresponding missions are eternally oriented toward *producing* the world. The Word comes forth from God, but not only

---

[27] The translation in the NRSV provides an additional witness to the lack of attention to the Christian hermeneutic of the Old Testament by translating רוּחַ as "wind" rather than "Spirit." In an understandable attempt to be sensitive to non-Christian readers of Genesis, the editorial committee effectively marginalized (literally! – "spirit" is relegated to a footnote) two thousand years of Christian effective-history on this text.

at the moment of creation; rather, at that moment, the "eternally begotten Word" is identified with the Word "through whom all things were made."

Continuing to act, and also continuing the plural self-identification, God says, "Let us make humankind in our image, according to our likeness" (Gen. 1:26). Because this creation will be in the image of God as named by a plural form, it too must manifest plurality and difference: "male and female, God created them" (Gen. 1:27). But lest we assume that this is a mutually exclusive (or "contrastive") difference, we are reminded (in Genesis 2) that both male and female have their source in the solitary earth-creature, אָדָם (adam). The traditional translation of this word as "man" obscures the change that takes place when the creature falls asleep. The English makes it appear that a man falls asleep, and that the same man wakes up (and finds a woman beside him). The Hebrew suggests that one kind of being falls asleep, and two wholly different beings wake up.[28] Only when male (אִישׁ, ish) and female (אִשָּׁה, ishshah) have been created out of this earth-creature (אָדָם) does the creation of the image of God begin to manifest polyphonic difference, and thereby fully embody the status that it is declared to have in Genesis 1: "good."

A genuine polyphony is offered by the two creation stories themselves, which differ without being mutually exclusive. Of course, they have also often been read in a homogenizing fashion (due perhaps to an imperative toward literal canonical unity) or as a sharp dichotomy (to emphasize their differing sources, or to make Hebrew myth appear highly "unscientific"). A polyphonic reading allows both stories to be heard, in their harmony *and* their dissonance. So, for example, the stories differ in that one places humanity near the end of the process of creation, and the other near the beginning; yet both of these positions in a series (first and last) are rhetorically effective tools for the placement of emphasis. Both stories thus suggest some kind of difference between humanity and the rest of the created order. Yet because both stories also treat the creation of human beings as only one part of the story, humanity is also integrally *related* to the rest of the created order: the difference here is mutually constitutive, rather than contrastive.

Christ the form of polyphony

Through the incarnation of the Word, we receive our most complete picture

---

[28] Contemporary Bible translations could surely do a better job of attending to this difference. See, inter alia, Phyllis Trible, "A Love Story Gone Awry," in *God and the Rhetoric of Sexuality*, Overtures to Biblical Theology (Philadelphia: Fortress Press, 1978), 72-143.

of divine polyphony. Christ bears witness to a God of harmonious flux and superabundant donation – a God in whom difference can exist without contradiction or confusion. The Gospel narratives provide us with a wide variety of such witnesses, many of which revolve around the rejection of any contrastive account of *action* and *passion* in God. The Gospels witness to a God who can be active (and wholly free) and yet also passive (submitting to the actions of others). Action and passion are not irreconcilable opposites, but are able to co-exist in God, just as do two simultaneously played notes in a piece of music. God acts without constraint, and yet enters into *relationships* with human beings – which means that God is willing to be "moved" by others.[29]

This dialectic is observable from the "first moment" of the incarnation (if it can be said, at least from the human perspective, to have a "beginning" in time). This is the moment in which the angel announces to Mary that she will bear the Savior of the world. This act should not be seen as a violent and forceful invasion of a woman by a patriarchal God, as it has sometimes been read.[30] Indeed, the event is incomplete until Mary confirms it in an act of her own will: "Let it be with me according to your word" (Luke 1:38).

And indeed the entire life of Jesus manifests this dialectic of action and passion. At times he is supremely active, narrating the nature of God's Reign, embodying that Reign through exorcisms and healings. At other times he is clearly acted upon: he is given birth, raised in a Jewish home, questioned by the religious leaders of the day, driven away by angry crowds, and – most obviously – arrested, interrogated, tried, stripped, mocked, and crucified. That the incarnate God can be "acted upon" by human beings in this way is a testimony to the polyphony of action and passion in God.

The narratives of Mary and Jesus thus bear witness not only to God's power,

---

[29] The relationship between God and creation remains asymmetrical, in that God is passive only to the degree that God chooses to be, whereas creatures often have no choice. God has an unlimited freedom to place Godself at the disposal of others. See Barth, *CD* IV/1, 186–7 [*KD* IV/1, 204]. See also the comments on asymmetry as a key aspect of Barth's account of the problem of double agency in Hunsinger, *How to Read Karl Barth*, ch. 7.

[30] Writers who have seen Mary only as a symbol of the oppression of women are wont to conflate the annunciation with Greco-Roman mythological portraits of male Gods raping women, e.g. the story of Jupiter and Io. But in many readings of Luke 1, and in her designation as "the first disciple," Mary's active consent seems fundamental. See Ivone Gebara and Maria Clara Bingemer, *Mary: Mother of God, Mother of the Poor*, trans. Phillip Berryman, Liberation and Theology (Maryknoll, NY: Orbis, 1989) [ET of: *Maria, Mãe de Deus e Mãe dos Pobres* (Petrópolis: Vozes, 1987)]; Geitz, *Gender and the Nicene Creed*, 47–50; John Macquarrie, *Mary for All Christians* (London: Collins, 1991); Rosemary Radford Ruether, *Mary – The Feminine Face of the Church* (London: SCM Press, 1979).

but to God's willingness to forfeit that power for the sake of humanity. This aspect of God's character is perhaps best summed up by St. Paul, who – using a hymn – reminds us of the polyphonic insight that Christ,

> though in the form of God,
>> did not regard equality with God
>> as something to be exploited;
> but, emptied of self,
>> took the form of a slave,
>> and was given birth in human likeness.
>> And being found in human form,
> he humbled himself
>> and became obedient to the point of death –
>> even death on a cross.
> Therefore God also highly exalted him
>> and gave him the name
>> that is above every name,
> so that at the name of Jesus every knee should bend,
>> in heaven and on earth
>> and under the earth,
> and every tongue should confess
>> that Jesus Christ is Lord,
>> to the glory of God the Father.
>
> (Phil. 2:6–11)

In God, "having power" and "giving it away" are not contradictory elements, nor are they even in tension with each other. Rather, it is of the very nature of God's power to be in a constant state of donation, always turned out from itself, always giving and forgiving, always *producing* the world. This dialectic of action and passion, power and gift, can be illustrated in a number of different ways by means of a trinitarian reading of some key biblical texts. In an effort to give more concrete form to this dialectic, I here examine three specific instances of the more general case.

Torah, freedom, and forgiveness
In a passage that has often perplexed and annoyed many readers of the Gospel of Matthew, Jesus says:

> Do not think that I have come to abolish the law or the prophets; I have come not to abolish but to fulfill. For truly I tell you, until heaven and earth pass away, not one letter, not one stroke of a letter, will pass from the law until all is accomplished. Therefore, whoever breaks one of the least of these command-

ments, and teaches others to do the same, will be called least in the Reign;[31] but whoever does them and teaches them will be called great in the Reign. For I tell you, unless your righteousness exceeds that of the scribes and Pharisees, you will never enter the Reign (Matt. 5:17–20).

This passage is always something of a trouble-spot for students who have just worked their way through a text like Romans or Galatians and are glorying in the freedom of the Christian believer. What kind of new legalism is here being established?

Interpreters have often sought a quick exit from these difficulties, describing Matthew's account as idiosyncratic to his own context, or recasting this passage (and the entire Sermon on the Mount that follows it) as a discourse in which Jesus so intensifies the commandments of the law as to make them impossible to keep. But are such devices really the only way to understand these diverse passages? If they were, it would be hard to account for the simultaneous inclusion of all of them in the canon of scripture – nor for the ability of so many Christian interpreters through the ages to make some sense of them (and not simply to dispose of one of them by labeling it "Matthew's redaction" or "Paul's particular obsession" or whatever).

What seems to be at work in Matthew's gospel, as in Paul, is a reconfiguration of the notion of *law*. We typically think of a law as a *rule* – something set up to keep order by restraining our freedom. We are expected to obey it, and if we don't, we are subject to punishment. Moreover, we believe that such punishment ought to be carried out; if it is not, we feel that justice has not been done. This provides a very good example of how contemporary readings of the Bible are shaped by the assumptions of the modern nation-state. As I suggested in chapter 1, the state profits from generic portraits of God (which can be easily adapted to reinforce its own ideology). The portrait of God as divine lawmaker gives greater leverage to various interests of the nation-state: its desire to demand obedience, its arrogation to itself of the means of punishment, and its unwillingness to provide space for forgiveness.

But for the writers of the New Testament, the Greek word for law (νόμος) would have had among its sources the Hebrew word תּוֹרָה (*Torah*), which is not merely a generic term for law, but refers to the first five books of the

---

[31] For ἡ βασιλεία τῶν οὐρανῶν I offer simply "the Reign," seeking to respect the polyphony of the text (Matthew's form is different from that of Mark and Luke), while recognizing that it is probably a circumlocution to avoid the word *God*. The traditional translation ("kingdom of heaven") has led generations of students to conflate Matthew's phrase with a highly simplistic notion of "heaven," thus restricting the claim to the afterlife – with most unfortunate results (theological, spiritual, and socio-political).

Hebrew Bible. As such it is not understood primarily as a "book of rules," but rather as the *story* of God's gift to the people Israel. It is thus not law on the model of the nation-state – i.e., a constraint that (often) serves the interest of ruling classes. It is not meant to break the people by undermining their freedom, nor is it promulgated out of some politically-popular concept of "law and order." Unlike the laws of nation-states, the Torah is the story of God's constant love for the people of Israel.

In this respect it would perhaps be better to think of Torah not as "law" at all, given that word's resonances for modern readers. The Torah certainly includes divine commands, but it is also gift: God does not impose it merely as an assertion of divine power. The Torah is a story that seeks to orient Israel toward God, to encourage the covenantal relationship between God and the people to flourish. The Psalms, especially, often describe the Torah as a praiseworthy *gift* (not a view that many people take toward "the rules"):

> The Torah of יהוה is perfect,
>   reviving the soul;
> the decrees of יהוה are sure,
>   making wise the simple;
> the precepts of יהוה are right,
>   rejoicing the heart; . . .
> More to be desired are they than gold,
>   even much fine gold;
> sweeter also than honey,
>   and drippings of the honeycomb.
>
> (Ps. 19:7–10)

Thus, Torah might be best understood by analogy to the narrative forms of guidance offered by every good parent for a child's own protection. The story of God guides the children of Israel to cultivate good habits and to avoid various dangers, just as we tell stories to guide our own children to eat good food and not to accept rides from strangers.

Of course, these attempts to provide guidance can sometimes fall out of focus, blindly enforced "just because that's the way we do things" rather than being grounded in love for our children. In our family, for example, some of our elder daughter's toys are kept in a room that is inaccessible to our younger (one-year-old) daughter, because some of their parts present a choking hazard. Now, however, the younger one no longer mouths everything in sight, and can play with small objects under supervision. Nevertheless, we have continued to describe the room as "Monica's space" and to deny Emily all access to it. Is this story still "for her own good"? Or is it merely for *our* convenience, since we don't want to be bothered to monitor her closely when she plays with small toys? And is this "strict interpretation" of the "law" likely to result in all kinds of future difficulties (jealousy, failure to share toys, excessive desire for "forbidden fruit")?

Like any effort at guidance that is originally developed for another's good, Torah can cease to function as an expression of love, and can become a mere convenience for those in power. Abstracted from the story of which it is a part, it becomes merely a set of rules that then take on a life of their own, becoming their own ends. Moreover, for those who are *subject* to these rules, they can cease to function as a praiseworthy gift, "sweeter than honey," and become nothing more than a burden (or worse). Some such shift seems to have provoked Jesus' critique of certain interpretations of the Torah; for many, it had ceased to be gift, and had become duty, burden, bondage – or perhaps merely a convenient way of maintaining relationships of power. This explains why Jesus sometimes seems to urge a "relaxation" of certain interpretations of the Torah. Consider the following passages:

> Then he said to them, "The sabbath was made for humankind, and not humankind for the sabbath; so the Son of Man is lord even of the sabbath." (Mark 2:27-28; cf. Matt. 12:1–14 // Luke 6:1–11; Luke 13:14–16)

> Then he called the crowd again and said to them, "Listen to me, all of you, and understand: there is nothing outside a person that by going in can defile, but the things that come out are what defile." (Mark 7:14–15)

> [The scribes and the Pharisees] bind heavy burdens, hard to bear, and lay them on the shoulders of others; but they themselves are unwilling to lift a finger to move them. (Matt. 23:4)

These passages suggest that Jesus understands the Torah, not as a burden, but as a gift. On the other hand, he does not advocate anarchy; indeed, he makes some elements of the law *more* stringent, *more* difficult to follow. At least, this is what he seems to teach about laws concerning adultery and divorce (Matt. 5:27–32, 19:3–9; Mark 10:2–12; Luke 16:18), murder (Matt. 5:21–26), and the honor of one's parents (Mark 7:9–13). This appears to make Jesus' teaching on the law quite confusing; after all, are not laws such as these also "heavy burdens, hard to bear"?

They may be; but they also serve to protect potential victims – people who are cast off by their upwardly-mobile spouses, or dishonored by their ungrateful children, or abused and insulted by another person's murderous anger. This is perhaps why, when asked to summarize the law, Jesus focuses on theft, murder, adultery, bearing false witness, and attitudes toward parents (e.g., Matt. 15:19, 19:18–19; Mark 7:21–3, 10:19; Luke 18:20). In all these cases, someone is directly injured by the abrogation of the law, as opposed to those violations that are perhaps "victimless" – e.g., those concerning the sabbath and food.

On the other hand, this affirmation (and even strengthening) of certain laws should not be seen as a new legalism, for two reasons. First, Jesus emphasizes that the keeping of the law – even of those laws that he has identified as particularly important – does not exhaust the duties of the true disciple. This point comes through clearly in the story of the rich man:

> As he was setting out on a journey, a man ran up and knelt before him, and asked him, "Good Teacher, what must I do to inherit eternal life?" Jesus said to him, "Why do you call me good? No one is good but God alone. You know the commandments: 'You shall not murder; You shall not commit adultery; You shall not steal; You shall not bear false witness; You shall not defraud; Honor your father and mother.'" He said to him, "Teacher, I have kept all these since my youth." Jesus, looking at him, loved him and said, "You lack one thing; go, sell what you own, and give the money to the poor, and you will have treasure in heaven; then come, follow me." When he heard this, he was shocked and went away grieving, for he had many possessions. (Mark 10:17–22)

This passage is surely an indictment of attachment to possessions; but it is also a commentary on the insufficiency of the law. No matter how steadfastly we may keep the law, we will always tend to construct obstacles between ourselves and God. Thus, Jesus' response is (like all good rhetoric!) crafted with attention to the person being addressed – a point that helps us understand why Mark comments that Jesus, looking at the man, "loved him." Jesus focuses on *this man's* particular obstacle – possessions. For others, the chief obstacle may be different, but the general point is the same: no one wins salvation through the keeping of the law. This point is, of course, thoroughly underscored in the writings of St Paul (Rom. 5–7, Gal. 1–4, and *passim*).

A second element of Jesus' teaching further emphasizes that his commentary on the Torah is not legalistic: his insistence on the importance of forgiveness. "If the same person sins against you seven times a day, and turns back to you seven times and says, 'I repent,' you must forgive" (Luke 17:4). Despite the affirmation that the law will not pass away, its enforcement must not become an excuse to fail to love. And conversely, forgiveness is only meaningful if we take seriously the law or covenant that is broken; if we are able to say, "Oh, it's nothing," then we are implicitly denying that a "forgivable" offense has occurred.

Three notes are thus sounded simultaneously: (1) Torah is not an arbitrary set of laws, but a gift – the story of God's love, protecting potential victims and establishing the covenant with Israel; (2) we cannot earn salvation, even by a resolute keeping of the Torah, and in this sense we are "freed" from it; and yet (3) those who fail to receive it as a gift need to ask for, and be offered, forgiveness. It would be a mistake to play any of these three off against one another, suggesting that forgiveness makes the law irrelevant, or that Torah and freedom are incompatible. Precisely in the simultaneous sounding of these three notes, God's polyphonic character is revealed to us. God is lawgiver, liberator, and forgiver; and these three are one.

Power, temptation, and obedience
God's polyphonic character is further revealed by the interrelated roles played in the life of Christ by power, temptation, and obedience. Again, we miss the point if we turn these into a zero-sum game, as has occurred all too frequently; in such interpretations, the temptations of Jesus are described as unreal (his divine nature could not do otherwise than make the right choice) and Jesus' obedience is considered a mere ruse of powerlessness (he could have escaped his fate at any moment). Such portraits are reinforced by prayers and hymns that describe Jesus' humanity as something of an exceptional case, as in the following verse of an otherwise quite lovely Christmas hymn:

> If Jesus had wanted for any wee thing
> A star in the sky or a bird on the wing
> Or all of God's angels in heaven for to sing
> He surely would have it – for he was the king.

The infant Jesus is here described as insulated from the want, grief, and pain that is an essential part of human existence for all the rest of us. At work here – and in the claims that Jesus' temptations were unreal and that his obedience was a ruse – is the ancient heresy of docetism, in which Christ only *seemed* to be human, but actually remained aloof from the shadow side of human existence.

In contrast, a polyphonic reading of these narratives would recognize that supreme power can still be compatible with a submission to the will of the other; that a complete picture of *incarnation* requires the taking on of all aspects of human life, including all that it lacks; and that, when tempted, one may actively consider a variety of options (and thus truly have a "choice") without thereby compromising one's holiness. Again, these elements need not be understood as mutually exclusive or contradictory; like the differing notes of a chord, they can be sounded (and heard) simultaneously, without compromising the unity of the whole.

Let us consider, briefly, how all these elements are at work in the scriptural texts. These texts certainly seem clear about the *power* of Christ. From the very start, for example, Mary clearly recognizes the power of God at work in her, having "scattered the proud in the thoughts of their hearts, . . . brought down the powerful from their thrones and lifted up the lowly, . . . filled the hungry with good things, and sent the rich away empty" (Luke 1:51–3). And Jesus is described as teaching with authority, not as the scribes (who must rely on the teachings of the rabbis, who in turn must rely on written texts). He works signs that testify to his power, healing the sick and restoring sight to the blind.

But on the other hand, this power is not absolute or tyrannical; it is capable of submitting to others, and can consider options and make choices. Mary *chooses* to accept her role as the bearer of the Savior; Jesus *chooses* to accept the necessity of his own gruesome death after his prayer in Gethsemane. At the outset of his ministry, Jesus is tempted in the wilderness; the devil encourages him to place obstacles in God's way. Traditional readings of the temptation accounts have tended to be especially docetic, portraying Jesus as aloof from the power of temptation – silencing Satan with quick, witty rejoinders, as though unaffected by forty days without food. The canonical temptation accounts are exceedingly brief, of course, and they do not automatically bring to mind the idea of painful struggle and difficult choice. But if we are to take seriously the text's use of the word *tempt*, we have to imagine that various results were possible. If Jesus *could not help* but make the right choices, in what sense were these temptations?

This is why an important purpose is served by Nikos Kazantzakis' novel *The Last Temptation of Christ*, as well as the film based on it.[32] For all their flaws, these two pieces of imaginative interpretation depict Jesus as a creatively struggling human being, seeking to respond rightly to the voice inside his head that says "you are God." Only if this struggle is kept in mind does his obedience really become meaningful. Moreover, we begin to understand the trinitarian virtue of polyphony only when we are able to predicate of God, not only power and authority, but obedience and temptation as well. Jesus' activity in this regard is a logical extension of the activity of Israel; in both cases, God's *word* (as *Torah*, and as *logos*) must be "enacted" by a human agent, and the struggles inherent in any such enactment are themselves revelatory of the

---

[32] Nikos Kazantzakis, *The Last Temptation of Christ*, trans. P. A. Bien (New York: Simon and Schuster, Touchstone Books, 1960); film of the same title, directed by Martin Scorsese, Universal Pictures, 1988.

character of God.[33] As a reflection of God's simultaneous action and passion, the relationship between God's authority and God's obedience tells us something about God's character, and about the virtues that we too are called to embody.

Our reading of divine power has been too heavily influenced by the theories of power in the modern nation-state, where it is almost always understood as a zero-sum game. If one group of citizens gains power, it must do so at the expense of another group. The extension of certain rights to one segment of the population is almost always opposed by other segments, whose members feel their own power thereby threatened. And indeed, such fears are often legitimate, for the state intentionally develops the language of "rights" such that the power of citizens are always played off against one another, rather than threatening the power of the state itself.[34]

But a Christian conception of the relationships among authority, obedience, and temptation is not based on the language of "rights." It is not a contrastive structure, which assumes that any element of obedience must denote a corresponding loss of power, or that any "temptation" in which there is a serious consideration of alternatives represents a lack of real power. In the Christian narratives, these elements are held together, so that the consenting peasant girl is also glorified as Queen of the Universe, and the perfectly dutiful servant is also the Lord of All. In this sense, Christ reveals to us something of the polyphonic character of God, in whom the "going forth" that is involved in the divine processions does not represent any reduction in the reality of God, but is in fact part of the very essence of who God is.[35]

Life, death, and resurrection

The close-knit relationships among these elements of human existence are similarly revealed to us by the person of Christ. As I have already noted, the incarnation – in its fullest sense – means the taking on of *all* aspects of humanity, from pregnancy and birth to death and beyond. We are reminded

---

[33] "In the Bible, Israel's sonship is indissociable from the carrying of the word; a careful reading of St John's gospel would suggest, not merely that Jesus is the perfectly obedient Son who passes on the words of the Father, but that as creatively struggling human being he assumes an enacted form which in its universal significance is the word of the Father, and that *thereby* he is the co-equal Son" (Milbank, "The Second Difference," 219–20).

[34] Karl Marx saw this with more clarity than most; see, e.g., "On the Jewish Question," in *Karl Marx: Early Writings*, trans. and ed. T. B. Bottomore (New York: McGraw-Hill, 1964), 22-31.

[35] See Balthasar's comments on obedience and freedom as constitutive of God's Triunity in, e.g., *T-D* III:520–1 [*TD* II/2:477].

of this by the intertwined joys and sufferings that Mary took upon herself in her willingness to be the God- bearer: the burdens and delights of pregnancy, the pain of childbirth, the gift of nursing her son, and the myriad anxieties known to all parents as they worry about the health, safety, and flourishing of their children. But add to this the extraordinary pain of seeing one's own child rejected and eventually put to death: surely Simeon did not exaggerate when he described this as a sword that would pierce Mary's soul also (Luke 2:35). In these joyful and sorrowful mysteries, Mary reveals to us the simultaneity of joy and sorrow, not just in our own lives, but in the very life of God. Nietzsche was surely not the first to recognize that those who know the most profound joy also experience the deepest grief in loss.[36]

Of course, these features of human life – its simultaneous joys and sorrows – can be learned through experience by any human being; we need not rely on a special revelation through Christ to know this. On the other hand, in that revelation, we learn that these features, which have always marked human existence, also mark the life of God. In choosing, before all time, to become incarnate in the flesh of Mary's womb, in the flesh of Jesus of Nazareth, God chooses to "experience" the full range of human sorrow and joy. The ancient theologians believed that "what is not assumed is not saved" – which is to say that God did not merely take on a fragment of human life, not merely the pleasant and glorious bits, but also (and perhaps especially) the painful, sorrowful, ugly aspects of human existence. Even *these* aspects of human existence are taken up into the life of God, and thus are revealed as constitutive of who and what God is.

And something else is learned from Christ that cannot be learned from "human experience" alone. For in the case of both Mary and Jesus, death does not have the final word. Indeed, here the revelation is quite extraordinary, something wholly other, something that not only transcends human experience, but which also cannot be learned from the "wisdom of the Platonists," nor even by means of the revelation of God to Israel. Jesus reveals to us *the resurrection of the body*, and *eternal life*. Here again we recognize the simultaneity of action and passion in God: God acts (by raising Jesus); God is acted upon (by being raised); and God is the vehicle of the action (the Spirit in and through whom Christ is raised). This event is understood as the first fruits of what will come to all who have fallen asleep, as Paul testifies in 1 Cor. 15 – a promise that is exemplified, and thereby strengthened, in the story of Mary's "dormition" or "assumption." That the life of *God* might be understood as eternal – this was well known to Hebrew and Greek sages, and to many other civilizations

---

[36] A common refrain in both *Die fröhliche Wissenschaft* and *Also sprach Zarathustra*.

ancient and modern. That this might also apply to human life was imagined, for example by Plato, but only in a realm of pure spirit or mind. What is so extraordinary about Christian revelation in this regard is that eternal life could be *embodied* eternal life: that the body might retain its integrity even in death.[37]

Only a "musical" mode of thought can begin to make sense of this claim. The idea of continuity of a body through the most monumental moment of differential flux that we know – the moment of life passing into death – is beyond the scope of the most complex metaphysic hitherto imagined. It makes sense only within a fully polyphonic understanding of God, in which life and death, body, and soul can be "sounded" simultaneously. In the light of the resurrection of Jesus and the dormition of Mary, we can perhaps begin to sound the depths of the well-loved Psalm (139:7–13):

> Where can I go from your spirit?
>   Or where can I flee from your presence?
> If I ascend to heaven, you are there;
>   if I make my bed in Sheol, you are there.
> If I take the wings of the morning
>   and settle at the farthest limits of the sea,
> even there your hand shall lead me,
>   and your right hand shall hold me fast.
> If I say, "Surely the darkness shall cover me,
>   and the light around me become night,"
> even the darkness is not dark to you;
>   the night is as bright as the day,
>   for darkness is as light to you.
> For it was you who formed my inward parts;
>   you knit me together in my mother's womb.

There is no logical contradiction, no irrationality, in God's simultaneous presence in heaven and in Sheol, in life and in death. This is the ultimate revelation provided for us in the body of Christ, through the incarnation of the Word.

---

[37] For a discussion of how thoroughly this claim influenced medieval theology, see Caroline Walker Bynum, *The Resurrection of the Body in Western Christianity, 200–1336* (New York: Columbia University Press, 1995). Contemporary studies of this doctrine are rare; see Leonardo Boff, *Vida para além da morte* (Petrópolis: Vozes, 1981); Friedrich-Wilhelm Marquardt, *Was dürfen wir hoffen, wenn wir hoffen dürften? Eine Eschatologie* (Gütersloh: Gütersloher Verlagshaus, 1996), III:144–63. Some interesting literary-theological reflections appear in Graham Greene, *The End of the Affair* (New York: Penguin Books, 1951).

The Body of Christ

We now turn from one sense of "the body of Christ" to another sense – and thus conclude this brief sampling of the biblical witness to polyphony. Paul claims that the Church, like the human body, is not a homogenous unity, but is made up of members whose difference from one another entails neither subordination nor mutual exclusion. The passage is well-worn, but still worth quoting in full, as a reminder of just how thoroughly saturated is the Church with the polyphony of the triune God.

> The body does not consist of one member but of many. If the foot would say, "Because I am not a hand, I do not belong to the body," that would not make it any less a part of the body. And if the ear would say, "Because I am not an eye, I do not belong to the body," that would not make it any less a part of the body. If the whole body were an eye, where would the hearing be? If the whole body were hearing, where would the sense of smell be? But as it is, God arranged the members in the body, each one of them, as God chose. If all were a single member, where would the body be? As it is, there are many members, yet one body. The eye cannot say to the hand, "I have no need of you," nor again the head to the feet, "I have no need of you." On the contrary, the members of the body that seem to be weaker are indispensable, and those members of the body that we think less honorable we clothe with greater honor, and our less respectable members are treated with greater respect; whereas our more respectable members do not need this. But God has so arranged the body, giving the greater honor to the inferior member, that there may be no dissension within the body, but the members may have the same care for one another. If one member suffers, all suffer together with it; if one member is honored, all rejoice together with it. Now you are the body of Christ and individually members of it. (1 Cor. 12:14–27)

Most worthy of note, perhaps, is what is here ruled out. There is to be no elimination of difference; the body cannot be made of all eyes or all ears, any more than a true symphony orchestra could consist of bassoons or piccolos alone. There is also to be no homogenization into an undifferentiated unity ("If all were a single member, where would the body be?") – just as no single instrument, no matter how grandiose (say, a pipe organ), can replace an orchestra. Nor is one member or set of members to be elevated among any other – the melody of a fugue cannot cast out the counterpoint, nor can the orchestra get along without the soloist when playing a concerto.

Paul does not explicitly model this picture of the Church on the Triunity of God, but such a connection can be easily made; in reading this text, we are

alerted to the importance of difference, the inappropriateness of homogenization, and the radical equality of the members of the body. All of these
elements, constitutive as they are of the Body of Christ, also reveal to us
something about the character of God.

Indeed, the Church is able to manifest this revelatory character precisely
because it is *the Body of Christ* – the continuing embodied manifestation of
God's presence in the world. This implies that the various members of this
Body must be able to coexist in non-contrastive and non-exclusionary ways.
But it also suggests that these members must be "connected" to one another
in profound and mutually-determinative ways. I will explore this aspect of the
Church when I turn to the trinitarian virtue of *participation* in chapter 5.
Meanwhile, I will conclude the present chapter by developing a triune mark
to illustrate the trinitarian virtue of polyphony.

Polyphony and Literature

Through Christ, the triune God has been revealed as polyphonic; and some of
the contours of that polyphony have been made explicit. Nevertheless, this
need not mark the end of our thinking about divine polyphony. By holding this
category firmly in mind, we can construe and narrate the created order as
marked by polyphony in ways that illuminate the doctrine of the Trinity and
make it more persuasive. As I noted in the Introduction, works of imaginative
literature can provide an especially useful space for such construals. I offer one
such example here – first examining the theory, and then explicating the
practice.

Bakhtin on polyphony

The Soviet literary theorist Mikhail Bakhtin (1895–1975) has recently arisen,
out of the ashes of obscurity, to become one of the most important voices in
contemporary literary criticism. I will not here rehearse the history of his life
and work, nor his overall importance for Christian theology, both of which
can be gleaned from other sources.[38] Instead, I want to focus on the
programmatic chapter of Bakhtin's *Problems of Dostoevsky's Poetics*, in which
he introduces and defines *polyphony* as a literary category.

[38] For Bakhtin generally, see Katerina Clark and Michael Holquist, *Mikhail Bakhtin*
(Cambridge, Mass.: Harvard University Press, 1984); for theological reflections, see David
Dawson, *Literary Theory*, Guides to Theological Inquiry (Minneapolis: Fortress Press,
1995), 85–124.

In this text, Bakhtin argues that one of Dostoevsky's most important innovations – a technique which revolutionized the form of the novel – resulted from his ability to bring to life, simultaneously, a number of fully developed characters, each of whom was able to speak in a fully valid voice. Here is Bakhtin's own statement of his thesis:

> *A plurality of independent and unmerged voices and consciousnesses, a genuine polyphony of fully valid voices is in fact the chief characteristic of Dostoevsky's novels.* What unfolds in his works is not a multitude of characters and fates in a single objective world, illuminated by a single authorial consciousness; rather a *plurality of consciousnesses, with equal rights and each with its own world,* combine but are not merged in the unity of the event.[39]

According to Bakhtin, Dostoevsky peopled his novels with "fully valid" characters – able to change, to surprise us, to break out of the psychological boxes in which the reader is often tempted to place them.

Bakhtin notes that a number of critics recognized this aspect of Dostoevsky's fiction, but treated these differing voices as varying articulations of the one "real" message of the book, or as "planes" or "stages" through which the reader is led, or as diverse elements that are fused together to announce the author's perspective.[40] Against these views, Bakhtin argues that in Dostoevsky's characters, various constitutive elements exist simultaneously yet remain truly differentiated. Whatever unity they achieve must be a "musical" unity of differential flux, not a fusion or synthesis that is achieved at the expense of their diversity. Although Bakhtin does not think that Dostoevsky's achievement can be adequately summarized in a single image, he does offer some theologically suggestive hints – commenting that, if we "were to seek an image toward which this world gravitates, an image in the spirit of Dostoevsky's own worldview, then it would be the church as a communion of unmerged souls, where sinners and the righteous come together."[41] In attempting to articulate a literary polyphony, Bakhtin draws our attention back to Paul's image of the members of the body, and thus to the polyphonic nature of the Church as the Body of Christ.

---

[39] M. M. Bakhtin, *Problems of Dostoevsky's Poetics,* ed. and trans. Caryl Emerson, with an Introduction by Wayne C. Booth, Theory and History of Literature, vol. 8 (Minneapolis: University of Minnesota Press, 1984), 6.

[40] Bakhtin attributes these views to Vyacheslav Ivanov, Boris Engelhardt, and Leonid Grossman, respectively, in his discussion of their work (and that of other critics) in *Problems,* 10–27.

[41] Bakhtin, *Problems,* 26–7, slightly altered.

Indeed, Bakhtin believes that this "ecclesial" insight helped to shape Dostoevsky's anthropology, in which human beings were understood, first and foremost, as members of a community. As such, they are complex creatures; they cannot be reduced, without remainder, to particular psychological motives or physiological features. On the human plane, at least, polyphony is not a feature of isolated individuals, but of a community of persons.[42] Similarly, God is one, but we can still speak of divine polyphony – for God is also three. As we noted in the previous section, God's image does not inhere in *one* human being, but in a plurality of human beings: "male and female God created them." As both Dostoevsky and Bakhtin recognized, the isolated individual consciousness cannot begin to mirror the multi-voiced nature of God; we can think of humanity as created in the image of the triune God only when we think communally – not when we limit our focus to individuals.

Bakhtin's discussion of polyphony thus helps us better understand the radical equality that this musical term implies – both in God and in the created order. As I noted in chapter 3, theologians have always been tempted to hierarchize the Three, setting them in some sort of logical or temporal sequence. But the musical analogy points us away from such hierarchies, since the relations among the constitutive parts of polyphonous music do not exist in stable hierarchies. If I play a C-major chord on the piano, three notes are sounded simultaneously; there can thus be no temporal ordering. And who can say which note is "most important" or "logically foundational"? We refer to the chord by referring to one of its notes, but this is merely a convention of naming. The triad would be just as incomplete without the E or the G as it would be without the C.

Music is able to invoke the category of non-contrastive difference because it encourages us to consider, alongside the linear (and therefore implicitly hierarchical) relationships of temporal sequence, the non-linear relationships of location in space. Bakhtin saw this shift as fundamental to Dostoevsky's perspective.

> The fundamental category in Dostoevsky's mode of artistic visualizing was not evolution, but *coexistence* and *interaction*. He saw and conceived his world primarily in terms of space, not time. . . . Dostoevsky attempted to perceive the

---

[42] "Dostoevsky found and was capable of perceiving multi-leveledness and contra-dictoriness not in the spirit, but in the objective social world. In this social world, planes were not stages but *opposing camps*, and the contradictory relationships among them were not the rising or descending course of an individual personality, but the *condition of society*." Ibid., 27.

very stages [of literary development] themselves in their *simultaneity*, to *juxta-pose* and *counterpose* them dramatically, and not stretch them out into an evolving sequence. For him, to get one's bearings on the world meant to conceive all its contents as simultaneous, and *to guess at their interrelationship in the cross-section of a single moment.*[43]

Such a shift – from temporal to spatial categories – can help us better understand the divine processions without recourse to logical or temporal hierarchies, and thereby to glimpse the truly radical equality that characterizes the triune God.[44]

Throughout this section, I have hinted that Bakhtin's development of the concept of polyphony had profoundly theological roots. In their biography of Bakhtin, Clark and Holquist note two aspects of Russian Orthodox thought that especially influenced him: "The first of these is a radical communality (*sobornost'*); the second is a profound respect for the material realities of everyday experience."[45] These convictions were clearly at work in Bakhtin's analysis of Dostoevsky's fiction. And other critics have suggested that they may have been at work in Dostoevsky's own writing as well.

For example, commenting on Dostoevsky's relationship to Russian Ortho-doxy, Julia Kristeva remarks that "it would be impossible to understand Dostoevsky without it."[46] She admits that his polyphony sprung from many sources, but that, among them, one should not neglect that of the Orthodox faith and its understanding of the Trinity. She characterizes that doctrine as one of "difference and unity of the three Persons," in which the supposedly neat coherence of "subjectivity" is invited to display all its actual and potential contradictions.[47]

Other critics[48] have noted that Dostoevsky was influenced by Vladimir

---

[43] Ibid., 28.

[44] A discussion of the relationship between the Trinity and time is beyond the scope of this book. See, inter alia, Jenson, *The Triune Identity*, 138-48 and ch. 5; Peters, *GOD as Trinity*, part 4; Richard H. Roberts, "Barth's Doctrine of Time: Its Nature and Implications" and Rowan Williams, "Barth on the Triune God," both in *Karl Barth: Studies of His Theological Method*, ed. Stephen W. Sykes (Oxford: Clarendon Press, 1979), 88–146 and 147–93, respectively.

[45] Clark and Holquist, *Mikhail Bakhtin*, 85.

[46] Julia Kristeva, "Dostoevsky, The Writing of Suffering, and Forgiveness," in *Black Sun: Depression and Melancholia*, trans. Leon S. Roudiez (New York: Columbia University Press, 1989) [ET of: *Soleil noir: Dépression et mélancolie* (Paris: Éditions Gallimard, 1987)], 214.

[47] Ibid.

[48] e.g., Konstantin Mochulsky, *Dostoevsky: His Life and Work*, trans. with an Introduction by Michael A. Minihan (Princeton: Princeton University Press, 1967), 566.

Solovyov, and attended the latter's "Lectures on Godmanhood." The lectures were highly critical of individualism,[49] and many of them focus on trinitarian themes. Solovyov's lectures may have especially influenced Dostoevsky as he wrote his last novel, *The Brothers Karamazov*. This novel, on my reading, is trinitarian to its very core — a point that I have developed at length elsewhere.[50] Here, it will provide us with an illustration of a Christocentric, communally-embodied form of trinitarian polyphony.

Polyphony in The Brothers Karamazov

A plot summary of this 800-page masterwork is out of the question here; I will mention only a few details that are essential to my analysis. The novel explores the lives of three brothers — Dmitri, Ivan, and Alyosha — all of whom have good reason to despise their father, Fyodor, a complete buffoon and a self-indulgent sensualist. When Fyodor is murdered, each of the brothers must grapple with his responsibility for the act, even though none of them held the weapon. Suspicion falls on Dmitri, who was near the house when the murder took place, and whose passionate and reckless nature seems capable of such an act. But it was Ivan who, in his intellectual aloofness and his celebration of the radical claim that "everything is permitted," inadvertently encouraged the murderer to commit the crime. And Alyosha, too, must struggle with his own role in the affair: having entered the monastery and attached himself to the elder Zosima, he is painfully aware of having allowed the lives of his father and his brothers to fall into chaos.

Precisely because they are *three* brothers in *one* family, Dostoevsky is able to shift the reader's attention away from the individual consciousness of the

---

[49] See the comments of Peter P. Zouboff in the introduction to his translation: *Vladimir Solovyev's Lectures on Godmanhood* (n.p.: International University Press, 1944), 55–6. See also Hans Urs von Balthasar's commentary on Solovyov in *The Glory of the Lord: A Theological Aesthetics*, vol. 3, *Studies in Theological Style: Lay Styles*, ed. John Riches, trans. Andrew Louth, John Saward, Martin Simon, and Rowan Williams (San Francisco: Ignatius Press, 1986) [ET of: *Herrlichkeit: Eine theologische Ästhetik*, bd. 3, 2e. Aufl. (Einsiedeln: Johannes Verlag, 1969)], 279–352 (with specific comments on Solovyov's influence on Dostoevsky at 294–5 and 343–4).

[50] Initially in "Trinitarian Rhetoric in Murdoch, Morrison, and Dostoevsky," in *Literature and Theology at Century's End*, ed. Gregory Salyer and Robert Detweiler, American Academy of Religion Studies in Religion, no. 72 (Atlanta: Scholars Press, 1995), 189–213; and, in more detail, in *"The Brothers Karamazov* as Trinitarian Theology," in *Reading Dostoevsky Religiously*, ed. George Pattison and Diane Thompson (Cambridge: Cambridge University Press, forthcoming).

"hero," toward a simultaneous recognition of oneness and difference. The three thereby mirror the divine Three in that their individuality is defined by their mutual participation (they are, to a degree, "subsistent relations"). But we may also say that "these three are one"; just as their given names divide them, so their family name draws them together.

It may seem outlandish to try to discern a "triune mark" in the midst of a family that would, in the contemporary world, simply be labelled as "dysfunctional." But Dostoevsky wrote with the *sacramental* insight that the glory of God can be discerned in the most mundane elements of the created order. As one of the novel's characters remarks, "those who renounce Christianity and rebel against it are in their essence of the same image of the same Christ, and such they remain."[51] As such they can serve to illustrate some of the Christologically-centered elements of polyphony that I developed earlier in this chapter.

First, the novel reminds us that the all-powerful triune God is also a loving God and a forgiving God. The seeds of this claim are already planted in Ivan's parable of the Grand Inquisitor, when he is prompted by Alyosha to give it an ending. The contrast could not be greater: on the one side, the talkative Inquisitor, with his supposed "love" for humanity (but only in the abstract, of course; individual human beings he happily burns). On the other side, we have Christ, who "suddenly approaches the old man in silence and gently kisses him on his bloodless, ninety-year-old lips."[52] And then Ivan speaks words loaded with irony: "That is the whole answer." The answer is *love*—love for one's enemies, which has the power to defeat them. The prisoner is let out into the dark squares of the city; and as for the old man, "the kiss burns in his heart, but [he] holds to his former idea." "And you with him!" replies Alyosha to his brother. For Alyosha knows that Ivan cannot reconcile the idea of power with the idea of love and forgiveness. For Ivan, this is a strict either-or distinction; to love, to forgive, is to renounce the power and freedom that he holds so dear.

By the end of the novel, Ivan seems to have learned the necessity of such love, even if the process of education has devastated him. And the novel gives us many examples of those who do love humanity in all its fallenness. The elder Zosima provides the prototype of such love in the novel – a love which is all-encompassing. Zosima offers the following exhortation:

---

[51] Fyodor Dostoevsky, *The Brothers Karamazov*, trans. Richard Pevear and Larissa Volokhonsky (New York: Random House, Vintage Books, 1990), 171. The remark is made by Father Païssy to Alyosha.

[52] Dostoevsky, *The Brothers Karamazov*, 262.

Love man also in his sin, for this likeness of God's love is the height of love on earth. Love all of God's creation, both the whole of it and every grain of sand. Love every leaf, every ray of God's light. Love animals, love plants, love each thing. If you love each thing, you will perceive the mystery of God in things. Once you have perceived it, you will begin tirelessly to perceive more and more of it every day. And you will come at last to love the whole world with an entire, universal love.[53]

Such a self-discipline of love is possible only if we allow ourselves to be formed by God. It cannot achieved by our own efforts; it is possible only because God has shown us the way through the incarnation of the Word.

No one is capable of perfection in this regard; even Zosima laments of his failures. When he dies, his body proves itself to be as corruptible as any other. But the true miracle, as Alyosha finally realizes, is not incorruptible flesh, but the incarnation of Zosima's love – or more precisely, of Christ's love – in the most unlikely places.[54] For this love is recognizable not only in Alyosha, but even, at times, in Dmitri and Ivan. Dmitri expresses his love often in the text – sometimes too carnally, to be sure, but often and unexpectedly in ways that resemble God's love. (His sense of responsibility and love is evoked by a dream he has, in which he sees peasants whose village has been burnt to the ground; he focuses especially on a baby – "the wee one," Dmitri says – who is dying of frostbite and hunger.) Despite their obvious love of power, neither Dmitri nor Ivan can insulate himself from the power of love.

Secondly, triune polyphony posits an integral relationship between life and suffering. The doctrine of the incarnation describes God as having participated in human affairs by being born into the world and suffering it. Dostoevsky illustrates this notion as well; for him, innocent suffering can be redemptive, because it rearranges our usual assumptions about responsibility and forgiveness. Because God is willing to be responsible for the sins of humanity, we are called to a similar sort of responsibility and to forgiveness. Kristeva writes: "Confronted with that stay of time and actions within the timelessness of forgiving, we understand those who believe that God alone can forgive. In Christianity, however, the stay – divine to be sure – of crimes and punishments is *first* the work of human beings."[55]

---

[53] Ibid., 318–19.

[54] For some helpful comments on the ways in which the traditional concept of "miracle" is refigured into "love" in the novel, see Stewart R. Sutherland, *Atheism and the Rejection of God: Contemporary Philosophy and* The Brothers Karamazov, Values and Philosophical Inquiry, ed. D. Z. Phillips (Oxford: Basil Blackwell, 1977), 118-20.

[55] Kristeva, "Dostoevsky," 200; translation slightly altered.

This idea is present in the portrait of Christ in Ivan's parable, who suffers the Inquisitor's harangue and appears quite ready to suffer at the stake as well. It is also present in the elder, Zosima, as well as in the stories of his brother Markel and of the boy Ilyusha (both of whom suffer and die at a young age, but in doing so bring about profoundly positive changes in the lives of others). But it is most markedly (and remarkably) present in the character of Dmitri, who eventually comes to consider the possibility that his own innocent suffering may be redemptive.

Dmitri's actions, from the time of the murder to the end of the book, clearly parallel the sufferings of Jesus – from his "last supper" at Mokroe, to his arrest and apprehension (at which he is unjustly accused, questioned, mocked, and stripped). He will later be tried; false witnesses will be brought against him, and he will be found guilty, much to the delight of the crowd assembled for the spectacle. But he will endure it, because he has come to believe what Zosima teaches – though he did not learn it from Zosima. He has learned that we are all "responsible to all and for all," even to the cold and hungry "wee one" about whom he dreamed. Dmitri wakens from that dream, and notices that someone has, out of compassion, placed a pillow under his head. This tiny act of unmerited grace seems to awaken in him a recognition of his own responsibility "to all and for all." Suddenly, he announces that he is willing to sign the transcript of his arrest interview, even without reviewing it. He knows that, even if he did not hold the weapon that killed his father, he is nevertheless responsible – and therefore he is, in a very real sense, in need of repentance and forgiveness.

Finally, the polyphonic character of God is illustrated in the created order by means of the novel's accent on mutuality and communion. Each of the three brothers is at his worst when he is isolated from others – whether towering above them, fleeing from them, or being abandoned by them. This tendency toward romantic individualism and even isolationism – so much a part of the intellectual furniture for those of us in the West – leads only to alienation and violence. Dostoevsky believed that "the ultimate source of all social ills is the spiritual disintegration and dissociation of human life, the decay or decrease of brotherhood among men."[56]

How is this alienation to be avoided? Dostoevsky believes that it requires us to participate *in* and *with* the lives of others – not only in the ultimate sense countenanced by Zosima in the novel ("responsibility to all and for all"), but also in our mutually participative relationships. Dostoevsky insists that the

[56] Georges Florovsky, "Three Masters: Gogol, Dostoevsky, Tolstoy," *Epiphany: A Journal of Faith and Insight* 10 (Summer 1990): 43–58; here, 51.

human being must learn to be "a 'conciliar person,' a member of the Body of Christ" – to move from a focus on the individual "self" to a focus on the community.[57] Of course, one could read all this as merely a lesson in social psychology, an invitation to break free from loneliness and isolation and to join the human race. But something else may be at stake here – a harmony of the singular and the multiple, which is at the root of the Christian doctrine of God. "The trinitarian nature of God as recognized in Christianity implies the ideal harmony of the personal attributes of God in the Father, Son and Holy Spirit within the *koinonia* and the dynamics of *symphonia* for the 'unity of all in all.'"[58]

No *one* of the characters, not even Alyosha or Zosima, can, alone, bear God's image. As I noted above, the image of God belongs not to any one human being, but – according to the Genesis account – to human *beings*. Thus, at the end of the novel, the gathered children do not shout "Hurrah for Alyosha" – as many commentators seem to have done (since he is usually thought to be the most commendable of the three brothers). Rather, they shout "Hurrah for Karamazov." This forces us to recognize how all three brothers – and even their father – contribute to the polyphonic character of this name. Somehow, Dostoevsky manages to make each of the three into the story's "main character":

> Any one of the three brothers, from a particular point of view, is the centre of the story. Dmitri commands the plot; Ivan is the ideological centre; Alyosha is the spiritual climax. As the novel has a plot, an ideology, and a destination, none of them can be neglected and all must be held together at every turn of the road.[59]

The novel is highly successful at holding together the elements of oneness and difference by telling the story of three very different brothers, all of whom are still Karamazovs.

Why have the trinitarian elements of *The Brothers Karamazov* typically been so difficult to discern? One explanation may be that critics have often focused on the human psyche as the primary object of Dostoevsky's interest. They have called him a "psychologist" or an "anthropologist." But of course, in the Orthodox tradition especially, anthropology is always grounded in theology

---

[57] N. A. Zabolotski, "Fyodor Mikhailovich Dostoevsky Today," *Scottish Journal of Theology* 37, no. 1 (1984): 41–57; here, 46–7.

[58] Ibid., 47.

[59] A. Boyce Gibson, *The Religion of Dostoevsky* (London: SCM Press, 1973; reprint, Philadelphia: Westminster Press, 1974), 175.

– and more specifically, in the doctrine of the Trinity. For human beings are created in the image of God, and they are also perfected in God, ultimately by being taken up into the divine life. Thus, whenever Dostoevsky is described as having provided a particularly compelling portrait of concrete human beings, the astute reader will also be aware of the claims about God that are implicit in such portraits.

This is not to suggest that Dostoevsky collapses the distinction between God and humanity. Rather, as I have already suggested, we find in his novels a radically *sacramental* worldview. He believes that God is made manifest in the mundane aspects of the created order as well as its most glorious aspects. Janine Langan finds this most clearly expressed at the end of the novel, when the boys gathered at the stone shout "Hurrah for Karamazov."

> Beyond all Romantic judgmental aggression, it is a pledge of solidarity with all the Karamazov adolescents encountered in the book, not only Alyosha but his father and brothers as well. For they, too, are icons. However crippled, however involved in myth, they testify through their growing pains and twisted faces to the irresistible presence in them of an ineradicable seed: God's image and likeness.[60]

Even the most debased, fallen characters point us back to the perfect, polyphonic communion of the inner life of God: the communion that informs and underwrites our common bond of humanity, and the communion whereby even we "great sinners" are called into profound mutual participation.

[60] Janine Langan, "Icon vs. Myth: Dostoevsky, Feminism and Pornography," *Religion and Literature* 18, no. 1 (Spring 1986): 63–72; here, 72.

Chapter 5

PARTICIPATION

In chapter 1, I noted with appreciation the attention that has been given in recent trinitarian thought to *relationality*. But I have also suggested that this concept can be misleading, since we usually assume that relations exist *between* things – that they are possible only after we have already established the independent existence of two or more discrete entities. And this tendency is compounded by the modern understanding of human persons as, first and foremost, *individuals* (who can choose to enter into relationships – or choose to avoid them). We thus find it extraordinarily difficult to imagine how anything could be exhaustively described by the category of relation.

And yet, this is precisely what I have argued that we should affirm about God – that God is *wholly constituted* by relationality. In other words, God is not (first) three independent entities who (then) decide to come into relation with one another; God is, rather, "relation without remainder." Thus, the Three are *mutually constitutive* of one another. This claim, which I describe as the trinitarian virtue of *participation*, will be the primary focus of this chapter: the Three *participate* in one another in a profound way, undermining any attempt to understand them independently of one another. Furthermore, the trinitarian virtue of *participation* can come to mark our own lives as well. It can help us begin to think about what it might mean to dwell in, and be indwelt by, the lives of others. It thus encourages us not simply to value "relationality" in the abstract, but to think about the *character* of our relations.[1] After all, such relations are not a good in themselves; they can be trivial, insincere, abusive, or worse. In the contemporary context, especially, relationships are often entered into for one's own convenience. By contrast, the doctrine of the

---

[1] Colin Gunton attends to this problem by advocating a "perichoretic" relationality (*The One, The Three, and the Many*, 169). I examine the advantages and the limits of περιχώρησις in the middle section of this chapter.

Trinity encourages us to understand ourselves not as "individuals" who may (or may not) choose to enter into relationships, but rather as mutually indwelling and indwelt, and to such a degree that – echoing the mutual indwelling of the Three – all pretensions to wholly autonomous existence are abolished.

Dwelling in, and Being Indwelt by, the Other

The mere decision to use the word *participation* will not, by itself, solve all the problems that I have just described. The word needs to be given concrete content, so that it can come to describe something more than merely accidental relations between two otherwise independent entities. In this section, I offer my own construal of the word *participation*, and explore some of its conceptual associations; I then consider its concrete embodiment in the practical life of the Church.

Participation, fellowship, communion

The standard definition of *participate* is "to take part in"; this usually refers to an activity in which we are joined by others. We "participate" in sports, in meetings, in worship. At first glance, then, *participation* would seem to suggest bringing human beings (or the Three) together for the purpose of performing some activity; however, this is not how I want to construe the word. I am interested in those instances in which we take part, not in some*thing*, but in some*one* – an *other*. For example, to "participate in the sufferings of another" is to make another's pain one's own – perhaps by subjecting oneself to similar treatment, or empathizing with another to the greatest possible degree. Similarly, if I ask you to "take part in" my life, I am asking for a very significant degree of emotional, physical, and spiritual intimacy. This is the idea of participation that I am attempting to call forth: not merely of working alongside others in a common activity, but of dwelling in, and being indwelt by, one another.

Thus, it may help us to join the word *participation* to the words *fellowship* and *communion*, in an effort to emphasize this mutual intimacy. Admittedly, the notions of *fellowship* and *communion* have sometimes been understood along the same lines as the more "distant" and "disengaged" forms of participation mentioned above – as when we assume that exchanging a few words with some casual acquaintances constitutes "fellowship." But *communion* and *fellowship* can also be associated with the kind of intimate mutual indwelling that I am attempting to describe here. If we express a desire to "be in communion with" others, this will certainly require spending time with them and sharing mutual interests. But it also requires something more: it means that we must be willing to allow others to shape our lives in profound and fundamental ways.

Under such circumstances, the lines of identity between "I" and "you" are blurred. Those who participate fully in one another's lives are no longer "persons" in the dominant modern sense (individual consciousnesses that are fundamentally detachable from the rest of the world). In the event of true mutual participation, there are no longer substantively and permanently distinguishable subjects and objects, for this would imply a definitive separation or division. Rather, subject and object are best understood as *rhetorical* categories, denoting the whence and wherefore of our communication. Under the influence of the trinitarian virtue of participation, the apparently "individualizing" labels of *subject* and *object* are recast as purely temporary and relational features of the process of communication.

In the case of God, this means that it is impossible to isolate any one of the Three as "pure subject" or "pure object" without introducing fundamental distortions into the doctrine of the Trinity.[2] Unfortunately, such distortions have become a common tendency; the Three are sometimes described as subjects – individuals who "work" and "act" relatively independently of one another.[3] This tendency has been buttressed by the ease with which the Christian tradition fell into the habit of "naming" the Three. That it did so was certainly understandable; Christians narrated the story of salvation as involving very specific persons, and one certainly expects such persons to be named. But the extension of this naming – from the story of salvation back to the inner life of God – eventually made it difficult for Christians to hold fast to the claim that "these three are one." By assigning each of the Three a single name, and treating these names as exclusive, Christian theology made it relatively easy for them to be separated and discussed as individuals.

I have already commented on the hazards of this enterprise in my discussion of the divine relations in chapters 2 and 3. Anything that "has a name" – that is, any object named by a noun – is easily isolated from its context and transferred to other contexts. Of course, this feature makes names very useful; and through most of Christian history, it posed little cause for concern, since pride of place in the construal of meaning was accorded to *verbs*, not to nouns.

---

[2] See the useful discussion in Staniloae, "Holy Trinity," 77–8.
[3] Particularly in Weinandy, *The Father's Spirit of Sonship*, 119–21; see also Torrance, *Persons in Communion*, *passim*, and LaCugna, *God For Us*, esp. chap. 8.

Thus, St Thomas (and much of the trinitarian theology that preceded him) claimed that the divine processions and relations were more fundamental than the "names" of God, which varied widely.[4] According to Michel de Certeau, only from the time of the "dethroning of the verb"[5] in the fifteenth century did substantives come to be seen as the authoritative "containers" of meaning. If this claim is accurate, then we face a most interesting problem: the use of easily-recognized (and almost universally-accepted) substantives for the Three necessarily has a very different impact in the modern era than it did through much of Christian history. Previously, the names would have been recognized as mere shorthand for the (more fundamental) verbal forms (the processions and relations), which were in turn grounded in the economy of salvation. But today, these verbal forms are lost from view; the names are usually seen as primary, which makes it difficult not to think of the Three as isolated individuals.[6] And yet, from the earliest era of trinitarian speculation, theologians had argued that nothing positive could be said of any of the Three that could not also be said of the others. The mutual participation of the Three is so complete that none of them can be invoked without invoking the others as well.

The earthly mirror of this complete mutual participation is the Church. "Those who are called out" (ἐκκλησία) from the world are – or should be – bound together in quite profound ways; indeed, their lives implicate and are implicated by one another. Recalling Paul's extended analogy in 1 Corinthians, they are like the members of the body: they form an organic whole. Any member that is separated from the body ceases to be what it truly is. One may dissect the body for scientific study; but in the process, its organic wholeness is lost. Paul's analogy is an extraordinarily apposite one, precisely because we are not usually tempted to attribute any real independence to an isolated body part that has been "cut off" from the whole. But when we transpose the

[4] I will return to this point, and provide bibliography, in chapter 6.

[5] Michel de Certeau, *The Mystic Fable*, vol. 1, *The Sixteenth and Seventeenth Centuries*, trans. Michael B. Smith (Chicago and London: University of Chicago Press, 1992) [ET of: *La Fable Mystique, XVIe–XVIIe Siècle* (Paris: Éditions Gallimard, 1982)], 125. My thanks to Nicholas Lash for pointing me toward this passage; note also Lash's own use of verbal forms throughout *Believing Three Ways*.

[6] Ironically, the advocacy of a single name for each of the Three, however "biblical" those names might be, tends to obscure their profound mutual participation, since these names can be so easily disconnected from the narrative contexts in which they originated. Alternative names, such as those that I offer in this book, are admittedly never grouped as a formula in current translations of the biblical text; nevertheless, by evoking the processions and relations, they direct us back to the narratives that they summarize.

analogy back to groups of human beings, we tend to stop thinking in terms of "participation" and to think instead of individuals involved in accidental relations (from which they can extricate themselves at will).

Other examples may perhaps help. The mutual participation described here is mirrored again in the family, where the relations among the members should, at least in the ideal case, be marked by *communion* and *participation* in one another's lives. However inadequate my own practice of this particular trinitarian virtue may be, I think I understand what this *should* mean in my own family. I am "related" to my wife and my daughters, yes, but more than this: I dwell in their lives and they in mine. They are fundamentally constitutive of who "I" am. Therefore, when you ask me how "I" am doing, my answer will reflect how "they" are doing as well. The modern era has tempted us to think of ourselves as autonomous individuals; but upon deeper reflection, we recognize that such absolute distinctions fail to describe the communion and mutual participation we seek to embody.

We can also return, once again, to the example of pregnancy. The word *relationship* is probably too weak to describe the connection between "mother" and "child" – and I put these names in inverted commas ("scare quotes") in an attempt to call into question the assumption that they can be separated by assigning them differing names. They participate in one another to such a degree that no clear line can be drawn between them. What happens to one happens to the other. Indeed, depending upon the stage of the pregnancy, the death of one can bring about the death of the other – and conversely, the life of one is dependent upon the life of the other.

In sum: the notion of a pure, isolated "individual" is a highly disputable human construction. In God, there are no individuals; the Three dwell in each other so completely that we cannot divide them, one from another. And so we too are called to live lives of mutual participation, in which our relationships are not just something that we "have," but are what constitute us as human beings. God is pure mutual participation – relation without remainder. Admittedly, our status as created beings rules out any perfect imaging of God's internal participation. But we should not underestimate the power of the Spirit, working in us, to do infinitely more than we can ask or imagine – such that we too might dimly reflect, however inadequately, the complete mutual participation within God.

In the modern era, however, we find it relatively easy to place obstacles in the way of this gracious gift; and so, too often, our lives fail to offer even a very dim reflection of this particular characteristic of the triune God. In the next section, I offer some brief observations of why this is particularly so in the culture of modernity.

Individualism run amok

Among its many legacies, the Enlightenment left us with the apotheosis of the ostensibly solitary human being. The quest for intellectual, spiritual, moral, political and physical independence is one of the most dominant features of the seventeenth, eighteenth, and nineteenth centuries. The French and American Revolutions are only the most obvious outcroppings of this phenomenon, which can be found, in some form, in almost any Enlightenment treatise, even if chosen rather at random. Here, I will provide only a brief (and admittedly oversimplified) sketch of the more obvious indicators of this phenomenon.

When Descartes undertakes his *Meditations*, he does not convene a gathering of close friends and trusted colleagues to discuss the nature of existence. He describes himself as alone in his room; and although he can potentially make contact with other people through his own writing, he does not enter into any direct conversation with others. He is a solitary individual, thinking deep thoughts. His reflections on God, the world, and the nature of things seem to be the product of his unencumbered, solitary mind; he is completely, thoroughly, absolutely *alone*. What is more: his argument suggests that he is able to achieve the degree of insight that he here achieves *precisely because* he is alone – with no one to lead him astray or to muddle his thoughts with irrelevant details.

Similarly, Immanuel Kant, in his invocation of "the starry firmament above, and the moral law within," provides us with an image of the clear-minded philosopher, standing alone under the night sky – knowing the truth in his heart, and not being dependent on any other human beings for these two absolute certainties. The moral law and the starry skies would be there, even if every other human being vanished from the face of the earth.

The individualism of the Enlightenment, like its rationalism, has extended itself quite forcefully into the twentieth century. Consider Jean-Paul Sartre's prototypical modern hero – Orestes (in *The Flies*) – who does not flee in terror from the Furies as did his literary predecessor (in the *Oresteia* of Aeschylus). No indeed: in Sartre's play, Orestes marches out to the crowds and displays his bloody hands, silencing the moral outrage of the people by his proclamation of self-sufficiency:

> You see me, you men of Argos, you understand that my crime is wholly mine;
> I claim it as my own, for all to know; it is my glory, my life's work, and you
> can neither punish me nor pity me. That is why I fill you with fear. . . . But have
> no fear, people of Argos. I shall not sit on my victim's throne or take the scepter

in my blood-stained hands. A god offered it to me, and I said no. I wish to be a king without a kingdom, without subjects. Farewell, my people. Try to reshape your lives.[7]

Orestes is such an absolute individual that he does not even covet political power; for this would bring him into contact with others, make him "dependent" on them (in the same way that, as Hegel saw it, all masters "depend" on their slaves). Comparing himself to the piper of Scyros who led the rats from the town, Orestes strides out into the light, and the Furies fling themselves after him. But he will not feel the terror of his Aeschylan predecessor; for to him – as to Sartre – the Furies are merely flies. Annoying, yes; but hardly capable of inflicting the kind of nightmarish terror that seemed to be the hallmark of these personifications of moral outrage. That would require that the views of others were relevant – and in the mind of the pure individualist, they are not.

Modern individualism poses significant challenges for the Christian faith – calling into question the ideal of mutual participation both within the believing community and within God. Christians have understood themselves as called into communion with each other because they bear the image of the triune God; consequently, to raise doubts about the indispensability of the common life is to raise doubts about the trinitarian conception of God. According to the assumptions of the Enlightenment, "persons" are autonomous, fully self-determined, and fully distinct from one another; they determine their own goals and need only consider their own desires. "Unlike God, in whom each person is for the other two, the person never *is* for others"; the Enlightenment conception of personhood thus "came to mean freedom of position and the creation of self by self."[8] The notion of the self as subjective consciousness displaced the centrality of mutual participation, both in the doctrine of God and in the Christian understanding of human community. The outcome is visible all around us; in its glorification of the isolated individual, our culture is profoundly antitrinitarian. At every level, through practically every system and structure, we are discouraged from allowing our lives to become too tightly intertwined with those of others.

Needless to say, such a fundamental cultural tendency as modern Western hyperindividualism is not going to be overcome by fiat. But being aware of

[7] Jean-Paul Sartre, *The Flies*, trans. Stuart Gilbert, in *No Exit and Three Other Plays* (New York: Random House, 1989) [ET of *Les Mouches* (Paris: Gallimard, 1943)], 123.

[8] Francis Jacques, *Difference and Subjectivity: Dialogue and Personal Identity*, trans. Andrew Rothwell (New Haven: Yale University Press, 1991) [ET of: *Différence et subjectivité: Anthropologie d'un point de vue relationnel* (Paris: Aubier-Montaigne, 1982)], 68.

this context may help us to understand the influence it has exerted on our readings of God's life – and of our own. Certainly, the biblical narratives can provide a perspective from which to critique the modern cult of the self; but we will tend to read these narratives through highly individualistic lenses unless we also allow our lives to be formed by the trinitarian virtue of participation. Such formation occurs through practices that allow us a glimpse of triune participation – not only within God, but in God's interaction with us and in our relationships with one another. One practice that clearly embodies this virtue is the gathering of Christians around a common table, in order to give thanks to God and to come into fellowship with God and with one another. It is known by many names: the Lord's supper, communion, eucharist.

Participation in the body and blood of Christ

In 1 John, we are told that one of the "three who bear witness on earth" is "the blood." Some commentators have seen this as a reference to Christian martyrdom, and this may well have been the writer's intention. On the other hand, very early in the history of the Church, Christians had begun to recognize the eucharist as one of their most distinctive practices – one that set them apart from the cultures in which they lived. (Early polemic against Christians often drew attention to their "barbaric practice" of eating the body and blood of another person.) The long-term endurance of the rite helped to make "the blood" of the eucharistic cup an essential witness to the cause of Christ.

In the eucharist, participation is manifested on many different levels. We participate in one another by sharing the bread and the cup, allowing ourselves to be formed into the Body of Christ. We participate in God through our reception of Christ's body and blood. Finally, the eucharist also weaves together the stories of the Three in various ways, and thereby testifies to the complete mutual participation within God. This practice thus provides one of the most important sites for our formation in the trinitarian virtue of participation; and, in turn, it helps us to "see the form" of that participation in the triune life of God. How does it achieve this end?

First, the eucharist takes place within the context of a rehearsal of the story of our salvation. Despite the many differences among Christian theologies of the eucharist, most rites include an *anamnesis*, a memorial recapitulation of the acts of God that have brought about our redemption. These acts include the creation of the world, the saving of a remnant from the Flood, the gift of promise to Abraham and Sarah, the deliverance of the Israelites from the bondage in Egypt, the establishment of the Davidic monarchy, and the voices of the prophets. The focus narrows as the narrative describes the incarnation of the Word in the womb of Mary and the birth of Jesus. It goes on to describe the life, death, resurrection, and ascension of Jesus, the pouring out of the Spirit, and the promised return of Christ to earth.

The story of salvation is a story of intimate mutual participation. God participates in our lives – most obviously in the incarnation, but also in the entire litany of mighty acts that are meant to bring us into newness of life. Obviously, we have often failed to "participate in God," and we have never done so with the degree of constancy and perseverance that God has manifested toward us. So can this meaningfully be called *mutual* participation? Perhaps it can, if we recognize that God works in us to "complete what is lacking" in our own participation in God. Indeed, we could say that we are "participated" by God – taken up into the divine life and, by grace, brought into a communion which we would otherwise be incapable of achieving.

God's participation in our lives becomes most sharply focused at the moment in the eucharist when God's *presence* is invoked. Here, different rites vary widely; some include a direct *epiclesis*, in which the celebrant asks that God's Spirit descend upon the gifts of bread and wine, that they might become the body and blood of Christ. In those traditions that focus on the common table as a "memorial" of Christ's sacrifice, this presence is invoked by the process of *calling to memory* Jesus' last meal with the disciples. In either case, an effort is made to bring Christian believers "into contact" with God in a more direct, even immediate, way. While the narration of salvation history provides a *context* for this mutual participation, it would (by itself) be insufficient; it would remain something that happened a very long time ago and very far away. In contrast, the "presencing" of God that takes place in the eucharist is an acknowledgment of the ongoing reality of God's participation in our lives.

A further "participative" element of the eucharist can be found in the elements themselves. Both bread and wine are appropriate signs of divine–human interaction, for they show that God is both the source and the perfecter of all human work. Human beings cannot make bread or wine by themselves; they must draw on the elements of the created order (grain, fruit). On the other hand, bread and wine themselves do not occur in nature; they require human activity to bring them into existence. Both aspects are nicely summarized in the prayer over the gifts in the Roman Catholic rite:

> *Celebrant:* Blessed are you, Lord God of all creation, through your goodness we have this bread to offer, which earth has given and human hands have made. It will become for us the bread of life.
>
> *People:* Blessed be God forever.

Celebrant: Blessed are you, Lord God of all creation. Through your goodness
we have this wine to offer, fruit of the vine and work of human
hands. It will become our spiritual drink.
People: Blessed be God forever.

An additional feature of bread and wine should be noted: in both cases, human beings do not merely extract raw materials from creation and manufacture something for themselves. Rather, the human "product" requires a further intervention – an act of grace? – to make it what it is: bread must rise, and wine must ferment. As such, both elements remind us that whatever effort we may put into the process of "sustaining ourselves," we do not do so alone; our work is ultimately completed and perfected by God.

Moreover, in Jesus' naming of the bread and wine as his body and blood, we are given a further avenue for reflection upon the trinitarian virtue of participation. However we may understand this process of "re-naming" – and again, Christians have understood it in widely varying ways – it sets the stage for a profound degree of mutual participation between God and human beings. How much more deeply could we participate in someone than to enter into that person's body, or to allow that person's body to enter into our own? The language has lost its capacity to startle us, perhaps because we have heard it so many times, or because we would really rather not think about it. I here offer three brief meditations on how this language might be brought back to life.

1   "You are what you eat," as Feuerbach solemnly declared. In our culture, food has become so commodified that we rarely think of ourselves as being "in relationship" with that which we eat. We see food as a means to an end: the satisfaction of desires, the production of a certain kind of body, the display of a certain social class. But the food that we eat did not suddenly materialize on our plates; it has a history, having been prepared, purchased, harvested, grown, raised, and/or planted by other human beings. In some cases it was also *killed* by human beings; and in still other cases, it *killed* human beings on its way to our stomachs. Much of the food we eat is produced under barbaric conditions, both to the animals that produce it (or die to "become" it) and to the human beings who are employed or enslaved for the sake of its efficient sojourn to our palates. If we were to bring these elements to mind as we shop for and prepare our food, rather than simply seeking out the best bargain or the most delectable tastes, we might begin to recognize that eating something actually *does* bring us into relationship with it – we truly *are* what we eat. We participate in the lives of that which we eat: through our choices, we put the chickens in the cages, we kill the fish, we contribute to the migrant

farmworkers' misery. They are a part of who we are – however much the food-processing industry has succeeded in blinding us to these matters. A more "participative" outlook on our eating practices would perhaps engender a clearer perspective on the eucharist as well.

2   One of the most obvious ways that we "are nourished by the body" of another human being is through breastfeeding. Because our culture does not tend to hold this activity in pride of place, we rarely attend to its theological significance. But nursing mothers (and their children) know what a profound experience of mutual participation breastfeeding can be. Again, cultural imperatives toward independence and autonomy have tended to encourage early weaning and technological replacements for a mother's milk. In doing so they have also obliterated one of our most obvious avenues for thinking about what it means to inhabit, or be inhabited by, the body of another – which is precisely what Christians claim occurs in the eucharist. This is part of what is being described by Mother Julian of Norwich's description of Christ as our mother, who nourishes us bodily.[9]

3   Mutual physical participation is also central in erotic relationships. A wide variety of mystical writers have drawn on sexual imagery to convey the intimacy of the relationship between God and human beings.[10] Unfortunately, because Christian theology has never developed a deep and significant theology of sex, it never fully realized its potential to explicate and exemplify the mutual physical participation described by the claim that we "eat and drink the body and blood of Christ." Physically erotic relationships involve taking another person's body into our own, and/or having our bodies received into the body of another. This is the kind of "intimacy with God" that is being invoked in the eucharist. Recognizing the connection might not only give us a renewed appreciation for the eucharistic rite; it might also force us to think in theologically serious ways – perhaps for the first time – about the meaning of erotic love.

All three of these meditations touch on "uncomfortable" subjects; this is quite intentional. The main problem with the Christian experience of the

[9] Julian of Norwich, *The Revelation of Divine Love in Sixteen Showings*, trans. M. L. del Mastro (Garden City, NY: Image Books, 1977).
[10] E.g., Mechthild of Magdeburg, Hadewijch, St Teresa of Avila, and many others. See the commentary in Mark McIntosh's forthcoming study, *Mystical Theology* (Oxford: Basil Blackwell, 1998), ch. 2.

eucharist, in my view, is that it is not nearly uncomfortable *enough*. For many of us, it has become such a ritualized or sentimentalized event that its profundity has evaporated. It no longer seems to have the cosmic dimension that was once so central to it: here, in this earth-shattering moment, we participate in God and in one another at the deepest and most intimate level.

One last point – and here I return to the reflection on "blood" with which I began this section. The eucharist also binds human beings together; we participate not only in God, but in one another as well. This too has often been obscured: by the proliferation of "individualizing" elements (individual wafers, individual cups, and a pattern of partaking that requires no movement among the congregation); and "rationalizing" elements (denying the eucharist to some of the baptized, and/or claiming that one must "understand" what is taking place in the rite). As an alternative, we need to focus on the element of *blood* as central to the eucharist. We all have blood; it is essential to our lives; and it needs to be shared with others. Christ's willing donation of blood is a gift to us, but also a reminder of that which binds us together. People once mingled their blood as a sign of profound mutual participation; today, it seems a much more negative symbol, as the carrier of disease from one organism to another. But this too can be a reminder of the profound meaning of the eucharistic event: we are "sharing blood" with those with whom we have gathered. For many, this is a frightening thought indeed. Nevertheless, the blood that binds us together is a chief reference point of the eucharist, by which it draws us into mutually constitutive relationships with one another that can reflect, however dimly, the mutual participation of the triune God.

Christians who have been formed in the common practice of eucharist have already learned something about the trinitarian virtue of participation. As such, they are able to read the biblical texts, and the history of the interpretation of those texts, as witnesses to the complete and perfect participation within God. In the next section, I offer my own reading of those witnesses – once again focusing on the incarnation as the chief site of revelation.

The Form of Trinitarian Participation

Christ reveals to us the contours of a specifically trinitarian account of participation. This occurs on three levels. First, because "God was in Christ" (2 Cor. 5:19), we have come to know something of the profound mutual participation that constitutes the life of the triune God. Secondly, this participation is mirrored in the intimate union of Christ and Christian believers. And thirdly, it points us to the interweaving of these believers' lives with one another in the concrete practices of the Church.

Mutual participation within God

In chapters 2 and 3, I described trinitarian theology as based on the claim that "there are two processions in God." If we keep this claim in mind, it will be relatively easy for us to recognize the profound mutual participation among the Three – for they are also One. Christians tell a story of one God in whom there are two processions and therefore three subsistent relations; we can make no sense of this story unless we affirm that the Three indwell one another to the greatest possible degree.

As I have already observed, these rather abstract claims about the inner life of God are merely a systematic account of the scriptural narratives. One of the warrants for this account is the πατήρ-υἱός language in the text of the New Testament. Here, the mutual participation of Christ in God and God in Christ is described as very intimate, like that between parent and child, or perhaps between the master and the apprentice, or between one's ancestors and one's present generation – all of which are possible translations of the Greek words.[11] We can make sense of one "half" of each of these pairs only with reference to the other half: there can be no parent without a child, no apprentice without a master, no present generation without ancestors. We can speak of the mother as the "cause" of her daughter, but only if we also recognize the daughter as "retroactively causative" of her mother.

The New Testament sometimes describes this mutual participation simply through the use of prepositions such as *in* and *with*. For example, Jesus says, "I am *in* τῷ πατρὶ and ὁ πατὴρ is *in* me" (John 14:11). A similar motif is sounded in the prologue to John, where the Word is described as being "with" God from the beginning. And (as we have already noted) the baptism of Jesus provides a similar witness: the body of Jesus, the voice of God, and the descent of the dove are not three isolated events, nor are they merely accidentally related. Rather, they draw together the agent, the object, and the vehicle of the anointing of Jesus as God's messiah.[12] Irenaeus recognizes in this event a very clear *vestigium trinitatis*; he describes the Three as one who has anointed,

---

[11] I provide concrete arguments for this claim in "On Translating the Divine Name," especially 427–8.
[12] McDonnell, *The Baptism of Jesus*, 118-19.

one who has been anointed, and the ointment.[13] Note again how the Three *constitute* one another in this act: there can be no process of "anointing" without an actor, a recipient, and an ointment. Remove one of the three, and the result is not simply deficient or incomplete; it vanishes altogether.

The Nicene claim that the Wellspring is "of one being" with the Source is another attempt to express the depth of mutual participation described in the scriptural narratives, in which Jesus' divine attributes are emphasized throughout. His names (in Matt. 1:21–3, for example) reflect his saving power ("Jesus" = "one who saves") and his identity with God ("Emmanuel" = "God with us"). After his resurrection, he is called "my Lord and my God" (John 20:28); these words suggest a strong association with יהוה. Nor is this identification absent from Jesus' own lips: if his repeated use of the phrase "I am" was too subtle a reference for some, they seem not to have missed the point of the comment, "Very truly, I tell you, before Abraham was, I am" – for immediately, "they picked up stones to throw at him" (John 8:58-59).

Paul testifies frequently to the mutual participation of God, Christ, and the Spirit. His letters often open and close with greetings and benedictions that weave the Three together. Another good example of this mutuality occurs in Romans 8:9-11; here, Paul speaks of God, Christ, and the Spirit – and even of the Spirit of God and the Spirit of Christ – in ways that witness to their participation in one another.

> But you are not in the flesh; you are in the Spirit, since the Spirit of God dwells in you. Anyone who does not have the Spirit of Christ does not belong to [that One].[14] But if Christ is in you, though the body is dead because of sin, the Spirit is life because of righteousness. If the Spirit of the one who raised Jesus from the dead dwells in you, the one who raised Christ from the dead will give life to your mortal bodies also through his Spirit that dwells in you.

Here, as often, Paul's language seems to refer to the Three *not* as individuals who happen to have come into relation with one another, but rather to a reality that is so mutually self-participative that distinctions can no longer be drawn. Thus he can claim that justification comes "in the name of the Lord

---

[13] *in Christi enim nomine subauditur qui unxit et ipse qui unctus est et ipsa unctio in qua unctus est; et unxit quidem Pater, unctus est uero Filius, in Spiritu qui est unctio.* Irenaeus, *Adversus Haeresis* 3.18.3. I owe the reference to McDonnell, *The Baptism of Jesus*, 119.

[14] Interestingly, the Greek pronoun αὐτοῦ is ambiguous; identical in masculine and neuter genders, it could theoretically refer to Christ, the Spirit, or God. The fact that Paul apparently saw no need to relieve the ambiguity is perhaps a further warrant for the point that I am making here.

Jesus Christ and in the Spirit of our God" (1 Cor. 6:11); that "No one can say 'Jesus is Lord' except by the Holy Spirit" (1 Cor. 12:3); and even that "the Lord is the Spirit" (2 Cor. 3:17–18).

Despite the claims of many historical-critical interpreters, these passages need not be read as a testimony to Paul's confusion. I would suggest that they testify to the intimacy among the Three, and thereby discourage us from separating them into three discrete entities. Needless to say, Paul did not write under the guidance of a full-fledged, systematic doctrine of the Trinity. Nevertheless – as Frances Young and David Ford note in their study of 2 Corinthians – the "grammar" of Paul's references to God are in accord with the "grammar" of the doctrine of the Trinity that was developed at a later date.[15] Paul is thus employing the same patterns of speech that came to shape trinitarian discourse – and especially, in this instance, patterns that emphasize mutual participation within God.

> The temptation to identify God simply with a concept of absolute transcendence, or with Jesus of Nazareth, or with "spirit" understood either cosmically or as indwelling human beings is negated by the requirement always to include each element. The rule is: never refer to God in one way without intending also each of the others.[16]

It seems to me that this is precisely what Paul is doing, and that he thereby underscores the mutually participative nature of the Godhead.

The scriptural testimony to the mutuality of divine participation was taken up and emphasized among early Christian theologians.[17] St Athanasius, in his Letter to Serapion, moves from the mutual participation of Christ and God (John 14:11) to a similar understanding of the indwelling of the Spirit.[18] Thus (to cast his point in the language I developed in chapter 2), if we partake of the Wellspring we possess the Living Water, and if we partake of the Living Water we possess the Wellspring. Similarly, St Hilary of Poitiers comments that it seems impossible that the Three can mutually "contain" one another, but the nature of God makes this possible.[19] We can thus say that the Source, as source, contains all things; the Wellspring, as the perfect image of the

---

[15] *Meaning and Truth in 2 Corinthians* (Grand Rapids, Mich.: William B. Eerdmans, 1988), 256.

[16] Ibid., 256–7.

[17] My treatment here follows that of G. L. Prestige, *God in Patristic Thought*, 2nd edn (London: SPCK, 1952), ch. 14.

[18] Athanasius *ad Serap.* 4.4.

[19] Hilary *De Trin.* 3.1.

Source, must have the same properties as the archetype, and so must also contain all things. This implies a profound mutual participation; as the Source is reflected in the Wellspring, so is the Wellspring reflected in the Source. In this image, God "contains" God in mutual ways.

These sorts of reflections became the foundation of the idea of περιχώρησις. This word, as employed by Sts Gregory Nazianzus, Maximus the Confessor, and others, was originally used to describe the reciprocal participation of the two natures of Christ. It was the sixth-century writer known to us as "pseudo-Cyril" who first applied the term to the mutual participation within the Trinity.[20] The word is not easy to translate; "interpenetration" is perhaps most commonly employed today, especially by theologians who describe the Three as "persons in communion" (since it helps to offset the "isolating" tendencies of the modern use of the word *person*). "Coinherence" is another rendering, which comes fairly close to the "participatory" language that I have described in this chapter. Indeed, something like "mutual and reciprocal participation" might even be a possible translation of the word. Not wishing to silence any of these elements, I will usually leave the word untranslated.

A number of different images have been offered to attempt to describe περιχώρησις. It is something like three sources of light placed in a room; the lights interpenetrate each other with the result that the (single?) resulting light somehow remains multiple. Another useful analogy is that of the three dimensions of physical objects – height, width, and depth. Each dimension implies the other two, so that changing any one of the three changes the whole. Seeking a less static metaphor, and noting that the word is closely related to another Greek word meaning "to dance around,"[21] some theologians have referred to περιχώρησις as "the divine dance."[22] There are certainly advantages to the analogy, which suggests order and symmetry in the midst of diversity. But it is not a wholly happy image, since dances are always done by *dancers*, thus returning us to the original problem of "relationality": how to prevent it from devolving into a picture of three separate entities who are only accidentally related to one another. When picturing "the triune dance," it is hard not to think of *three people*. And even if their dance is sufficiently elegant and harmonious so that they blur into one, it is hard for

---

[20] See the discussion in Prestige, *God in Patristic Thought*, 280–1 and 297–8.

[21] περιχωρέω (to go around) vs. περιχωρεύω (to dance around).

[22] See, inter alia, Nicholas Lash, "Human Experience and the Knowledge of God," in *Theology on the Way to Emmaus*, 154–7; building on Lash's account, Jones, *Transformed Judgment*, 94–5, 116; and, with apologies concerning the lack of a direct etymological connection, LaCugna, *God For Us*, 271–2.

us to resist the notion of three individual agents, each of whom is motivated by a (relatively) isolated will.

Some of the same problems are at work in the common translation of περιχώρησις as "interpenetration." The related verb, *interpenetrate*, strongly suggests movement from one place to another; it thus underscores the strongly active sense that many writers seem to appreciate in περιχώρησις.[23] Unfortunately, this "active" sense of the word makes it difficult to imagine a scene of "threefold interpenetration" that does not involve three *actors* or *agents*. This is somewhat less of an issue for the term *coinherence*, since its relatively static quality – sometimes claimed to be a weakness[24] – at least has the advantage of mitigating our tendencies to connect it to images of three agents or "individual persons."

The rediscovery of περιχώρησις is a praiseworthy attempt to prevent the isolation and separation of the Three – a tendency that has been reinforced by continued use of the language of "persons," despite its highly individualistic associations in the modern era. One always wonders, though, whether this very rich Greek word would need to play such a prominent role, if we were to begin with a less individualistic portrait of the Three in the first place. It seems as though, having defined the Three as individuals, we desperately need to find ways to keep them in conversation with one another. As an alternative, we might simply begin with the claim that they mutually constitute one another to such a degree that we cannot speak of them as "individuals."

That God may evermore dwell in us, and we in God

The incarnation of the Word also reveals to us the potential for a profound mutual participation between God and human beings. According to the Chalcedonian definition of the faith, Christ is truly human and truly divine, and these two natures dwell together "without confusion, without change, without division, without separation."[25] It would be hard to imagine a more thoroughgoing instance of mutual participation between humanity and God. Of course, one might admit this and still argue that Christ is a special case; that this is our singular example of such thoroughgoing mutual participation, something to which the rest of us cannot aspire. But such an interpretation narrows the incarnation to an isolated historical event, and misses its truly

---

[23] Jüngel, *The Doctrine of the Trinity*, 32–3 [*Gottes sein*, 43–4]; Boff, *Trinity and Society*, 134–6; Gunton, *One, Three, Many*, 163.

[24] This is Colin Gunton's position (*One, Three, Many*, 163n10).

[25] *Denz* 301, 302.

cosmic significance. Christ provides a focal point for this participation, to be sure; but the significance of the incarnation is precisely its revelation of a more intimate relationship between God and human beings than was ordinarily thought possible.

In the New Testament, the word that most commonly signals the potential intimacy between God and the world is κοινωνία (*koinōnia*). This word implies an intensely close relationship; in Greek literature, it was often used to refer to marriage, since this was understood to be among the most profound and intimate connections between human beings.[26] In the New Testament, some of its most common English translations include "fellowship," "communion," and "participation." It can even invoke the idea of a *mutual* participation between God and human beings – even though this relationship remains, at some level, asymmetrical (since our participation in the life of God is possible only because God first chose to participate in us).

In 1 Corinthians 1:9, Paul claims that God has called us "into fellowship" (εἰς κοινωνίαν) with Christ. Some commentators have suggested that the "fellowship" here described is a merely collection of human beings, and that Christ's role is simply as the one *through whom* we are called into this association.[27] But elsewhere Paul is not hesitant to suggest a mutual indwelling of Christ and human beings; in Philippians 3:10 he speaks of "participating in Christ's sufferings" (κοινωνίαν παθημάτων αὐτοῦ). A similar passage is found at 2 Corinthians 13:13, where Paul speaks of the "grace of our Lord Jesus Christ, the love of God, and the fellowship [κοινωνία] of the Holy Spirit." At first glance, these seem to be mere attributes, distributed among the Three; but given that Paul requests that these gifts might "be with" those to whom he is writing, we need not understand them as applicable only to God. Rather, they flow from God to human beings, and thereby draw us back up into the life of God. Grace makes possible our faith, and God's love for us makes possible our love of God. Similarly, God's internal triune fellowship grounds the mutual participation between God and humanity.

The mutual participation of God and human beings is further emphasized by the extension of πατήρ-υἱός language such that it applies not merely to Christ's relationship to God, but to *our* relationship with God as well. Jesus

---

[26] William F. Arndt and F. Wilbur Gingrich, eds., *A Greek-English Lexicon of the New Testament and Other Early Christian Literature*, 2nd edn (Chicago and London: University of Chicago Press, 1979), s.v. *κοινωνία*.

[27] This tendency among some New Testament scholars is noted by Justo L. González, *Faith and Wealth: A History of Early Christian Ideas on the Origin, Significance, and Use of Money* (San Francisco: Harper and Row, 1990), 82–3.

urges his disciples to pray to God as πατήρ, and various human beings are called "children of God."[28] Paul is especially fond of this language, using the image of *adoption* to make this connection – and thereby implying a close relationship between Christ (as the prototypical child of God) and those who have "become" children of God (Rom. 8:15, 8:23, 9:4; Gal. 4:5; Eph. 1:5).

Finally, I would once again emphasize the role of the eucharist as especially valuable in helping us to understand the mutual participation between human beings and God. Especially in those traditions that speak of a "real presence" of Christ in the elements, we are presented with the image of a body inhabiting the body of the other; we take Christ's body into ours and in this act become the Body of Christ. The eucharist has thus been important for a wide variety of mystical theologians, who have used the language of "inhabitation" to describe both God's presence in us and ours in God.[29] God is "our dwelling place" (Ps. 90), but we also speak of "inviting God into" our hearts and souls, and of our bodies as "a temple of the Holy Spirit" (1 Cor. 3:16, 6:19). Many eucharistic rites make use of this language of mutual participation; here, we pray that through our participation in the body and the blood, God may evermore dwell in us, and we in God.

Participating in one another

The trinitarian virtue of participation also marks, or can come to mark, the relationships among human beings. Created in the image of God, we participate in one another's lives to a much greater degree than the modern obsession with individualism would ever admit. The Romanian Orthodox theologian Dumitru Staniloae comments that:

> The responsibility that one believer feels for another, the prayer that is offered on behalf of another, represent imperfect degrees of this permanent and reciprocal substitution of the divine persons, imperfect degrees of a permanent identification that is able nevertheless to respect and maintain separate identities.[30]

[28] E.g., peacemakers (Matt. 5:9); the resurrected dead (Luke 20:36); all who received the true Light (John 1:12); all who are led by the Spirit (Rom. 8:14-21); all who believe in Christ (Gal. 3:26); all who receive the love of God (1 John 3:1); those who conquer (Rev. 21:7).

[29] A specifically eucharistic analogy is developed in the writings of Mother Julian of Norwich; in the case of St Teresa of Avila, a broader portrait of "inhabitation" suffuses her descriptions in *The Interior Castle*.

[30] Staniloae, "Holy Trinity," 78, trans. slightly altered.

Staniloae will even speak of human beings as bearing a "consubstantiality" with one another that reflects, however dimly, the claim that the Three are "of the same substance" with one another.[31]

This claim is underscored in the New Testament, and again the word κοινωνία plays a key role. For example, in Acts 2:42, we are told that the members of the Jesus movement "devoted themselves to the apostles' teaching and fellowship (κοινωνία), to the breaking of bread and the prayers." As already observed, the word *fellowship* may be inadequate here, as its current usage tends to allow for a rather disengaged relationship. It is often used of people who get together merely because they share a common interest; it can also simply denote shared feelings, or companionship.[32] But the context in Acts suggests that the earliest Christians experienced a rather more intense level of involvement in one another's lives, in at least two senses.

First, they "broke bread" together: they shared meals. This may refer to an early form of the eucharist; it can be usefully juxtaposed to Paul's account in 1 Corinthians, where he uses the word κοινωνία to describe the event: "The cup of blessing which we bless, is it not a participation in the blood of Christ? The bread which we break, is it not a participation in the body of Christ?" (1 Cor. 10:16, RSV). On the other hand, the passage in Acts may refer to a more general form of table-fellowship (sometimes called an "agapē meal"). In either case, the earliest Christians engaged in the practice of sitting down together at a common table. It is something of a commonplace in studies of the ancient world to note that table-fellowship was a very important matter; the willingness to eat with others signified a certain degree of acceptance of that person. Thus Jesus was condemned for eating with tax-collectors and sinners (Matt. 9:11 // Luke 5:30; Mark 2:16), and the New Testament often uses the language of table-fellowship to denote a willingness to participate in the lives of others (e.g. Acts 10–11).

This practice continues to be important in many cultures today, and at least to some extent in our own. We commonly share meals with those with whom we live and work – those "others" in whose lives we most fully participate. The activities that surround a meal – procuring and preparing food, setting the table, nourishing our bodies, engaging in conversation, and cleaning up – involve us in one another's lives in various ways. For example, we must take account of the various dietary restrictions (physical, psychological, or moral) and the aesthetic and gustatory preferences that each person brings to the table. This may mean giving up certain foods (or giving up certain restrictions), at

---

[31] Ibid., 82.
[32] González, *Faith and Wealth*, 82–3.

least temporarily, in order to share a truly "common" meal. Common meals – good ones, at any rate – require patient listening practices, careful discernment of the needs of others, and the observance of certain culturally-encoded rituals ("table manners"). None of this is possible unless we are willing to participate in some significant ways in the lives of those with whom we "sit at table."

Returning now to the passage in Acts 2: there is a second element that makes this description of κοινωνία a more intense affair than is normally associated with the modern English word *fellowship*. As the context of the passage makes clear, the followers of Jesus shared a common economic life. This seems to be a very important test of *participation* among human beings: are they willing to give up the idea of *possession*? We know how difficult this can be even within the realm of family life. (To student couples who asked whether it was ethically acceptable for them to live together out of wedlock, Stanley Hauerwas used to reply – probably only half-jokingly – that it was fine, as long as they had a joint checking account.) Whatever platitudinous remarks we may make to one another about the importance of our life together, we have not really indicated a willingness to *participate* in one another's lives until we do so in the regions that are most important to us. Many of us are, in this respect, very much like the rich young man to whom Jesus spoke; we have great possessions. That man "went away grieving," for he could not imagine living as the apostles did: "All who believed were together and had all things in common; they would sell their possessions and goods and distribute the proceeds to all, as any had need" (Acts 2:44–5).

Scholars are divided as to the precise form that this practice took, and how widespread it might have been;[33] but my point does not depend upon these precisions. I want to emphasize how very different *any* kind of economic sharing is from our common economic practices today (with a few exceptions, such as religious orders and other intentional Christian communities). About the closest that most of us come to this kind of life is our willingness to give money to the Church – an activity that, though certainly praiseworthy, cannot truly exemplify the trinitarian virtue of *participation*. We "give" money, meaning that we transfer a certain sum out of our own (individual) account and into the (individual) account of the parish. It is simply a business transaction, in which money always "belongs" to someone; the title of ownership is merely changed. Thus, we do not allow the idea of *participation* to critique our culturally-normed assumptions about possession and property. What we miss, in the process, in any sense in which a common economic life

---

[33] For a useful discussion, see González, *Faith and Wealth*, 79–86.

might actually come to draw us more deeply into a life more profoundly marked by mutual participation.[34]

But the passage in Acts does hold out to us the possibility of such participation, even if it is rarely practiced today. The community that undertakes to share its meals and its money, as well as less tangible goods (e.g., its processes of education), is a community in which real "participation" is possible. We are called into such participation within the Christian community because of that community's bond with Christ. As Douglas Meeks notes in his study of theology and economics, "Having a share in Jesus Christ means 'giving a share' in the household of life."[35] And we might trace this back one step further: we are called into an intimate bond and mutual participation with Christ by the mutual participation that always already characterizes the very being of God.[36]

Thus, on three levels – within the life of God, between God and human beings, and among human beings – participation is an essential feature of Christian life and thought. We gain our clearest understanding of this profound mutual participation through the revelation of God in Christ, and we embody it through practices such as the eucharist, table-fellowship, and economic life. But this trinitarian virtue can also be recognized in other elements of the created order; and in the remainder of this chapter, I offer construals of its role in the process of human communication and in human relationships. These comments represent a further instance of the practice of parallelling, as outlined in chapter 3; they thus seek to render trinitarian doctrine more intelligible, more relevant, and more persuasive.

Participation in Theory, Practice, and Malpractice

This section begins with an exploration of the theoretical analysis of human communication in the work of Francis Jacques. I then turn to one of the novels of Iris Murdoch, which will provide a concrete example of both the practice and the malpractice of participation – illustrating not only the positive role that it can play, but also the disastrous effects that result when human relationships *fail* to embody this particular trinitarian virtue.

[34] For some interesting reflections on this possibility, see Stephen E. Fowl, "Making Stealing Possible: Criminal Reflections on Building an Ecclesial Common Life," *Perspectives* (September 1993): 12–16.

[35] Meeks, *God the Economist*, 207n34.

[36] Meeks explores the specifically trinitarian warrants for the reshaping of economic life throughout *God the Economist*. See also Ackva, *Dreieinen Gott*.

Human communication

In his fascinating study *Difference and Subjectivity*, Francis Jacques offers a postmodern account of human personhood. He observes that the notion of subjectivity that we inherited from the Enlightenment – one that is focused on thinking alone, as exemplified in Descartes and Kant – is being replaced with theories that focus on the subject's ability to speak and to communicate. He approves of this development, but fears that the legacy of Descartes and Kant is so strong that the process of communication will continue to be understood as a transparent transference of the subject's *intention* into particular linguistic forms that "contain" meaning. Jacques calls this "a highly improbable doctrine, according to which the subject of the utterance is seen as the master of meaning and pertinence."[37]

In contrast to this view, Jacques offers what he believes to be a more complete account of the process of communication. The utterance is not really the "property" of the speaker or writer, but is "just as much the activity performed by the person who listens. . . . The utterance is then a joint discourse-creating activity in which speaker and listener are the terms of a real-time relationship."[38] Jacques goes on to consider the implications of this understanding of communication and meaning for our description of human personhood. "What happens to the philosophical status of the person if we replace the individual's *cogito* with the proposition 'I speak, but *we* say'? . . . At the very least, we are led to a different view of the discourse-producing agency, taking account of the fact that speaker and spoken-to are from the first only defined as such in relation to each other."[39]

I discussed this approach to the production of meaning briefly in chapters 2 and 3. In my comments on revelation, I suggested that God speaks, but "what is said" (that is, the content of communication) involves active participation, *both* by the one who speaks *and* by the one to whom something is spoken. Jacques's study reinforces this point, and makes a number of additional observations that will be useful in developing the trinitarian virtue of participation. For example, he examines the role of another node in the communicative network – someone who "participates" in the process, even while remaining largely absent from view.

Jacques observes that, if someone is *spoken of*, yet excluded from the actual interplay of speaker and listener, a "third person" appears: *she* or *he*. Thus, the

---

[37] Jacques, *Difference and Subjectivity*, 4.
[38] Ibid., 7.
[39] Ibid., 9, emphasis added.

three grammatical "persons" are not arbitrary; they are the three possible relationships that can be found within discourse.

> I, you, and he/she are the three positional values in any communication act. They are not inventions of grammar. In one form or another, ... an oppositional structure between *I* and *you* on the one hand, and that "personality correlation" with *he/she* on the other, exists in every language. It imposes its mark on all communication, and as a result it plays a constitutive role in the concept of person.[40]

Jacques then goes on to speak of the "mutual dependency" among these three. Martin Buber argued that the human being can only become an "I" through a contact with "you"; Jacques argues that this is a necessary condition, but not a sufficient one. "A person only becomes someone, an *I*, under the extra test of what we may call the *he/she*: the other not as an allocuted *you*, but as a *him* or *her*."[41] Jacques is not talking about the wholly negative notion of an I–It relationship, which Buber (and others, like Emmanuel Lévinas) urge us to avoid. For Jacques, the third person is not necessarily a "non-person," but is a person who, though technically absent, is *made present* by the use of grammatical third-person forms. So "she" or "he" is always only *relatively* absent; the whole point of referring to the absent person, using third-person pronouns, is to render this "absent other" into presence – and to emphasize that this person may have been (and may well again be) more directly involved in acts of communication (as an "I" or a "you").[42] Jacques stresses that the third person is not simply an "optional extra" in the realm of human discourse; even if not mentioned explicitly, the "other" must exist to make human communication meaningful. In order to define those to whom discourse is directed ("you"), we must be able to define those to whom it is *not* directed – the third person, she/he/they.[43]

---

[40] Ibid., 31, emphasis added.

[41] Ibid., 34.

[42] The invocation of the third person bears certain family resemblances to the rhetorical technique of "presencing": bringing to the forefront – of a conversation or argument – something that is not elaborated in detail, but that an audience can reasonably be expected to recognize and understand. See Chaïm Perelman and Lucie Olbrechts-Tyteca, *The New Rhetoric: A Treatise on Argumentation*, trans. John Wilkinson and Purcell Weaver (Notre Dame, Ind.: University of Notre Dame Press, 1969) [ET of: *La Nouvelle Rhétorique: Traité de l'Argumentation* (Paris: Presses Universitaires de France, 1958)], 115–20.

[43] For additional reflections on the trinitarian implications of the personal pronouns, see Staniloae, "Holy Trinity," 82–3, 95–6, and *passim*.

Jacques's analysis reinforces the description, in chapter 3, of the process of rhetorical invention as a *vestigium trinitatis* (though he develops the analogy somewhat differently). Indeed, Jacques is very interested in the connections between the doctrine of the Trinity and human communication; he believes that one can construct a normative model of *human* personhood on the model of the threefold divine personhood that trinitarian theology describes. He examines, for example, Thomas's relational account of the Three; but he also notes that Thomas does not provide a similarly relational account of *human* persons.[44] Jacques finds this somewhat surprising; in his view, the process of human communication is a reflection of God's Triunity in the midst of the created order:

> In my opinion, the personal identity of communicating persons is the most beautiful mirror of the Trinity. . . . The identity of human persons is revealed by the fact that they are able to differentiate themselves from the other persons in the relation in which they are involved, while still remaining each other's equals. . . . Each new communicational commitment partially composes, decomposes, and recomposes the concept of self.[45]

This continuous process of the composition, decomposition, and recomposition of the self is what I am trying to invoke with the category of *participation*. We are not isolated entities; we exist as "persons" only insofar as we participate in others, and they in us, to such a degree that the construal of the "self" is constantly being broken down, and reconstituted anew, in the intimacy of this mutual participation.

Jacques's analysis of human communication allows him to understand something about the doctrine of the Trinity that a good many theologians have missed – namely, that God is not three "persons in relation." Rather, God is pure mutual participation: relation without remainder.

> The Trinity founds within the divine Being itself nothing less than the relation by which persons are constituted. Metaphysically, how can this be? I shall go so far as to say that God *is* relationally. God is the One who is, the One who

---

[44] Jacques, *Difference and Subjectivity*, 66. My own reading of Thomas would tend to confirm this judgment. For human persons, Thomas seems wholly satisfied with the definition offered by Boethius – "an individual substance with rational nature" (*ST* Ia.29.1, trans. Velecky, VI:41). Thus, his potentially revolutionary description of divine personhood does not get transferred, even as a *desideratum*, to human personhood. "It is one thing to look for the meaning of 'person' in general and another to look for that of 'divine person'" (*ST* Ia. 29.4, trans. Velecky, VI:59).

[45] Jacques, *Difference and Subjectivity*, 68–9.

makes relations possible, because God is a relation. It is the Word that makes us human beings because that primary relation is constitutive of the Word. The doctrine of the Trinity casts a disturbing light on depths that human reason finds it difficult to penetrate.[46]

Even though Jacques is not writing as a Christian theologian, this seems to me a remarkably perceptive account of the mutually participative life of the triune God, and of our lives as created in the image and likeness of God.

The practice and malpractice of participation

I have preferred the language of *participation* over that of *relation* because, while it is certainly possible for human relations to mirror the absolute relationality of the triune God, such language frequently drifts away from this goal. In our own lives, relationships are often trivialized; we often enter into them, and leave them, without much consideration. This tendency, due in part to the hyperindividualism of our culture, displays its symptoms everywhere: from the easy abandonment of spouses and children to the amazing popularity of drive-through restaurants. Great or small, these symptoms remind us that "relationships" have become for us an accidental enterprise: we have them when we want to, and we avoid them when we (think that we) need to.

In order to illustrate more clearly why our relations ought to be marked by the trinitarian virtue of *participation*, I turn to a novel by Iris Murdoch entitled *The Time of the Angels*.[47] The characters in this novel are clearly "in relation" with one another, but this doesn't seem to help; they still understand themselves as fundamentally isolated and autonomous agents. They enter into relationships for their convenience; thus, these relationships are never really constitutive of who they are. Yet at the same time, the novel also offers an alternative: a very subtle image of complete mutual participation, which provides a silent but steady critique of the various characters' easy acceptance of the utter disposability of their own relationships. Murdoch thus provides us with a useful comparison of the "practice and malpractice" of participation – that is, a comparison between relationships that are formed by this virtue, and those that are not.

The novel is set in a rectory in South London. Significantly, the church building to which it was once attached no longer exists; it was bombed out in the Blitz, and all that remains is the bell tower. The rector, Carel Fisher, was

---

[46]   Ibid., 69.
[47]   Iris Murdoch, *The Time of the Angels* (1966; reprint, Harmondsworth: Penguin Books, 1968). Some of these reflections appear in a different form in "Trinitarian Rhetoric."

installed in this sinecure because it seemed a relatively safe place for him. (He had been behaving in an increasingly eccentric manner, scandalizing his parishioners with his atheistic cosmological speculations.) He spends most of his time in his darkened study, and has instructed the housekeeper – a woman of mixed Irish and Jamaican descent, named Pattie – to turn away all visitors. The rectory, usually enveloped in a dense fog, soon takes on the aura of a fortress: isolated, self-sufficient, impregnable. The rectory's other inhabitants include Carel's daughter Muriel, her invalid cousin Elizabeth, the porter Eugene Peshkov (a refugee from Russia), and Eugene's son Leo (a self-styled anarchist). These six characters are clearly "in relation" with one another – they have to be. The rectory's isolation, together with Carel's general suspicion of the outside world, leave them little choice.

We soon learn that Carel has taken Pattie as his lover – indeed, that he had done so even before the death of his wife – and that she has submitted herself to his control in a thoroughly pathological way. She is thus the target of scorn from Muriel, who blames her for the death of her mother and for her rotting relationship with her father, whom she now fears. Muriel sees him rarely; their conversations are businesslike, almost contractual. Her real interest is in her cousin Elizabeth (a flashback suggests early romantic desire). The two women spend most of their time together – reading Greek poetry, doing jigsaw puzzles, and smoking cigars. Muriel has become something of a full-time nurse to Elizabeth, whose ailment, never precisely specified, is severe enough to confine her to her room. This is a source of constant anxiety to her legal guardian, Marcus (one of the few characters in the book who lives outside the rectory). Marcus is Carel's brother, and is concerned about the latter's obvious isolation and eccentricity. But his real enthusiasm is for Leo, to whom he would like to impart the wisdom of the ages (though a more-than-merely-intellectual interest is also suggested).

Leo seeks Muriel's affections, but she instead pursues Leo's father, Eugene; he finds her advances incomprehensible and keeps her at a great distance. Instead, he becomes involved in a romantic relationship with Pattie (one of the few potentially positive relationships in the novel). But Muriel, jealous and angry for having been romantically displaced by (of all people) her archenemy, destroys their affair by telling Eugene about Pattie's former relationship with her father. Meanwhile, Leo – having been rejected by Muriel – develops a fascination for the inaccessible Elizabeth. Muriel takes him to a closet so that they can observe her through a crack in the wall. But when she looks into the room, she sees Elizabeth in bed with – Carel. In her haste to usher Leo out of the linen closet, Muriel trips over him and they fall to the floor of the closet entangled in an embrace – just as the door is opened by Marcus, with Pattie at his shoulder. And as though Carel's incestuous relationship with his niece were not bad enough, Muriel soon discovers that Elizabeth is not actually her cousin at all, but her half-sister – which is to say, she is actually Carel's *daughter*.

In short, the characters in the novel are involved in an intricate web of relationships – some good, most bad, and none taken very seriously. They fall into and out of love with one another with some regularity, and exhibit a voyeuristic interest in the exchanges among others. Many of their relationships are dominating and abusive. The characters' problem is not that they lack relationships; indeed, none of them sees him- or herself as a wholly isolated individual. Nevertheless, their relationships are ultimately destructive.

The novel thus reminds us how morally empty is all talk of "relationality." Relations are not necessarily a good; they need to be given some concrete content. And my description of the novel thus far doesn't offer much in that regard; indeed, one would have to have some sympathy with the flummoxed reviewer who could only manage to describe the plot of this novel as one in which "Marcus loves Leo, who loves Muriel, who loves Eugene, who loves Pattie, who loves Carel, who loves Elizabeth."[48] What most critics did not notice, however, was that the novel also offers, in a very subtle way, a point of severe contrast to the relationships-of-convenience among the human characters. Its subtlety is due to the fact that it is not a human character at all, but rather an *icon*.

And not just any icon: it is a copy of Rublev's fifteenth-century masterpiece, "The Holy Trinity." It depicts the three messengers of God, visiting Abraham and enjoying a bit of table-fellowship by the oaks of Mamre. In the text of Genesis 18, these three are also identified as "the Lord"; this passage thus became, for many Christian interpreters, a reference to the Trinity. In the novel, the icon comes into contact with almost all the people in the story, and in doing so, reveals the true character of their relationships. Consider, for a moment, a retelling of the story from the point of view of the icon itself.

The icon is owned by Eugene. Early in the story, it is stolen and pawned by Eugene's son, Leo. But it is of such value to Eugene that Muriel, the Rector's daughter, tries to convince Leo that he should recover it. It is purchased from the pawn shop by Marcus, and it provides him with an excuse to enter the often-barricaded rectory. But before it can reach its intended recipient, both the icon and its bearer are intercepted by Carel; the icon is thus present during the novel's most sustained discussion of the nature and existence of God. At the end of that discussion, Marcus is too mesmerized to

---

[48] Anastasia Leech, review of *The Time of the Angels*, in *The Tablet* (September 24, 1966): 1074.

retrieve the icon, so it remains in the study. It is taken from the study by
Muriel, who hopes that she will win Eugene's affections by returning it to him.
But Muriel is intercepted by Leo, who announces that he is in love with her.
The icon is placed on a side-table, while Muriel dispatches Leo. There it is
discovered by Pattie, who returns it to Eugene.

Of course, *The Time of the Angels* is not told from the point of view of
Rublev's masterpiece. Most critics assumed that the icon was nothing more
than an archaic item of religious devotion – the equivalent of an unused rosary,
or a relic which is known to be fabricated. The critics, like the iconoclasts of
Christian history, failed to treat the icon *as an icon*: they saw its surface, but
were unable to look "through" it to the reality beyond. Murdoch set them up
for it, of course, by having one character describe the icon as "three angels
confabulating around a table." Its role thus seemed primarily illustrative – of
the book's title and of the Rector's cosmology, in which "the death of God
has set the angels free. And they are terrible."[49]

About the best the critics managed was to see the icon as a symbol for God,
both graphically and metaphorically, and thus to understand its haphazard
sojourn as an indicator of God's low cultural status. But this assumed that the
icon simply represented God *in the abstract*, rather than in the concrete
specificity of God's Triunity. For the reader who reads with trinitarian
convictions, the icon becomes the central focus: not simply a scrap of wood
being casually tossed about, but rather the only fixed point of reference in the
story. It brings to presence pure mutual participation, willing donation,
unbounded agapic love – everything that the novel's human characters lack.
It thus reveals the isolation of the characters – and their trivializing approach
to relationships – by the ways that they treat it, describe it, and relate to it.

For example, the icon highlights Carel Fisher's inner conflict about the
nature of God. He has come to believe that the philosophers were wrong in
affirming that the Good is "one, single, and unitary." In conversation with his
brother, he argues that "There is only power and the marvel of power, there
is only chance and the terror of chance. And if there is only this there is no
God, and the single Good of the philosophers is an illusion and a fake."[50] But
his only alternative to unity is chaotic multiplicity, which he believes to be the
essence of evil.

There are principalities and powers. Angels are the thoughts of God. Now he
has been dissolved into his thoughts which are beyond our conceptions in their

[49] Murdoch, *The Time of the Angels*, 173.
[50] Ibid., 172.

nature and their multiplicity and their power. God was at least the name of something we thought was good. Now even the name has gone and the spiritual world is scattered. There is nothing any more to prevent the magnetism of many spirits.[51]

These are the only choices for Carel: either the unity of the Good (which seems impossible in the light of the evil of the world), or the multiplicity of many spirits (the terrible angels who pull us into the void). Interestingly, however, when he sees the icon, Carel is stopped for a moment by its power. He first murmurs a single word which has been used throughout the novel to emphasize power: the word *tall*. Then he speculates: "They would be so tall." When Marcus points out that the icon represents the Trinity, Carel is yanked back into his version of reality. He quickly dismisses both his brother and the doctrine of the Trinity with the assurance of a logician: "How can those three be one? As I told you. Please go now, Marcus."[52]

Throughout the novel, the icon points to the quiet desperation of the characters, because it embodies what they all lack: peaceful, non-contrastive difference, perfect harmony, pure mutual participation. Many art historians and theologians have commented on the success of Rublev's effort. One sample: "Similarity and difference, rest and movement, youth and maturity, joy and compassion, restraint and pity, eternity and history, these all come together. There is no separation or confusion or subordination of the Persons."[53]

But the icon of the Trinity is not simply a glimpse of the inner life of God. If we are to take seriously the claim that we are created in the image of God, then this icon must also be a portrait of humanity, or at least, of humanity's proper destiny. Rublev's

image of the divine Trinity rules out all egotism – whether individual or collective – all life-destroying separation, any subordination or leveling of persons. It invites all humanity to make this world a permanent eucharist of love, a feast of life. Created in God's image (Gen. 1:26), humanity is called to live in the image of the divine life and to share its daily bread together.[54]

[51] Ibid., 173.
[52] Ibid., 176.
[53] Dan-Ilie Ciobotea and William H. Lazareth, "The Triune God: The Supreme Source of Life. Thoughts Inspired by Rublev's Icon of the Trinity," in *Icons: Windows on Eternity: Theology and Spirituality in Colour*, ed. Gennadios Limouris (Geneva: WCC Publications, 1990), 202–3.
[54] Ibid., 203.

This powerful description of the icon trades heavily on the Christian image of the eucharist – which, as I have suggested, is a centrally determinative practice for the trinitarian virtue of participation. In stark contrast, the characters that inhabit the novel practice a sort of anti-eucharist: they all live in separate rooms somewhere in the darkened rectory; they often even eat their meals there, alone; the walls that divide them become a towering symbol of isolation.

The characters of the story are ultimately still isolated individuals, even in the midst of their relationships. Such is life in the modern world, and most critics have read *The Time of the Angels* as symptomatic of post-enlightenment individualism. But the icon clearly offers another possibility, drawing our attention to the mutual participation and communion that is manifested by the triune God. Interestingly, however, the icon does not present what some might consider to be the only real alternative to isolationism – that is, it does not portray a homogeneous uniformity in which all distinctions are ultimately meaningless. Instead, the icon is able to offer the possibility of true mutual participation which somehow does not allow the Three to be eclipsed by the One, but calls us to rejoice in the communion of their perfect and glorious particularity.

Chapter 6

PARTICULARITY

I suspect that some readers may, at this juncture, be a bit nervous about the general direction of my project. The previous two chapters have been consistently critical of individualism; they advocated musical consensus and mutual participation. But even if one acknowledges the importance of these trinitarian virtues, one may still worry that they are not sufficiently attentive to difference – that they allow no space for "the particular," for the obvious distinctions between human beings. Doesn't Christianity create a space for particularity through its description of a God who, although One, is also Three? And are not human persons ultimately distinct from one another, at least in their bodily existence? Must we not allow for a region of *difference*?

The answer to these questions must be a firm "yes and no." Before unpacking that resolutely contradictory claim, I want to emphasize that the previous two chapters should not be construed as minimizing particularity and difference. Indeed, I often described polyphony as a *difference* that is not contrastive, not exclusionary. And while the chapter on participation clearly emphasized the importance of dwelling in, and being indwelt by, the lives of others, it did (after all) still speak of *others*. In other words, in my own practice of trinitarian theology, I have already created a space for "difference."

And yet, our culture is so focused on the individual, and on the creation of distinction, that I have felt it necessary to begin with the more "communal" and "mutual" virtues of polyphony and participation, before turning to what differentiates us. In the modern age, especially, it seems relatively easy to take note of the distinguishing features that set human beings apart from one another (and sometimes against one another); it is rather more difficult to recognize that we are bound together in harmonious and mutually participative ways. Too strong an accent on difference may serve only to condone our hyperindividualism; hence, this chapter is the last of the three. Moreover, the claims of the previous two chapters will also pervade this one: the particularity described here implicates, and is implicated by, the musical consensus of polyphony and the mutual indwelling of participation.

Divine particularity is manifested in a number of different ways: in the fact that the Three are not simply identical to each other; in the specificity of the narratives of יהוה, Christ, and the Spirit; and in our appropriation of the external acts of God to each of the Three in different ways. These basic elements of trinitarian doctrine provide some initial pointers toward particularity as a trinitarian virtue. Nevertheless, in order to keep this notion of particularity from collapsing into a simple individualism, we will need to revise certain dominant assumptions about its constitution; this will be the focus of the first section of this chapter. I will then describe how this particularity marks the triune God; finally, in the last section, I will suggest how it can come to mark the lives of human beings.

Rethinking the Particular

Ordinarily, we understand "the particular" as specifying the distinctiveness of a thing, group, or category; it is thus the opposite of "the general" or "the universal." In the realm of trinitarian discourse, it is often applied to the Three, who have been variously called persons, hypostases, identities, or modes of existence. Whatever nuances of meaning these terms may evoke, they all attempt to designate something that is real and relational, something that can "be" and "act"; such entities are rightly described as "particulars." On the other hand, the oneness of God requires that these terms not be interpreted in a radically individualistic sense; the abilities of these particulars to "be" and to "act" cannot operate in a state of supreme isolation, without the participation and agreement of others. Unfortunately, the word *particularity* sometimes evokes precisely this individualistic shade of meaning; it suggests that which *separates* one entity from another, that which seeks to prevent its freedom from being obstructed by another. It evokes the notions of distinction, separation, exclusion, and even isolation. Under the entry *particularity*, one thesaurus offers a general heading of "the quality of being individual," and goes on to list the following synonyms: individuality, separateness, singularity, discreteness, distinctiveness.[1]

And yet the doctrine of the Trinity is ultimately about none of those things. Nor are Christians called into isolation, separateness, or singularity. Indeed, given the modern inheritance of the word *particularity*, my use of this word to

---

[1] *The American Heritage Electronic Dictionary* (Houghton Mifflin, 1991), s.v. *particularity*.

name a "trinitarian virtue" may be considered not altogether felicitous. Nevertheless, whatever word is chosen will require significant redefinition; accomplishing this process is the goal of the present section. I want to develop a conception of particularity that is radically anti-individualistic, and that thereby enables us to critique the modern celebration of separation and autonomy – even while it provides a space for difference. Because God is Three, particularity is necessarily a trinitarian virtue; and yet, because God is also One, we are called to construe this particularity in an anti-individualistic way.

Particularity without individuals

Personal identity is communally constituted. Although I may speak of "my identity," it is not really "mine" in the way that we usually intend this language; it is not something which we "own," something over which we have complete control. Our identities are profoundly shaped by our encounters with *others* – others with whom we have come into contact over the course of our lives. Thus, it is misleading to couple particularity with "individuality," as though we were our own creators, shaping our lives in splendid isolation. Our particular existence is something we have *as a result of* our participation in a diverse world, not "in spite of" that participation.[2]

A useful illustration of this process has been offered by Alistair McFadyen, who describes personal identity as "sedimented" from previous "acts of communication" (which he defines, quite broadly, as actions "in which there is change and exchange and in which information is transformed and transferred").[3] The metaphor of "sedimentation" helps us recognize that our identities are something that, in some sense, happen *to* us; others are highly involved in this process, even though it results in a particular "person" who can be identified and thus distinguished from others.

The metaphor of "sedimentation" might become even more useful if we were to give it a more precise description than does McFadyen. It could be taken in at least two different ways, depending upon whether one thinks of "sediment" as something that creates layers of solid rock, or something that creates the rather less "fixed" surface at the bottom of a river. In the first case, the image tends to evoke an excessively static description of personhood – a slow, relentless, "geological" process, in which our lives are permanently

---

[2] Colin Gunton makes a similar claim in *The One, The Three, and the Many*, 194.

[3] Alistair I. McFadyen, *The Call to Personhood: A Christian Theory of the Individual in Social Relationships* (New York: Cambridge University Press, 1990), 26–8; 313.

determined by forces beyond our control. But in the second case, the metaphor becomes quite appropriate, signifying a dynamic process that always allows for the decomposition and recomposition of previous "sediments." A riverbed has its own particular shape, form, and composition; but its "particularity" is shaped, formed, and composed only through an encounter with others (with the river, and especially with certain elements carried along by the river).[4]

We are thus "particular" persons, but only because of our location in a network of encounters and relationships. As McFadyen puts it, personal identity

> is not something purely private, for it has been derived from the history of relations which has taken place around this particular social location and in which this person has participated as subject. It is through the person's own participation in and interpretation of this history or interaction that it takes a particular character, becomes centred on the person in a particular way and builds up an idiosyncratic identity.[5]

One's "personal identity" is thus bound up much more intimately with the lives of others than it first appears to be.

Indeed, even the most "distinctive" elements of human existence are the products of our communication with others. Consider, for example, our particular *bodies*:[6] the obvious fact of human embodiment can easily make all claims about mutual participation seem counterintuitive. How can we really dwell in, and by indwelt by, other persons, when we are so obviously and physically "separated" from them? Yet our bodies, too, are the products of human communication. They come into being as a result of physical, organic interactions, and they learn to behave in certain ways according to our encounters with others. We even take on certain physical marks as a result of these interactions. As McFadyen notes, there can be "no strict separation between the physical and the social dimensions of life":

> The body is essentially communication, rather than the stationary fencing closing off an asocial personal identity. It is engaged in dynamic processes of exchange and cannot therefore be a static substance. . . . Similarly, there is no static organ of identity (e.g. self or soul) made up of some other kind of substance

---

[4] Thanks to Bill Cavanaugh and Phil Kenneson for conversations on some of the rhetorical effects of the word *sediment*.

[5] McFadyen, *The Call to Personhood*, 317.

[6] I draw this example from the commentary in McFadyen, *The Call to Personhood*, 86–90.

over and above the body. Personal identity is a sedimented history of response, that which endures through time; it is not a static substance but an entire historical corpus of response which includes the body, for it is only as a body that such a history has taken place.[7]

This is an excellent reminder of the ways that "our selves, our souls and bodies" are interwoven with, and indeed constituted by, our communication with others.[8]

At this point, one might justifiably ask whether there is any point in speaking about "the particular" at all. If our identities, and even our bodies, are not really our "own" in any private sense, perhaps we can only speak meaningfully of the group, the community, or the world. Here again, though, the process of human communication is a key reminder of the importance of the particular. Even though our identities are constituted by others, we still need to be able to focus on the "object" that is communally constituted; minimally, we need to account for the various roles this object plays in the process of communication. "Particular" human beings, though their identities are shaped only in their encounter with others, must still function variously as the source, the destination, or the subject-matter of human communication. They speak and write; they listen and read; they are spoken about or written about. The shape of our "sedimented identities" may be constantly in the process of recomposition, churning about like the sand at the bottom of a river; but all the while we continue to be involved in acts of human communication. We need to be able to pick out these "sedimented identities," from the thousands of interdependent objects and events that surround us, in order to be able to *talk* about them; moreover, this process of identification needs to be repeatable, in order to establish continuities among our acts of communication.[9] Thus, even if we are rightly dubious about the notion of an "isolated individual," we still need the concept of the particular – because these "particulars" are the subjects, objects, and destinations of the process of communication.

As we have already noted, human communication is a fluctuating and highly unstable process, in which various actions are always being displaced

[7] Ibid., 89.

[8] Much more could be said here, of course – especially with respect to theological notions such as "the resurrection of the body" and "the Body of Christ." Some initial reflections appear in my comments on the eucharist in chapter 5, and my discussion of "body matters" in chapter 8.

[9] These aspects of personal identity are noted, with attention to their trinitarian application, in Jenson, *The Triune Identity*, 108–10.

by new events. A person speaks, and so for a moment is an "I," an agent of communication; but soon afterwards, that person listens to another, and becomes the destination of communication, a "you." At another time, or even at the same time, the same person may be spoken *about* by others, and thus become a "he" or "she" (or perhaps part of a "they"). As we noted in the previous chapter, the personal pronouns are not references to static entities; rather, they describe communicative relations. McFadyen makes a similar point: "Personal pronouns function to identify 'where' speech, for example, is coming from. . . . Personal pronouns mark the contribution and engagement of people in a particular network of communication."[10]

The difficulty, of course, is that this is not how we commonly think of the personal pronouns; they are more typically understood to be *individuating* devices, descriptions of distinctions which separate us from the rest of the world. Consider, for example, Descartes's use of the word *ego* (a personal pronoun, after all); here "I" becomes something that is radically isolated from the rest of the world, seemingly detached from its particular place in the communicative network. For Descartes, and for the philosophical tradition that followed him (and in which we are still very much ensconced), the rhetorical nature of the personal pronoun is lost, as the *ego* seems to become a "thinking thing" whose very activity is thought to be the foundation of its own existence.

Thus, the personal pronouns have tended to lead theologians away from the kind of anti-individualistic particularity that I am attempting to develop here. Consider Colin Gunton's protest against the claim that we are all inextricably connected to one another: "What is wrong," he asks, "with saying that you are you and I am I in our own proper distinctness, concreteness, and particularity?"[11] And yet there *is* something wrong with this way of putting the matter; more precisely, we need to interrogate this "obvious" distinction between *you* and *I*. Is the difference really a substantial one, as this quotation would seem to imply? I would suggest, instead, that the difference is a rhetorical one – and no less real for that – but dependent primarily on the way that the speaker ("I") and the listener ("you") are constructed in the specific context. Their "proper distinctness" appears quite dubious when we transpose them into the realm of human communication, where the first and second persons do not name substances but rather a locutionary space, a relation ("from" or "to") rather than an essence.

In sum, then, particularity does not render us into isolated individuals; it

---

[10] *The Call to Personhood*, 81.
[11] *The One, The Three, and the Many*, 195.

recognizes that we are different from one another, but understands this difference as a product of our interactions with others. It also recognizes that human begins are constantly in the process of being formed and re-formed by these encounters. Thus, when we speak of "I" or "you," we are not speaking of stable, fixed entities; we are simply attempting to locate, tentatively and temporarily, the intersection of various interactions, such that they may become the agents, objects, or destinations of human communication. We are particular, but only through the process of engagement with the *other*.

Perhaps I can shed some additional light on this description of particularity by means of an extended example, focusing on one of the more common ways that we employ the language of *particularity*. When it comes to art (and specifically painting), I would say that I have my own *particular* tastes. By this I mean (or think I mean) that my preferences for certain forms of painting are real, that they are my own, that they do not belong to anyone else. Thus, when you show me a painting by Kandinsky, I am likely to say: "that's not my style." By which I mean: I have little interest in that painting, because my own preferences, which are particular to me, do not include a preference for Kandinsky's style.

Having thus established the particularity of my tastes, I tend to use them as a bulwark against those who would like to introduce me to something new. You say to me, "Let's go to this Kandinsky exhibition," and I say, "No thanks, he's not really to my taste." Note that this is the end of the argument – *de gustibus non est disputandum*: there is no accounting for taste. Particularity thus becomes an argument for a radical individualism (in this instance, in aesthetics): I do not have to listen to your claims about the beauty and depth of Kandinsky's paintings, because I have my own particular tastes, and they are inaccessible to you; they are uniquely my own.

But in what sense "my own"? The starkly individualistic claim that "my tastes are purely my own" can survive only in a radically decontextualized account of my life. It is meaningful only if I am able to isolate my "particular tastes" from everything about my life that led to the development of those tastes. My taste in art is not an innate quality; it is a learned phenomenon, and it has a great deal to do with my experiences in life. For example, my mother, who taught grade school for much of her life, made an effort to introduce her students to the great traditions of painting. My earliest exposure to art came from wandering around in her classroom, looking at the reproductions of Rembrandt, Vermeer, and the Impressionists that hung on the walls. I picked up bits and pieces of the classical tradition in later years of schooling, but I never took a course in art history; indeed, until college, I had rarely been in an art museum. As an undergraduate, I did have courses in European intellectual history and in the history of France; these, of course, tended to reinforce my early predilections for Northern Renaissance and Impressionist art, as do the facts that my wife teaches French and that I became a Christian theologian.

Moreover, these previous communicative encounters remain *present* – and not just unconsciously – during conversations with others about my "particular" tastes in art. In fact, such conversations often lead me to refer to those whose artistic tastes have influenced my own. Here we have a reminder of the role of the "third person" in the process by which human communication forms personal identity: My dialogue partners have included not only those who were then addressing me (trying, for example, to persuade me of the aesthetic bankruptcy of French Impressionism), but also people who were not present at the time: my mother, my friends, my wife, and others who loved the work of the Impressionists and whose testimony meant much to me. We are products of communicative activities – not only with "you" (the other who is present) but also with "she/he/they" (who are "absent," and yet continually made "present" through the use of the third person in discourse).

Thus, my "particular" tastes in art are not "my own" in any individualistic understanding of those words. They developed over a period of time because of a network of influences; hence "I" played a relatively minor role in the development of "my own" artistic tastes. They are *particular* tastes, but they are not mine in any exclusive or private sense. These tastes have been particularized in very fundamental ways by other human beings, by accidental occurrences, and by various choices that I made while completely oblivious to the effects they would have in shaping my tastes in art.

My broader point should be clear enough: that which is "particular" to one person is neither an individual achievement nor a personal possession. Others have shaped this particularity to such a degree that there may even be some question about the extent to which we can call it "our own" – though we do indeed tend to use this form of speech quite frequently. As I suggested in my comments on *fellowship* in chapter 5, the trinitarian virtues call into question the rather cavalier and permanent ways in which we use possessive pronouns and other self-identifying language (e.g., "my own"). The trinitarian virtue of particularity is non-individualistic, non-contrastive, and non-exclusionary. It provides a space for human interaction within which we can recognize our utter dependence upon others and upon God.

Thus, my particularity does not make me an "individual," even though it may be necessary to construct me as one in order to speak to (or about) me. When you ask me about "my" tastes in art, you speak to me as though I were an individual, and I answer the same way; but this is a temporary construction, and one which often obscures – yet cannot completely evade – the ways in which my "particular" tastes are really the product of previous (and ongoing) acts of communication.

I have now said more than enough to describe my specific construal of the word *particularity* as a trinitarian virtue. But a construal of the word is not enough, for *practices* give words their sense. Trinitarian theology becomes meaningful only in the light of practices in which Christians are involved – practices through which they enact and embody the language of the doctrine. Through their participation in the believing community, they come to recognize the ways in which personal identity is never a matter of abstracted individuals, but is always formed in relation to other human beings and to God through a pattern of call and response. In the next section, I will examine a specific set of practices that seem to me to bear witness to the understanding of particularity that I have been describing here – a particularity that is constituted by others, constantly in flux, and most clearly meaningful in the context of human communication.

A witness to particularity: the Spirit

In the first epistle of John, the Spirit is identified as one of the "three who bear witness on earth." From very early in the history of the Christian communities, the Spirit was understood as the One who draws Christians together, assuring that their solidarity with one another would not diminish – even though Jesus' ascension into heaven meant that they could no longer "hold onto" him (at least not in the same way as they had done before). The Spirit is described as "another advocate" who will do the work of Christ (John 14:16) and bear witness to Christ (John 15:26). The Spirit protects Christians, in fulfillment of Jesus' high-priestly prayer: "Holy Father, protect them in your name that you have given me, so that they may be one, as we are one" (John 17:11). This petition is offered in the context of Jesus' recognition that his followers must continue to live in the world: "Now I am no longer in the world, but they are in the world, and I am coming to you." The "worldly" lives of Christians will require them to differ from one another – to become particular, to allow themselves to be "sedimented" by the various circumstances in which they find themselves. This will require diversity and freedom; and it would almost certainly result in a scattering of Christians to the winds, were they not held together by God.

That the Christian life will demand a *particularized* response to diverse circumstances is especially apparent in Acts 2. The scene is Jerusalem, and the time is the feast of Pentecost – which meant that the city was filled with pilgrims from a diverse assortment of lands. In order to encounter these people in all their diversity, the apostles had to be empowered to speak in different ways, so that all who were present could hear the message in their own native languages (Acts 2:4–8). God provides this empowerment through the sending of the Spirit – the Living Water poured out on the apostles. The Spirit thus attends to the particular, so that Christians can proclaim the Gospel to others in a way that recognizes that they differ from one another, yet without allowing this difference to become a source of isolation or privitization. The Living Water energizes and enlivens Christians, so that they can give the message the shape it must have in order to be "heard" by varying audiences.

A number of Christian practices seem especially oriented toward the particular, and are thus dependent on the Spirit's attention to both unity and difference. For example, the work of evangelism must take into account the particular circumstances of varying audiences, in order for the Gospel to be rightly heard by each. Christianity's first missionary was clearly aware of this; writing to the church at Corinth, St Paul declares,

> Though I am free with respect to all, I have made myself a slave to all, so that I might win more of them. To the Jews I became as a Jew, in order to win Jews. To those under the law I became as one under the law (though I myself am not under the law) so that I might win those under the law. To those outside the law I became as one outside the law (though I am not free from God's law but am under Christ's law) so that I might win those outside the law. To the weak I became weak, so that I might win the weak. I have become all things to all people, that I might by all means save some. (1 Cor. 9:19–22)

The "particularizing" imperative of evangelism is further exemplified by the translation of the biblical and liturgical texts into other languages, as well as the recognition that missionaries must know a great deal about the cultures into which they bring the Gospel.

Another obvious example of a Christian practice that requires attention to the particular is the activity of *preaching*. The preacher must recognize that each audience is different. Its members are formed by their own histories of encounter with others, and it is ultimately ephemeral; that is, the congregation is differently constituted each time it assembles and hears a sermon. A good preacher must therefore respect the particularity of the present moment – which of course does not mean treating it as isolated from all other moments. Precisely the opposite: because the audience is shaped by its encounters with others, the preacher must be attentive to at least some of those encounters, in order that the Word of God might be heard. Rowan Williams has put the point well:

A sermon is a particular *event*, far more than a text. It is a moment when you try to make a connection between a specific group of people in a specific time and place, and the resources of the Christian vision in its historic wholeness. You try to bring to bear a vast range of words, pictures, doctrines on the problems of the here and now, and you also allow your perception of the needs of the here and now to shape your view of the tradition you draw on, to direct you to *this* rather than *that* in the Bible or the creed. . . . Good sermons happen when the twofold listening – to tradition and to the present – really becomes a listening to and for God, so that something emerges almost begging to be put into words.[12]

The particularity of a sermon – at least of a good sermon – can never be equated with pure individualism, separated from the social and communal locus which gives it life. The sermon must ultimately respect communally-constituted particularity of those who are addressed.

Christian practices of preaching and evangelism combine "words of wisdom," "words of knowledge," and "teaching," which are three of the "gifts of the Spirit" that Paul describes in 1 Corinthians 12. These gifts witness to a non-individualistic particularity; the one Spirit is manifested in different ways among different Christian believers. Each member of the body is particular; each performs a different function. But this particularity does not make the members into isolated individuals, nor does it occur through private acts of the will. Rather, this particularity is received as a gift. All the members manifest the same Spirit; and yet, we can still "pick them out" and describe the ways that they communicate with one another.

Thus, we can speak of the "identity" of a Christian believer, but only with attention to the way that this identity is shaped through a process of mutual participation with others. Again, Paul's analogy of "the body and its members" plays a key role, by simultaneously affirming two very important claims: that Christians are particular members of the Body, and that this particularity is useless in isolation from the one Spirit that animates the whole body. "Now you are the body of Christ and individually members of it. And God has appointed in the church first apostles, second prophets, third teachers; then deeds of power, then gifts of healing, forms of assistance, forms of leadership, various kinds of tongues" (1 Cor. 12:27–8). These varying gifts are animated by the same Spirit, the same Lord, the same God (1 Cor. 12:2–4). Nevertheless, they are diverse; God makes the members of the Body *particular* through the bestowal of diverse gifts.

---

[12] Rowan Williams, *A Ray of Darkness: Sermons and Reflections* (Cambridge, Mass.: Cowley Publications, 1995), vii. [Published in Great Britain as *Open to Judgment* (London: Darton, Longman and Todd, 1994).]

Moreover, the use of these gifts helps to form Christians into a people for whom the notion of a "communally-constituted particularity" is a meaningful concept. In an average congregation, some people teach, others preach, others feed the hungry. The Living Water nourishes and sustains the various members of the Body of Christ in differing ways. In this sense it particularizes them, such that no two members are precisely identical. But these gifts also bind them together, reminding each of them that one's identity is not one's "own" in a private or individualistic sense. The particular manifestations of the Spirit's gifts are worked out in relation to others in the community.

At the center of all these manifestations is the person of Christ, who gives them their proper form and content. "No one speaking by the Spirit of God ever says 'Let Jesus be cursed!' and no one can say 'Jesus is Lord' except by the Holy Spirit" (1 Cor. 12:3). Thus, the particularity of Christian believers is bound to the particularity of Christ. The Gospel narratives describe God as particular – as having encountered the world in certain ways (and not in others). God has a particular history with the people of Israel; God becomes incarnate in the flesh of a particular Jewish woman and is born as a particular child; God is poured out on the apostles at a particular place and time to inaugurate the continuation of Christ's work in the world. These narrative accounts of particularity are embodied by Christians who manifest the gifts that Paul describes. By dwelling in community, and by learning to recognize the variety of gifts as given by the same Spirit, Christians learn that particularity is not a matter of individualism and isolation. Nor (on the other hand) does the unity of the Church require that every person march in lock-step formation. Within the context of the believing community, we are formed as particular persons – who are nevertheless aware of how thoroughly our particularity depends upon the "others" in community with whom we are formed.

Triune Particularity

How does the notion of particularity that I have been developing here apply to the triune God? We can say that the Three are particular in that they, too, are the subjects, objects, and destinations of various forms of communication. The doctrine of the Trinity posits processions and relations in God; thus it also posits particularity in God (identifying a source of the processions, and two processive "events"). And even though the external works of God are indivisible, we still want to claim that each of the Three may carry out these works in differing ways (as for example in the divine missions of incarnation and inspiration). Moreover, when we do speak of one or another of the Three, we need to be able to do so in ways that will allow us to identify this same one at another point in time, and allow our listeners to understand some continuity between these two references. This does *not* mean that there can only be one word or phrase to identify each of the Three; but it does mean that I may sometimes need to make it clear that (for example) the Living Water to whom I referred in chapter 2 is the same Living Water to whom I am referring in this chapter.

I have suggested that particularity is best understood as a tentative and temporary construction, necessitated by the process of communication. It is a locutionary space that allows us to refer, to "identify," in ways that are always tentative and context-dependent. With respect to the doctrine of the Trinity, we render God's particularity in order to be able to *talk* about the Three, and to allow this talk to develop some degree of continuity of reference over time. Traditionally, the Three have been particularized by the use of *names*; hence, this section begins with an exploration of the process of naming, before turning to a more general consideration of the Three as markers of divine particularity.

Nouns and names

Earlier in this chapter, I suggested that we have tended to understand particularity in a highly individualistic way. This tendency is underwritten, at least in part, by certain assumptions about nouns and names. We often think of these structures as serving primarily to *isolate* and *individuate* objects, rather than setting those objects in a narrative context and thus emphasizing the ties that bind them to other objects. This approach to nouns and names encourages us to abstract them from their contexts and think of them in isolation. For example, when I use the word *desk* to refer to the object on which my computer is sitting, this allows me to isolate it from its surroundings – including the work that went into its construction, its various owners over time, and so on. These relational aspects of the desk are part of what constitutes its particularity; often, however, these aspects are obscured when I give the object a name (and thus allow it to be abstracted from its context).

Sometimes this process of abstraction is useful, as when we are teaching or learning a language. If my daughter frequently refers to the alley behind our house as a "parking lot," and I want to teach her to call it an "alley," I may need to abstract it from its context, at least temporarily, to show her why I use a particular word for it instead of some other word. I might show her some other alleys, and then show her some parking lots, so that the referential differences between the two words will become clear. But this process of abstraction is never an end in itself; the whole purpose of naming things is to narrate them, to be able to communicate about them. Learning to call something an "alley" would be a fairly trivial pursuit if we did not need to *talk* about alleys – to offer (and receive) directions to them, to ask people to shovel snow from them, or to discuss with our neighbors how we might go about beautifying them.

The things that we name are always already involved in a wide range of narrative relationships; they are deeply embedded in the context of our discursive practices. This is true not only for common nouns, but for many proper nouns as well. The naming of streets and roads, for example, is done not simply for the pleasure of having a word to associate with a particular slab of concrete, but rather to say what role the road plays in the larger context of which it is a part (how it is related to other roads, to vehicles and pedestrians, to cities and buildings and underground tunnels). For example, roads are sometimes named for the town to which they lead. So Cambridge has a Barton Road, a Grantchester Road, a Girton Road, and so on – each leading to a town of the same name. In time, such names become "attached" to particular roads, and in theory this connection could endure, even if the town for which the road is named disappeared altogether. But even this would not alter the road's history, which gave rise to its name: "This is (or was) one of the (several) roads leading to Grantchester." Sometimes a name provides further information about a road's context: *road*, *avenue*, *boulevard*, *close*, *circle*, and *way* often indicate (or perhaps once indicated) different shapes, widths, directions, and purposes. The name of the road tells us very little "the road itself," that is, the road as abstracted from its context. The names of roads, like the names of many things, tell us not what they "are" in isolation, but how they fit into the whole – that is, what part they play in the larger story.

Human names have this function too, though this is now often lost from view. Names might be chosen as a reference to a relative, an ancestor, a saint. They might have interesting etymologies which help to say something about the person (explanations of which are often found among Old Testament names, for example). Part of a name might indicate lineage (Ivanovna = daughter of Ivan), place of origin (Theodore of Mopsuestia), or title (Alexander the Great). Again, these names *can* be used to individuate a person, and sometimes they are very useful in this regard ("No, not Cyril of Jerusalem, I mean Cyril of Alexandria"); clearly, however, this does not render a person into a private or isolated individual. Indeed, a closer look at the "individuating" features of names and nouns reminds us that they usually achieve this end only by reference to the narrative networks within which this "person" is located.

Nevertheless, the contextualizing aspect of nouns and names is often obscured today, for a number of reasons. First, our general individualizing tendencies – already explored at length – lead us to take note of what is unique about a person or a thing before we admit it to a particular group. Consider, for example, the practices of governments, which need to able to individuate their citizens in order to carry out a number of tasks, such as the enforcement of property laws. Here, names are often replaced by numbers, which insure that this individuation is efficient and complete; this also obscures a person's context, since the number is always at least partly arbitrary and says little about one's origin, family, and so on. In this case, the "naming" of persons with numbers isolates them to an extreme degree. Secondly, technological invention and the rapid flow of information has created an explosion in the number of different entities that we are likely to encounter in the average lifetime, which means that new names must constantly be invented in order to distinguish this new thing from everything that has preceded it. This process is underwritten in capitalist societies by planned obsolescence and by the importance of marketing everything as "new." Finally, with respect to human names, we no longer tend to name in ways that show lineage, place of origin, or title. The etymologies of most names are lost to us (though recovered momentarily in baby-naming books), and the practice of naming children after saints and relatives seems to have waned somewhat. We do still have the practice of retaining last names that connect us to (some of) our forebears, but this is a relatively small remnant of the "connecting" power that names once had.[13]

Thus, when we use names to identify people – to posit their *particularity* – we tend to think that we are isolating them from others, abstracting them from their context in order to individuate them. But we are also contextualizing them, linking them (sometimes in very specific ways) with events, stories, places, and other people. We name our children, for example, not only to differentiate them from one another (and thus avoid the fate of Mrs McCave, the unfortunate Dr Seuss character who "had twenty-three sons and she named them all Dave"). More importantly, we name them in order to involve them in an ongoing story of which we are also a part.

And so it is also with the names of God. They do individuate, for the purpose of communicative reference; they attempt to indicate that we are talking about God (and not someone else), and about the triune God (not some other imagined god). But in doing so, they also evoke a wide range of

[13] The difficulties raised by "what to do with names" in marriage further reinforces this point. We are torn between the desire to narrate the life of each person as connected with his or her parents, and the desire to narrate the couple as united to one another.

associations and connections, which may vary dramatically among readers and listeners. The names of God provide us with a way of referring to God's *particularity*, which is not the same thing as saying "God's individuality" or "God's isolation." Rather, it means offering a temporary and tentative linguistic construction of God, for the purpose of understanding how God enters into the communicative process (as speaker, listener, or referent). Thus, as we turn to a survey of the divine names as an indicator of God's particularity, we need to remember their tentative and temporary nature. They do not merely distinguish God from the world (and the Three from one another); they also involve God in various narrative contexts.

On the divine names

The Bible offers a great many names for God.[14] (In this section, I leave many of these names untranslated, even untransliterated, since I am primarily making a point about their variety, not their meaning.) In the Old Testament, אֵל שַׁדַּי, יהוה, אֱלֹהִים, and various specifications of אֵל are all common. These have typically been identified with different "streams" of the literary tradition; but this may not be the most important feature of the plurality of names. If the goal of the biblical writers were to identify God in a way that abstracted God from the narratives, and thus made God into a private, distant individual, the best way to have done so would have been to use only one name (or perhaps a number!), and do so consistently. When rendering persons as discrete individuals is important (as it is for governments), it becomes important not to allow a single person to be known by a wide variety of names. Someone who is known by a wide variety of different names is a bit hard to pin down; that person is not so much a discrete individual, but is more like a node in a variety of overlapping networks. That the writers and redactors of the Old Testament books were content to leave multiple names in place suggests that their goal was not the substantive isolation of a distinct entity, but rather the need – different in differing narrative contexts – to speak about God, and to recognize that God speaks.

Nor does this process stop in the New Testament. According to the gospel accounts, when Jesus speaks of God, he uses the name πατήρ, but also ἀββά

---

[14] The *locus classicus* for the entire discussion, including a very comprehensive list of names, is Pseudo-Dionysius, *On the Divine Names*. English translation in *The Complete Works*, trans. Colm Luibheid, with a Preface by René Roques, with an Introduction by Jaroslav Pelikan, Jean Leclercq, and Karlfried Froehlich, with a Foreword by Paul Rorem, Classics of Western Spirituality (New York: Paulist Press, 1987).

and ἐλωΐ and, quite frequently, θεός. Jesus himself is called ὁ κύριος, and occasionally even ὁ θεός; he identifies himself as ὁ υἱὸς τοῦ ἀνθρώπου or simply as ὁ υἱός; I have already commented on Jesus' self-identification by means of the words "I am" (ἐγώ εἰμι: John 6:35, 48, 51; 8:58; 10:9, 11, 14; 15:1). Similarly to the Living Water, a host of names is given: πνεῦμα, πνεῦμα ἅγιον, τὸ πνεῦμα τῆς ἀληθείας (John 14:17, 26; 15:26; 16:13); παράκλητος (John 14:16, 26); πνεῦμα θεοῦ and πνεῦμα Χριστοῦ (Rom. 8:9). God is thus being particularized in a variety of ways, associated with various narratives that describe God and God's acts. These manifold expressions of particularity are in no way exclusive of one another. This point is made especially clear by the names for the Living Water, which offer a number of intra-trinitarian connections – to God, to Christ, and to truth – and also identify it with certain divine activities (such as inspiration and advocacy).

By assigning names to God, the biblical authors sought to identify the particularity of the Three without rendering them into isolated individuals. This occurred in at least three ways. First, the use of certain names tended to invoke certain narratives. In Exodus, for example, Moses learns one name while trying very hard to resist the call to deliver the Israelites from bondage. He protests that he will have no response when asked for the name of the one who sent him. He is thus offered a mysterious phrase, and then told to say, first, that אֶהְיֶה ("I am," Exod. 3:14), and then, that יהוה (3:15) has sent him. The name יהוה thus particularizes God in ways that serve to remind (at least some) listeners of the event of the Exodus. Similarly, the noun ὁ λόγος ("Word") will invoke, for Christians, the narrative of creation and redemption in the Johannine prologue. Some listeners may have associated Jesus' self reference, ὁ υἱὸς τοῦ ἀνθρώπου, with the narrative of Daniel 7. Many other narrative invocations are probably lost to us today, since we do not always have knowledge of the stories that would have been familiar to the audiences to whom the Gospels were originally addressed.

Secondly, certain names tended to identify the particularity of God (or of one of the Three) by means of their etymology. Whether the etymologies stand up under philological scrutiny is not the point here; after all, the process of naming is not intended as an exercise in the construction of dictionaries, but as a means of connecting a name to a narrative. I have already mentioned the various names of Jesus in Matthew 1, such as Ἰησοῦς and Ἐμμανουήλ; clearly, Χριστός (christos) functions this way, since its etymology leads us back through the Hebrew מָשִׁיחַ (messiah) to the idea of "anointing." In this last instance we have a good example of how the connective and associative elements of names can become hidden from our sight; the name "Jesus Christ" has become so assimilated to our modern notion of a "name" that the actual function of *Christ* – as a title, with all sorts of associative references – often goes unrecognized.

A Christological hermeneutic of the Old Testament dramatically increases the range of names for God. For example, Isaiah proclaims that the coming savior "is named Wonderful Counselor, Mighty God, Everlasting Father, Prince of Peace" (Isa. 9:6). Similarly, the Living Water is given a variety of names in the Old Testament, in those instances where the immanent presence of God is emphasized in some way. First, there is the Hebrew word רוּחַ, frequently signifying the Spirit of God. Similar (though less explicit) suggestions appear in Psalms and Proverbs. Indeed, the Wisdom tradition provided a number of texts which were read as witnessing to the self-differentiation of God. For example, יהוה says, "You are my child [בְּנִי]; today I have given you birth" (Ps. 2:7), thereby reminding the people that יהוה is not exhaustively defined by isolation, but is related to an Other, as a parent is to a child.

A third way that biblical names render God's particularity is through the activities that they imply. The names often have verbal forms of one sort or another; we have already seen some examples of this, as in παράκλητος (from a verb meaning "to give counsel" or "to advise"). But there are many more. For example, Jesus' mission – "not to be served but to serve, and to give his life a ransom for many" (Mark 10:45) – is emphasized by his identification as "the lamb of God" (since the lamb was an animal of sacrifice), in addition to the use of specific messianic titles (Matt. 16:16–17; John 4:26). Similarly Paul identifies ὁ υἱός with descriptions that accent parent-child motifs: "the image of the invisible God, the firstborn of all creation" and the "firstborn of the dead," in whom "all the Fullness [of God] was pleased to dwell" (Col. 1:15–19).

Sometimes these activities are not formed into concrete names, but are still associated with one of the Three; and this provides yet another way of rendering God's particularity without separating the Three into discrete individuals. I have already noted the role of the Spirit and the Word in creation. Similarly, even though the role of redemption is specifically attributed to Christ, we are also told that "God was in Christ, reconciling the world" (2 Cor. 5:19); and believers are marked with the seal of the Holy Spirit for the day of redemption (Eph. 4:30). The activity of "giving signs" is also clearly predicated of each of the Three, and of various combinations thereof – signs from God (the voices at baptism and the transfiguration, the dramatic cosmic events surrounding the crucifixion), signs from Jesus (such as those related in sequence in the Gospel of John, beginning with the Wedding at Cana), and signs from the Spirit (such as the gifts to which Paul refers in 1 Cor. 12–14).

In summary, we have noted, first, that the Bible employs a wide variety of names in reference to God; and second, that the function of these names is to identify God according to the specific narrative context, rather than to abstract the Three from those contexts and treat them as distinct entities. By connecting God to various narratives, etymologies, and activities, the names – far from systematically isolating the Three – unite them in polyphonous, mutually participative difference. Their particularity results from the need to speak about them, and to recognize that they speak; it should not be taken as positing their independent substantial existence, nor as any diminution of their full mutual participation. There is no question, of course, that names have a distinguishing and identifying role; but we misunderstand this role if we isolate it from its context.

Here, we can make good use of the word that Greek theologians often used to categorize the three – the word ὑπόστασις, one meaning of which (in Aristotle) was "that which settles under" something else. In other words, the Three "settle from" something; indeed, we could describe them as "sediments." They thus cannot be understood as self-enclosed entities, but are always already related to that from which they are sedimented. By construing the word ὑπόστασις as related to McFadyen's description of human personhood as "sedimented," we can summarize the purpose of assigning names to the Three. We are identifying them, *tentatively and temporarily*, as that nexus of relationships that constitute them, in order to refer to them as agents of action and speech. This is probably a necessary process, in order to be able to speak of them at all, and especially to do so with the flexibility required by a variety of rhetorical contexts. But as the language of "sedimentation" reminds us, these nominal descriptions are not primary; we must always take one step back, to think about where this "sediment" comes from, and thereby remember that the Three are "relation without remainder." Since we must sometimes name these relations with nominative forms, and since the rhetorical contexts in which we must do so are many and various, we ought to employ a *variety* of names – and to find ways of reminding ourselves that all such names are but tentative and temporary particularizations. Long before we had names with which to name them, the Three were *relations*.[15]

One step remains in our investigation of divine particularity: a consideration of the impact of the foregoing analysis on the question of divine action.

---

[15] Thus, as I noted in chapter 2, I hope that the language of "Source, Wellspring, and Living Water" will be used liturgically and catechetically, but not that it will become a single universal standard for English translations of the Greek terms. I also hope that it will evoke the (logically prior) processions and relations in God.

It may be all very well to speak of, for example, a particular road as simply a "locutionary space," a form of language that we use to place it in a specific rhetorical context. The road does not have a will of its own; it is not an actor. But for human persons, and for God, we also need to inquire into how the particular can *act*. How can this "locutionary space" *do* something? How can a "tentative and temporary identification" of the "nexus of relationships" be said to act? Or do we, perhaps, need to rethink what we mean when we predicate *action* of one or more of the Three?

Particularity and action

When a particular activity is predicated of one of the Three – that is, when one of the Three is named as the subject of a sentence – this is an attempt to account for the fact that, even within the most profoundly mutually participative relation, we can still speak meaningfully of *agency*. When we say that one of the Three "does" something, we are trying to be more specific about where an action is coming from – even though we know that the entire Trinity is necessarily involved in the process. Particularizing the Three by naming them is an attempt *to specify the orientation of activity* within a relational whole. I will attempt to unpack what I mean by this rather cumbersome phrase by means of an extended example.

I have often used the example of pregnancy to suggest the idea of complete mutual participation; I have also noted that any attempt to separate this reality into discrete entities is misleading at best. We use terms such as *the expectant mother* and *the fetus* and *the placenta* to attempt such separation, but in our more reflective moments we know that these are somewhat arbitrary lines of division: the mother contains the fetus and the placenta; the placenta interpenetrates both mother and fetus; and so on. How can we speak of these "three" in ways that still recognize that they are also "one"? Can we speak of them as *particularities* in the sense that I have been developing here? Can we meaningfully claim that any one of the three "does" something? Or must we give up the attempt to pick any one of them out as an object, subject, or referent of a sentence?

We know that, within the complex unity of pregnancy, *activity* occurs: something acts, something else is acted upon. We know that there is circulation of the blood, sustaining and being sustained, kicking and being kicked. These actions are, on one level, all-involving; and yet we want to be able to give them some directionality, to *specify the orientation of activity* within the whole. If we are able (despite the obvious difficulties) to imagine a relation that is truly subsistent – that does not describe something "between" two endpoints, but that exhaustively constitutes whatever is being described – we can still posit something like "directionality" within the whole; that is, we can attempt to say where an activity comes from, and where it goes.

Thus, even though we cannot meaningfully separate this mutually participative reality into discrete constituent parts, we can particularize its internal activities. For example, we can speak of nurturing, of being nurtured, and of conveying nurture. In doing so, we "orientate" the activity of nurture – specifying that it comes from somewhere, that it is a particular kind of action, and that it has a destination. Of course, none of the three can exist in isolation from the others; these three are one. Nevertheless, this process of orientation does provide us with a tentative and temporary way to identify three "somethings," thus allowing us to *speak* of them in their particularity. This is what I mean by suggesting that we can particularize by "specifying the orientation of activity."

Additional support for this way of thinking about activity within a relational whole can be gleaned from some of the terms that were proposed, in the early Church, as attempts to answer the question "three whats?" (I have already observed that we do not, in fact, need to answer this question; but some of the answers that have been offered will help us think about how the Three act.) In the Orations, St Gregory of Nazianzus refers to the various nominal forms as the "personal names" of the Three.[16] This was especially useful in his rhetorical context, since one of his primary goals was to argue, against Eunomius and other neo-Arians, that the description ἀγέννητος ("unbegotten") was not the single exhaustive "name" of God. By pointing to the great multiplicity of names for God, Gregory was able to defuse the idea that the name was a clue to the very essence of some reality.

St Basil used the term ἰδιότης, which refers to that which is one's own, a property or peculiar nature; often translated "particularity," this term reinforces the general argument of the present chapter. The differences among the Three, says Basil, consist in their plurality and in the "particularities" which characterize each.[17] But Basil makes it clear that the purpose of these particularities is mainly to identify the Three – that is, to be able to speak about them, to attribute to them speech and action, rather than to imply any substantive distinction among them. He thus calls them γνωπιστικαὶ ἰδιότητες, "identifying particularities." Later theology employed the term ἰδιότητες ὑποστατικαί,[18] which (following my analysis of the word ὑπόστασις at the

---

[16] e.g., *Or.* 30.17-21.

[17] Basil *Contra Eunomium* 1.19; see Prestige, *God in Patristic Thought*, 244–5.

[18] Pseudo-Cyril *de ss. Trin.* 9.

end of the previous section) could be translated "sedimented particularities."

A final hint about what it means to speak of the Three as "acting" comes from yet another Greek term – τρόπος ὑπάρξεως, which seems to be almost universally rendered into English as "mode of existence" or occasionally as "mode of subsistence." The predominance of these translations is due in part to the influence of Karl Barth and Karl Rahner, who recommended the phrase (translating it into their German as *Seinsweise* and *Subsistenzweise*, respectively).[19] In addition to the modalist implications of the English translations (which I noted in chapter 1), they also obscure the importance of mutual participation among the Three.

For the rhetorically-trained Greek thinker, one obvious reference of the word τρόπος would have been what we would call "figures of speech" (we also have the English word *tropes*).[20] The tropes are what one uses, in a particular rhetorical context, when the usual words that would otherwise be available simply do not fit. Old words must be pressed into new service, trying to evoke meanings that – though probably uncommon and perhaps even considered a bit eccentric at first – can still get the point across, usually with an economy of language and perhaps with a flash of wit as well. The standard tropes included metaphor, metonymy, synecdoche, and hyperbole.

It would be misleading to contrast such language with "literal" language, as though one set of words had their meanings physically attached, whereas the others did not. The question is simply whether a particular usage is *common* or *familiar* to a particular audience; the tropes are employed where more commonly-used language is unavailable, inappropriate, or simply fails to produce the right effect. Language that is originally used "tropically" can become so commonplace that it loses its figurative character; indeed, much of what we call "literal" language may have originated as a trope. For example, whoever first spoke of the "stem" of a wine glass was employing a metaphor, borrowing from the world of flowers to describe the world of glassware. But today, the term is so common that its figurative evocations are usually unnoticed.

Thus, a τρόπος ὑπάρξεως is a figure of speech. A figure for what? The word ὑπάρξεως, ultimately derived from the verb ὑπάρχω, can suggest not only the idea of "existence" (which strikes most English-speakers, at least, as a rather static quality), but also the more dynamic notions of emergence and

---

[19] Barth, *CD* I/1, 359-68 [*KD* I/1, 379–88]; Rahner, *The Trinity*, 103–15 [*Der dreifaltige Gott*, 385–93]; see also Jüngel, *Doctrine of the Trinity*, 25–9 [*Gottes sein*, 36–41].

[20] See the listings of this and other uses in G. W. H. Lampe, ed., *A Patristic Greek Lexicon* (Oxford: Clarendon, 1961), *s.v.* τρόπος, 1414–15.

origin.[21] Both translations are of course possible, but given the dynamic, processive, and relational qualities of the Three, it would seem preferable to focus on the word's evocation of "where something comes from" – its origin, direction, or orientation. I would thus describe a τρόπος ὑπάρξεως as a "trope of origin and direction" – a figure of speech that is being used to describe the way in which something emerges, to *specify the orientation of activity* in God. In other words: we know that God is a relational whole, simultaneously Three and One; how shall we attribute action to God? Since it would be misleading to speak of God only as a unified subject, we need to postulate some kind of internal activity in God; but this cannot be achieved by means of our readily available linguistic constructs. Thus, we employ a figure of speech, a trope, attempting thereby to describe the internal activity of God in ways that give it order and direction. We ought not to allow these tropes to transform the divine relations into quasi-independent entities, since they are simply an attempt to speak of the Three without denying that they are subsistent relations. These "tropes of the orientation of activity" allow us to identify the Three as subjects and objects in theological discourse – and to do so differently in differing rhetorical contexts.

We can now gain a better understanding of the ancient trinitarian principle, "the external works of the Trinity are indivisible." It must be so, of course, because if we were to think of any one of the Three as acting alone, always and eternally, to "do" something with respect to the created order, we would be positing a pure individual. By saying, for example, that "the Source alone creates," we would be positing the Source as an independent entity, doing something in isolation from the Wellspring and the Living Water. We would be describing – as though it were a substantive entity in its own right – something which is better understood as a figure of speech that characterizes God in a tentative and temporary way for a particular rhetorical context. The word *Source* does not name an essence, a substantial entity that could then be the agent of an independent action toward the world. On the other hand, these "tropes" *can* identify specific *internal* actions of the Trinity (for example, "the Wellspring flows eternally from the Source"). Indeed, in order to describe God's internal self-differentiation, some such language is *required*. The names thus specify God's particularity by providing a figure for the origin of activity within God; they are attempting to do precisely the same work as the relational language that we developed in chapter 2. To say, for example, that "the Living Water flows out from the Source" is a way of speaking about the divine relation of emergence.

---

[21] See the extracts in ibid., *s.v.* ὕπαρξις and ὑπάρχω, 1434–5.

But in addition to describing these "internal" divine actions, we would also like to be able to speak about each of the Three as engaged with the world in various ways – to say, for example, that "the Wellspring is the redeemer of the world." Such a claim should not exclude the roles of the Source and the Living Water, for they are also rightly called "redeemer." This is an instance of "appropriation," in which we posit one of the Three as the agent of a particular divine action – not because that One is alone responsible for it, but because such descriptions can make the point more clearly and persuasively. Here too, the recognition that the names for the Three are *tropes* can be very helpful: as figures of speech, they are appropriate in particular rhetorical contexts (such as the narration of the stories of Mary, of Jesus, and of the early Church). They should not be taken as identifying substantive entities that would exclude the agency of the other Two.

Similarly with respect to the divine missions: we speak of the birthing of the Wellspring and the pouring out of the Living Water, but this does not deny that the Three all have a part to play in both these events. On the other hand, the tropes do allow us to speak of the *particular* role that each of the Three plays in these events. We say, for example, that "the Wellspring became incarnate and dwelt among us," and that "the Living Water was poured out on the Church." It would be inappropriate to say, for example, that the Source was poured out on the Church, or that the Living Water became incarnate. But these strictures of theological grammar do not deny that God (as a whole) is active in the missions. The Source *sends* these two on their respective missions, and each is intimately involved in the mission of the other (the Spirit announces and confirms and sustains the incarnation, and the incarnate Word "breathes out" the Spirit upon the disciples). The two missions demonstrate that divine particularly can be *embodied*, in two ways: in Christ as the incarnation of the Word, and in the Church as the locus of the Spirit.

Changing the Subject[22]

In analyzing the *vestigia* tradition in chapter 3, I suggested that we should be able to construe certain aspects of the created order as reflecting the Triunity of God. Thus, if God's particularity bears the non-individualistic and "communicative" character that I have described here, we ought to be able to illustrate this description by focusing on certain elements in creation. In the

[22] Title purloined from an important study by Mary McClintock Fulkerson, *Changing the Subject: Women's Discourses and Feminist Theology* (Minneapolis: Augsburg Fortress, 1994).

process, we may gain some sense of how we can come to embody this virtue as well. One fruitful avenue for approaching this task is to examine recent discussions of what it means to be a "subject."

The last few decades have witnessed a declining confidence in the portrait of human subjectivity that was developed in the Enlightenment – the notion of an autonomous self, capable of exercising its freedom in supreme isolation from the rest of the world. The subject has been "de-centered" – though no one seems very certain about precisely what that might mean, or how it can still allow us to account for human speech, thought, and action. Here, I want to consider the work of two writers who have meditated upon these questions – one a philosopher, the other a novelist. Neither of them employs trinitarian categories explicitly; yet both of them help to illustrate the trinitarian virtue of particularity, by redefining subjectivity as a locutionary space that is constituted in the midst of our encounter with others.

The space of subjectivity

Calvin Schrag recognizes the inadequacies of the Enlightenment conception of the subject (as a free, isolated, autonomous center of consciousness). Yet he rightly observes human beings still participate in communicative activities, including speech, writing, and action (activities that he groups together under the term "communicative praxis"). Moreover, this activity has a *source*; it comes from somewhere. Schrag refers to this "somewhere" as the "space of subjectivity." This space need not be inhabited by an autonomous subject; however, there must be some such space for us to make sense of human action and discourse.

> The questions "Who is speaking?" "Who is writing?" and "Who is acting?" take on a renewed urgency in the aftermath of the deconstruction of the subject. . . . The subject as speaker, author, and actor is restored, not as a foundation for communicative praxis but as an implicate of it. . . . The subject emerges via its co-constitution with other subjects as the narrator, actor, and respondent within the human drama of discourse and social practices.[23]

Thus, what I have been describing in this chapter as "particularity" is very close to what Schrag is attempting to describe with the phrase "the space of subjectivity."

What occupies this space? We could perhaps say "nothing"; it is not

---

[23] Schrag, *Communicative Praxis*, 137–8.

occupied by a "subject" in the dominant modern sense, nor by any substantive entity. Yet this space still plays an urgently important role in the process of human communication – an activity that Schrag understands in very broad terms (not unlike those offered by McFadyen) as including a wide variety of human interactions. The subject – speaker, writer, or actor – is not a pre-existing being, but is rather *implicated* by the process of human communication.

> The subject is not a *pre*-given entity; so also it is not a *post*-given entity. . . . It is not an entity at all, but rather an event or happening that continues the conversation and social practices of mankind and inscribes its contributions on their textures.[24]

"It is not an entity at all": precisely right. We have typically conceptualized the *subject* (and the *particular*) in substantialist terms, and have thereby been unable to think about it except as an *entity*. Schrag's important contribution is to provide us with good reasons to stop thinking about the subject in such terms, and instead to think of it as a node in the communicative network.

> The speaking subject is not the inventor of language, the authorial subject is not the creator of textuality, and the agentive subject is not the producer of social practices. The speaking subject always speaks in and from a background of delivered forms of textuality; and the subject as agent is socialized by the communal patterns in which he acts.[25]

This is a radically de-centered subjectivity, but it can still make sense of agency in discourse and action; it allows us to speak of the "whence" of human communication. In this respect, Schrag appreciates the following comment of Derrida: "I don't destroy the subject; I situate it. That is to say, I believe that at a certain level both of experience and of philosophical and scientific discourse one cannot get along without the notion of subject. It is a question of knowing where it comes from and how it functions."[26]

Given his perspective, Schrag knows he has a natural ally in the rhetorical tradition. Rhetoric allows us to speak of human communication with reference to its specific activity: *whence* it comes, *to whom* it is directed, and

---

[24] Ibid., 121.

[25] Ibid.

[26] Cited in Schrag, *Communicative Praxis*, 129, from *The Languages of Criticism and the Sciences of Man: The Structuralist Controversy*, ed. Richard Macksey and Eugenio Donato (Baltimore: Johns Hopkins University Press, 1970), 271.

what kinds of *effects* it produces (among those *by whom* it is actually heard). As Terry Eagleton has noted:

> Rhetoric, which was the received form of critical analysis all the way from ancient society to the eighteenth century, examined the way discourses are constructed in order to achieve certain effects. . . . It saw speaking and writing not merely as textual objects, to be aesthetically contemplated or endlessly deconstructed, but as forms of *activity* inseparable from the wider social relationships between writers and readers, orators and audiences, and as largely unintelligible outside the social purposes and conditions in which they were embedded.[27]

Toward the end of his book, Schrag's analysis takes a self-consciously rhetorical turn, arguing that the primary activity within the "space of subjectivity" is the rhetorical activity of persuasion. This means that it has very definite ethical outlines, since meaning and truth are established within the interpretive community.

Schrag provides a way of thinking about subjectivity, and thereby a way of thinking about the implications of particularity for human beings. His observations can be given a specifically trinitarian application, as a way of helping us move from God's particularity to our own. I will conclude my reflections on his work by adopting, to my own argument about trinitarian particularity, his discussion of three terms that designate how the "space of subjectivity" reorients our notion of agency and personhood. His terms are temporality, multiplicity, and embodiment.[28]

The doctrine of the Trinity describes God as involved in the *temporality* of the world. This entails a rejection of the classical metaphysical claim that God wholly transcends time and therefore must remain distant from the ever-evolving world. A trinitarian account of the divine life demonstrates that God is not subject to the metaphysical assumptions of classical theism; rather, God can be involved in time, can change, can suffer. We know this through the incarnation of the Word: here, God is revealed as intimately involved in the history of the world, "producing" it in a way that is not distant and disengaged, but which involves changing and suffering and even dying.

Schrag's analysis suggests that something similar is at work in human personhood. Our particularity is related to our temporality: we are involved in time, and this involvement means that our particularity is constantly

---

[27] Terry Eagleton, *Literary Theory: An Introduction* (Minneapolis: University of Minnesota Press, 1983), 205–6.

[28] Schrag, *Communicative Praxis*, 145–57.

evolving. We are always facing new circumstances and new constellations of relationships to "others"; each new moment may demand a new series of responses. A Christian account of human personhood can extend this analysis, noting that we learn to respond rightly to these changing circumstances by recognizing that God, too, is involved in the temporality of the world. The practices that I discussed earlier in this chapter (with reference to Paul's account of the "gifts of the Spirit") provide a good starting-point for thinking about the ever-changing contexts of the Christian life.

Secondly, Schrag's comments on *multiplicity* provide a useful illustration of this chapter's development of the concept of "particularity without individuals." A trinitarian account of God's particularity does not imply isolation or a radical individualism; it describes God as complex, relational, and self-differentiated. The particularity of each of the Three gains its own proper contours only through its relation to the Others. In more general terms: the particular has its own shape, yes, but only because it has allowed itself to be shaped by others. Schrag accents this element of human particularity, arguing that the self is not isolated or private, but is necessarily multiple. He quotes with approval Nietzsche's comment:

> The assumption of one single subject is perhaps unnecessary; perhaps it is just as permissible to assume a multiplicity of subjects, whose interaction and struggle is the basis of our thought and our consciousness in general? . . . *My hypothesis*: The subject as multiplicity.[29]

This recognition of the inherent multiplicity of the human subject provides a much better illustration of divine particularity than does the supreme, isolated self as postulated in much Enlightenment thought. In God, subjectivity is not univocal, but multiple. As Schrag suggests, this multiple particularity is especially obvious in the process of human communication: while it obviously has a "source," this source cannot be understood as isolated from the others to whom it is directed and to whom it refers.

Still, there is an important difference between Nietzsche's account of "the subject as multiplicity" and the trinitarian virtue of particularity. This difference resides in Nietzsche's claim that this multiplicity necessarily involves "struggle." Human interaction may indeed be bound up in agonistic structures of controversy, struggle, and even violence; but it is not so with

---

[29] Friedrich Nietzsche, *The Will to Power*, ed. Walter Kaufmann, trans. Walter Kaufmann and R. J. Hollingdale (1967; reprint, New York: Vintage Books (Random House), 1968) [ET of: *Der Wille zur Macht* (1883-1888)], #490, cited in Schrag, *Communicative Praxis*, 148.

God. In God, particularity manifests itself within difference in a way that is
wholly harmonious: the path of peaceful flight.[30] Thus, while Christians are
called to understand particularity as defined by a certain multiplicity, they are
also called to allow their lives to be shaped by the peace and peaceableness of
a truly *trinitarian* particularity.

Thirdly, we have described God's particularity as *embodied*, most obviously
in the particular missions of incarnation and inspiration (the birthing of the
Wellspring and the pouring out of the Living Water). These bodies – the
womb of Mary, the flesh of Jesus, the Body of Christ – are socially related
bodies, bodies that are formed and shaped and "sedimented" through their
contact with others human beings and with God.

Schrag argues that human subjectivity is also necessarily embodied. Unlike
Enlightenment conceptions of the self (which objected to the notion of
embodiment because it seemed to imply fragility and the potential for ultimate
dissolution), the decentered subject need not fear embodiment.

> The introduction of embodiment into our considerations of the space and
> posture of the decentered subject opens up new dimensions of the phenomenon
> of presence. The presence of the subject is a *bodily* presence. This immediately
> shifts the emphasis away from a preoccupation with an elusive seat of unification
> of mental contents and a fugitive epistemological point. It is precisely such a
> center, sought for in modern philosophy of mind and epistemology, that is
> decentered. This shift makes all things new with regard to the meaning of
> presence.[31]

This too will have a number of implications for Christian ethics, which I will
explore in detail in part three of this book. Specifically, it calls us to practices
of pluralizing, in which embodied difference should be recognized and
validated (rather than reduced to a homogeneous economy of the same).

Schrag's description of the "space of subjectivity" helps to explicate the
account of divine particularity that I have offered in this chapter, as well as
helping us begin to think about how it might shape concrete Christian
practice. Schrag's description of the temporal, multiple, and embodied nature
of human subjectivity bears a strong family resemblance to the particularity of
the Three. Moreover, by following his advice to think about the human
subject, not as an "entity," but as a space from which and to which
communication and action are directed, we can recognize that such subjects

---

[30] See John Milbank, *Theology and Social Theory*, 6, 434, and *passim*. I offer some concrete
reflections on this claim in the next chapter.
[31] Schrag, *Communicative Praxis*, 152.

are not wholly independent of the contexts in which they are located, but are communally constituted in ways that reflect the trinitarian virtues of polyphony, participation, and particularity.

Beloved

I now turn to a literary development of particularity – one which also redefines subjectivity in a way that casts doubt on all pretensions to pure individualism, instead demanding communal engagement and relation to the other. As was the case with Schrag's work, traditional trinitarian categories are not explicit here; but for the reader who reads with trinitarian concerns, these categories seem to spring immediately to mind.[32]

"124 was spiteful. 124 was loud. 124 was quiet."[33] These are the opening sentences of the major divisions of Toni Morrison's *Beloved*, and those who have not yet read this masterpiece of fiction might be surprised to learn that "124" is a *house*. 124 Bluestone Road is inhabited by Sethe, a woman who attempted to escape the violence of slavery by travelling the underground railroad to southern Ohio. It is inhabited by Denver, her daughter – the only one of Sethe's children still willing to reside in this very mysterious house. It is inhabited by Baby Suggs, Sethe's mother-in-law, whose power as a leader in the community prompts everyone to tack on, to the end of her name, a sanctifying epithet: like "Yahweh, blessed be he," she is "Baby Suggs, holy." And from time to time, it is also inhabited by the ghost of a child, Sethe's own child, the child whose grave is marked only with the word *Beloved*: the child whom (Sethe once decided) would be better off dead than enslaved.

Our first indication of the novel's revision of what it means to be a subject appears in the way in which characters are *named*. We have noted throughout this chapter that names help to provide a context for particularity by connecting persons to narratives; this feature is amply demonstrated by the names of the characters in *Beloved* (as in many of Morrison's other works). Almost every name evokes a story: "Denver" is so named because the woman who helped Sethe through her difficult labor was named Amy Denver. One man names himself "Stamp Paid" because he had faced such horrible circumstances in his life that he felt as though any debt he might possibly have owed, to God or to anyone else, had been paid. "Paul D" is one of a number

---

[32] I have explored these categories in more detail in "Trinitarian Rhetoric in Morrison, Murdoch, and Dostoevsky."

[33] Toni Morrison, *Beloved* (1987; reprint, New York: New American Library, Signet Classics, 1991), 3, 207, 293.

of Pauls – slaves on the plantation who were differentiated by the assignment of random letters after their names (Paul A, Paul B); thus, even the slavemaster's attempt to abstract the man from his narrative context becomes *part* of the story (and thus underscores the inherently contextualizing feature of names).

So the persons in this story are indeed *subjects* – they act and speak and think – but they are subjects who are never isolated from the contexts and the narratives of which they are a part. The novel is thus able to depict persons who are in the process of coming to terms with their own particularity. They cannot do so in isolation from one another; but neither are they defined as mere "cogs in the machine," an unimportant segment of an undifferentiated whole.

Morrison's fiction subverts our usual assumptions about both oneness and difference. She achieves this goal by means of a number of strategies, one of which is her use of various triads with a family or household, in which each member's particularity is shaped and formed in a process of triangulation with two others. This suggests that human particularity is sedimented by a complex process of affirmation and negation, not simply with respect to a *single* other ("I define myself as like, or unlike, that person"); it is a more dynamic process, whereby some "third element" always disrupts and realigns the emerging particularity of each.

One such triad is that of Baby Suggs, Sethe, and Denver, whose shifting alliances and relationships keep the whole household in a state of non-hierarchical flux. In some senses, Sethe is clearly "in charge" in this household; Denver is her child, and Baby Suggs is in Sethe's care. But Baby Suggs maintains some clear seniority by means of her age and her sanctity; and Denver, who is learning to read, points us toward the authority of the future. As the characters change, the structures of authority continue to shift and fluctuate. When the dead child returns, incarnate, as the 18-year-old Beloved, a new triad forms with her mother and her sister, and all enter into a new experience of the pleasure and pain of communion – most beautifully reflected by three poetic soliloquies (in which each woman reflects upon her relationship with Beloved), and by the section that follows them, in which the three voices are woven together into a tapestry of participation and difference.

Thus, even though particularity does differentiate persons, allowing them to act and speak as subjects, it can never be achieved without others. One of the novel's memorable images occurs in the narration of Paul D's imprisonment as a member of a chain gang in Georgia. Suffering horrible physical, emotional, and sexual abuse from their masters, many of the men chose death rather than abiding such a life. One night, heavy rains weakened the muddy walls of their temporary cells, and the prisoners made a break for freedom.

They were, of course, still chained together, so they had to act in concert; if any one of them failed to escape, they would all fail. When they were finally far enough from the guards and the tracking dogs, they could break their chains apart and head toward freedom; they all gained their "independence," but none would forget how this came about; they did not achieve it "independently," but only because each man made sure that those to his left and to his right would also prevail. They become particular – and free – only in the context of communal activity.

The category of *freedom* is very useful for thinking through the question of human particularity, and Morrison wrestles with it throughout the novel. Does freedom for one person necessarily imply the subjugation of others? Is particularity ultimately a zero-sum game, in which individual freedom is always purchased at the expense of human relationships, and in which participation in a community prevents a person from having any truly distinctive identity? Sometimes it seems so, even within the novel – as when an extravagant party creates distance and jealousies such that the neighbors fail to warn Sethe of the arrival of the slavecatchers, or when Sethe's wholesale devotion to her children makes her unable to hear Paul D when he tells her, "You your own best thing, Sethe" ("Me?" she responds – "Me?").[34]

Nevertheless, Morrison seems to be seeking a way of breaking out of the apparent dilemma posed by the relationship between freedom and community. In this novel, the authority of each character is constantly being mitigated, tempered, supplanted, or supplemented by others. I have already noted the shifting lines of authority among those who live at 124 Bluestone Road. One could also point to the ways in which the novel's male characters – especially Paul D and Stamp Paid – take on a certain temporary and tentative authority, and then move away from the house or fade into the background while other characters become the chief actors. By allowing some of her characters to "participate" in the authority of other characters, Morrison calls into question some of our typical assumptions of authority – not only of masters over slaves and men over women, but of property-owners over interlopers, parents over children, and adults over their aging parents. These authoritarian dualisms are always being broken up by the intervention of an "other" – a third force which disturbs the false equilibrium, and unmasks the creeping tyranny. Denver realizes this late in the novel, when her mother's renewed relationship with Beloved threatens to collapse in on itself. "Whatever was happening, it only worked with three – not two."[35]

[34] Ibid., 335.
[35] Ibid., 298.

Essential to this portrait of the particularity of each character is a sense of participation in the lives of others: call and response, an interchange of properties, traditionally emphasized in trinitarian theology through the use of the term περιχώρησις. That one can still be particular, and yet inhere in another, is marvelously exemplified in the novel's depiction of Baby Suggs, preparing the crowd for her preaching at the Clearing:

> After situating herself on a huge flat-sided rock, Baby Suggs bowed her head and prayed silently. The company watched her from the trees. They knew she was ready when she put her stick down. Then she shouted, "Let the children come!" and they ran from the trees toward her.
>
> "Let your mothers hear you laugh," she told them, and the woods rang. The adults looked on and could not help smiling.
>
> Then "Let the grown men come," she shouted. They stepped out one by one from among the ringing trees.
>
> "Let your wives and children see you dance," she told them, and groundlife shuddered under their feet.
>
> Finally she called the women to her. "Cry," she told them. "For the living and the dead. Just cry." And without covering their eyes the women let loose.
>
> It started that way: laughing children, dancing men, crying women and then it got mixed up. Women stopped crying and danced; men sat down and cried; children danced, women laughed, children cried until, exhausted and riven, all and each lay about the Clearing damp and gasping for breath. In the silence that followed, Baby Suggs, holy, offered up to them her great big heart.[36]

The children, men, and women do not lose their particularity, but these categories do not remain precise and distinct. Instead, they blur together, interpenetrate one another, until each has so informed and altered the others that any claim to complete separateness cannot be maintained.

Because the characters of the novel move about one another in this way, we as readers are invited to do the same. We are invited to participate, not just in the plot, but in the characters themselves: to allow their memories to become our own. In an interview essay with the author, Sandi Russell describes the process clearly:

> The key to these forms of expression is participation: "There were spaces and places in which a single person could enter and behave as an individual within the context of the community. A small remnant of that you can see sometimes in black churches where people shout. It is a very personal grief and a personal statement done among people you trust. Done within the context of the

[36] Ibid., 107.

community, therefore safe." Just as the black preacher or the blues singer leaves room for the hearer's response, so Toni Morrison argues, "I have to provide places and spaces so that the reader can participate."[37]

In the lives of the characters, as in the lives of the readers, nothing is more antithetical to true humanity than separatedness, aloneness. And so, as "particular" readers, we too are reminded that our particularity is meaningful only in relation with those in whose lives we participate.

Morrison's novel can also help us understand how the virtue of particularity has been manifest in other trinitarian analyses – even in places where it is least expected. For example, St Augustine's triad of "memory, understanding, and will" does not seem, at first glance, to provide much space for particularity; it is usually interpreted as a description of three faculties that operate within a single center of consciousness (the isolated human mind). Thus, many contemporary commentators have drawn a straight line from Augustine to modern forms of individualism.

But for Morrison – and for St Augustine as well – memory, understanding, and will are *not* isolated individual faculties (as the modern age has tended to depict them). Rather, they are *communal* faculties which cross the barriers of "individuality" that we have erected around particular persons. For Morrison, memory is always "rememory": it is a recalling to mind of something out of the past, something that always involves others. We may have willfully forgotten it, but this forgetting cannot last, because others are always there to urge us to make the event present again through an active un-forgetting.[38] Likewise, the will is not the private property of an isolated center of consciousness, but always a communal activity: a product of so many external influences, a conjunction of various "sediments" without which there would be no particular "self." If we could learn to read Augustine's trinitarian analogies, not through the dominant Enlightenment culture in which we have been schooled, but through the communal, participative categories operative in Morrison's fiction, we might begin to understand why Augustine consid- ered the communally-shaped human mind, which exists only in relation to others, to be an entirely appropriate *vestigium trinitatis*. And then both

---

[37] Sandi Russell, " 'It's OK to say OK' " (1986), in *Critical Essays on Toni Morrison*, ed. Nellie Y. McKay, Critical Essays on American Literature (Boston: G. K. Hall and Co., 1988), 43–7.

[38] For further helpful reflections on this point, see Marilyn Sanders Mobley, "Memory, History and Meaning in Toni Morrison's *Beloved*," in *Toni Morrison*, ed. with an Introduction by Harold Bloom, Modern Critical Views (New York: Chelsea House Publishers, 1990), 189–99, esp. 191–5.

Morrison's novel and Augustine's analogy could be recognized as manifesting the trinitarian virtue of particularity – and thus creating a space for difference that is equally constituted by a profound mutual participation and a rich, multi-voiced polyphony.

LIVING WATER: TRINITARIAN PRACTICES

INTRODUCTION TO
PART THREE

The final third of this book examines some of the practices that inform, and are informed by, the trinitarian virtues elaborated in part two. This process is a circular one. Particular practices help to form us in the trinitarian virtues; thus, the discussion of virtues was already also a discussion of practices (such as baptism, eucharist, and the gifts of the Spirit). But on the other hand, the virtues direct us toward specific forms of practice as well. God's role (in both parts of this process) is traditionally appropriated to the Holy Spirit – the Living Water that flows through the Church in this "time between the times" (that is, between the first and second comings of Christ). The mission of the Spirit is to build up the Church, conveying grace in the virtuous formation of Christians by sustaining them in specific practices.

God has nourished us with this Living Water throughout the history of salvation – not only in the act of creation (Gen. 1:2), but in the continuous process of "producing" the world. According to the Old Testament, the Spirit is present in those who are called out by God for special tasks – people such as Belazel (Exod. 31:3), the seventy elders (Num. 11:25), and especially the prophets, through whom God spoke (and continues to speak):

> You shall know that I am in the midst of Israel, and that I, יהוה, am your God and there is no other. And my people shall never again be put to shame. Then afterward I will pour out my spirit on all flesh; your sons and your daughters shall prophesy, your old men shall dream dreams, and your young men shall see visions. Even on the male and female slaves, in those days, I will pour out my spirit. (Joel 2:27–29)

God's Spirit comes upon Mary (Luke 1:35) and rests on Jesus (Isaiah 11:2, Matt. 3:16 par.); moreover, this nourishing, life-giving, Living Water has been poured out upon the followers of Christ, empowering them to continue God's work in the world (Acts 2; John 14–16, 20:22–23).

The mission of the Spirit contributes to the development of certain practices which should *flow from* the trinitarian virtues, even while helping to *shape* us in those virtues. Any attempt to speak of the relation of Christian practices to the Christian doctrine of God must therefore grapple with the same questions of agency that arose with respect to the language of "virtue" in part two. Here again, we should not think of divine and human agency as essentially contrastive. Indeed, the biblical witness to the Spirit seems to underscore a stereoscopic vision of God and human beings as the agents of Christian practices. We act, but the Spirit acts through us – providing us with speech, prayer, and perhaps even the potential for deification:

> When we cry, "Abba! Father!" it is that very Spirit bearing witness with our spirit that we are children of God. (Rom. 8:15–16)

> Likewise the Spirit helps us in our weakness; for we do not know how to pray as we ought, but that very Spirit intercedes with sighs too deep for words. (Rom. 8:26)

> And all of us, with unveiled faces, seeing the glory of the Lord as though reflected in a mirror, are being transformed into the same image from one degree of glory to another; for this comes from the Lord, the Spirit. (2 Cor. 3:18)

In all these passages, divine and human agency are both at work: we speak *and* the Spirit bears witness; we pray *and* the Spirit intercedes; we see *and* the Spirit transforms. This "double agency" will be apparent throughout this part of the book, as we examine the role of the trinitarian virtues in the development of particular practices.

I have grouped my reflections under three headings: Peacemaking, Pluralizing, and Persuading. These practices underscore one of the principal claims of this book: that, for God and for us, "these three are one" in a way that requires us to re-think our understanding of oneness and difference. On the one hand, I have argued against the notion that oneness is achieved only by means of homogeneity; or, to use the language of part two, that the kinds of difference embodied in polyphonic music or table-fellowship are also constitutive of unity. And on the other hand, I have resisted the notion that multiplicity is necessarily a scattering to the winds, leading to naïve forms of relativism and isolationism; the trinitarian virtue of particularity does not exclude the possibility of harmonious consensus and mutual participation.

When transposed into a discussion of specific practices, these claims have direct and potentially far-reaching implications for our lives as Christians. Of first importance in this regard is the practice of *peacemaking*. Violence springs from the drive toward homogeneity: the desire to eliminate one's enemies, to efface or consume the otherness of the other, to exercise power in such a way that the difference implied by an opposing force is subordinated and ultimately extinguished. Peacemaking is possible only when the potential plurality represented by the other is allowed to flourish – that is, when it is no longer understood as a threat to oneness. The more thoroughly the trinitarian virtues inform Christian practice, the more obvious and effective will be their role in shaping us into instruments of God's peace.

Secondly, *pluralizing*. Christianity must not only "make room" for multiple modes of discourse and multiple forms of practice; it is in fact *defined* by such multiplicity. Christian practice can be, and indeed must be, both "catholic" and "evangelical" in the broadest senses of these terms: it must be "manifest throughout the whole" and it must "proclaim the Good News." In order to achieve these ends, we must acknowledge the diversity of the world "throughout the whole" of which the Good News is to be proclaimed. This diversity requires a pluralistic approach to doctrine and ethics. This does not mean, of course, that just *any* practice or *any* belief will do; it does mean, however, that multiple voices must be heard in the contexts of (for example) Christian worship and family life.

And finally, *persuading*: because the decision to act, even in the midst of difference, can be helpfully illuminated by analogy to the faculty of rhetoric. We can describe God as engaged in the process of persuasion with respect to the created order; this in turn has implications for our interactions with one another. The trinitarian practice of persuading will affect the Christian exercise of authority – which has, too often, been modeled on the coercive power of the nation-state, rather than the persuasive power of the triune God. We are called to exercise authority in ways such that the Body of Christ is truly *one* body with *many* members – which is to say that it can be neither a bland, homogeneous "melting pot" nor a chaos of meaningless divergence. In concrete terms, this means that the Church must rethink its understanding of the teaching office, reconceiving it in rhetorical rather than quasi-military categories – employing not the technique of command, but the art of persuasion.

The concrete nature of these discussions will bear the mark of all such efforts (already described in chapter 1) – contingency, provisionality, and an absence of definitive, tautological finality. In addition, the move from the abstract to the concrete requires one to operate increasingly out of one's own experience. I am "particular," in the sense described in the previous chapter; I am shaped by others, but I can also be differentiated from others (I am male, married, a father, an Anglican, and so on). Here, readers will find a "particular" slant on

Christian practices; and as such, my claims are much more likely to provoke disagreement. Nevertheless, I hope that this part of the book will not be rejected simply on the basis of such disagreement. While I would certainly like to persuade readers of the positions I advocate here, this is not my primary goal. First and foremost, I would like to bring about a shift in our conversations about Christian practices, such that we attend more closely to their relationship to trinitarian doctrine. In other words, I ask not so much that my "positions" be accepted, but that we take trinitarian concerns into account when addressing questions such as these.

To those many readers who will disagree with my claims, I would like to say: I hope that your concrete alternative positions will take their cue from the doctrine of the Trinity, rather than ignoring that doctrine or considering it irrelevant to matters of praxis. I will have achieved most of my purpose in writing this part of the book if those who disagree with my views about (for example) Christian worship will make their arguments in the following form: "No, the doctrine of the Trinity doesn't underwrite *that* practice; instead, it calls us to . . ." This in itself would be a great improvement over the prevailing mode of contemporary theological discourse, in which Christian practices are advocated, enacted, and evaluated with very little attention to trinitarian doctrine.

One of the reasons that issues of concrete practice engender so much disagreement is that they can only begin to make sense if they are *lived*, rather than merely discussed. Thus, the practices that I describe here can only be fully persuasive when one participates in them as a member of the Christian community. Indeed, my goal throughout this book has been to coax trinitarian theology out of its typical surroundings (the ethereal world of verbal abstraction) and into the context of concrete practice. Readers might thus want to ask themselves, not merely whether point A flows logically from point B, but also whether my comments ring true – or whether ways might be found to *enable* them to ring true – in the day-to-day practices of actual Christian communities. For it is through such communities that God, the Living and Life-Giving Water, is most clearly discerned, received, and poured out upon the whole world.

Chapter 7

PEACEMAKING

Peaceableness and peacemaking are central elements of the Christian witness. In the earliest period of Christian history, especially, this was one of the aspects of the new faith that clearly distinguished it from the civil religion of the Roman Empire, and from many strands of Judaism as well. Christians, by and large, did not participate in the Roman army during the first two centuries, both because the army was thoroughly dominated by pagan religious rituals and because of an aversion to killing. The early Christian apologists, including Justin, Hippolytus, Tertullian, and Origen, speak very eloquently against Christian participation in the military in particular – and indeed, against any form of collaboration with violence.[1]

This general pacifism began to shift in the years leading up to the conversion of Constantine, and after that time took a dramatic leap. The new consensus on peace and war is often attributed to St Augustine – though his willingness to countenance violence was limited, and his views on this matter are often misunderstood and are rarely given the nuanced treatment they deserve.[2] Along with this shift in Christian attitudes toward state-sanctioned violence came a diluted sense of the importance of non-violence in one's personal relationships. Thus, for a number of historical, cultural, and hermeneutical reasons, the pacifist consensus of early Christianity lost its foothold, and has never fully recovered – despite having received an important infusion of energy from many of the Radical Reformers of the sixteenth century, as well as their heirs in the contemporary era.[3]

[1] For a review of recent historical scholarship on this point, see David G. Hunter, "A Decade of Research on Early Christians and Military Service," *Religious Studies Review* 18, no. 2 (1992): 87-94.
[2] For two valuable exceptions to this rule, see Rowan Williams, "Politics and the Soul: A Reading of the *City of God*," *Milltown Studies* 19 (1987): 55-72, and John Milbank, *Theology and Social Theory*, ch. 12.
[3] For the great variations on this issue among the Radical Reformers, see George H.

Historians may well want to dispute the details of this thumbnail sketch. I offer it only to provide a very general benchmark against which to measure just how much more significant the practice of peacemaking might become, were the doctrine of the Trinity to play a more active role in our thinking about various elements of Christian practice. Typically, those Christians who have emphasized the practice of peacemaking have appealed primarily to the ethical teachings of Jesus, the importance of relying on God as one's sole defense, and/or the idolatrous practices inherent in the many coercive and violent practices of the modern nation-state. Such appeals are important, and this chapter has no intention of minimizing them. But they can be strengthened and woven together by the recognition of peacemaking as a trinitarian practice. The Triune God is a God of peace; and God's peace, through the grace of the Living Water poured out upon us, nourishes and strengthens us to participate in the practice of peacemaking. In so doing, we are taken up into the peace of God, restored to the image of the God of peace. Through God's work in our lives, we have the opportunity to become a peaceable and peacemaking people.

The Path of Peaceful Flight[4]

By *peace*, I mean harmonious relations; among human beings, the word refers to the ability to face and negotiate the strife, quarrels, and disagreement that mark our daily existence without resorting to violence. Somewhat ironically, "peace" is meaningful only in those circumstances in which strife, quarrels, and disagreement can potentially occur. Thus, when we speak about peace, we are necessarily speaking about multiplicity – and, more specifically, about multiple or divided wills that can come into conflict with one another. And while we might claim that inanimate objects can have peaceable effects on our lives ("a peaceful meadow"), or personify them as "peaceful" (the "Pacific" Ocean), we also recognize that such objects cannot really be "at peace" with someone (or with themselves). We can speak of peace only when will(s) can, at least *potentially*, differ – and can thus potentially come into conflict.

Williams, *The Radical Reformation*, 3rd edn (Kirksville: Sixteenth Century Journal Publishers, 1992); for one of the most influential contemporary voices, see John Howard Yoder, *The Politics of Jesus: Vicit Agnus Noster*, 2nd edn (Grand Rapids, Mich.: William B. Eerdmans, 1994).

[4] The closing line of Milbank, *Theology and Social Theory*, 434.

On the other hand, peace also implies unity, or oneness, or at least coexistence; it implies a decision to give up or sublate whatever could bring one into conflict with another, whatever disrupts harmonious relations. To pursue peace is to come to agreement, or at least to negotiate difference, rather than turning to violence. We can meaningfully speak of peace only when some potential for conflict *exists*, yet is not *actualized* – that is, when there is difference that could potentially lead to conflict, but which is not allowed to escalate into strife and violence.

Why, then, do we sometimes speak of someone being "at peace," e.g., "at peace with herself"? Such statements necessarily assume that human beings can be divided against themselves. If the human will were indivisible, there would be no potential source of conflict which, by being checked, could warrant the description "at peace." Christian anthropology has typically posited a divided will; St Paul testifies to it in Romans 7, and Augustine describes it in Books 7 and 8 of the *Confessions*. Such an anthropology makes it possible to speak meaningfully of being "in conflict with oneself" or "at peace with oneself" – at least with respect to human beings.

These same human beings, it will be remembered, are "created in the image of God." To what extent can this division of the will be predicated of God? At first glance we might assume that this particular human attribute – the divided will – is a result of the Fall, or perhaps simply necessitated by our created state. God, surely, does not have a divided will. And yet, if God's will were understood as simple, wholly unified, and incapable (even hypothetically) of such division, then it would makes little sense to attribute "peace" to God, any more than we would attribute conflict or disorder. Why, then, do we find several biblical texts wherein God is called "the God of peace"?

The God of peace

The word *peace* is very common in the Bible, especially when compared to non-biblical literature of the time.[5] In the Old Testament, the English *peace* commonly translates the Hebrew שָׁלוֹם (*shalom*); this word is translated in the Septuagint as εἰρήνη (*eirēnē*), which is also translated by the English *peace*. In both Testaments, God is frequently described as bringing peace and granting peace to the people; in some cases this refers to a peaceful relationship between

[5] Ceslas Spicq, O.P., *Theological Lexicon of the New Testament*, ed. and trans. James D. Ernest, 3 vols (Peabody, Mass.: Hendrickson Publishers, 1994) [ET of: *Notes de lexicographie néo-testamentaire*, 3 vols (Fribourg: Éditions Universitaires, 1982)], *s.v.* εἰρηεύω, I:424–38.

the people and God, and in other cases the reference is to peace *among* people. But in some cases, at least, peace seems to be predicated of God.

The only Old Testament occurrence that might be interpreted this way is Judges 6:24, where Gideon calls an altar שָׁלוֹם יְהוָה, thus juxtaposing the notion of peace with the name of God. This could be read as a predication; however, the fact that the phrase is used in order to *name* something makes its context unclear. Most commentators seem to believe that Gideon is here making a claim about God as the *giver* of peace – an interpretation which seems consonant with much of the Old Testament.

In the New Testament, however, we find a wider range of examples. In five instances, the NT writers speak of "the God of peace,"[6] and in one instance (2 Thess. 3:16) of "the Lord of peace." Again, in these passages – as in Judges 6:24 – God might be construed as the source of peace; this too would be consonant with the other uses of εἰρήνη in the New Testament. But all six passages could also be read as implying that peace can actually be predicated of God. One passage in particular seems more intelligible if read this way: "Now may the Lord of peace give you peace at all times in all ways" (2 Thess. 3:16). While allowing for stylistic parallelism and other possible explanations, it seems rather odd that Paul would feel compelled to say something like "May the Lord, who gives peace, give peace." Here, especially, the text can be construed as describing God not only as a "dispenser" of peace, but as actually *marked by* the quality of peace. What could this mean?

In a radical monotheism which allowed no "otherness" in God, such an attribution would be meaningless – or at least, it would differ radically from our normal use of the word. This may explain why some readers of the passage in Judges have found it odd to imagine that *shalom* could properly be predicated of God; such readers assume (perhaps wrongly) that there is no space for otherness in יְהוָה.[7] In any case, in the Christian doctrine of God, there *is* space for otherness; could this also imply a potential for difference of will? If so, perhaps it *is* meaningful to speak of peace as an attribute of God – that is, to speak of "the God of peace."[8]

---

[6] Most of the occurrences are Pauline: "The God of peace be with all of you" (Rom. 15:33); "The God of peace will shortly crush Satan under your feet" (Rom. 16:20); "the God of peace will be with you" (Phil. 4:9); "May the God of peace sanctify you entirely" (1 Thess. 5:23). One reference to "the God of peace" occurs in the Epistle to the Hebrews (13:20).

[7] Relevant questions have been raised about this claim. See, for example, Wyschogrod, "The 'Shema Israel' "; Wyschogrod, "A Jewish Perspective on Incarnation," and Elliot R. Wolfson, "Iconic Visualization and the Imaginal Body of God," both in *Modern Theology* 12, no. 2 (April 1996): 195–209 and 137–162, respectively.

[8] This is not to suggest, of course, the New Testament writers had worked out the details

We already observed that peace requires a potential for division that is not actualized. Here too it may be useful to speak of God's "division" or "difference" under two headings: the *potential* for division and *actual* division. What we discover, in Paul as in many later construals of Christian theology, is that in God, there is difference, and thus the *potential* for strife (thus making the language of "peace" meaningful); but that God – unlike human beings – chooses not to allow this potential for strife to be actualized. I have already quoted Philippians 2, which lauds the decision to forgo strife. The choices described in that passage – not to exploit one's equality with the other, to empty oneself, to become obedient unto death, and to exalt the other – are the choices made by God. Here below, matters are otherwise; in our lives, we often *do* seek to exploit our equality with another; we *resist* the ideas of self-emptying, obedience, and death; we *avoid* the exaltation of the other, seeking to exalt ourselves instead; and so on. God does not follow the course that we might follow; in God, each of the Three acts *for the sake of* the Others.[9]

The Gospel of John offers a similar image concerning the Three: "And I will ask the Source [τὸν πατέρα], who will give you another Advocate, to be with you forever" (John 14:16). Here, we read of wholly peaceable relations among Christ (who asks), the Source (who gives), and the Living Water (who is given) – even though this Living Water will in some sense do the work of the Wellspring (and is thus called "another" advocate). Despite their differences, the Three work harmoniously to achieve a common goal (in this case, the mission of the Spirit to the Church). There is no hint of the jealousy, discord, and strife that are so common whenever human beings attempt to cooperate in a common endeavor.

Again, though, this is not to say that there is no *potential* for strife. In a number of biblical texts, we are given a clear indication of that potential, even though strife and violence do not ultimately occur. In chapter 4 I discussed the Temptation of Jesus, where we must assume at least a *potential* for conflict within God; otherwise the entire scene becomes meaningless, or a ruse at best. Similarly, Christ's prayer in Gethsemane suggests a potential for difference, in its request for an alternative course of action. Two wills are described as tending in opposite directions; Jesus speaks of his own will, and then speaks of "your will." The conflict does not actually occur, for Jesus submits his "own" will to the will of the Other – or, in the light of our above discussion

---

of this conception when they employed the phrase. But here, as often in the NT, we find a proto-trinitarian theology, even though all its nuances were not yet in place.
[9] Cf. Staniloae, "Holy Trinity," 89.

of particularity, we might say that he recognizes how thoroughly his will is (or should be) *shaped* by the will of the Other. In any case, without some potential for difference, the entire narrative would be unintelligible.[10] The Three are never in essential conflict with one another, yet such conflict must be theoretically possible because of their difference (the Three are certainly non-identical, as the pseudo-Athanasian Creed makes clear). God is *capable* of being internally conflicted, but chooses otherwise; and thus we can meaningfully claim that the triune God is a God of peace.

This notion of God's interior peaceableness is echoed throughout the early period of Christian theological reflection. Tertullian says that the Three are "distinct, not divided," "discrete but not separated";[11] he thus implies difference in God, but asserts that this difference does not lead to strife. Origen construes a model for the peaceful co-existence of the Three on the basis of the diversity of spiritual gifts described in 1 Corinthians 12; he argues that Paul "thereby explains very clearly that there is no separation in the Trinity, but that what is called the 'gift of the Spirit' is ministered through the Son and worked by God the Father."[12] St Gregory Nazianzus rejects polytheism precisely because it involves faction and hence leads to lack of order, which, in turn, leads to disintegration.[13] Yet according to Gregory, monarchy or monotheism is *not* defined as "the sovereignty of a single person (after all, self-discordant unity can become a plurality)," but rather "the single rule produced by equality of nature, harmony of will, identity of action, and the convergence toward their source of what springs from unity."[14] Note especially the phrase "*harmony* of will": the description here is not of a narrow monism, but of *difference* that is nevertheless brought into some form of polyphonic agreement. In this way, Gregory is able to describe a monotheism which is not monolithic but rather fully trinitarian, and thus one to which the attribute *peace* can meaningfully be applied.

In the contemporary era, intradivine peace and harmony has been empha-

---

[10] An even stronger instance of potential conflict is Jesus' cry of dereliction from the cross; but it is a more complicated one, since some have argued that here, conflict within God is not merely potential but actual. See the response of Karl Barth in *CD* IV/1, 185ff [*KD* IV/1, 202ff]; Barth denies "even the possibility" of conflict in God (186), but does not clarify what sense this makes of the word *peace* when predicated of God.

[11] *distincte, . . . non divise; discreti, non separati* (*Adv. Prax.* 2.11).

[12] Origen, *On First Principles*, I.3.7, my translation from the Latin text of Rufinus (most of the original Greek text is lost): *Ex quo manifestissime designatur quod nulla est in trinitate discretio, sed hoc, quod donum spiritus dicitur, ministratur per filium et inoperatur per deum patrem.*

[13] *Or.* 29.2.

[14] Ibid., trans. from Norris, *Faith Gives Fullness*, 245.

sized in the work of theologians associated with a social doctrine of the Trinity. For example, Jürgen Moltmann argues:

> The one God is a God *at one* with Godself. That presupposes the personal self-differentiation of God, and not merely a modal differentiation, for only persons can be at one with one another. . . . The unitedness, the at-oneness, of the Triunity is already given with the fellowship of the Three.[15]

Similar descriptions appear in the work of Leonardo Boff.[16] Building on these insights, John Dear has offered an explicitly pacifist interpretation of the Trinity: "The God of peace lives in eternal community – nonviolently."[17] Dear describes God as not only living *in* community but as *being* a community – a description that I would also advocate, so long as the word *community* is understood along the lines of Paul's analogy of the members of the body (and not taken to mean a group of discrete individuals who come together in accidental and temporary ways). Even better, perhaps, is Dear's description of the Trinity as a *communion* – a word that implies both difference and harmony, and seems less likely to be interpreted individualistically.

To summarize: "God is a God not of disorder but of peace" (1 Cor. 14:33). In its affirmation of difference that does not devolve into strife, the doctrine of the Trinity establishes the theological priority of peace. God is internally differentiated, but the resulting potentiality for conflict is faced and negotiated by means of mutual love and abundant donation – not through coercion, strife, or violence. In this polyphonic orchestration of oneness and difference, Christian thought finds its highest good and greatest perfection. It is, however, a vision that meets with considerable contrast in the everyday life of human beings.

The fall to violence[18]

Created as we are in the image of God, human beings bear the stamp of God's likeness and are capable of modeling the peaceableness of the triune God. That

---

[15] Moltmann, *The Trinity and the Kingdom*, 150, translation altered [*Trinität und Reich Gottes*, 167].

[16] For example, Boff, *Trinity and Society*, 49.

[17] Dear, *God of Peace*, 50.

[18] This phrase is employed by Marjorie Suchocki in *The Fall to Violence: Original Sin in Relational Theology* (New York: Continuum, 1994). While I do not agree with her nearly complete equation of sin and violence, I think that the two concepts share many features – and that Genesis 1–11 can profitably be read as describing a Fall (or "Falls") that accent these connections.

we have, in most cases, failed miserably even to approximate this state, testifies to the catastrophic event of the Fall. Theologians have typically located the Fall in Genesis 3, and specifically in the decision of the man and the woman to eat the fruit of the tree of the knowledge of good and evil. But the whole range of pre-Abrahamic stories in Genesis describe human beings as progressively distancing themselves from the image in which they were created; and thus I would prefer to speak of a rather more complex Fall, perhaps even a series of "Falls," in which human beings allow difference to devolve into conflict, strife, and (usually) violence.

In Genesis 1–11, we are provided with five different instances in which human beings mistreat or otherwise abuse that which they have been given. In Genesis 3, having been given a garden with food aplenty, the man and woman partake of the only thing which was forbidden to them; they are exiled from the garden, but they are not cursed (though the serpent and the land are). In Genesis 4, Cain kills his brother, ignoring God's advice to "master sin"; as a result, he *is* cursed (though protected). Again, in Genesis 6, the multiplication of people upon the earth is greeted not with gratitude but with wickedness; the earth is "filled with violence" (Gen. 6:11,13). After the flood, the re-establishment of the covenant with Noah is followed by an act of sexual license (its precise nature is somewhat ambiguous), which leads to the curse of Canaan (Gen. 9:25). And finally, the decision on the part of human beings to build a city with its tower in the heavens (and thereby "make a name for themselves") results in the abandonment of their building project, the confusion of their languages, and the scattering of the people over the face of the earth (Gen. 11:1–11).

Examined as a whole, this narrative helps us to understand the connection between the Fall and violence more completely than does a focus on Genesis 3 alone. The Fall consists not only of humanity's having fallen prey to a trick of language (a conclusion drawn by many readers of Genesis 3). Its scope is much larger: it concerns our unwillingness to accept the *otherness* of the other; for us, difference tends to become a warrant for violence, rather than a reflection of the peaceable image of God. All five stories describe an attempt to elevate one's own significance at the cost of the other. The man and woman eat the fruit because they believe it will elevate them in relation to God; Cain kills to obliterate his rival; Ham enjoys some kind of sexual license at another's expense; the builders at Babel seek their own fame, demanding that others recognize their superiority. At the center of the five stories is that of the flood, in which the general and thoroughgoing obliteration of the other – described here in the general terms of wickedness, evil, and violence – is sufficient to bring about the deluge.

These stories narrate the desire to subjugate the other and to elevate the self; they thus contrast markedly with the internal life of God, in which the Other is recognized to be "of one being" with the Self. The stories describe acts of violence against the other, though the violence is clearly greater in some cases than in others – ranging from murder to the violation of a piece of fruit. This latter violation (the first in the order of the narrative) would appear innocuous enough at first glance; but the fruit is protected by divine sanction, and its violation is thus a violation of God's trust. Interestingly, most of the stories seem to imply the penetration or piercing of an "other": the fruit, the body, the bedchamber, the heavens. This desire to violate the other – to enter it, in order to consume it or to gain pleasure from it, without regard for its integrity and otherness – is characteristic of the "fall to violence." Indeed, it represents a turning against *ourselves*; the violation of the other is ultimately a violation of self. This follows necessarily from the claim that all human beings are created in the image of God, and that their particularity does not isolate them from one another. Yet time and again, we fail to do what the triune God does by nature: to know and to love the Self in the Other.

The Genesis account also helps us to understand why Christian claims about interior peaceableness of God have so often gone unnoticed. The God described in these chapters seems rather violent – expelling the couple from Eden (3:23–24), sentencing Cain to wander the earth (4:12), and, most starkly, choosing to "blot out from the earth" the human beings and all living creatures (6:7). Once human beings have chosen not to live in the peaceable image in which they were created, God apparently chooses to speak to them in terms they can understand – that is, in violent terms. God's violent activity toward creation is manifest in a wide range of biblical narratives.

But even as we survey the "body counts" in various parts of the Bible, we should not lose sight of three important truths. First, not all of the carnage is of divine origin; much of it is brought about by human beings. Secondly, the internal life of God remains peaceable, even though the process of producing the world requires actions that appear (to us, at least) to be strikingly violent. (Gardeners probably seem violent to the inhabitants of gardens as well.) Finally, and most importantly: according to the Christian narrative, God is not merely a propagator of violence against the world, but also one who *suffers* the world's violence. Indeed, the ultimate salvation of humanity will come about by means of a human act of violence – an act not propagated by God, but rather one propagated by human beings upon God. In the crucifixion and resurrection of the incarnate Word, we are offered a way out of the violence to which we have fallen. At first, this does not seem to be of earth-shattering significance, since the biblical stories often attest to the unpleasant consequences of violence (even for the perpetrator); people might well be expected to seek an alternative to violence at every turn. But matters are not so simple, because violence is never easy to escape.

The fall to violence tends to be perpetuated, because every act of violence – every attempt to obliterate or consume the otherness of the other – is met by a reassertion of otherness (by the other or by his or her protectors) and by a corresponding attempt to obliterate the original perpetrator of violence. I have already commented on this cycle in the Genesis account, and have noted that even God acts violently toward the world; similar examples may be found elsewhere in the Bible. This account seems consonant with René Girard's description of violence as rooted in mimetic desire – a desire that is difficult to eliminate. Violent acts engender a desire for retribution; and if this fails, says Girard, "violence seeks and always finds a surrogate victim."[19] Each act of vengeance is seen as a new transgression, and the cycle continues. According to Girard, societies have sometimes sought to *prevent* this cycle by systems of sacrifice. "The sacrificial process furnishes an outlet for those violent impulses that cannot be mastered by self-restraint; a partial outlet, to be sure, but always renewable, and one whose efficacy has been attested by an impressive number of reliable witnesses. The sacrificial process prevents the spread of violence by keeping vengeance in check."[20]

In modern societies, the judicial system provides this outlet for vengeance – not by eliminating it, but by codifying it and demanding that it be carried out anonymously (and dictating that no vengeance be sought, in reaction, upon the system of justice itself). It is generally more effective than systems of sacrifice, but, as Girard notes, "it can only exist in conjunction with a firmly established political power. And like all modern technological advances, it is a two-edged sword, which can be used to oppress as well as to liberate."[21]

Whether the deflection of this tendency toward revenge takes place through judicial, political, or religious channels, it must maintain a "transcendent" character, so that the punishment that it distributes does not become a warrant for further violence. Once it loses this transcendent character, "there are no longer any terms by which to define the legitimate form of violence and to recognize it among the multitude of illicit forms."[22] And such breakdowns are inevitable, according to Girard, since all such attempts to stop the cycle of violence are ultimately human institutions, and

---

[19] René Girard, *Violence and the Sacred*, trans. Patrick Gregory (Baltimore: Johns Hopkins University Press, 1977), 2 [ET of: *La violence et le sacré* (Paris: Grasset, 1972), 15].

[20] Ibid., 18 [35].

[21] Ibid, 23 [41].

[22] Ibid., 24 [43].

their artificiality will eventually be recognized. ("The only true scapegoats," says one of Girard's collaborators, "are those we cannot recognize as such."[23]) Once this recognition occurs, the mechanisms of restraint are revealed to be fraudulent; they have not actually *put an end* to violence, but have simply carried it out in quieter ways. As this becomes obvious to more and more people, they lose confidence in the ability of the system (the judiciary, the politicians, the priests) and instead find ways of intervening directly for the purpose of revenge – thus reinaugurating the cycle of violence.[24]

Whether or not one accepts Girard's *explanation* for the perpetuation of violence, he does at least seem to have described – with an appropriate level of bleakness – the circumstances in which we find ourselves today. Violence does seem endemic to our culture; in the past, it was contained by officially sanctioned acts of violence against which revenge was impossible, but this mechanism no longer inspires much confidence. What, we might well ask, is to prevent the resumption of the war of all against all?[25] The widespread violence that we know today seems very closely related to the disintegration of the mechanisms of its containment.

One can easily see how the Torah functioned as a transcendental check on violence of the sort that Girard describes. An act of wrongdoing was described as punishable by violence, even death; but this act could not be revenged, because it was justified transcendentally (that is, it was said to be sanctioned by God). Some of Jesus' commentary on the Torah can be understood as a recognition that current interpretations of the Law were doing little more than *masking* the desire that breeds violence. In Matthew's Gospel, he frequently reminds his disciples that they have "heard that it was said" that transcendentally-sanctioned violence of one sort or another was legitimate. This was true for acts of revenge generally ("an eye for an eye and a tooth for a tooth," Matt. 5:38), and for attitudes toward one's enemies (Matt. 5:43).

It hardly need be noted that these justifications of revenge still hold sway in our own culture – even though the state, rather than God, is now the only entity that seems able to impose (with at least occasional success) a transcendent quality upon the violence it dispenses. This, of course, does not prevent innumerable acts of violence and revenge from taking place on a daily basis. Here I refer not simply, or even primarily, to the acts of murder, rape, and

---

[23] Guy Lefort, in René Girard, Jean-Michel Oughourlian, and Guy Lefort, *Things Hidden Since the Foundation of the World*, trans. Stephen Bann and Michael Metteer (Stanford: Stanford University Press, 1987), 129 [ET of: *Des choses cachées depuis la fondation du monde* (Paris: Grasset, 1978), 152].

[24] Girard, in ibid., 128–9 [151].

[25] Cf. the account of Lefort, in ibid., 137 [160].

torture, of which our various forms of mass media make us so thoroughly (though highly selectively) aware. I refer also the myriad ways in which we "return evil for evil" – whether in thought, word, or deed – at our jobs, in our communities, and among our families and friends. Can this cycle be broken?

The peace of God

The cycle *can* be broken, but only by God. Our sinful condition does not naturally incline us away from violence; indeed, it inclines us toward revenge. If we had retained the fullness of the image of God, as described in the creation account, we would have also retained God's peaceableness; but we have fallen to violence (a fall not only enshrined in the primeval histories of Genesis, but re-enacted daily among human beings). Peace can only be restored by God's gracious act of self-giving, through which we come to participate in the peace of God. In this process, God's Triunity plays a key role: in their polyphony, mutual participation, and non-individualistic particularity, the Three form us – through specific communal practices – into a peaceable and peacemaking people.

That God wills peace for the created order is shown implicitly in the Genesis narrative. There is originally no enmity between the serpent and the woman, as can be inferred from the later curse (3:15). Indeed, human beings do not seem to be at odds with animals until after the flood. The animals are named peaceably (2:19–20); they live together on the ark (Gen. 6–7). Only plants and fruits, not animals, are originally provided as food for human beings (Gen. 1:29). Only after the flood are human beings permitted, for their own purposes, to exercise violence against animals (Gen. 9:3).[26]

Enmity *among* human beings is also excluded from the original plan of creation. This is strongly implied by God's outrage in reaction to violence – both to Cain's murder of Abel (4:10–11) and to the general violence that breaks out among human beings (6:11). Ancient Israel looked forward to a restoration of the peaceable kingdom, memorably described in Isaiah's image (11:6–9):

> The wolf shall live with the lamb
>> the leopard shall lie down with the kid,
>> the calf and the lion and the fatling together,
>> and a little child shall lead them.

[26] The apparent exception, Abel's sacrifice of the "firstlings of his flock" (Gen. 4:4), is not for his own gain but as a return of the gift to God.

The cow and the bear shall graze,
>   their young shall lie down together;
>   and the lion shall eat straw like the ox.
The nursing child shall play over the hole of the asp,
>   and the weaned child shall put its hand on the adder's den.
They will not hurt or destroy on all my holy mountain;
>   for the earth will be full of the knowledge of יהוה
>   as the waters cover the sea.

According to Isaiah, the peaceable kingdom was to be ushered in by a shoot "from the stump of Jesse" (11:1), who will judge the poor with righteousness and "decide with equity for the meek of the earth" (11:4). Christians came to understand that prophecy as having been fulfilled in the person of Jesus. Through the birthing of the Wellspring, God reasserted the reality of humanity as the image of God in all its peaceableness. As "the image of the invisible God" (Col. 1:15), Christ offers us a portrait of true *humanity* as well – a humanity untouched by the Fall and by the cycles of mimetic violence that have become so commonplace that they almost seem to be a part of the human condition. Mary and Jesus provide us with a portrait of true humanity in its original, uncorrupted, nonviolent state.

The angel brings Mary news without violence ("Do not be afraid," Luke 1:30), and she accepts it without violence ("Let it be with me according to your word," Luke 1:38). Mary's child preaches peace and peaceableness, and enacts it in his ministry. He specifically replaces the counsels of mimetic violence that had been gleaned from the Torah with counsels of nonresistance.

> But I say to you, Do not resist an evildoer. But if anyone strikes you on the right cheek, turn the other also; and if anyone wants to sue you and take your coat, give your cloak as well; and if anyone forces you to go one mile, go also the second mile. Give to everyone who begs from you, and do not refuse anyone who wants to borrow from you. . . . Love your enemies and pray for those who persecute you. (Matt. 5:39–44)

The healings, feedings, and restorations that Jesus accomplishes seek to restore wholeness to that which has been divided, often against itself. Jesus thus provides us with a model of peaceableness which marks true humanity, as opposed to the woefully fallen image that we have come to describe as "the human condition." Moreover, in addition to making peace a hallmark of his own ministry and teaching, Jesus enacted it in his death. As he had counseled others to do, he did not resist evildoers, but loved and forgave his enemies to the end. To his disciples, he gives peace – not "as the world gives," but the true peace of God. In doing so, he reveals to them "what has been hidden from the foundation of the world" (Matt. 13:35).

This passage was chosen by René Girard as the title of one of his books, in which he interprets these "hidden things" as the cycles of violence upon which the world, even in its more peaceful moments, has been built. Girard sees the Jewish and Christian scriptures "as a set of texts which reveal the violence on which peace within communities has ordinarily been founded."[27] More specifically, they point out the "founding murder" upon which the systems of vengeance and sacrifice are based, and thus reveal the whole idea of transcendentally-justified violence as a grand deception. Jesus uncovers these mysteries; and for his efforts, he is put to death.

> Jesus engages in decisive struggle with these particular powers. And it is at the very moment when they apparently triumph – at the moment when the speech that brings them out into the open and condemns them as being basically murderous and violent has been reduced to silence by the crucifixion, that is to say by a new murder and new violence – that these powers, believing themselves to be victorious once again, have in fact been vanquished. It is at that point, in effect, that the secret of their operations, which has never before been revealed, becomes inscribed quite explicitly in the gospel text.[28]

This interpretation, Girard believes, is born out in the letters of Paul, who sees Christ's death as a victory over the powers of death and revenge.

One might, of course, immediately object that Christ's death came to be seen as a sacrifice as well, and that transcendentally-justified violence was thus perpetuated, not eradicated, by Christianity. Girard sees this as a decisive wrong-turn, endorsed primarily (though not exclusively) by the Epistle to the Hebrews. That this interpretation was later taken up by the Church and given a certain pride of place, especially in the medieval period, is (according to Girard) simply further testimony to the powerful desire to justify the perpetuation of violence and revenge. Christianity tended to use its power to persecute, and its perpetuation of violence was harshly condemned by atheistic humanism – Nietzsche being a prime example of this critique.[29]

I have come into conversation with the work of René Girard for two reasons: first, he helps us understand why violence tends to perpetuate itself, and how difficult it can be to break that cycle; and secondly, he recognizes that

---

[27] Fergus Kerr, O.P., "Rescuing Girard's Argument?" *Modern Theology* 8, no. 4 (October 1992): 389.

[28] Girard, in *Things Hidden*, 191 [*Des choses cachées*, 215].

[29] Ibid., 225–6 [248–50].

the Christian narrative has a central role to play in breaking that cycle. But he fails to give a thorough account of *how* it breaks that cycle, because he does not discuss how the Christian narrative points us back to the triune God, in whom peace can always already be discerned.[30]

For Girard, Jesus is ultimately a wise man who absorbs (and does not return) the violence that is inflicted upon him; his story ends with the crucifixion. But for Christians, the crucifixion is clearly *not* the end of the story; it is inextricably linked to the resurrection (a linkage that makes sense only in light of God's Triunity). Jesus is not merely a wise man, but is the Wellspring who became flesh and dwelt among us; thus, the one who suffers (and absorbs, and does not return) the world's violence is *God*. In the resurrection, we are called to recognize the Crucified One as the Word of God made flesh – which witnesses to God's internal self-differentiation. Jesus' words, "I proceeded and came forth from God" (John 8:42, RSV) no longer appear to be the words of a prophet, speaking metaphorically about his own authority, but rather a description of procession within God: a God in whom oneness and difference are interwoven in a complex polyphony.

And thus, despite the human fall to violence, and even in spite of the violent acts of God within the created order, we can still speak of God as "the God of peace." The peaceable God creates a peaceable world; when human beings fall into a cycle of violence, God continues to "produce" the world by a revelatory act of redemption. This act gives us the potential to escape the cycle of violence; and yet we have rarely taken advantage of this opportunity. Indeed, the past century has been the site of atrocious forms of large-scale violence – what one writer has called "man-made mass death."[31] If the peace of God is to play any role in the midst of this violence, then this too must be not only our own work, but God's as well: the work of sanctification. In this process, we are formed in practices that allow our lives to reflect, however inadequately, the God of peace in whose image we were created. It is, at the very least, a place to begin.

> The Trinity itself, after all, with its vision of mutual deference among equals and its identification of a crucified preacher of peace as the Word of God incarnate, offers a starting point for condemnation of the world's violence. Christians in

---

[30] Nor is this the only theological fault-line in Girard's argument. See the critique in Milbank, *Theology and Social Theory*, 392–8; and, in partial response, Kerr, "Rescuing Girard's Argument?"; also John Milbank, "Stories of Sacrifice," *Modern Theology* 12, no. 1 (January 1996): 27–56.

[31] Edith Wyschogrod, *Spirit in Ashes: Hegel, Heidegger, and Man-Made Mass Death* (New Haven and London: Yale University Press, 1985).

various eras have made passionate christological and Trinitarian witness against violence's evil.[32]

Developing more explicit connections between the doctrine of the Trinity and practices of peace will be the main focus of the remainder of this chapter.

We can examine these connections from two angles, bearing in mind the dialectical relationship between *virtues* and *practices* that I discussed just prior to the beginning of this chapter. First, we can consider the role of those Christian practices that are already deeply rooted in the doctrine of the Trinity – practices in which the trinitarian virtues of polyphony, participation, and particularity are already highly visible. If, as I have argued, the triune God is a God of peace, then such practices ought to help generate peaceableness and peacemaking among Christians. If we practiced them more frequently, and with more attention to their triune character, our communities might become better and more consistent witnesses to the peace of God. Secondly, we can examine Christian practices that are less obviously connected to *either* the doctrine of the Trinity *or* the practice of peacemaking. Here, we can ask: if we were to allow such practices to be guided by the trinitarian virtues, might they too be reshaped into a witness to God's peace? These two approaches will be examined in turn; in each case, I offer two examples (first an extended one, and then some very preliminary comments toward the development of another).

Trinitarian Practices of Transformation

Some common Christian practices are already deeply rooted in the doctrine of the Trinity – even though this close connection may be all but lost, even to those who regularly participate in the practice. I begin by tracing the trinitarian roots of a practice that I discussed in a previous chapter, here changing the focus slightly to consider how it forms us into a peaceable people, an image of the God of peace.

The peacemaking eucharist

In chapter 5, I described the Christian participation in the body and blood of Christ as a central trinitarian practice. In the eucharist, we call upon the Holy Spirit to sanctify the gifts given to us by God – gifts that take on a renewed

---

[32] Placher, *The Domestication of Transcendence*, 173.

meaning in the context of the narratives of the Word of God made flesh. The eucharist is an outward sign of God's gracious act in which we are drawn into communion with one another – here we feed on, and thus become, the Body of Christ. In this process, the trinitarian virtue of participation becomes clearly manifest, even though we remain "many" and therefore particular. And this in turn forms us in the practice of peacemaking, since it allows us to recognize difference in a way that does not lead to estrangement and violence.

Eucharistic practice is already trinitarian, almost every step of the way.[33] In recapitulating the history of God's involvement in the world, it necessarily speaks of the divine processions (begetting and issuing) and their correspond-ing "missions" (Incarnation and Inspiration). In the *epiclesis*, the Spirit is called down to transform the gifts of God into the Body of Christ. In the closing doxology, the triune nature of God is once again invoked, folding the entire rite into the glory of the Three who are One:

> Through Christ, and with Christ, and in Christ,
> all honor and glory are yours, almighty God and Father,
> in the unity of the Holy Spirit, for ever and ever.[34]

Much of what is said and done in the eucharist would be largely meaningless outside of the concrete narratives of God's activity in the world (and their later philosophical formalization in the Christian doctrine of the triune God). Because the eucharist is a thoroughly trinitarian practice, and because the triune God is a God of peace, the eucharist itself underwrites the practice of peacemaking. Here, I want to mention five distinct elements of the rite that can help to form us into a peaceable and peacemaking people.

First, before the eucharist begins, we offer one another a sign of peace. This very important act recalls the words of Christ concerning the appropriate preparation for approaching God:

> So when you are offering your gift at the altar, if you remember that your brother or sister has something against you, leave your gift there before the altar and go; first be reconciled to your brother or sister, and then come and offer your gift. (Matt. 5:23–24)

This moment of reconciliation requires more than just a mental note to

---

[33] For full-scale developments of this theme, with attention to varying confessional practices, see Geoffrey Wainwright, *Eucharist and Eschatology* (New York: Oxford Univer-sity Press, 1981), and Marshall, *Trinity and Truth*, ch. 2.

[34] Eucharistic Prayer D, *The Book of Common Prayer*, 375.

ourselves that we ought not to hold a grudge. It requires contact – physical contact – in which we join our bodies to the bodies of others. As such the "sign of peace" is an outward sign of the uniting of our bodies into one body – the Body of Christ – in the act of communion itself.

Unfortunately, this practice has often been minimized. What was once a "kiss of peace," uniting bodies in an almost frighteningly intimate way, now often consists only of a tentative handshake and a mumbled greeting. Of course, this does still provide an opportunity to meet the other face to face, body to body; and so even the most minimal forms of this practice are preferable to its complete omission. But even when these handshakes become hugs and the "peace" becomes a fairly lively affair, it rarely brings us into contact with anyone other than those who are seated closest to us; and this is unfortunate, for often these are not the people with whom we most need to be reconciled. Christians would be well-served by giving more time to this portion of the eucharistic rite, and encouraging freedom of movement, so that we might all be encouraged to "make peace" with those with whom we are estranged (i.e., frequently, the ones whom we've deliberately avoided when choosing our seats). The sign of peace reminds us of our participation in one another's lives, and thus prepares us to be taken up into the triune life of God.

Secondly, the eucharist involves retelling the story of the death and resurrection of Christ, thereby reminding us of the revelation of God as the God of peace. It recapitulates salvation history – beginning with the initial donation of the peaceable creation, and pointing forward to its consummation at the end of history. At its center, it focuses on the acts of violence perpetrated against Jesus, reminding us that they were not, and *should* not be, revenged; instead, Jesus prays, "Father, forgive them" (Luke 23:34). That he is then raised up by God is a prophetic call for us to renounce the cycle of violence, just as Jesus did. Without denying the enormous distance separating Jesus from his enemies (and us from ours), the eucharist liberates us from the urge to take revenge upon them, freeing us to love them.[35] "Christ our passover is sacrificed for us," as the liturgy reminds us; but we are not asked to respond to this act with another round of vengeful sacrifice. Instead, we "keep the feast," offering a "sacrifice of praise and thanksgiving," allowing God to shape our selves, our souls and bodies, into instruments of peace.

Thirdly, by calling upon the Holy Spirit to descend upon the gifts, we

---

[35] That Christians have failed to heed this call through much of their history (especially with regard to their persecution of Jews) is a failing that we should never fail to recognize as such; for this reason, it perhaps should be incorporated into the eucharistic prayer itself.

pledge to set ourselves apart as that community that will not be drawn in to our culture's love of violence; this is the significance of the rite's description of the elements as "holy gifts for a holy people." The word *holy* deserves special attention here. Whatever it may mean with respect to the "substance" of that which is described as holy, it certainly tells us something about that person's or thing's relationship to the rest of the created order. The word *holy* is related to the verb *to hallow* – to "set apart," to "designate for a special purpose." What makes "holy water" holy? At the very least, it differs from ordinary water in having been set apart – specially designated for its purpose – through an act of consecration. Similarly, the Church is called "a holy people," not because it can do no wrong, but because its members have been "called out," set apart from the world.

Like the word *Church* itself (or at least, the Greek word ἐκκλησία which it translates), the word *holy* urges us to rethink precisely what sets us apart from the world. These "holy gifts" have been set apart for a "holy people," but this language makes no sense if Christians are not in various ways distinguishable from other members of society at large. Thus, this part of the eucharistic prayer reminds us of the many things that set us apart, including our belief in a God in whom "these Three are One" – in whom difference is acknowledged and negotiated without strife or violence.

Fourthly, in the eucharist we re-enact a moment of the table-fellowship. This practice – so central to the history of Israel, the story of Jesus, and (as I have already noted) to the early Church's understanding of κοινωνία – has fallen out of favor in the modern age. A great many cultural forces push us away from the practice of sharing a common table: the extraordinary rush of our daily lives, the desire for conveniences of all kinds, and our growing preference for machines rather than people. But the complete mutual participation of the triune God calls us to turn away from the isolationism espoused by our culture and to *participate* in one another's lives. Table-fellowship requires time, energy, and various sorts of sacrifice; but true *participation* is impossible without it.

Thus, St Paul chastises the members of the church at Corinth who violated the spirit of table-fellowship (1 Cor .11:17–22). They allowed their divisions and factions to overwhelm the Lord's supper, making it into an event of separation ("each of you goes ahead with your own supper") and allowing huge disparities to persist ("one goes hungry and another becomes drunk"). Paul invokes Jesus' words to his disciples to remind the Corinthians that the eucharist should bind them together, not break them apart. It thus calls them to certain standards of behavior ("wait for one another"; "if you are hungry, eat at home") and provides an interior critique of their factions and divisions.

In a more general sense, we can say that table-fellowship is a peacemaking activity because – let's face it – it's difficult to enjoy a good meal in the midst of a fight. Playful banter, yes; antimated argument, yes; but a knock- down, drag-out fight is just not very good for the digestive system. In David James Duncan's brilliant novel *The Brothers K*, the Chance family fails to realize how completely their peace depends upon their dinner table.[36] The meal had always begun with their father's rapidly spoken, nearly meaningless, but somehow comforting prayer: "GiveusgratefulheartsourFatherandmakeusevermindfuloftheneedsofothersthroughChristourLordAmen." When the schedule changes and Papa Chance is no longer at the dinner table, the other family members take on the task in turns – launching into freestyle prayers which beg God for special favors or otherwise express a personal theology (or lack thereof). These prayers bring to light differences that disrupt the common meal and issue in a grimly funny yet ultimately painful period of family history (the narrator calls it "Psalm Wars"). The episode is a clever and clear reminder that the inability to sit down together to eat is very closely related to the inability to be at peace with one another.

Table-fellowship is not a miraculous cure-all; nothing can assure that fights will not break out, even in the midst of a solemn eucharist (though I've never seen it happen). And in many forms of eucharistic practice, the "common" and "unifying" element can be undermined by exclusionary or isolating practices (as I noted in chapter 5). Nevertheless, sharing a meal together can often have uniting and peacemaking effects beyond whatever may be obvious in the moment. Given the manifold pressures exerted by our culture against regular and meaningful table-fellowship, those Christian communities that do not already make the eucharist a regular (at least weekly) practice should seriously consider doing so. It may not prevent the ecclesiological equivalent of the Chance family's Psalm Wars, but its power as a peacemaking practice should not be underestimated.

Fifthly, and finally, the eucharist is not merely an "internal" celebration of peaceableness, but is meant to prepare us to turn our lives outward, leading peaceable lives and becoming peacemakers beyond the walls of the Church. Many forms of the "prayer after communion" accent this element:

> Eternal God, heavenly Father,
> you have graciously accepted us as living members
> of your Son our Savior Jesus Christ,

---

[36] David James Duncan, "Psalm Wars," chap. in *The Brothers K* (New York: Bantam Books, 1993), 165–91.

And you have fed us with spiritual Food
in the Sacrament of his Body and Blood.
Send us now into the world in *peace*,
and grant us strength and courage
to love and serve you
with gladness and singleness of heart;
through Christ our Lord. Amen.[37]

Having refreshed ourselves with the peace that the world cannot give, we are empowered to enter that same world "in peace"; and this claim is reinforced in the closing words of the rite, exhorting us to "go in peace to love and serve the Lord."

A very successful literary description of the peace of the eucharist occurs in Graham Greene's novel *The Heart of the Matter*. The book's main character, Henry Scobie, finds himself unable to take communion because he is not at peace (with himself, with his wife, with his work). On several occasions, he is described as sitting through the eucharist, painfully aware of the rite's many references to peace. By concentrating on the word's frequent recurrence, Scobie becomes aware of just how much peace God has to offer.

Peace seemed to him the most beautiful word in the language: My peace I give you, my peace I leave with you: O Lamb of God, who takest away the sins of the world, grant us thy peace. In the Mass he pressed his fingers against his eyes to keep the tears of longing in.[38]

And yet, Scobie also has enough integrity to recognize that he will be unable to accept this gift as long as he refuses to discipline himself in peaceable and peacemaking practices. He is in the midst of an adulterous love affair; he is involved in a complicated cover-up in his work as a police officer; he thus cannot avoid feeling that, in the midst of such wretchedness, God's offer of peace seems to come too cheap.

Pax, pacis, pacem: all the declinations of the word "peace" drummed on his ears through the Mass. He thought: I have left even the hope of peace for ever. I am the responsible man. I shall soon have gone too far in my design of deception ever to go back. . . . At the foot of the scaffold he opened his eyes and saw the old black women shuffling up toward the altar rail, a few soldiers, an aircraft mechanic, one of his own policemen, a clerk from the bank: they moved

---

[37] *The Book of Common Prayer*, 365, emphasis added.
[38] Graham Greene, *The Heart of the Matter* (1948; Harmondsworth: Penguin Books, 1962), 60.

sedately toward peace, and Scobie felt an envy of their simplicity, their goodness.[39]

Scobie knows that the eucharist will not eliminate, nor even necessarily reduce, the strife and conflict that people experience in various facets of their lives. But he does recognize it as a sign of God's perpetual willingness to help negotiate those conflicts. His flaw, as Greene paints his character, is that he does not also recognize the circular and reciprocal nature of this relationship. He cannot accept God's help until he is at peace; but he fails to see that he cannot be at peace until he accepts God's help. Instead, he attempts to negotiate his conflicts alone – without the help of God, and without the help of others – and this effort finally breaks him.

Peace is not easy to achieve. If we try to negotiate all our conflicts as though we were solitary individuals, we will surely fail; we need others, and we need God. This blending of energies into a polyphonic chord of peace is enacted in the eucharist. Here, we unite our lives with those around us, coming into full communion with them and participating in one another as the Body of Christ. The triune God calls us to a more regular practice of the eucharist; for here we learn to participate in one another's lives in ways that can reflect, however dimly, the peaceful mutual participation of God. Here, the followers of Jesus learned to participate in his body and blood; here, they learned love and the forgiveness of sins; and here, they learned that it was necessary that the Messiah should suffer and then enter into glory. Let us join with them, and learn once again to sit at table together, so that we may tell others what has happened to us, and how the Lord has been made known to us in the breaking of the bread.

Practicing the Creed

The "confessions of faith" – the Nicene and Apostles' Creeds – are deeply rooted in the trinitarian faith of the Church. And yet, even in those denominations in which they are regularly recited, they do not always carry much freight. Perhaps this can be explained in part by Wittgenstein's dictum that words only becoming meaningful in the light of practices – and for most of us, the creeds are "just words." What might we do to transform "saying the Creed" into a *practice*, such that its words were given sense by the context in which it was said? What would it mean to "practice" the Creed?

I suspect that, if the deeply trinitarian creeds were no longer treated as a form

---

[39] Ibid., 224–5.

of words, but as practices to be enacted, they could become a witness to the practice of peacemaking. Here, I cannot defend this claim in detail, but I hope to say enough to encourage others to try out the idea in the concrete life of the worshiping community.

By saying the Creed, we declare that we believe in *this particular* God, the triune God, the producing God, who has created and redeemed the world and who continues to sanctify it. This is the God in whom we believe: the God of Abraham and Sarah, the God of Mary, the God of Jesus. We do *not* believe in a generic "Supreme Being," nor the god "under" whom citizens declare themselves to be "one nation" when they pledge their allegiance to a colorful piece of drapery. The effort to distinguish between such generic portraits of God and the triune God of Christian belief is one of the most important functions of the Creed. If we could find ways of making this contrast salient every time the Creed is recited, it could become an intervention on behalf of peace, and against violence.

As I noted in chapter 1, nation-states have found it relatively easy to co-opt generic portraits of God, painting these portraits in such a way that they seem to underwrite whatever mischief the nation-state may be up to. Very frequently, of course, that mischief has been very much more than mischief: it has been violence, horrible violence, cruel and arbitrary and faceless violence, perpetrated against those least able to defend themselves. A generic portrait of a supreme being can easily be molded into the kind of God who would support such activities – especially if a strong connection is invented between God and whatever nation-state happens to be carrying out that violence. But the violence of the nation-state cannot be so easily underwritten by the highly specific portrait of the triune God, whose particularity we emphasize every time we say the Creed.

Transforming the recitation of the Creed into a peacemaking practice will require, first, a careful examination of those community practices with which it is *incompatible* – practices that suggest an allegiance to a very different god. For example, church buildings are often adorned with the trappings of the nation-state, including flags, monuments to various political leaders, and memorials that glorify war rather than protesting or mourning it. These are the trappings of violence – of an institutional system which will not, indeed by its very constitution cannot, renounce coercion. They are thus at odds with the claim that the God who is worshiped in this space is not the generic god of the state, but the triune God, in whom there is perfect harmony and peaceable co-existence.

To think of the recitation of the Creed as a *practice* is to recognize that it challenges the violent and usurping gods in whom our culture increasingly places its faith. It thus calls us actively to renounce these gods and to declare our belief in the God of peace. In most of our church buildings, this will require some significant housecleaning, dismantling the trappings of war that are clearly incompatible with the practice of the Creed. The Church might thereby learn to practice peacemaking *as only the Church can* – through nonviolent witness and forgiveness, rather than violence and coercion. This is what it means for the Church to offer an *alternative politics* to that of the nation-state.[40] "The nations before God are like a drop from a bucket, and are accounted as dust on the scales" (Isa. 40:15).

The Trinitarian Transformation of Practices

Needless to say, not all Christian practices bear the marks of the triune God so clearly as do the eucharist and the Creed. Indeed, in the cases that I will discuss below – the stewardship of the earth, and (much more briefly) the reckoning of time – few readers will initially discern anything "trinitarian" at all. But if the doctrine of the Trinity is really at the core of the Christian narrative, as I have suggested that it is, then we should attempt to think in trinitarian terms – even (indeed, perhaps especially) about those practices that bear no obvious connection to the doctrine of the Trinity. Here, I want to suggest that – in the case of these two practices, at least – doing so will help us to discover some potential practices of peacemaking in some surprising places. By allowing these common Christian practices to be more fully imbued with the trinitarian virtues, we can refine them into practices of resistance to violence – practices that witness to the peaceableness of the triune God.

Stewardship of the earth

The past twenty years have seen a flurry of books and articles advocating the adoption of an "environmentalist" position by Christians.[41] In general, this

---

[40] See the accounts of Stanley Hauerwas in such works as *Against the Nations: War and Survival in a Liberal Society* (Minneapolis: Winston Press, 1985), and *In Good Company: The Church as Polis* (Notre Dame, Ind.: University of Notre Dame Press, 1995). For a careful critical assessment of Hauerwas that prefers his approach to that of Moltmann, see Arne Rasmusson, *The Church as Polis: From Political Theology to Theological Politics as exemplified by Jürgen Moltmann and Stanley Hauerwas* (Notre Dame, Ind.: University of Notre Dame Press, 1995).

[41] Even a lengthy list of books would be terribly selective; I mention here two collections and a bibliographical resource: Richard N. Fragomeni and John T. Pawlikowski, O.S.M.,

stance seems altogether appropriate; various biblical texts have too often been construed as encouraging human beings to do whatever they liked with the earth, rather than counseling an attitude of care and stewardship. Unfortunately, however, much of this recent "eco-theology" is composed of roughly 95 percent ecology, with theological considerations entering the picture only in order to buttress a position that was already ecologically warranted. And even when a more theological approach has appeared, it often veers toward a vague pantheism. If God is understood as being "in" the earth, or even as *being* the earth, then (it is assumed) Christians will be ethically inclined not to injure the earth, for they would thereby be injuring God.[42]

But such pantheistic approaches are ultimately incompatible with Christianity, which has always stressed a distinction between God and creation. In my view, however, this distinction can be maintained without thereby leading to ecological malfeasance.[43] The created order is not God, but that does not mean that God wills that human beings should treat it carelessly. Recall, here, our discussion (in chapter 2) of God's activity of "producing" the earth. To produce – in the sense of producing a play, or producing of a garden – is not simply to create something and turn it over to others who care nothing for it. Rather, the producing God is constantly at work, redeeming and sanctifying the world, while not depriving human beings of the freedom that they enjoy as bearers of the image of God. In this sense, God's production of the created order is not merely an exercise in divine self-glorification; human beings are given a gift which they can freely choose to return in the form of worship and praise.[44]

The Ecological Challenge: Ethical, Liturgical, and Spiritual Responses (Collegeville, Minn.: Liturgical Press, 1995); Fred Van Dyke, David C. Mahan, Joseph K. Sheldon, and Raymond H. Brand, Redeeming Creation: The Biblical Basis for Environmental Stewardship (Downers Grove: InterVarsity Press, 1996); Peter W. Bakken, Joan Gibb Engel, and J. Ronald Engel, Ecology, Justice, and Christian Faith: A Critical Guide to the Literature, Bibliographies and Indexes in Religious Studies, vol. 36 (Westport, Conn.: Greenwood Press, 1995).

[42] In spite of her efforts to guard against it, Sallie McFague's description of "the earth as God's body" seems to result in a vague pantheism. See The Body of God: An Ecological Theology (Minneapolis: Fortress Press, 1993).

[43] For a wide-ranging discussion of divine transcendence as compatible with political action, see Kathryn Tanner, The Politics of God: Christian Theologies and Social Justice (Minneapolis: Fortress Press, 1992).

[44] We can still speak in terms of mutual gift, even if this implies some form of exchange. See, inter alia, Jacques Derrida, Given Time: I. Counterfeit Money, trans. Peggy Kanuf (Chicago: University of Chicago Press, 1993); Marion, God Without Being; Milbank, "Can a Gift?"; and Webb, The Gifting God.

Remember the parable of the vineyard: the owner is not always immediately present, but is nevertheless concerned about the proper operation of the vineyard. So he is always engaged with it, even from a distance – sending various messengers, and finally his son, to inquire about it and counsel its proper use. That the workers treat these messengers badly is a worthy parallel to the ways that we have often treated those who have counseled us about the proper operation of the vineyard called "earth."

So even though creation is not identical with God, Christians are still called to care for the created order and to preserve it. Unfortunately, here (as in so many realms of Christian ethical discourse) the prevailing assumption seems to be that this activity must be carried out primarily by large institutions – those that can ultimately have some "measurable effect" on the large-scale problems that we face. Thus, we have tended to expend most of our ecological energies trying to get the state to regulate, preserve, tax, or guarantee, all in order to carry out a strategy of "earth-keeping." And even when the focus is not on the activity of the state, it tends to mimic the state by justifying certain ecological strategies on the basis of their economic and aesthetic value alone.

As long as this "care for the earth" is carried out according to strategies which are not shaped by the trinitarian virtues, it seems very unlikely to become a practice of peacemaking. As we have already noted, the nation-state is not naturally inclined toward peace; and, in more general terms, it is not devoted to the care and preservation of that which is other (including the created order generally). The state may be cajoled into adopting some of the same policies that Christians might, on theological grounds, recommend – but this will not occur unless the state perceives that its own interests are at stake in doing so. Christians are called to care for the earth *not* because doing so is in their interest, but because the triune God created the earth and continues to produce it by sending the Word and pouring out the Spirit.

It seems to me, for example, that the trinitarian virtue of *polyphony* calls us to listen to the entire orchestration of creation, and not to allow the apparently minor melodies to be silenced. Ecological work to protect endangered species would clearly be part of this work, even if such protection comes at some cost to human beings (which seems likely since, after all, these species often became endangered in the first place precisely because human beings sought their own profit first). Attention to the polyphony of creation requires us to think about the differences between the creation which God has *produced* and the particular *uses* to which we have subjected it. This difference calls for serious discernment about the degree to which our lives actually *require* us to subjugate the created order – as opposed to the subjugation that we carry out simply because it is profitable, pleasurable, or merely convenient.

Secondly, the trinitarian virtue of *participation* underwrites a sense of interconnectedness within the created order. Augustine's doctrine of creation implies that all creatures can be construed as bearing the mark of God, even if they do so with increasing remoteness (in the case of, for example, inanimate objects). We are woven into a web of participation, not only with God and with other human beings, but with the entire creation. Odd, then, that so many ecological commentators (including Christian ones) seem to believe that such participation is advocated only in native American spirituality or other non-Christian traditions, when in fact it seems to be intricately bound up with the doctrine of the Trinity. (One fiction writer who seems to have recognized something of this relationship is Barbara Kingsolver, whose fine novel *Animal Dreams*[45] draws on both Hopi and Christian narratives to describe the web of creation into which human beings are woven.)

Finally, the *particularity* of creatures, while clearly manifesting difference (human beings are not cats, cats are not rocks) ought not be allowed to obscure their interconnectedness. We are constituted by that with which we come in contact – not only other human beings, but cats and rocks as well – and conversely, their particularity is partly constituted by their encounter with us. This calls us to examine our interactions with the created order somewhat more carefully than we are normally in the habit of doing. This creature – God's creature, remember – will be *particularized* by my action. I thus bear a certain responsibility for that outcome, as does every other human being who has (or will) come into contact with that creature. This is, I think, one of the reasons why Christians understand themselves as called "to rule and serve all God's creatures":[46] one can more easily recognize one's responsibility in shaping the particularity of other creatures if the two terms of this apparent paradox – dominion *and* service – are recognized as implying one another.

All of this would seem to point toward an ethic of minimal interference in creation. The God of peace calls us to make every effort not to damage, displace, and re-order the created world any more than is necessary. Admittedly, this is a difficult matter of judgment; but most of us could (at the very least) find ways to reduce our consumption of goods, since their production always requires some degree of displacement of and damage to creation. We are called to be stewards of the earth, preserving its created state as best we can and recognizing that the overwhelming majority of whatever we manage to "create" (in a derivative sense) *will not even be comparable* with the beauty and goodness of what God has created "out of nothing."

[45] Barbara Kingsolver, *Animal Dreams* (San Francisco: Harper/Collins, 1990).
[46] *The Book of Common Prayer*, 373.

If the Christian practice of stewardship takes the trinitarian virtues seriously, it will be marked by this "ethic of minimal interference" – which is itself a peaceable and peacemaking practice. Examining it in detail would take much more space than I am able to devote to it here. In general, though, most of us recognize that, in the industrialized West, our habits of consumption are very closely tied to violence – violence against human beings (to minimize the prices of manufactured goods), violence against animals (to maximize the efficiency of food production), and violence against natural resources such as water, air, and land. Allow me to close this section with a brief meditation on one of these forms of violence, and a possible alternative practice.

Each year – in order to manufacture many kinds of food and clothing, to test the efficacy of new medical procedures, and to develop a wide range of toiletries, cosmetics, and household goods – we slaughter millions, and probably billions, of animals. This violence is so overwhelmingly accepted in our culture that many people seem almost pre-programmed to darken various regions of their moral imaginations whenever the topic is raised. There are, undoubtedly, circumstances in which we may feel compelled to commit some violence against at least some kinds of animals (though I will not attempt to work through this question in detail here). Unfortunately, however, the inevitability of some minimal level of violence too often serves as a warrant for not thinking about the subject at all. This decision ignores the fairly brutal fact that a great deal of our violence against animals is committed in order to achieve a very marginal reduction in the price of goods, to cater to carefully-constructed "gourmet tastes" or "standards of fashion," or to develop products which consumers do not even want (until a "need" for such goods is created by advertising).

If this issue strikes some readers as rather far removed from the doctrine of the triune God, we might recall that animals, clothing, and especially food are given an extraordinary amount of attention in the biblical texts from which we draw our central narratives of faith. According to the book of Genesis, the original relationship between God and the created order was one in which peaceableness extended to the relationships between human beings and animals. As we noted above, the human inhabitants of the garden are given "every green plant for food"; not until after the flood and the establishment of the covenant with Noah is meat-eating permitted (thus, human violence toward animals appears to be part of that "fall to violence" narrated in the early chapters of Genesis). Only in a world in which the violations described in those stories have become commonplace can the violation of the animal fail to seem – at the very least – troubling.

Even after the covenant with Noah, which seems to recognize that human beings have chosen to live with violence, the treatment of animals is rather closely regulated (for example, in the Levitical codes). There seems almost to be a recognition that a people's treatment of animals will be related to its general tendencies toward violence and injury. Because we have become accustomed to treating animals as a means to the "greater" end of our own personal satisfaction, it becomes relatively easy for us to justify violence on the basis of those ends. For example, if we wish to dine on veal, then (we have decided), this "wish" is considered sufficient to justify the violence that is demanded by the production of veal: the separation of the infant from its mother, the isolation of the animal, the maltreatment, the early and violent death. Every effort is made to conceal these details from the person who actually *eats* the animal, for this narrative is (at least) unpleasant, even if it is not universally recognized to be a failure to attend to God's will for the created order.[47] But even if we *know* about these details of the treatment of animals, we rarely pause to observe that they result directly and solely from our desire for a food that can be produced only through by such means – in other words, our desires, our tastes, are the cause of the violence. We maltreat and kill the animal by purchasing the food, the clothing, the cosmetics, the medicine.

This, of course, is a most unpleasant thought – doubly so for those goods that we could get along quite well without – and yet more so for Christians, who are called to lives of peacemaking. Because it is such an unpleasant thought, it is usually studiously avoided, and this helps to sever the connections between our desires and tastes (on the one hand) and whatever needs to take place in order to satisfy those desires (on the other). This dissociation makes it so much easier for us to allow our own tastes (needs, values, preferences, and politics) to justify violence on a yet grander scale – including violence against human beings, and (as some recent research has suggested) perhaps especially violence against women.[48]

Christians are called to seek to restore the peace of creation, to recognize that Christ has put an end to the cycle of violence. The Reign of God, the true vision of a peaceable kingdom, calls us to the profound peaceableness inherent in a world in which even the most culturally-acceptable, ordinary, everyday forms of violence – such as that which we perpetrate against animals – is no longer understood as part of what it means to be a human being, created in the image of the triune God.

---

[47] On this point, see Stanley Hauerwas and John Berkman, "The Chief End of All Flesh," *Theology Today* 49, no. 2 (July 1992): 196-208.
[48] For a compelling account of this connection, see Carol J. Adams, *The Sexual Politics of Meat: A Feminist-Vegetarian Critical Theory* (New York: Continuum, 1990).

The reckoning of time

For most of us, the reckoning of time is never questioned; we assume that, for reasons of efficiency and cultural unity, we must all operate on the same calendar. We thus tend to accept our culture's definitions of the shape of the day, the reckoning of weeks and months, and the designation of the year. I here offer a few preliminary thoughts as to how a more "polyphonic" reckoning of the passage of time could lead us to a more integrated, thoroughgoing, and peaceable vision of the Christian life.

Our common cultural conception of time is extraordinarily linear; effects follow their causes in strict, logical sequence. Time (or so we assume) moves straight down the hourly slots in our appointment books, straight across the neatly arranged rows of our wall calendars, straight across the "Great Events" timelines in the margins of our history books. But certain elements of Christian practice urge us to think of time according to patterns that are more circular than linear. Our regular cycles of prayer, of scripture readings and feast days, and even the circular nature of the worship service itself (often marked by procession and recession) – all reflect, in small ways, the cosmic significance of the Christian reckoning of time. St Augustine and St Thomas referred to this reckoning with the words *exitus* and *reditus*: the whole creation moves out and away from God – and yet always longs to return to God, and thereby close the circle. "You have made us for yourself," says St Augustine, "and our hearts are restless until they rest in you."[49]

The trinitarian virtue of polyphony encourages us to listen for this alternative accounting of time, not in an attempt to obliterate our culture's linear perspective (an impossible feat at any rate!), but rather to hold open the possibility of another accounting that can be observed alongside that which dominates our culture. If we listen carefully to this delicate counterpoint, we may begin to imagine a conception of time that is dependable, recognizable, and marked by constancy and peace – rather than by novelty, anxiety, and constant conflict.

On the most obvious level, the Christian accounting of time provides constancy and stability by celebrating every Sunday, without exception, as a feast of the Lord. Regardless of what degree of chaos may beset the outside world, the Church's time continues to cycle in uninterrupted fashion. We should not underestimate the peaceful effect of this regularity; in contemporary society we have very few institutions or practices that can be relied upon to take place regularly and consistently. Our culture seems to thrive on

---

[49] Augustine *Conf.* I,1

innovation, and there is very little that we can count on to be the same as it was last *week* – let alone last year. Keeping one ear inclined toward the very different calendar of the Church may help us to put time on our side again – to understand our lives as peacefully borne along by time, rather than being forced, often against our will, to face the uncertainties of each "new" day.

The Church offers an alternative reckoning of the day (which begins in the evening), the week (which begins *and ends* on Sunday), and the year (which begins on the first Sunday of Advent). Through these alternative reckonings, and even in its recognition that time *has* a beginning and an end, the Church invites us to relativize the supreme importance we often attribute to the temporal details of our lives – the next deadline at work, or the fact that the sale at our favorite store ends today. If we are able to conceive time only as our culture conceives it, then we will surely inherit not only its harried, frenetic pace, but also the bothersome feeling of emptiness with which we seem to "end" each day. If we allow ourselves, in a polyphonous spirit, to "hear" the Church's alternative accounting of time, we might begin to feel a surprising reorientation: the day, week, and year begin not with a frenetic rush of the business, but with a time which, for most of us, is *not* occupied by labor. Instead, it provides an opportunity for the community to gather, to share a common meal, to offer praise to God, to think and learn and experience life together.

Other time-related practices could be mentioned here: the discipline of sabbath-keeping; the designation of the day according to its assigned feast or fast, saint or memorial, rather than only its number or national holiday; observing the times of preparation for Christmas and Easter according to their liturgical designations (Advent and Lent), rather than attending to when stores set up their displays of holiday goods; and so on. If nothing else, reminding ourselves of the Christian reckoning of time may provide an alternative to the strife and conflict that we tend to associate with time. As such, it can contribute to the trinitarian practice of peacemaking.

The School for Peace

Where do we learn to live such lives? How can we possibly expect to counter the massive weight of our culture's attention to violence? The culture itself will not change on its own; that is the other lesson of the Fall. We can expect violence to endure, and to increase, until that time when time shall be no more. But the Church can provide a space away from the violence of our culture, if it learns once again to be a truly alternative community, "called out" from the wider culture, proclaiming the Reign of the God of Peace – instead of the reign of the nations, the reign of violence.

The Church will function as the "school for peace" only if it tells stories and habituates practices that allow peaceableness to shape our lives. These are the stories it has always told: of God's grace, of repentance and forgiveness, of kindness and mercy, of care for the other. These are the stories of the creation of the world, of the building of the temple, of the good Samaritan and the prodigal son. Above all, it is the story of the Christ: of Mary, who gave birth to Jesus – and of their sufferings, both upon the cross and at its foot. Lives that are shaped by these stories are peaceable lives. But if these stories are seen merely as a sideline to the living of a life – merely as something engaged briefly on Sunday mornings, and not allowed to shape our very existence – then we will instead be shaped by the stories of the world: stories of warfare and hatred, of revenge and murder. These are not the stories of the God of peace.

And the practices that the Church must habituate are also those that it has always sought to develop in the members of its body: practices of forgiveness, of kindness and mercy, of care for the other. To refuse to return injury for injury, to forgive not seven times but seventy times seven, to bind up the wounds of the downtrodden: Lives that are shaped by these practices are peaceable lives. But again, if these practices are seen merely as something to do in one's spare time – as a sacrifice to be made once a month, or perhaps a bit more often during Lent – then we will instead be shaped by the practices of the world: self-aggrandizement, wish-fulfillment, evasion of responsibility, and scapegoating. These are not the practices of the school for peace.

The peaceableness of the triune God is the model for human living. We are created in this peaceable image, and we constantly fall away from it. Through the reconciliation brought about through Christ, we have been restored to that image; but we must still decide to accept this gift. Thus far in Christian history, it seems that relatively few members of the Body of Christ have been willing to allow their lives to be shaped in fundamental ways by the practices and stories of the God of peace. Doing so requires us to make the Church the center of our existence – a difficult task indeed.

One test of the matter might be this: at the end of many worship services, there is a call to peace and peaceableness: "Go in peace to love and serve the Lord." But for how long (after the end of the worship service) does that peace really take hold of our lives, and become our "first principle"? Most of us don't need to be "out of Church" for too long before peaceableness slips away. We might say that, when this occurs, it is time to go "back to Church" – whether physically (to the building, to a worship service), or in prayer, or in our reading and study, or in our decisions about how to spend our time. In order to live lives of peaceableness, in the image of the Triune God, most of us will need to "go to Church" more than once a week.

This is not to say that a life of peace can only be lived by those who spend 24 hours a day within the walls of the Church. From the very beginning, Christians have lived in the world. But also from the beginning, they have needed regular contact with the "school for peace" in order not to be shaped fundamentally by the violence of that world. Only through repeated, regular, life-centered contact with the triune God can we expect to depart from the Church in peace, according to God's word. For here, our eyes learn to see the salvation which God has prepared for all people – a light to enlighten the nations, and a glory to the people Israel.

Chapter 8

PLURALIZING

I have described the practice of trinitarian theology as the attempt to rethink the categories of oneness and difference – and thereby to create a space in which we can claim, without reserve, that "these three are one." The task is a difficult one; as I noted in chapters 1 and 2, many theologians have felt that they must ultimately follow one of only two possible paths. They assume that they must choose between "the One" or "the Many," and then offer a tip of the hat in the opposite direction, in an attempt to avoid the (inevitable?) criticism that they have over-emphasized singularity and neglected difference (or vice versa). In a sense, this division among trinitarian theologians is simply a microcosm of contemporary theology in general, in which theologians assume that the world is divided into two camps: those who revel in the scattering of widely divergent perspectives, and those who foretell the doom that is sure to ensue unless we are able to restore unity.

As long as oneness and difference are understood as a zero-sum game, modern theology will continue to be beset by this "disjunctivitis." To set these two categories against one another is to force Christian theology to work against itself: the more one argues in favor of difference, the less one is committed, it seems, to a specifically Christian identity. And on the other hand (according to this way of thinking), the more one seeks to merge everything into a single, undifferentiated whole, the more remote one's theology becomes from the obvious differences that mark the world in which we dwell. On this "contrastive" account, there can be no "happy medium"; *both* ends of the spectrum (oneness and difference) are positive goods, greatly to be desired; every advance toward one of them is offset by a distancing from the other.

Throughout this book, I have been attempting to deconstruct this very contrast – and to develop a trinitarian theology that cannot be located on a spectrum that stretches from oneness to difference. In fact, *there is no such spectrum* – for oneness and difference are not mutually exclusive, nor even contrastive. Rather, they interpenetrate one another in ways that confound our typical mathematical certainties. "These three are one": every bit as much a stumbling block to modern culture as was the message of "Christ crucified" to Paul's audiences, two thousand years ago.

God's Triunity is not merely a compromise between the one and the many. Rather, it grasps both concepts simultaneously and defines them as requiring one another. Concretely, this will entail practices of *pluralizing*: practices that define oneness as most truly "one" when it is involved in a process of self-differentiation, and difference as "different" only when we can recognize the lines of convergence within it. *Pluralizing* is not the same as "pluralism," which in our cultural context often refers to the celebration of pure multiplicity – "letting a thousand flowers bloom." In contemporary pluralism, oneness is not considered a desirable end (or is simply assumed to pervade all difference, under some abstract description of "our common humanity"). Hence the proliferation of choices is considered to be the highest good, even if these choices ultimately become meaningless. But the triune God calls us to difference *and* to oneness; and so I have employed a verbal form, *pluralizing*. I hope thereby to evoke a dynamic of differentiation and convergence, in which nothing holds still long enough for us to pigeonhole it into the supposedly discrete categories of "the one" and "the many."

The doctrine of the Trinity provides us with the archetypal account of "pluralizing": the divine processions mark God's eternal self-differentiating movement, while the indivisibility of God's external works mark the harmonious convergence of the Three. Can human beings begin to echo this eternal differentiation and convergence? Can we be formed and re-formed into the image, however imperfect, of the "eternally pluralizing" triune God? If this is possible at all, it will occur only through a grace-filled engagement in practices in which we are habituated to recognize both oneness and difference. For the triune God, the Self is always Other and the Other is always Self; living in the image of the triune God thus means learning to recognize ourselves in others and others in ourselves. It means attending to the lost melodies in the polyphony of creation; engaging in practices of mutual participation; and recognizing that particularity is not "ours," but that we are nodes in a network of life that is larger and more differentiated than we (from our own "particular" perspectives) can imagine. The eternally pluralizing triune God calls us to pluralize our practices of worship and of family life, such that these two arenas of the Christian life more adequately reflect oneness *and* difference.

Pluralizing Our Worship

Picture one of the great medieval or renaissance cathedrals: Reims or St Paul's, St Peter's or Ulm. Imagine it filled, not with the usual throng of camera-wielding tourists, but with faithful Christians who have come to the building for purposes directly related to their faith. Imagine that they are all inside the building, practicing that faith in word and deed. Indeed, imagine the most ideal scene of Christian practice imaginable. What would this picture look like?

For most of us, the mental image will be an improved version of a worship service in our own churches, perhaps on a holiday significant enough to fill the pews. The worshipers will be standing, their hymnals open, all singing a hymn or reciting a prayer in unison. Everyone's attention will be fixed on the singular purpose of the worship service. There will be no irrelevant distractions: no one is nodding off to sleep, no one is singing out of tune, and all the children are "well-behaved," which in our culture tends to mean that they are being "seen but not heard."

But this is not the picture that my initial paragraph is meant to evoke – for these cathedrals were not built as places in which only one thing can happen at a time. By their very architecture, they invite the practice of pluralizing. Side chapels offer venues for various services to occur simultaneously; confessionals provide space for sins to be confessed and forgiven (before, during, and after worship services); ample foyers and aisles allow room for onlookers (and distracted participants of any age) to move, to play, or to observe; and the "main worship service" – if there happens to be one in progress – may be taking up only a small part of the nave, or perhaps only the choir. In the back pews, several different groups gather, perhaps to plan a pilgrimage or to learn the catechism.

I would not wish to wax nostalgic about the era in which these buildings were built, nor the circumstances of those for whom they were the focus of Christian life. Nevertheless, the medieval cathedral provides us with an initial image of pluralizing: a beehive of activity, in which many people are doing many different things at once. In the midst of their diverse activities, they are held together by their common focus on Christian worship and the Christian life. They do all meet under one roof; but their activities are many and various, and no one seems particularly concerned that other people, in other parts of this great room, may not be doing the same thing. Rather than being distracted by this great swell of activity, people seem to thrive in it, and to concentrate their attention all the more fully on their own particular acts of participation in the Christian life.

Can only one thing happen at a time?

Unfortunately, this is not the picture of a "busy church" for most Anglo-American Christians today. Diverse activities may take place, but they are all closeted in separate rooms so that they cannot interfere with one another. One large room is reserved for the "main worship service"; but again, at any one time, only one thing is allowed to take place here. In many cases, this room is called the "sanctuary" – an interesting terminological shift. The sanctuary (literally, "holy place") was once a very small part of the whole building, sometimes located behind a curtain or screen (as in the "Holy of Holies" of the Jewish temple, and in most Orthodox churches today). This relatively small space was the only place that needed to be reserved for "one thing at a time." The rest of the building could have multiple purposes and was often subject to multiple uses. Today, the word *sanctuary* usually names the largest room in the building, and it is typically off-limits for most of the week. It is used only when enough people can be gathered who are willing to do the same thing; thus it is used rather rarely. Like the "living rooms" of many modern middle- and upper-class Western households, it is not really used for "living"; it is kept spotless, with all random activity banned, so that it will be ready for those rare occasions when it is really needed.

This "sanctuary" is often used only once a week, usually on Sunday mornings; in a typical month, occasional weddings or funerals might also take place in this space. In particularly active congregations, the sanctuary (or at least a corner of it) may be used for a service or two on some weekdays as well. Most of the time, however, it is empty. It is designed and built so as to encourage everyone inside it to do the same thing at once. If built in the older "basilica" style, with columns along the side-aisles, the spaces between the columns are rarely filled with side-chapels; instead, they are opened out and filled with additional pews, so that the people who use this space can be encouraged to do the same thing that everyone else is doing (even though it is often impossible to see what is happening from this space). Otherwise, a church may be built "in the round," with all seats facing the center, in a well-meaning (and sometimes moderately successful) attempt to provide the whole congregation with a sense of community and a common focus – but, in the process, often discouraging any use of the space in which many things take place at once.

Contemporary Christian worship space is no longer easily divisible into a number of smaller spaces; the working assumption (at least as reflected in recent architecture) seems to be that only one thing ought to take place in one space at one time. Why has this shift occurred? Initially I attributed it to certain tendencies in modern culture, since we tend to place a certain amount of value in "time alone," "getting away from it all," and "a quiet space, without distractions." But then again, most of us are in the habit of doing a number of things simultaneously: we cook and listen to the radio and direct traffic within the household; we drive while talking on the phone and perhaps even while reading a newspaper (frightening!). Our workplaces, homes, and even our cars are designed to encourage a number of things to happen at once. Why not our churches?

I do not think it too farfetched to connect this tendency in church architecture to diminished attention to the doctrine of the Trinity. If God's internal self-differentiation has become a matter of purely intellectual interest, it should be no surprise that differentiation among the ways that God is worshiped would not rank terribly high among the priorities of most Christian believers. In his book *The Domestication of Transcendence*, William Placher includes a chapter entitled "The Marginalization of the Trinity." Corroborating Michael Buckley's claims in *At the Origins of Modern Atheism*, Placher details the dramatic shifts that took place in the seventeenth century: the doctrine of the Trinity, which had been central for Thomas, Luther, and Calvin, had become – by very early in the Enlightenment era – largely irrelevant to Christian theology.[1]

Placher does not directly comment about the ways this shift was reflected in architecture, but the cover of his book reproduces a seventeenth-century Dutch painting of a church in Haarlem "after cleaning" – meaning that the walls have been whitewashed and all the iconography removed. The stained glass that once differentiated every side chapel has been replaced with clear glass, so that every part of the building looks the same. There are no secret, dark corners; the interior is painfully bright, so that nothing that transpires here could possibly go unnoticed. It is difficult to imagine more than one thing happening here at a time.

Now, undoubtedly, the "cleaning" of church buildings was undertaken for a wide variety of reasons. But whatever its purpose, it produced an architectural form that was entirely in keeping with the Enlightenment portrait of God. Placher describes that portrait as follows:

> Christian theologians increasingly thought of God as comprehensible in human terms, as the First Cause of the universe (who might or might not subsequently intervene in its affairs), and as the support of human efforts at moral improvement. Their imagining of this God primarily as a cosmic ruler and supporter of

---

[1] Placher, *The Domestication of Transcendence*, ch. 10.

ethical standards put the divine on the side of most of the dominant forms of social order.[2]

Such a god is most appropriately worshiped in a bright, well-lit, wide-open building, in which only one thing can happen at a time. After all, social order is difficult to maintain if a wide variety of different activities are going on in a variety of dark corners of the church. People need to be focused on the "one thing" that transpires in this space, so that they can be properly shaped into whatever moral shape the dominant social order finds convenient.

All the more ironic, then, that such "totalitarian" architectural forms came to dominate an "enlightened" culture, while the medieval cathedral, in all its manifestation of difference, is typically assumed to be the site of single-minded indoctrination. Consider the opposite possibility: the cathedral's construction made it difficult to exercise the kind of totalitarian control that such "enlightened" societies secretly wished to exercise. This would help to explain why the medieval cathedrals have so many idiosyncrasies (gargoyles, widely varying keystones, different capitals at the top of every column), while the typical modern building is a dreary edifice of sameness. More significantly, it may explain why, during the French Revolution, the gothic churches of Paris (for example, Notre Dame, St Eustache, and St Germain l'Auxerrois) were typically used for storage (primarily of forage, vegetables, and animals, respectively), and not as places to rally the troops. After all, who knows what kinds of anti-revolutionary plots might be hatched in those side-chapels?

Some medieval architectural elements cannot easily be removed; but in the United States, where *all* church building took place during or after the Enlightenment, only a handful of neo-gothic imitations provide the kind of differentiated, articulated space that encourages many things to happen at once. And among modern Western Christians in general, whatever degree of conformity was not achieved through architecture has been established through other totalizing practices. The "sanctuary" – whether it lends itself to multiple activity or not – is usually a place where "only one thing" happens. Those who "disrupt" the service must go elsewhere; often these persons are children, so their usual destinations are cry-rooms, nurseries, or space for "children's church." When someone who speaks another language comes to the service, she or he is typically asked to forsake that language for another, in order to participate fully. (When enough such people congregate, particularly mission-oriented parishes may allow the sanctuary to be used for an additional service, in another language – always, of course, at some other time,

[2] Ibid., 178.

when the "difference" that such persons impose will not be too threatening.) Activity in the side chapels (if they exist) must cease when the "sanctuary" is in use.

Our typical contemporary use of the church building thus mirrors, all too well, our more general failure to translate the trinitarian virtues into concrete practices. We have tended to require that worship take place in one voice, rather than many: prayers, songs, and readings are offered by one person (or, if collectively, always in unison). We do not allow much deviation from the script: if a child cries, or someone sings out of tune, or a teenager dozes off, or someone uses a novel form of language in a prayer or reads from a new translation of the Bible, we feel that something is out of place. We do not pause to ask whether this expression, too, may be an example of true and right worship of God. Because it differs, we assume it to be inadequate, or at least out of place. And indeed, some of it may be; the problem is that we never seem to ponder that question very carefully, never spend the time required to develop practices of serious discernment. We just assume that difference is a problem.

There are, of course, exceptions to this tendency; I will note a few of them later in this chapter. In my own experience, however, homogeneity is the rule in any single worship service. And even in those (relatively rare) cases where difference *is* welcomed, a similar problem may, ironically, arise; few people may feel compelled to think about whether something is out of place – to participate in practices of discernment – because anything and everything is automatically accepted. Both instances exhibit a failure to understand unity and difference as mutually constitutive of one another.

God's Triunity calls such assumptions into question. If God's difference does not compromise God's oneness, why are we so quick to assume that the unity of our worship is compromised by multiplicity? Recall the discussion of polyphony in chapter 4: a variety of different lines of music can be heard at once, without compromising the beauty of the whole and without silencing any of the various voices. God may also be praised by the baby who cries, the old man in the back who recites the Lord's Prayer during the first hymn, or the toddler who yells "why is it so quiet, Mommy?" at a particularly somber moment.

Some of this may seem not so much like multiplicity as disorder – and a word must be said on this subject, especially since I have already called attention to St Paul's claim that God is not a God of disorder, but of peace (1 Cor. 14:33). I am not arguing in favor of disorder in Christian worship; but I do believe that we need to re-think our construction of the categories of order and disorder. We have always assumed that we guarantee order most fully by guaranteeing homogeneity – by separating people from one another and by excluding from the worship service those whose intellect, sense of propriety, or attention span does not allow them to do what everyone else is doing. This does insure a certain kind of monotonous order within the worship service itself; but it hardly reflects the polyphonic order of the triune God.[3]

Moreover, we rarely think about what the enforced homogeneity of much Christian worship does to those who must be excluded from it in order to insure its uniformity. While the "quiet adults" are sitting in church, those who are excluded are unable to experience the "embodied witness"[4] that can be offered by Christians whose worship practices reflect the story according to which they live. Instead, those who are excluded tend to drift relatively easily into culturally-validated forms of discourse and practice. In many parish settings, the nursery or child-care space is not equipped to introduce children to the narratives and practices of the Christian faith, but to allow them to continue to participate in the prevalent activities of their culture. Toys, games, and activities may have no relationship to the Christian story at all; indeed, sometimes they are diametrically opposed to it, encouraging violence, nationalism, and cultural conformity. Even if the Christian narratives are a part of a church's ministry to children, they often come in a very watered-down form – a form believed to be meaningful to children, but often giving them a very distorted understanding of the meaning and message of the Gospel.

Those who do not fit in to the worship service need not be physically removed in order to be "excluded." Consider this scene (it occurs with some frequency): the parents of an occasionally noisy infant are told, "we do have nursery that you can use," and the parents respond by saying that they would like to keep their children in church if at all possible. The next week, or perhaps later in the same service, the same offer is made, and the parents offer the same response. If this process is sustained for long enough, the unspoken message is eventually heard: "we don't want your children making noise in our service. Please take them away." Indeed, this message is sometimes produced without any words at all; churchgoers have developed a whole range of nonverbal cues to express their desire to exclude those who aren't doing things rightly.

---

[3] See the comments on the trinitarian reinvention of order in Milbank, *Theology and Social Theory*, 428–30.

[4] For a development of the notion of Christian practice as "embodied witness," see the forthcoming study by Philip D. Kenneson, provisionally entitled *Beyond Sectarianism: Re-Imagining Church and World*, Christian Mission and Modern Culture, ed. Alan Neely, H. Wayne Pipkin, and Wilbert Shenk (Philadelphia: Trinity Press International).

In the end, the desire for order and homogeneity – which so often motivates the exclusion of otherness from the worship service – turns against itself. By moving children and other "non-conformists" out of the worship service (in order to guarantee its "good order"), we encourage those who are so excluded to develop their own set of practices and narratives, or to follow those of the prevailing culture, rather than ordering their lives according to the stories of Christianity. And because these divergences usually take place in other rooms, other buildings, and other cultural universes, we rarely realize just how divergent they have become – until we attempt to bring the excluded persons back into the worship service, and then express surprise that they don't seem to understand what transpires there.

Some alternative practices

What can we do, concretely, so that our worship services better reflect the eternally self-pluralizing triune God whom we worship? In general, we can habituate ourselves into allowing different things to happen in a single space in our churches. We should drop the misappropriated term "sanctuary," restoring this word in its proper reference, that is, to the area around the altar or communion table, the analogue to the Holy of Holies in the Temple, where (quite properly) "only one thing" occurs. The rest of the worship space can then be opened up to many simultaneous uses. During the worship service, especially, we can learn to allow different things to happen at once. Rather than worrying whether a person is reading the prayer precisely as printed in the bulletin, we might simply ask whether the triune God is being worshiped. A child's noisy curiosity may be an entirely appropriate act of worship, as may the prayer of someone who speaks, or seems to speak, a language with which we are not immediately familiar.

This does not mean that every kind of behavior is therefore appropriate. Someone who sits in the back of the church and utters curses against one and all is not worshiping God, and it is certainly the responsibility of the whole Church to point this out and to seek to correct such behavior. But this requires discernment – not an automatic ejection of the would-be worshiper simply because "that's not what it says in the service-book." Someone who does not participate in lock-step with others usually has reasons for doing so, and it is very much the business of the Church to listen to those reasons and to try to understand them.

Consider Paul's discussion of semi-disruptive worship practices in the Corinthian community, specifically concerning the practice of speaking in tongues. He does not attempt to guarantee uniformity in the worship service, but instead encourages Christians to undertake practices of discernment in evaluating various forms of worship, so that it provides a truthful witness both to believers and to outsiders. Paul asks the Corinthians not to forbid speaking in tongues, but he also asks that someone interpret these signs of the Spirit's presence (1 Cor. 14:27–28, 39). Prophetic words are not to be shunned; yet the gathered community must still "weigh what is said" (14:29). In general, Paul asks not for unity but for faithful witness and evangelical results: "Let all things be done for building up" (14:26).

Of course, this requires us to undertake practice of discernment – and such practices can be very difficult. The woman who refers to God as "she," the child who cries throughout the service, and the man who mutters insults under his breath – all are trying to tell us something, and Paul's injunction that we "discern the spirits" means that our first response to such apparent disorder should be to listen and to attempt to hear their various messages. Simply to exclude them because "they aren't doing it our way" is to fracture the Church, to rend the Body of Christ. Such exclusion, unless undertaken with careful discernment and appropriate pastoral care, will simply make it more difficult for the excluded person to encounter the witness that Christian worship is supposed to offer. Eventually, those who are excluded will migrate to a more hospitable place; and we, who once had the opportunity to welcome them, will lose all influence over the stories by which they live and the practices in which they are engaged.

Here, as often, any alternative practices will need to be attentive to local circumstances, and I cannot provide a general blueprint for action. Nevertheless, I will close this section by tracing the outlines of two practices that seem to me a necessary part of the practice of pluralizing.

Making space for children
Children tend to be the first victims of an excessive quest for homogeneity in the worship service. Their differences from adults cannot be hidden; and in a society that so highly values "rational activity," a child's love of nonsense automatically appears out of place. I will have more to say about these assumptions in the next section; for the present, I simply want to emphasize that the inclusion of difference within the Body of Christ could most profitably begin here.

This does not necessarily require devoting one segment of the worship service exclusively to children. In fact, such practices (for example, the addition of a "children's sermon" to the order of worship) do not necessarily mitigate the problems I have described here, since they still require something of a separation of adults and children – a strategy of "divide and conquer" rather than a multi-voiced polyphony. Nevertheless, such practices at least allow the two groups to hear and see what the others are hearing and seeing, which is certainly better than placing children in one room and adults in another. All the same, to "make space" for children in worship requires more than just carving out a particular niche for them in the service. It also requires adults to re-think their own expectations about the worship service, and to recognize that – if it is to be an act of the whole Body – it will require all members to accept the "otherness" of the other members.

Children must give up a great deal to be in the worship service: their usual expectations (concerning decibel level, freedom of movement, and the importance of interactive play) are suddenly extinguished, and they are expected to be silent, still, and wholly passive. This is not the life into which children are habituated, and in fact we would think there was something wrong with a child who exhibited these behaviors all the time. Certainly, the church is not the playground, and parents do need to help their children understand that; but parents (and other adults in the service) also need to develop realistic expectations. Children can be helped to sit quietly; they can enjoy books, snacks, and other diversions, while still taking in some aspects of the worship service. The arrangement of life at home will naturally influence a child's ability to negotiate life at church; and parental attentiveness to the needs of children certainly helps. In any case, the worship service should not be something that children learn to dislike. If it is understood only as a place of constraint and disapproval, the child will fly from the Church at the earliest possible opportunity.

More secure, I think, are those traditions in which the understanding of order and disorder is rather different than it is for white Anglo-American congregations. Black Church worship allows more freedom of movement and vocalization, and thus welcomes the noisy child much more readily. This also allows for a more general plurality in the worship space: there is a certain unity of spirit, held together (often) by a preacher. But here, preaching is not just the voice of one person addressed at the silence of the crowd; it is rather a dialogue of call and response, of communal commentary, movement, and song. Black Church worship has grasped the importance of "pluralizing" much more readily than has the worship of mainstream white denominations.[5]

[5] See my comments on the worship service at the Clearing in Toni Morrison's *Beloved*, which I discuss at the end of chapter 6. See also James H. Cone, "Sanctification, Liberation, and Black Worship," *Theology Today* 35, no. 2 (July 1978): 139–52; Robert C. Williams, "Ritual, Drama, and God in Black Religion: Theological and Anthropological Views," *Theology Today* 41, no. 4 (January 1985): 31-43.

My experience of black worship is very much second- and third-hand, but I have somewhat more direct experience with respect to Hispanic congregations. For the past several years, my own parish has helped to house and sponsor a Spanish-language mission congregation within our building. This has been a very important "pluralizing" experience for us, and one which I can heartily recommend. We have learned to share our building's space for worship, meetings, table fellowship, and teaching. We have developed a large number of bilingual services; many parishioners have learned Spanish or taught English. In the process, we have learned that it is possible, and sometimes necessary, to do things differently than we have done them in the past.

Specifically, with respect to the current topic, the Hispanic worshipers in our church often have a different sense of "appropriate activity" for children within the worship service, as well as a more flexible sense of time. This means that if a segment of the service goes more slowly than planned because, for example, children want to move about and look at something in a side aisle or to investigate the music leader's guitar, the members of the congregation are less likely to clear their throats loudly or look at their watches in irritation. Of course, this also means that worship services *never* start on time, which is an important cross-cultural discovery for those among us (primarily the Anglos in my parish) who are so used to punching clocks and/or living according to the will of our desk diaries and pocket calendars.

I am not suggesting that the cultural trappings of Hispanic and Black Church worship need to be infused in some large-scale way into other congregations in order for them to pluralize their worship. These elements reflect significant cultural differences, and Christianity (and Christian worship) must attend to these differences if it is to be true to the "multicultural" mandate of Acts 2 (in which the Living Water empowers the apostles to speak to all nations in language that they can understand). But various forms of cross-cultural worship experience help us recognize that the homogeneity that is often built in to much Christian worship is not a *necessary* attribute. God can be rightly worshiped, even when the setting does not depict everyone reading the same words from exact copies of the same books, all at the same time. And this realization leads quite directly to a second way in which we can pluralize our worship.

Pluralizing the language of worship
The headlines of church magazines and the "opinion" sections of popular theological journals are filled with comments about the language of our worship. One group calls for more feminine language for God, while another

side deplores such changes as pagan. One side demands the removal of military imagery in hymns and prayers, while another group laments the loss of words that they had treasured since childhood. The polemic is often heated, and often seems to be more about scoring debating points than about thinking carefully about worship and language. As Philip Kenneson noted recently, American congregations seem to lack the patience to articulate a coherent theology of worship, and are thus willing to allow the "free market" to dominate; the language of worship becomes a matter of "taste," "style," or "preference."[6]

Indeed, what is at stake in current debates over the language of worship is rarely a thoughtfully-articulated theological position. It is, rather, a particular taste or preference within worship, often developed on the basis of wholly untheological factors, which is then provided with some *ad hoc* theological justification to give it an aura of respectability. And then, this position (whether it be traditional, contemporary, or some blend) is then prescribed as an absolute for all. In other words, the main goal seems to be not so much innovation or continuity in worship, but rather, that everyone be made to say the same thing at the same time.

What no one seems to be asking is a question that would seem, at least, to be a prior one: *should* we all be saying the same thing at the same time? Is it always necessary that we do so? And, given that the meaning and reference of language varies among the members of the audience, how would we even know whether we were saying the "same" thing? From its very foundation on the day of Pentecost, the Church has proclaimed that its message can be preached in diverse languages. Different cultures will require different words, if we are to preach the "same" message to all. People are increasingly aware that we live in a world of diverse cultures, and that these cultures are increasingly intermixed with one another. Where did we get the notion that such diversity of culture could be adequately served by only one form of language in worship?

One of the first steps toward articulating a theology of worship would be a willingness to wrestle with the question of whether Christian worship, in order to be Christian, requires everyone to speak in unison all the time. It should be obvious that the answer to this is *no*; one need only examine the worship styles of the Black Church, much African and Latin-American

---

[6] See the comments in chapter 6 on the communally-formed nature of such particularities; and on the subject of worship language in particular, see Philip D. Kenneson, "Worship Wars and Rumours of Worship Wars," *Reviews in Religion and Theology* 1996, no. 2 (May): 72–5.

Christianity, and other non-wholly-European forms to understand the inappropriateness of the drive toward monolithic unity in worship. Whether this unity is demanded by so-called traditionalists or self-styled progressives, the result is the same: a worship style that demands homogeneity, but does not understand why. This result dramatically fails to speak to the particularity of those who worship; even if they are thoroughly catechized, they are not identical to one another, and the language of worship will evoke differing associations in every case.

One of the best things that can happen in a parish or congregation that is beset by "worship wars" is to pluralize worship. This does not mean dividing up the members of the congregation into discrete groups which hold worship services at different times and in different languages; this would simply recreate the problem of the "one thing at a time" mentality that I have already criticized. Rather, the various participants in these debates must learn to worship together, regardless of whether they actually use the same words at the same time. The result is a genuine polyphony in the Church: when the troublesome passage comes up in the hymn, some voices will sing the words that are printed on the page, while others will sing various alternatives.

There will be cases, of course, in which one group may doubt whether the other group is actually saying the "same" thing as they are. This will provide an important opportunity for discussion and serious thought, wherein a person or a group may become convinced that, in particular instances, the traditional language is better than the revised language (or vice versa). But the goal of such encounters should be – at least at first – to *listen* to and to *hear* what the other group is saying (rather than to leap into arguments that prove one's own position "right" or the other "wrong"). Before we can even talk about right and wrong forms of worship, we need to be able to articulate the purpose and goals of worship, and to ask how it should be formed by the biblical narratives, the experience of believers, and the theological claims of the Church (including, I would argue, the trinitarian virtues). And even after this discussion has occurred, the move to specific forms of worship language is not an easy one; and it is a matter that calls for tentativity and humility, rather than apocalyptic pronouncement.

Consider one example. The opening phrase of the Lord's Prayer, as it has customarily been translated into English, is "Our Father." Some Christians, saddened by the incessant masculinizing of Christian uses of *Father* over time (in art, preaching, and culture), have offered alternative language. Others have objected, citing "Father" as the most straightforward translation of the language of the Gospel (Matt. 6:9 // Luke 11:2) upon which the prayer is based. Both of these positions would appear to have their strengths and weaknesses, as has been pointed out in voluminous recent theological writings on the subject. In a congregation or parish that is struggling with this issue, I can think of no better solution than to allow alternative formulations to be used by worshipers who feel called to do so – and of course, to continue the conversation about the appropriateness of various forms. Christian believe that God is ultimately mystery, and their language for God must be tentative and provisional if they wish to make good on that belief. Recalling our various discussions of the names of God, it seems difficult to claim that only one form of words could ever be adequate or acceptable. The congregation that allows a variety of different voices to speak different names for God is a congregation that is fully aware of this mystery – especially if it is also willing to think seriously about the various forms of language it uses, and to make this part of the ongoing conversation of its life together.

This is not a complete solution to the problems we face, but it is an appropriate reordering of our priorities. Instead of assuming that vocalized unity must always be the touchstone of our worship practices, we should be willing to allow a plurality of voices within a single worship space. We must then be willing to come into conversation with those voices, so that the alternative formulations offered by one person or group are understood, even by those who choose not to follow the same path. Throughout this process, the focus must be on conversation and discernment, rather than on command and coercion. Surely such "pluralizing" is considerably more reflective of the triune God than is a demand for absolute homogeneity within worship, regardless of its ideological or political stripe.

But of course, we will continue to feel uncomfortable with such pluralized worship until we have learned to come to grips with plurality in other aspects of our lives – especially those aspects that we have usually thought of only in absolute or purely homogeneous terms. The second half of this chapter is devoted to one such aspect.

Pluralizing our Families

I have already noted the willingness of the modern nation-state to adopt and to alter certain elements of Christian discourse, such as its understanding of God, in order to serve specific political ends. Wars are justified with claims that "God is on our side"; vindictive punishments are meted out to protect "law-abiding Christians"; schoolchildren are coerced to participate in generic "prayers" out of a concern for their "spiritual well-being." Of course, none of these warrants is articulated theologically; most politicians know that only the most non-specific, broad-based appeals actually translate into electoral victories.

In the last few years, the word *family* has joined the words *godly* and *Christian* and *spiritual* as a theologically unspecified but politically effective tool for sanctifying one's own position and vilifying one's opponents. Most of the current talk of the importance of the family is merely of a piece with other attempts to champion the superiority of a particular race, gender, or economic class. To speak of "family values" in America today is a way of encouraging the electorate to ostracize anyone who is "not like us": a standard dogma of fascism, the American equivalent of *Blut und Boden*.[7]

Any Christian cooperation with such discourse is nothing short of idolatry. That there has been so much underwriting of this particular political tag-line by self-proclaimed "Christian" organizations is merely a reminder of the wholesale irrelevance of serious theological discussion in the ideological name-calling that passes for politics in the United States today. A Christian discussion of the family would need to consider, for example, how the doctrine of the Trinity bears on the understanding of what constitutes a family – and that would certainly not fit into a 30-second political advertisement! Moreover, a trinitarian account of the family would seem to point to a rather different picture than that envisioned by most advocates of so-called "family values."

The family and the Church[8]

In sociological discourse, the family is considered one of the basic units of organization. This does not mean that theological discourse must make the same assumption. In Christian theology, the basic unit of organization is the Church, and particularly the local parish or congregation. These parishes or congregations can be described as being composed of a certain number of "families," but such descriptions may grant sociological assumptions an excessive degree of importance; from the Christian perspective, these socio-economic entities are not autonomous, nor are they the "building blocks" of the Church. The true family is the Christian community – the local church, the parish, the congregation. This is why we speak of the Church as "the household of God" and describe ourselves as "sisters and brothers in Christ."

---

[7] I owe the analogy to Stanley Hauerwas.

[8] For an excellent overview of some of the issues at stake, see Rodney Clapp, *Families at the Crossroads: Beyond Traditional and Modern Options* (Downers Grove: InterVarsity Press, 1994), on which some of the following analysis is based.

The sociological unit called "family" is superceded by the ecclesiological family.

> Then his mother and his brothers came; and standing outside, they sent to him and called him. A crowd was sitting around him; and they said to him, "Your mother and your brothers and sisters are outside, asking for you." And he replied, "Who are my mother and my brothers?" And looking at those who sat around him, he said, "Here are my mother and my brothers! Whoever does the will of God is my brother and sister and mother" (Mark 3:31–35 // Matt. 12:46–50).

Unfortunately, however, when Christians talk about their "families," they rarely have this ecclesiological definition in mind. Instead, they have allowed political, cultural, and economic assumptions about what constitutes a family to hold sway over a theological description of the family.

And this tendency has, in turn, led to a certain idealization of the family, in which the fantastical constructions developed in American television programs in the 1950s ("Dad, Mom, two kids, and a dog") becomes the model of family life.[9] Obviously, a fairly large percentage of families – even according to the sociological definition of this term – do not conform to this supposed ideal. Some "families" consist of a single person; others of a single parent with children; another may consist of a woman, her daughter, and her granddaughter. But if the true Christian family is the Church, then these differences are theologically irrelevant. For Christians, the Church is "first family."[10] Indeed, it may behoove us to use a different term altogether to refer to those groupings of people who live together. Here, I will refer to these groups as "homes" or "the home" – so that the term *family* can also refer to the mutually participative life of the Church.

"Homes" might be thought of as small subdivisions of the church family. They are very difficult to define, because they vary so widely. They may be composed of people who are related to one another, but they need not be; their members may share common meals, common living space, and a common bed – or they may not. They may be bound together by marriage (certainly a theologically relevant notion), but then again they may not. Think about the variety of "homes" that make up the average congregation: no matter how homogeneous a group that congregation may be, the homes of its members will include a wide variety of socio-economic groupings: elderly

---

[9] For a critique of this non-existent ideal, see Stephanie Coontz, *The Way We Never Were: American Families and the Nostalgia Trap* (New York: Basic Books, 1992).

[10] Clapp, *Families*, ch. 4.

people living alone, or in groups that may be same-sex or mixed-sex; children living with their parents, with a grandparent, with an aunt or uncle or both, or with an extended family of whatever sort; college students living alone, living with their parents or siblings, living with one or more roommates of the same or the opposite sex. Whether or not these living arrangements actually constitute "families" in the classic sociological definition of the word, their differences do not seem of great urgency to the Christian notion of the family, since the family is, first and foremost, the local church.

Needless to say, a great deal of Christian worship, education, and pastoral care may take place in the home; nevertheless, Christians have relatively little at stake in the precise composition (number, age, age differences, gender balance) of these homes. On the other hand, Christians certainly *should* be concerned about how these groups are functioning. Are they marked by the theological virtues of faith, hope, and love? Are they places of mutual responsibility, physical safety, and an appropriate level of freedom? Unfortunately, the Church has rarely asked these questions when thinking about what goes on within the home. Instead, we have tended to adopt sociological and political language which concerns itself with only a small selection of demographic features about the home, rather than attending to theological judgments about whether faith, hope, and love dwell there.

We need to shift attention back to these theological concerns; and here, the doctrine of the Trinity can play an important role. The trinitarian virtues of polyphony, participation, and particularity provide us with a language for thinking about "families" on two levels: both at the level of the local congregation or parish, and within the home. Here, I will offer a few general observations about the potential impact of taking these virtues seriously within our smaller and larger "families." Then, in the remainder of this section, I will consider the impact of these observations on two areas of particular concern today: the role of children, and a group of concerns that I have collected under the label "body matters."

At the level of the parish or congregation, attention to the trinitarian virtue of *polyphony* will mean recognizing that the members of the Body live in a wide variety of homes, and that these varying structures are not arranged in some sort of hierarchical relationship to one another (with the stereotypical family from 1950s television sitcoms at the top, and the college students and nursing-home patients at the bottom). Every living arrangement – alone, with blood relatives, with others – is, on a formal level, equivalent. Needless to say, some homes may have special needs; one thinks of single parents, for example, or elderly persons living alone. But the Church should allow the different melodies of these different homes to be heard, without setting one or more of them up as the standard (against which all others are found wanting). The same virtue applies *within* homes; the various members of these groups may have very different roles to play, but they should not be understood in hierarchical terms. This is especially important when we examine the role of children, to whom I will return presently.

The trinitarian virtue of *participation* reminds us that the various homes in which the members of the Church dwell should not become fortresses that exclude and divide. Our culture tends to regard "families" as purely private enterprises, sealed off from one another by deadbolted doors. Here again, we have allowed our way of thinking to be dominated by cultural assumptions about individualism, privacy, and solitude, rather than biblical and theological warrants about community and mutual participation. This means, in practice, opening up our homes to one another, sitting at table with one another, and perhaps sharing certain aspects of a common economic life.[11] And within the home, this means the development of practices that bring people into contact with one another's lives – rather than a quick hello at the breakfast table, followed by a departure into discrete pigeonholes of the office, the school classroom, the coffee shop, and the pub.

Finally, *particularity* would seem to encourage us to allow our lives to be shaped by one another, rather than understanding ourselves first and foremost as individuals. We are members of the Body of Christ; we are members of a local congregation; we are members of smaller groups that live and eat and play together. Our primary responsibility is therefore not to our isolated "selves" (which, as we noted in chapter 6, do not exist), but to the others with whom we are always in the process of mutual formation.

Clearly, these comments only scratch the surface of the revisioning of family life that can be prompted by thinking through the implications of the doctrine of the Trinity. We need a much more thorough consideration of the practices that could begin to achieve these ends – something that I will be unable to offer here. Instead, I have chosen two areas of particular concern and controversy in current discussions of "the family," and have attempted to map out how a trinitarian ethic might address the issues that are at stake.

The authority of children

In the biblical narratives, children are generally understood as a *gift*. Eve describes Seth in these terms (Gen. 4:25); but the importance of children

---

[11] This aspect seems particularly important; unfortunately I have not been able to treat it at sufficient length in this book. See the trinitarian reflections on economic life in works such as Boff, *Trinity and Society*, and Meeks, *God the Economist*.

becomes much more obvious in the Abraham cycle. The child promised to Abraham and Sarah (Gen. 15:5; 17:6,16; 18:10) is central, as are the lines of descent through Isaac and Rebekah, Jacob and Leah and Rachel. Not only these children, but children in general, are the future and the promise to Israel, through whom the inheritance will be passed on (Lev. 10:14–15). Conversely, the lack of a child is a great woe (e.g. 2 Sam. 6:23 and often), as is the untimely death of a child (2 Sam. 12:14–19; Jer. 31:15). The raising of a child who is dead, or at the point of death, is an awesome miracle (1 Kings 17:21–23; 2 Kings 4:20–37; Mark 5:39–42 // Luke 8:49–56; John 4:47–53).

Stories of the birth and childhood of important figures such as Joseph, Moses, David, and John the Baptist are recounted in detail. Children are the bearers of tradition; they will learn and retell the story of the Exodus (12:26–27; Deut. 6:20–22), as well as other great events in the history of Israel (e.g. Josh. 4:21–22) and the traditions in general (Deut. 4:9–10; Ps. 78:4–6). The child becomes a symbol of salvation for Israel (Isa. 7:14, 9:6, 11:6); thus, the fulfillment of this prophecy, in the birth of Jesus to Mary, is recounted in detail (Matt. 1–2; Luke 1–2).

The notion of the people as the "children of God" – a role assigned occasionally to Israel in the Old Testament (see also Matt. 15:26 // Mark 7:27; Rom. 9:27) – becomes a frequent image for the Church (Matt. 5:45; Luke 6:35; John 1:12, 11:52; Rom. 8:14–21, 9:8, 9:26; Gal. 3:26, 4:5–7; Eph. 1:5; Phil. 2:15; 1 John 3:1–2, 5:19). The word *children* is used as a term of endearment by Jesus (John 13:33, 21:5), who would gather up children as a mother hen gathers chicks under her wing (Matt. 23:37 // Luke 13:34; Luke 14:5). It is also a term of endearment for Paul (1 Cor. 4:14, Gal. 4:19), and especially for the author of 1 John (2:1, 12, 14, 18, 28, 3:7, 18, 4:4, 5:21).

In Jesus' teaching, the child becomes a universal image of salvation and reconciliation with God. That the child's basic needs should be fulfilled by its parents is taken for granted (Matt. 7:9–11 // Luke 11:11–13; 2 Cor. 12:14). To children belongs the Reign of God, and whoever does not become childlike cannot be brought under God's Reign (Matt. 18:2–4; 19:14 // Mark 10:14–15 // Luke 18:16–17). Whoever welcomes a child welcomes Christ (Matt. 18:5 // Mark 9:36–37 // Luke 9:48). One of the missions of John the Baptist is to turn the hearts of the parents to their children (Luke 1:17, quoting Mal. 4:6). And at the end of time, a child will again be an instrument for the salvation of the world (Rev. 12).

This recapitulation should be a reminder of the significant and, overall, very positive role of children in the biblical narratives. It is certainly also true that a few texts seem to appeal to the cultural stereotype of children as foolish or rebellious; however, such texts are relatively rare (they are found primarily in the book of Proverbs). For the most part, childhood is given a very positive evaluation.

Nor is this positive image merely a reflection of the Greco-Roman milieu in which the New Testament texts were written. Precisely the opposite: as Thomas Wiedemann documents the matter in his comprehensive study, the Romans perceived children as vulnerable, liable to sickness, easily frightened, and consequently as "symbols of human fear as well as physical frailty."[12] Children were also unable to participate in warfare, which made them – like women and the elderly – unhelpful to the state.[13] The child was thought to lack capacity for reason; "the child's inability to communicate in the way adults do made him a symbol of non-participation in the rational world of an adult citizen."[14] The right of parents (specifically fathers) to discipline their children, by violence if necessary, was taken for granted. The only children whose status rose higher were those of elite families (especially those who held political office) and those who were far enough advanced in their education to pass, intellectually, as adults.

But among Christians, the matter was different. In fact, in the *Contra Celsum*, Origen quotes Celsus as accusing Christians of attempting to convert those whom he (Celsus) regards as irrational human beings, among them children.[15] Christians, however, were willing to wear this charge rather proudly; Irenaeus, for example, enthusiastically includes "newborns, infants, adolescents, and youths" among those who are saved through their rebirth in God.[16] And Cyprian "repeatedly insists that children are equal members of the Christian community."[17] The warrant for this claim came ultimately from Scripture, and was sealed by the practice of infant baptism. Speaking on behalf of sixty-six North African bishops, Cyprian writes:

> It is the judgement of all of us that the mercy and grace of God must be denied to no person who has been born . . . who has once been formed in the womb by God's hands. . . . Our trust in the Divine Scriptures makes it clear to us that God's gift is equally available to everyone, whether a child or an adult.[18]

---

[12] Thomas Wiedemann, *Adults and Children in the Roman Empire* (New Haven and London: Yale University Press, 1989), 18.

[13] Ibid., 19–20.

[14] Ibid., 21–2.

[15] Origen, *Contra Celsum*, III.50 and III.55; Origen defends this practice in III.56.

[16] *omnes, inquam, qui per eum renascuntur in Deum, infantes et paruulos et pueros et iuuenes*: Irenaeus, *Adv. Haer.*, II.22.4.

[17] Wiedemann, *Adults and Children*, 101.

[18] Cyprian, *Ep.* 64,2.1; 64,3.1, cited in ibid., 102.

Augustine continues this trend, treating children on the same level as adults (and even justifying physical discipline for this very reason!). As Wiedemann notes, part of this shift is due to Augustine's radical rejection of secular assumptions about children, the significance of whose lives transcended the temporal order.

> For the pagan, premature death was a disaster because the child's life was wasted; for Augustine, a child who died prematurely might have had as complete a life as a centenarian. He compares life-spans with musical intervals, or the hairs on one's head. Some are short, some are long, both may be perfect and complete. . . . The very vocabulary used by Augustine to talk about children shows that his contemporaries no longer saw them as a separate age grade, but as persons who happened to be younger than adults.[19]

In conclusion, Wiedemann suggests that Christianity's special affirmation of the significance of children meant that they were full members of the Church.

> By the fourth century AD, many churches, both Latin and Greek, incorporated children into the religious community as soon after birth as was practicable. This was at odds with the very obvious fact that babies and toddlers could not be thought to have accepted divine salvation in the same way as adults. Baptism could not serve a Christian society as a ritual symbolizing the progression from child to adult, leading to full participation in the community of adults. For the Christian, every baptised infant already belonged as completely as an adult.[20]

Children were full members of the Body of Christ; the distinction between adult and child had no lasting theological significance.[21]

Unfortunately, however, modern Christianity has been heavily influenced by its encounter with the Enlightenment; and through it, some aspects of the Greco-Roman attitudes toward children – which Christianity initially re-

---

[19] Wiedemann, *Adults and Children*, 105. He provides the following example of this shift in vocabulary: "*Parvuli*, 'little ones,' used by Fronto on those occasions when he wanted to express particular delight at children, has [for Augustine] become standard, replacing *liberi*" (ibid.).

[20] Ibid., 191.

[21] Paul's description of "putting away childish things" (1 Cor. 13:11) and his occasional negative comments on childhood (1 Cor. 14:20, Eph. 4:14) are clearly Greco-Roman rhetorical commonplaces; nowhere else does Paul develop any significant critique of childhood or "childish" behavior, and in fact (as I have already observed) he often uses the image of children as a positive description of the Christian believer's relationship to God.

jected – have been firmly reintroduced. Despite its haste to overthrow authoritarianism in favor of equality and fraternity, the Enlightenment was unable to extricate itself from the categories of dominance and subordination that were assumed to subsist within the familial order. The *locus classicus* here is Kant, who uses conceptual categories such as *immaturity*, *tutelage*, *coming of age* and *emancipation* in order to describe the difference between the enlightened and the unenlightened.[22] He thereby helped to re-establish the Greco-Roman portrait of children as spiritually inadequate, subordinate, and altogether lacking in wisdom – as opposed to the very positive understanding of children that seems to pervade the biblical narratives and early Christian practice.

Much can be gained by careful attention to the words of Jesus concerning the status of children. These are not simply as pious verses to be quoted in church-school; they are radical, counter-cultural claims about our assumptions about children. Jesus clearly recognizes that children are different; but at the same time he criticizes the general societal assumption that they should be subordinated to adults, and/or that they should not get in the way of adult concerns.

> People were bringing little children to him in order that he might touch them; and the disciples spoke sternly to them. But when Jesus saw this, he was indignant and said to them, "Let the little children come to me; do not stop them; for it is to such as these that the Reign of God belongs." (Mark 10:13–14)

Indeed, Jesus offers something of a reversal, suggesting that the true goal of human life is precisely not to "grow up," or "come of age" in Kant's sense (that is, to shed the qualities of childhood). Rather, those who have come of age are told that they will never be in a right relationship with God unless they "change and become like children" (Matt. 18:3).

What is being sought in this radical call? As is often the case with respect to the words of Jesus, we need to consider what we are (and are not) being called to do. For example, children often differ from adults in their size and physical features; but we take it for granted that Jesus was not arguing that a right relationship with God required one to be physically smaller. Instead, we turn to the rest of the Gospel, and discover that elsewhere, Jesus advocates certain human qualities that are also typically associated with childhood – qualities such as trust, compassion, and wonder. Apparently we are being

---

[22] As noted in Moltmann, *History and the Triune God*, 10 [*In der Geschichte*, 35–6].

called to allow some of these qualities, normally associated with children, to shape our adult lives as well.

How might the doctrine of the Trinity help guide us in thinking through these issues? At the outset, we should recall our observation in chapter 3 that classical trinitarian doctrine affirms that the Three are radically equal to one another, that none is subordinate to either of the others. If we keep complete co-equality of the Three firmly in mind, we can gain a very positive benefit from the traditional translations of πατήρ and υἱός as "father" and "son" or even as "parent" and "child": namely, that just as none of the Three is subordinate to either of the others, neither is the child subordinate to the parent. (This sounds counterintuitive, I know; I will return to it momentarily.) Unfortunately, the cultural pressures against children have often been read back in to the near-exclusive use of our English words *father* and *son* to identify two of the Three. As a result, the dominance of parents over children (so regularly validated in our culture) often becomes the standard for evaluating the relationship between the divine Father and the divine Son – thus contributing to the general tendency to place the Three into various sequences and hierarchies. And conversely, this trinitarian sequencing (which is actually rather widespread among Christians) has tended to reinforce cultural tendencies to understand parents as ranking above or over children. As Jürgen Moltmann comments, "A description of the relationship between Father and Son as one of 'rule and obedience' is unclear and likely to be misunderstood; for this also characterizes the relationship between master and servant."[23]

Moltmann's own solution to this problem is his "social" doctrine of the Trinity; his approach been echoed in the work of Leonardo Boff, Sallie McFague, and others. It seeks to break down the hierarchical relationships among the trinitarian hypostases, understanding the Three as a community of equals – that is, to turn the (ostensibly vertical) relationship of Parent and Child into a horizontal relationship of friends, lovers, committee members, or citizens. This is a well-intentioned attempt to avoid subordinationism; but sometimes this language can tend to obliterate the relational differences of the Three, describing them all as not merely *equal to*, but ultimately *indistinguishable from*, one another. Moreover, the interactions among (for example) friends or citizens reminds us that they are never purely mutual, purely reciprocal – especially not when viewed at any particular moment in time. Consider a human conversation: at any one moment, one person may be in temporary control of the dialogue – setting out the argument, asking or

---

[23] Moltmann, *In der Geschichte des dreieinigen Gottes*, 182, my translation (cf. *History and the Triune God*, 132).

answering questions in a way that determines the future course of the conversation. At other moments, a different person may take the lead. Admittedly, a certain degree of mutuality and equity can develop over time, as the participants carefully share out the roles of leader and follower. But as any two people in a long-term relationship know, there will always be temporary lapses into hierarchy and subordination; achieving long-term equity and mutuality is an extraordinarily difficult undertaking.

This is even clearer in parent-child relationships; parents and children are simply not "equals" in the way that one might want to describe an ideal relationship among citizens or friends. Clearly, parents and children must always negotiate structures of mutual submission. When the child exercises her freedom to touch the hot stove or play with the laundry detergent, parents should not hesitate to "subordinate" the child's will to their own, and the child must learn to submit. But what is not always noticed – and this may be the ultimate significance of the biblical account of children – is that in some circumstances, *parents must submit to their children as well.* Parents need to learn to listen to their children, to recognize and attend to the needs of children, and in general, to acknowledge that their status *as* children requires us to treat them *differently* – in order to treat them *equally.*

Thus, social trinitarians are quite right to insist on the equality within the Trinity, but they are wrong to model this equality on democratic political imagery or abstract accounts of friendship that tend to obliterate difference (or at least, to obscure the relations as orientations of activity) within God. The Three are equal because they are all characterized by free gift and superabundant love. The Three are never subordinate to one another; this is not because they all have "equal rights" within the Godhead, but because they are always about the business of giving themselves to one another – completely and absolutely. This is why "parent-child" language for the Three still needs to be given voice. For example, Hans Urs von Balthasar's account of the reciprocal, other-oriented divine activity may be of some use:

> We begin to discern the meaning of "fatherhood" in the eternal realm when we consider the Son's task, which is to reveal this Father's love (a love that goes to ultimate lengths, for example, the Parable of the Prodigal Son or of the Vineyard): such "fatherhood" can only mean the giving away of everything the Father is, . . . it is a giving-away that, in the Father's act of generation – which lasts for all eternity – leaves the latter's womb "empty."[24]

Steffen Lösel offers the following useful commentary on Balthasar's claim:

[24] *T-D* III:518 [*TD* II/2:475].

> The Father expropriates himself of his whole divinity and sets a second infinitely free agent within the one Godhead. In this original kenotic act, he renounces owning his divinity alone, i.e., to "be God for himself alone." With this eternal generation of the Son, he puts the divine unity and hence divine existence itself at risk, for if the Son did not return his divinity to the Father, he would destroy the unity which embraces the inner-divine substance. . . . The Son proves himself worthy of the Father's self-abandoning love by placing himself indifferently and obediently at the disposal of the Father.[25]

Balthasar's description reminds us that the "equality" within God is not the same thing as the "equal rights" of citizens. In their mutual activities of loving and giving, the Source submits to the Wellspring *and* the Wellspring to the Source.[26]

Thus, with respect to parents and children, our problem is not our (wholly appropriate) assumption that there must be moments of deference and submission. Rather, our problem is that we have interpreted these structures in an eternal one-way pattern – with parents always ultimately "in charge," and children always relegated to the role of receiving and obeying orders. Clearly, this does not fit the pattern of *polyphony* that I outlined in chapter 4. The activities of obedience and authority are not mutually exclusive activities, and they need not be parceled out to particular actors in an attempted "division of labor."

It is an easy enough mistake to make. Once we recognize the existence of structures of authority, we tend to choose the easiest option of negotiating them, which is to absolutize them – making the current leaders into permanent leaders and refusing to allow for any reversal of the lines of authority. And of course, raising children is extraordinarily difficult work; today's parents, so busy with other matters of concern, are always in search of easier approaches to the task. The Roman Empire's treatment of children as second-class citizens is much less troublesome than the trinitarian account, in which parents *and* children are involved in a mutual process of giving, listening, and submitting to the specificity of the other.

Obviously, in some stages of life (or moments of time), the lines of authority

---

[25] Steffen Lösel, "Murder in the Cathedral: Hans Urs von Balthasar's New Dramatization of the Doctrine of the Trinity," *Pro Ecclesia: A Journal of Catholic and Evangelical Theology* 5, no. 4 (Fall 1996): 427–39; here, 435.
[26] Lösel argues, however (ibid., 437–9), that Balthasar still tends to place the Holy Spirit in a subordinate role, and thus fails to work out a "trinitarianism without reserve." This is an important critique; see Milbank, "Second Difference"; Staniloae, "Holy Trinity"; and my comments on the "necessary third" in chapter 2.

will in fact flow as we have assumed: the parent leads, and the child follows. But at other stages of life or moments of time, the lines flow in the opposite direction. One obvious example occurs late in life, when (in most cultures) aging parents are cared for by their children. Our own culture's tendency to assign the task of the care of aged and dying parents to others has obscured this aspect of the parent–child relationship; but even for us, children must sometimes exercise the same kinds of decision-making authority over their parents that their parents once exercised over them.

But this inversion of our usual perception of parent–child authority structures is not limited to the later stages of life. It should be present from the very beginning: parents should learn to listen, to discern needs, and to serve. Infants ought to be "in charge" with respect to their schedules for feeding, sleeping, and other basic bodily functions. Again, this authority is often obscured in our culture by so-called "parenting experts" who legitimize many parents' attempts to resist any "submission" to the newborn's will in these matters – putting the baby on a strict feeding or napping schedule. (I have not yet read a book that advocates a strict diaper-changing schedule, but I wouldn't be surprised to find one.) The child has many other needs – for creative play, for time together and alone, for inquiry. Parents cannot and should not simply defer to all these needs; but parents do need to listen, to recognize these needs, and to attend to them.

Allow me to close this section by drawing on the trinitarian virtue of *participation* to suggest some practices that could help us validate and encourage, among parents *and* children, the kind of mutual, loving donation that we recognize in the triune God. I point to this trinitarian virtue in particular because it is very difficult to develop a relationship of mutual love and mutual gift with someone in whose life we do not fully *participate* (in the strong sense in which I have used this word). Such mutuality requires a constant contextual negotiation of actual and potential conflicts, and a willingness to submit to the other as easily as we expect them to submit to ourselves. Such negotiations are only possible in relationships of deep mutual participation.

And yet, we do not always cultivate practices that habituate us into mutually participative relationships with our children. I have already mentioned the tendency of the modern Western "family" to spend most of the day absent from one another. Certain practices can help to mitigate this tendency. Some of the alternative reckonings of time that I described in chapter 7 may be useful here – helping us to think about ways that we can reshape time in order to focus on the lives of others in the home and in the larger family of the Church. The various activities of the day, be they mundane or extraordinary, provide a context in which parents and children can truly participate in one another's lives. Another practice – more difficult in some cases, but worth attempting – is for parents and children who are *not* together during the day to spend time in one another's spheres of activity – which may mean bringing children to the workplace, spending more time at our children's schools, and going out of our way to find time to have meals together (since, as we have already noted, table-fellowship is such an important element of mutual participation). Finally, for those families who are able to undertake it, homeschooling provides an enormous opportunity for mutual participation of parents and children. Too often, Christian discussions of this practice are limited to worries about the teaching of evolution or sex-education in schools. A broader perspective would simply note that the Christian doctrine of God underwrites those practices which allow for the deepening and enrichment of mutual participation between parents and their children. For this reason alone it ought to receive prayerful consideration from those parents whose circumstances allow them to consider it as a live option.

In sum, the doctrine of the Trinity calls us to recognize the authority of children, as well as the authority of parents. It reorients our typical construction of "the family," urging us to find ways of allowing the trinitarian virtues to shape the relationships among family members, so that they are not seen as isolated individuals or boxes in a bureaucratic flowchart, but as members of the Body, each playing their own particular melody, and each needing to be heard. That these melodies will differ from one another goes without saying; the pluralizing of our concept of "family" does not entail the elimination of the particularity of its members. But that particularity is formed through practices of mutual participation, and especially through joint participation in the Body of Christ.

Body matters

I have suggested that, for Christians, the primary reference of the word *family* is the Church, and especially the local parish or congregation. Nevertheless, I have also suggested that the Church should be attentive to what goes on in the homes of the members of the Body – and that the doctrine of the Trinity might help us sort out what aspects of home life are of greatest concern. We should take an active interest, for example, in helping people who live together to find ways of participating as fully as possible in one another's lives. The home should allow space for particularity, but the particularity of the individual should not be made so significant that it compromises the polyphony of the whole. At this level, of course, such observations are terribly abstract; they certainly need to be worked out in the concrete circumstances of families – both in homes and in congregations. Here, I will try to provide some concrete specificity by narrowing the focus to a single issue: in what ways should the Church be attentive to the bodily relationships that take place among those who live together? If human beings are habituated in the trinitarian virtues, what kinds of behavior might we expect in this regard?

It might be easier to begin negatively. Clearly, there are *some* forms of bodily expression that would fail to model those virtues. For example, violence against one another is absolutely ruled out, as we noted in the previous chapter. Sexual expression that is attentive only to the desires of one person, and ignores the desires of the other, clearly fails to mirror the mutual participation of the triune God. This description is meant to refer, most obviously and most importantly, to those relationships in which sexual involvement is coerced through abuse or violence; but it also refers to a wide variety of bodily practices in which only one person's desires are taken into consideration. Nor can mutual participation really pervade a bodily relation-ship in which one of the members of the household is typically absent, or unfaithful, or otherwise failing to develop reciprocal and mutually participative relationships with the other bodies to which one is most closely "attached."

A very clear example of "bodily activity" that demonstrates a complete breakdown of the trinitarian virtues is violence against children and/or sexual activity with children. Such action represents a failure to allow for the otherness of children; it fails to recognize their authority as fully human "others" (as discussed above); it fails to address their needs for safety, protection, and bodily integrity. It ignores their particularity as human beings with memories and hopes and wills, all of which need time to grow and develop before they can think through the meaning and significance of physical force or erotic desire. Such activity ignores the fact that children sing a different tune, and refuses to allow that music be part of the polyphony of the home. In short, such acts fail to allow children *to be children* – to recognize that their experiences of such liaisons are categorically different than those of the adult who strikes or seduces them, and therefore such relationships are never marked by mutual participation.

This is certainly not an exhaustive description of the sorts of bodily activity that *fail* to exhibit the trinitarian virtues. Even so, it might help to consider what *positive* linkage there might be between these two realms of discourse. The most important link, I believe, is that the mutual bodily desire of two human beings can potentially reflect, however dimly, the internal mutual desire of the triune God. Moreover, it can also help us to think creatively about the mutual desire *between* human beings and God. In an important essay on the topic, Rowan Williams puts it this way:

Grace, for the Christian believer, is a transformation that depends in large part on knowing yourself to be seen in a certain way: as significant, as wanted. The whole story of creation, incarnation, and our incorporation into the fellowship of Christ's body tells us that God desires us, *as if we were God*, as if we were that unconditional response to God's giving that God's self makes in the life of the Trinity. We are created so that we may be caught up in this; so that we may grow into the wholehearted love of God by learning that God loves us as God loves God. The life of the Christian community has as its rationale – if not invariably its practical reality – the task of teaching us this: so ordering our relations that human beings may see themselves as desired, as occasions of joy.[27]

With respect to human sexuality in particular, this is a reminder that mutual desire is not for procreation alone; to construe it this way is to fail to recognize it as one of the many triune marks that human beings bear. Our own sexual desire – the total surrender of oneself to the other in an occasion of mutual joy – is an altogether fitting and indeed glorious *vestigium* of the triune life of God. From early in the Christian tradition, the inner trinitarian yearning, of God for God, was described with the Greek word ἔρως, of which human erotic desire is a pale reflection.[28]

It need hardly be noted that the human body is subject to, and capable of inflicting, horrific abuse. In this sense it is very much like many other elements of the created order, which can be abused but which are still good, and are pronounced so by God). But – as already noted – we can take steps toward identifying particular bodily practices as virtuous or vicious with the help of the trinitarian virtues. And the Church attempts to aid (though it certainly cannot insure) the virtuous pursuit of bodily desire by creating a space within which it seems mostly likely to retain a mutually participative character – the space marked by the covenant of marriage.

All of which brings us to a controversial and vexed issue in current discussions of human sexuality: the question of sexual orientation, and more particularly, the question of whether sexual desire can be virtuously pursued within monogamous same-sex relationships. An enormous amount has been written on this question, especially over the last few decades; I do not pretend

[27] Rowan Williams, *The Body's Grace: The 10th Michael Harding Memorial Address* (London: Lesbian and Gay Christian Movement, 1989), 3, now reprinted in Charles Hefling, ed., *Our Selves, Our Souls and Bodies: Sexuality and the Household of God* (Boston: Cowley Press, 1996), 56–68; here, 59.

[28] See, for example, Pseudo-Dionysius, *On the Divine Names*, 644A (trans. Luibheid/Rorem, 62); on Dionysius, and on the positive use of ἔρως in early Christian theology generally, see McIntosh, *Mystical Theology*, ch. 2.

to be an expert on its nuances. Many denominations have produced statements on human sexuality; meanwhile, scholars continue to debate the biblical, historical, and theological complexities of this issue. Not surprisingly, perhaps, few writers seem to have turned to the doctrine of the Trinity in an attempt to think through this difficult question; and yet, trinitarian theology may enable us to move this discussion forward in creative ways.

I have already suggested that the doctrine of the Trinity can help us to understand and evaluate the nature of the relationships among bodies, including relationships that involve sexual desire. The question which remains, is whether it necessarily limits those forms to opposite-sex relationships. And as far as I can see, there is nothing in trinitarian doctrine that has a word to say, in any *prima facie* sense, against monogamous gay or lesbian relationships. In such relationships, mutual participation is clearly possible, just as it is in opposite-sex relationships. The same-sex partner is still an "other," and fully capable of embodying the trinitarian virtue of particularity. The doctrine of the Trinity does not seem to address anatomical features of the desired body; God manifests yearning, desire, and love for the *otherness* of the other, but this otherness is not limited to – nor does it necessarily even involve – questions of sexual differentiation.

However, this should not be taken as suggesting that the triune God is not involved with *bodies*. God is involved, most obviously, with the Body of Christ – in three senses: the incarnate body that experienced the life and death of this world, in the womb of Mary and in the body of Jesus; the body broken for us, again and again, in the consecrated bread of the eucharist; and finally, in the Church as "the Body of Christ." In fact, one might well argue that, from a trinitarian point of view, the Body of Christ (in all these senses – Mary and Jesus, the eucharist, and the Church) should be the central image that gives meaning to the word *body*. In other words, all other descriptions of "the body" should derive their meaning and find their true center in the Body of Christ. Salvation is itself bodily, in that it depends upon the crucifixion of Christ, and on being taken up by God into the divine life.[29]

Thus, if we are to think in trinitarian ways about the body, we need to say something like the following: the triune God is always about the business of giving and loving, of "proceeding" in such a way that the divine "body"

[29] For this paragraph, and the one which follows it, I am dependent on an early draft of an article by Gene Rogers (to whom, many thanks), the title of which is "Sanctification, Homosexuality, and God's Triune Life," forthcoming in Saul Olyan and Martha Nussbaum, eds., *Sexual Orientation and Human Rights in American Religious Discourse* (New York: Oxford University Press).

(however we may understand that term) is always placed at risk, given over to the other, put at the disposition of the other; it thus also experiences the love of the other – the gift of the other – in return. The poetry of some mystical theologians traces the convergences between God's intratrinitarian love and erotic desire in some striking ways. Hadewijch writes:

> When he takes possession of the loved soul in every way,
> Love drinks in these kisses and tastes them to the end.
> As soon as love thus touches the soul,
> She eats its flesh and drinks its blood.
> Love that thus dissolves the loved soul
> Sweetly leads them both
> To the indivisible kiss –
> That same kiss which fully unites
> The Three Persons in one sole Being.[30]

Trinitarian theology gives us a number of clues as to how we ought to treat bodies – our own, as well as that of the other. What it does *not* say, however, is just how different those bodies have to be in order for mutual human love to reflect, however inadequately, the mutual love of the triune God.

Ultimately, trinitarian doctrine helps us to think about "bodily matters" by reshaping our priorities, encouraging us to ask what matters and what doesn't. Our political and cultural apparatus leads us to assume that sexual, biological, and other primarily physical features of a relationship are its most important features. Trinitarian doctrine leads us in a different direction: the body that really matters is the Body of Christ, and the bodily features of a relationship are relevant only with respect to whether they can be taken up into that Body. That question, in turn, depends at least in part on whether a bodily relationship is shaped by the trinitarian virtues, and whether it is enacts (or is at least in the process of learning to enact) trinitarian practices. A mutual and peaceable sexual relationship is always better than a hierarchical or violent one, regardless of questions about bodily form or sexual orientation. Bodily relationships should be marked by mutual participation, regardless of how legislatures and lawcourts choose to describe these relationships. As is so often the case, the Church has allowed itself to be conformed to this world and its judgments about what is important, rather than being transformed by the will of God. What is needed – though I have certainly been unable to develop it here – is

---

[30] Hadewijch, Poems in Couplets, 16, in *Hadewijch: The Complete Works*, trans. Columba Hart, O.S.B., Classics of Western Spirituality (New York: Paulist Press, 1980), 355. I owe the reference to Mark McIntosh.

a trinitarian theology of human embodiment, in which the virtues and practices operative in a relationship are the focal point, and the bodily specificity of persons is understood strictly in light of their membership in the Body of Christ.

A theology of embodiment that was truly attentive to the doctrine of the Trinity could also teach us how to analyze the arguments of those who seek to specify legitimate and illegitimate bodily relationships *without* attention to the triune life of God – whether they derive their results from "natural law" or "tradition" or a claims about "what the Bible says." This is not to argue that all ethical claims must flow directly from the doctrine of the Trinity; nevertheless, this doctrine is central for the Christian understanding of God and of the God-world relationship. If we can derive from this doctrine *nothing at all* about ethical norms with respect to the relationships among bodies, then we may discover that the "traditional" positions on these issues are as ideological and non-theological as were the "traditional" positions, held across the centuries, on gender, and race, and slavery.

With respect to sexual orientation in particular, one more point needs to be made. Some might argue that the trinitarian virtues seem to be empirically less evident in gay and lesbian relationships; that cultural and societal factors, for example, may militate against the constancy and mutuality so essential to any sexual relationship that seeks to conform to the triune life of God. I cannot here analyze the empirical evidence; I can only observe that, throughout most of the history of Christianity, almost every cultural institution has been hard at work making such constancy and mutuality *exceedingly difficult* for gay and lesbian couples to achieve. Sadly, the Church has contributed to this process – a process which might well be described as *deforming* human beings by pushing them *away* from the trinitarian virtues. Specifically, the Church has traditionally refused even to *consider* whether gay and lesbian couples might not merit the same degree of recognition, attention, and help that is offered to opposite-sex couples (however inadequate it may be in some cases). Given the history of the cultural structures designed to conceal, debase, or destroy gay and lesbian relationships, and especially given the Church's flagrant support of these structures, it seems a bit churlish to dismiss such relationships because they don't always seem to model the trinitarian virtues. Only after the Church has actually attempted to contribute to this formation can it have a word to say about the "empirical" evidence.

What kinds of practices might enable such formation to take place? Regardless of official and unofficial denominational positions on the applicability of "marriage" to gay and lesbian relationships, pastors and congregations need to demonstrate their willingness to provide the same kinds of pastoral care to committed same-sex relationships as they do to opposite-sex couples. Christians need to talk openly and honestly about the ways that sexual relationships can become distorted, and can fail to embody the trinitarian virtues (as noted at the beginning of this section) – and that this is just as much a danger in opposite-sex relationships as it is in same-sex relationships. Christian preaching and teaching need to become more conversant with the narrative of superabundant donation and mutual love that describes the triune life of God, and to talk about how human sexual relationships might come to reflect that life.

Pluralizing and Pluralism

To conclude this chapter, I want to return to my opening comments about the differences between the trinitarian practice of *pluralizing* and the more general contemporary enthusiasm for *pluralism*. I suggested that, while the latter is a very general celebration of difference, the former recognizes that difference is grounded in oneness, and reconverges toward that same point of focus. In my comments throughout the chapter, I have tried to emphasize that difference ought not to be glorified for its own sake, but only insofar as it mirrors the difference of God, which is also a unity: these Three are One.

The challenge for Christian theology is to recognize that these are not the opposite ends of a spectrum, but are mutually constitutive. The differences that Christians meet in one another – in matters of age, race, gender, class – can never lapse into relativistic chaos, for we are all bound by one Lord, one faith, one baptism. But that unity is always articulated in a threefold form; and so it can never be a warrant for absolute homogeneity. A general *pluralism* has no grounds for ruling anything out of court; every new perspective adds to the glories of diversity. The trinitarian practice of *pluralizing*, on the other hand, always directs our attention back to the One God. Here we find our true foundation, whose constancy, love, and perseverance have given us the freedom to listen to the music, to give thanks for communion, and to rejoice in difference.

Chapter 9

PERSUADING

Because the Church is "one body with many members," Christians often find themselves attempting to come together for a common purpose. Even if we are engaged in practices of pluralizing, we may still have to come to agreement on the (provisional and tentative) boundaries of difference. Moreover, as anyone who has spent much time in a local-church setting knows, these boundaries require fairly constant negotiation; Christians spend considerable time facing innumerable practical questions that require them to make relatively unified decisions. These decisions necessitate a certain level of (frequently verbal) interaction among the members of the Body, as they try to come to agreement concerning a common project.

What form should such interactions take? Should they primarily take the form of rules or laws, which some of the members of the Body compel others to obey? Or should we expect some sort of logical demonstration, in which "the facts" are examined so that all "rational people" can come to agreement? Or should we just sit back and wait for a clear sign as to what God would have us do? Perhaps some combination of the above?

A number of broad critiques could be lodged against any of these alternatives, on the basis of (for example) the significance of Christian freedom, the illusory nature of fact-value distinctions, the inherent conflict of interpretations, and so on. In any case, none of the descriptions offered in the previous paragraph provides an adequately *trinitarian* understanding of how we might interact with one another in order to carry out the mission of the Church. As an alternative, I want to suggest that our interactions with one another should be marked by an empathetic, mutual process of listening, speaking, and acting. I describe this process in the present chapter as the trinitarian practice of *persuading*.

The chapter begins with a construal of God as already involved in the activity of persuading.[1] From this account, I attempt to draw out some general implications for the Christian life. The remainder of the chapter builds on this description in order to re-think one specific problem that the Church faces today: the problem of *authority*. What authority do (or should) Christians exercise over one another? Especially in the context of Western democratic societies, where we have become so accustomed to (what we at least perceive to be) some degree of freedom with respect to both thought and action, any invocation of "authority" may sound vaguely sinister. It would usually be the *last* thing Christians would want to hear when they are facing a question of concrete practice, such as who should be admitted to communion, or what government policies one should protest, or what Sunday-School curriculum should be used. And yet, in one form or another, authority is always being exercised whenever decisions are made.

Although my comments in the latter sections of this chapter will focus on the issue of authority, I suspect that a fuller analysis of the trinitarian practice of persuading might help us rethink a wider range of issues faced by the Church today – including questions about liturgical language, ordination, and episcopal collegiality. These applications, and others like them, will need to be taken up elsewhere. I hope that this chapter's more restricted focus can at least provide some sense of the potential benefits of thinking about these problems through attention to the trinitarian practice of persuading.

Persuading as a Trinitarian Practice

What makes persuading a specifically *trinitarian* practice? I offered some initial reflections on this question in chapter 3, when I explored the process of rhetorical invention as a "triune mark." I suggested that the two rhetorical processions (the production of language and construction of the audience) help us to think more clearly about God's internal self- differentiation. Here, I want to extend the analogy, considering first its implications for God's relationship to human beings – and, in turn, how God's practices of persuading might shape and influence our own.

---

[1] I am aware that some process theologians predicate the language of persuasion to God, e.g. Lewis S. Ford, *The Lure of God: A Biblical Background for Process Theism* (Philadelphia: Fortress Press, 1987). Although I am familiar with some of this literature, it has not significantly influenced my approach.

The divine–human perspective

God and human beings are engaged in a process of mutual persuasion. This relationship is asymmetrical because, in a certain sense, our best efforts to "persuade" God are ultimately God's own (as suggested by those Pauline texts, already cited, that testify to the Spirit's activity in us, e.g. Rom. 8:15–16, 26). We have no arguments – we have "nothing to offer," to use the idiom of eucharistic donation – that did not come, ultimately, from God. Thus, my main focus here will be on God's activity toward us – activity that is ultimately characterized by persuasion, not by compulsion.[2]

This point too has trinitarian roots, and is bound up with the doctrine of creation. God does not, in any sense, "need" the world; even if God is understood as requiring "participation in an *other*" in order to be perfect, this otherness is always already a part of God (through the eternal flowing-forth of the Wellspring and the issuing of the Living Water). God creates the world in a wholly gracious act of love, and God's completeness and perfection are in no way dependent on a particular outcome of creaturely existence. Certainly, the proper destiny of human beings, and indeed of the whole creation, is that we might glorify and enjoy God forever; but even if we do not do so, God does not withdraw love and replace it with coercion. God's existence is not dependent upon the salvation of human beings; consequently God does not *compel* us to be saved, but rather seeks to persuade us. The Epistle to Diognetus makes this abundantly clear:

> And was the coming [of the Word], as human thought might suppose, in power, in terror, and in dread? Not so; it was in gentleness and humility. As a king sending his royal son, so God sent the Word; as God did God send the Word; as a human being to human beings did God send the Word – and did so because

---

[2] I recognize that, for those who are on the "receiving" end of these activities, it may not always be possible to tell the difference between persuasion and compulsion. Recent work in the sociology of knowledge, for example, has pointed out many historical cases in which compulsion is achieved by means that are assumed (by the "audience") to be instances of persuasion – which is to say that the audience believed it had some choice as to how to respond (the work of Michel Foucault comes especially to mind). Here, however, my focus is not on whether a particular human interaction is *perceived* to be an act of persuasion, but whether it is *intended* as such. The distinction is therefore most meaningful as a rubric for the self-examination of the Christian conscience. We can ask ourselves: in attempting to change the will of the "other," have I respected the otherness of the other? Persuasion (as I use the term here) requires that the members of the audience can choose among options without being subject to violence, ridicule, or other dehumanizing treatment.

God was fain to save us by persuasion, and not by compulsion – for there is no compulsion found with God.[3]

The word here translated "compulsion" (βιαζόμενος) could as easily be translated *force*, *oppression*, or *violence*. All three words stand in clear contrast with *persuasion*, which this early apostolic writing describes as characteristic of God's action toward the world. God chose to save us by persuasion – by means of a humble invitation, not a threatening demand.

Of course, one might object that these two approaches are not as different as they seem. Some recent theorists have suggested that a decision to use words (rather than weapons) does not necessarily imply the absence of coercion.[4] On the other hand, persuasion seems (at least in some circumstances) to be one of the few clear *alternatives* to coercive force. Some historians of sophistic rhetoric suggest that it arose in ancient Greece precisely as an attempt to overcome the reigning assumption that "might makes right."[5] Plato also suggests that language can provide an alternative to violence; in Book I of the *Republic* (327c), Socrates sets the dialogue in motion by raising a distinction between persuasion and force.

Fortunately, we need not settle this question here. We need only note that it is *possible* for persuasion to be coupled with a commitment to non-violence, whereas compulsion (in order to be effective) is usually backed up with (at the very least) the *threat* of violence. In other words, persuasion *can* be peaceable in that it can fully respect the freedom of the other to choose a different path, and need not humiliate, injure, or dehumanize those who do so. Compulsion, on the other hand, necessarily inflicts some kind of penalty on those who would deviate from the course they are being compelled to take. Because we believe that God produces a world in which we are free to respond, God's acts can be best understood through the category of persuasion.[6]

---

[3] *Diog.* VII.3–4, my translation, based in part on that of Maxwell Staniforth, *Early Christian Writings: The Apostolic Fathers* (Harmondsworth: Penguin Books, 1968), 178–9.

[4] See, among others, Robert Nozick, *Philosophical Explanations* (Cambridge, Mass.: Harvard University Press, 1981), 4; Douglas Robinson, *The Translator's Turn* (Baltimore: Johns Hopkins University Press, 1991), 5; and Stanley Fish, "Force," in *Doing What Comes Naturally* (Durham, N.C.: Duke University Press, 1989), 503–24.

[5] For example, Cole, *Origins of Rhetoric*, 28–9.

[6] Of course, this opens up a number of other issues. Are we fully free to respond to God's persuasive activity, or does God's eternal activity of election shape our response such that it is not really "our own"? Is the ultimate punishment ("hell," understood as the complete and eternal absence of God) something that we knowingly take upon ourselves – and if so, wouldn't divine compulsion more fully manifest God's love, since it would save us from such a fate? Pursuing these questions here would require another book, at least.

Obviously, this persuasion does not take the form of syllogisms. God's chief act of persuasion is the birthing of the Wellspring, the "sending of the Son into the far country" – an act that gains its persuasive appeal precisely because it so clearly manifests how thoroughly God loved the world (John 3:16). We are persuaded not because we recognize the logical clarity or the sheer reasonableness of God's "argument," but because God's superabundant gift awakens in us something that moves "the whole person" to belief and action.

God's "persuasive" approach to our salvation is closely related to God's *triune* character. As I have already noted, God's Triunity manifests an eternal self-differentiation (and therefore otherness) within God; God thus has no need to compel our salvation in order not to be alone. But there is something more: if God seeks to persuade us, this will require a certain "going forth from God" that mirrors the divine processions. This would not be necessary for an act of coercion; for example, if a government wanted its prison inmates to be isolated from one another, it could build solitary cells and place them there; it need not offer a persuasive argument in favor of solitary confinement in the hope that the prisoners will respond. Such a course of action is strictly an assertion of power; it requires no risk, no chance of being rejected, because the other is not treated as a fully valid agent. Persuasive activity is different; it requires putting oneself at some risk, knowing that one's offer may be rejected. To seek to persuade others is thus to "put something of oneself" into the process – to bind oneself to one's argument (which is why the character of the rhetor can influence the outcome).[7] The risk engendered by this process is sometimes fairly minor; perhaps our feelings are hurt, a bit, if our carefully-constructed arguments are rejected, or if someone ignores the obvious emotional attachment that we have to a certain point of view. Other acts of persuasion are much more costly; for example, to stand alone, unarmed, in front of a moving tank, while all the world watches – this is to venture an act of persuasion that risks almost everything.

God takes such risks – seeking to save us by means of persuasion (and giving us a role in the decision), and "giving away everything" in the eternal processions. This was intimated even before the details of trinitarian theology were worked out in full – for example, in the Old Testament narratives. God seeks to save the people of Israel by speaking to Moses in the burning bush,

---

[7] Indeed, for this reason some argumentation theorists have suggested that all persuasive arguments are ultimately *ad hominem* (though not therefore fallacious) – since all such arguments are bound to those who offer them. See, e.g., Henry W. Johnstone, Jr., *Validity and Rhetoric in Philosophical Argumentation: An Outlook in Transition* (University Park, Pa.: Dialogue Press of Man and World, 1978), esp. 53–61.

and by writing the Decalogue onto two tablets of stone. In these cases, we see a foreshadowing of divine procession – a "going forth from God" – in the speaking of a divine word. God speaks, and writes; and these rhetorical acts so thoroughly bear the mark of their author that they cannot be wholly separated from who God is: "the Word was God" (John 1:1). In each case, the audience is free to accept or reject the persuasive act – and there is some sense in which they thereby accept or reject God. Moses could have said no (indeed, he seems to have tried to do so); the people of Israel can, and do, say no to the Decalogue. God does not simply manipulate human beings as though they were puppets, thereby compelling a certain response; rather, God puts forth a divine word, a word which seeks to persuade the people but which can also be rejected by them. The "persuasive acts of God" revealed in the Old Testament do not provide a fully-developed trinitarian theology; nevertheless, descriptions of "God's Word" and "God's Wisdom" clearly helped to prepare the way for the language of the divine processions that would later come to mark trinitarian theology.

Implications for the Christian life

If persuasion marks God's activity toward the world, then we can already anticipate its importance in shaping Christian practices. Because we are created in the image of the triune God, our interactions should be marked by the same process of persuasion that marks God's action toward us: not an act of compulsion, but an attempt to portray the opportunity being offered as sufficiently attractive that others will be "delighted," and therefore "moved" to take advantage of it.

But our "practices of persuading" will only really begin to mirror those of the triune God if we are willing to allow our lives to be shaped by the trinitarian virtues – listening for the different themes that make up God's polyphonic orchestration of creation, participating more fully in one another's lives, and making space for a particularity that does not isolate us from one another. God's persuasive activity is marked by these virtues. Our own persuasive efforts – to negotiate our differences, to deliberate in order to take action, and to bring others to know the saving power of the triune God – can be formed by these virtues as well.

The process of persuasion among human beings, like its divine counterpart, is not limited to formal structures of logic. Indeed, it may not even take the form of speech; it is possible, and indeed probable, that we will be persuaded to shape our lives in particular ways primarily through our encounters with the *entire lives* of others – as we observe them, associate with them, and perhaps even desire to imitate them. Elsewhere in this book, I have referred to this process as the "embodied witness" that Christians should offer to one another and to the world. While the specific form of Christian persuasion must vary from case to case, I think we can say, with some confidence, that it should (1) never resort to violence or other means of pure compulsion, and (2) recognize that *the shape of the Christian life* is often a more powerful argument than the most carefully constructed syllogism.

Adopting "the practice of persuading" as the primary form of Christian interaction might bring about practical changes in the life of the Church that could conceivably extend far and wide; they might potentially affect the way we think about evangelism, catechesis, education, and a whole host of other Christian practices. In the remainder of this chapter, I will focus on one aspect of Christian practice that could be fundamentally reshaped if conceived in the light of the trinitarian practice of persuading.

The Problem of Authority

The central problem in current discussions of "authority" – and a pointer toward their solution – was articulated some twenty years ago by Nicholas Lash:

> For too long christian debates about authority (which must, in the last resort, be debates about the authority of God) have implied, however unwittingly, a thoroughly unchristian concept of God. The corrective that I have proposed is that we should continually remind ourselves that a christian doctrine of God, one which incorporates the principal features of the classical doctrine of the Trinity, may perhaps be the only guarantee of a theologically sound conception of authority in matters of christian belief and action.[8]

I wish to continue the development of Professor Lash's "corrective" by suggesting that the problem of authority can be best understood and addressed as an instance of the trinitarian practice of persuading. Put another way: if we attend to the trinitarian virtues when considering the proper exercise of authority in the Church, we will find it taking a shape that resembles that of the process of persuasion.

---

[8] Nicholas Lash, *Voices of Authority* (London: Sheed and Ward, 1976), 12.

What is authority?

The word *authority* is one of a cluster of words related to the Latin word *auctoritas*, which we customarily translate as "author." But this word is more than a category for bibliographical catalogues; an author is not merely, and not even primarily, "one who writes." Many ancient "authors" wrote nothing. *Authors* are people who have *authority*; which is to say, we take note of their words because we consider them worthy of attention on matters about which they speak. This is true equally for authors of novels and screenplays as for authors of encyclopedia articles, scholarly books, and home-repair manuals.

Now, precisely what makes the author "authoritative" will certainly vary according to the context. In a home-repair manual, the book's authority may depend upon a variety of factors: perhaps it has been published in a professional-looking format; perhaps it is sold in a home-repair shop (where people are supposed to be "authorities" on the subject); perhaps it is written, or promoted, or at least endorsed, by someone who does home-repair for a living – rather than only in the emergency situations faced by the average homeowner. But even all these features will be unable to rescue the book's authority if the reader – upon attempting to implement the book's instructions in actual practice – finds that they produce one colossal failure after another. In this case the book will eventually cease to be authoritative, no matter how charismatic the personality of its promoter.

I use this example as a reminder of where we find the actual locus of authority. It appears to reside with the person who is making the argument: the author of a book, the church leader, the writer of a home-repair manual. But these people are only one part of the overall structure of authority. People cannot be "authorities" in the abstract; there must be others who are willing, for one reason or another, to impute authority to them. Home-repair "experts" lose a great deal of their authority if those who attempt to rely on their advice find themselves with faucets that still leak and furnaces that still blow cold air. Conversely, authority can be magnified and attributed to those who actually know little or nothing about the subject in which they are thought to be "authorities." This is clearly exemplified in the current American fascination with talk-show hosts. Personalities such as Rush Limbaugh and Howard Stern, who have almost no knowledge or experience that would ordinarily count as "expertise" in the fields of discourse upon which they comment, are regarded as authoritative by millions of people.

Authority, then, is a complex process – and, I would want to say, a *rhetorical* process. Lines of authority are woven from the three threads that constitute every rhetorical context: the rhetor, the audience, and the argument. (As we observed in chapter 3, none of these is a distinct entity; all are relations that are bound to one another in reciprocal ways.) Someone speaks or writes; others listen or read; arguments are (or are not) taken to be authoritative. A wide variety of factors influence this attribution (or lack thereof), including the personality and style of the speaker or writer, the emotional state of the audience, the ways in which audience members understand themselves as bound together with one another (and/or with the rhetor), and the language in which the argument is cast. Whether or not one considers the more general notion of authority to have such rhetorical dimensions, there are good reasons for Christians to embrace this account with confidence – not least of which is God's own rhetorical act on behalf of our salvation.

> Where the authority of truth is concerned, no man effectively exercises authority in respect of others unless he persuades, by the quality of his life, and character, and speech. The God whom we confess is a God whose self-expression as a man has convinced us, wooed us, compelled us to answering recognition, love, and trust.[9]

Authority – Christian authority, at any rate – is ultimately a matter of persuasion.

We can clarify this point with reference to the New Testament account of Jesus, and of the authority he exercises. Jesus' authority is clearly not a result of his power to coerce conformity with his teaching. Indeed, given the outcome of the gospel narrative, we know that he quite deliberately surrenders any such power he might have had. Robert Murray comments that:

> The New Testament concept expressed in the word *exousia* [here translated "authority"] does not have the connotation of jurisdiction over others, much less the power to impose force on other persons, but rather the holder's rightful freedom to act. . . . The New Testament idea of authority, then, is very close to the idea of christian freedom given by the Spirit (cf. Gal. 5; 2 Cor. 3:17); and since this freedom is given to *all* who become children of God in Christ, it may not be used by those who have special authority in such a way as to infringe the freedom of the Spirit in others.[10]

---

[9] Lash, *Voices of Authority*, 11; here, *compelled* does not seem to imply coercion.

[10] Robert Murray, "Authority and the Spirit in the New Testament," in *Authority in a Changing Church* (London: Sydney, Sheed and Ward, 1968), 12–38; here, 33. Thanks to Nicholas Lash for pointing me toward this helpful article.

Because it respects the freedom of the other, this understanding of the exercise of authority is

> a witness to the truth, rendered in the Spirit and met by the working of the Spirit in the hearers. It does not so much impose as commend its message to the free human conscience. It will gain power from, or be frustrated by, the personal example of the authoritative witness.[11]

This means that, at least from the perspective of the New Testament, authority depends upon the *reception* of a teaching by those to whom it is directed; and further, that this reception will be affected by matters that are not driven by formal logic (for example, the character imputed to the one who exercises authority).

Some may regard this notion of authority as counterintuitive. In our cultural context, at least, authority is typically associated with coercion – with the forcing of another person to do something against his or her own will. This generally negative assessment of authority is clearly visible in the connotations of cognate words such as *authoritarian* and *the authorities* (words usually employed while slightly menacing music plays in the background). In fact, for many people, the negative connotations of these words are due in part to their association with the Church – even though, today, the Church has almost no power to force anyone to do anything that he or she doesn't want to do. However, at least one contemporary entity is still willing and able to rely on physical coercion to enforce its own authority – the modern nation-state (and its various organs and institutions).

It is certainly true that the shape of authority changes when one is willing to use violence to enforce it. In other cases we could say that a person actually needs to be *persuaded* to submit his or her will to that of the other – i.e., that the attribution of authority requires the consent of the one over whom that authority is being exercised. When I follow the instructions in my home-repair manual in order to fix my faucet, and the procedure fails, I simply stop regarding the book as authoritative in this respect, and I no longer follow its procedures. If, however, the publisher of the manual sent out an "enforcer" to threaten my physical safety if I were to disregard the book's precepts, then I might well, under such duress, decide to regard it as authoritative despite the ineffectiveness of its advice.

This rather comical scenario seems unlikely to transpire, but the same cannot be said for matters in which the nation-state has a significant interest.

---

[11] Ibid., 35.

Those who fail to regard its laws as authoritative may find their physical bodies subject to confinement, torture, or death. When physical violence enters the picture, authority passes out of the realm of persuasion altogether. And because we typically consider a fundamentally violent entity (the state) to be a preeminent source of "authority" in our lives, we fail to recognize that authority might also be construed as having a fundamentally persuasive character. Indeed, in most cases it *does* bear this character; and for those who live according to trinitarian convictions, it *should always* be exercised in this way.

On the basis of our discussion of peacemaking in chapter 7, it should go without saying that the Church must not turn to violence in order to exercise authority. Instead, it should operate through the channels of persuasion. In all cases, there must be someone who is exercising authority (whether through official Church pronouncements, charismatic personalities, individual interpreters of scripture, or various forms of "embodied witness"). Also, in all cases, there must be an "audience" of persons who are being asked to submit to this authority. And there must be actions or words that are persuasive toward this end.

What can we say about the character of this practice of persuading? The profound mutual attention to the circumstances of the Other, which marks God's triune life, should be the ultimate goal of the human exercise of authority. It requires respect for the freedom of the other. Of course, this does not mean that certain behavior cannot be condemned, or that discipline cannot be exercised. But discipline can be, and in the Christian context should always be, a very specialized form of the practice of persuading. Even the most severe acts of ecclesial discipline – such as shunning or excommunication – remain truly *Christian* only to the extent that they are ultimately understood as persuasive, rather than coercive or punitive techniques; their ultimate goal should always be the restoration of the excommunicated person to full fellowship. Communion is withheld in the hope that one's desire for it will be more persuasive than the desire to continue in whatever course of action divides that member from the rest of the Body. For this to function effectively, of course, other prerequisites must be in place; for example, Christians must be persuaded that full communion is something very positive, to be desired at all costs. Once the persuasive force of this claim is lost, then so is the persuasive force of excommunication.

Needless to say, questions such as these – as well as questions about who is competent to exercise authority, and to whom authority should be attributed – will be specific to particular structural definitions of the Church; and some of my comments will betray my own particular (Anglican) perspective. Most of my observations, however, will be more general; I want to suggest that the

problem of authority begins to take on a new shape, if we think of it as
constituted primarily by the trinitarian practice of persuading.

In order to show how this approach differs from the ways that authority has
often been perceived, I turn to a specific historical example. In this example,
two very different perspectives on authority are offered; but in the end, they
both turn out to be much more attentive to the assumptions of the modern
nation-state than to the doctrine of the Trinity.

The Peterson–Harnack correspondence

In 1928, Erik Peterson read a monograph by Adolf von Harnack, in which the
latter concluded that authority was not to be found in the Bible alone (a view
to which he refers as "biblicism"). Harnack wrote: "Biblicism receives its
healthy corrective in the authority of *the apostolic teaching*, which organizes and
delimits the authority of 'scripture.' "[12] Peterson agreed with this claim, but
thought that it highlighted the importance of having an authoritative teaching
body (a *magisterium*) within the Church, so that this "apostolic teaching" could
be rightly interpreted and enforced. Peterson thus felt that Harnack (a
committed Protestant) had in some sense provided an argument in favor of the
structure of authority operative within the Roman Catholic Church. There
followed a brief exchange of letters between the two theologians, in which
they discussed (among other things) the question of how authority should be
exercised in the Church.

While some of the issues of this exchange are not relevant to my argument
in this chapter, the letters do struggle with the problem of "locating" the authority of the Church. Both writers knew that it did not lie in the scriptural text
alone; they differed, however, as to the appropriateness of locating this authority
somewhere else. For example, did it lie in the authority of the Pope as the final
arbiter of dogmatic questions? Clearly Luther and many other Reformers had
rejected this view. Indeed, Protestant churches in general had tended to shy
away from the language of "dogma"; it seemed to connote an enforceable
teaching, when in fact, no one was considered qualified to enforce it.[13]

---

[12]   Michael J. Hollerich, trans., "Erik Peterson's Correspondence with Adolf von Harnack,
and an Epilogue," *Pro Ecclesia: A Journal of Catholic and Evangelical Theology* 2, no. 3 (Summer
1993): 333–44; here, 333; hereafter cited as "Peterson" or "Harnack." My comments here
appear in a different form in *Pro Ecclesia* 3, no. 3 (Summer 1994): 307–23.

[13]   "A dogma without infallibility means nothing. This was already settled by Luther's
position at the Leipzig Disputation, although Luther himself never fully realized the
implication of his assertions, nor was he ever clear about the unsatisfactory character of his
inconsistent substitute through a partial biblicism" (Harnack, "Correspondence," 337).

Interestingly, though, Luther (and many other Protestants) *did* accept the authority of a wide range of church teachings that are not found explicitly in the Bible. These included, especially, the canons of the early ecumenical councils, but also a wide range of authoritative teachings on the doctrine of the Trinity, the person of Christ, and even teachings about Mary (Luther clearly believed in the Immaculate Conception, for example). In practice, at least, Luther did accept the authority of at least some Church teachings; he raised objections, not to *the very idea* of extra-biblical authority, but to *particular* teachings that he took to be arbitrarily promulgated or insufficiently attentive to the Biblical witness.

Harnack seemed to believe that the Church had "outgrown" any need to rely on authority. Peterson, on the other hand, suggested that even Protestants, who did not recognize the authority of the Pope, still had their own versions of authority: he cites the 1580 *Formula of Concord*, with its acceptance of the early creeds and its rejections of heresies. And yet, Peterson also argued that such statements were of no value without an external authority to back them up; if that were not the Pope, then it needed to be the civil authority of the state, which could enforce the legitimacy of church teaching.[14]

Both writers seemed to assume that "authority" is something that only exists if someone can be compelled to accept it. Harnack takes this as a warrant for rejecting the whole idea of authority; Peterson considers authority necessary, but worries that, without some kind of enforcement mechanism (either papal or civil), it will be largely irrelevant. But are these the only two possible positions? Perhaps the Protestant Reformers were ultimately making a different kind of argument. Luther, for example, seemed to be claiming that "authority" – or the Christian exercise thereof, at any rate – was not the sort of thing that could be practiced by means of "enforcement." In the Leipzig Disputation, for example, he had argued that "No believing Christian can be coerced beyond holy writ."[15] This comment is often read as an invocation of Luther's appeal to "scripture alone"; but this cannot be the whole story, since (as already noted) Luther, like many other Reformers, continued to accept a large array of doctrines, from the early creeds to mariological dogmas, which were not elaborated explicitly in the Bible (though Luther would insist that they could not be inconsistent with the Bible). Given Luther's acceptance of at least *some* non-biblical church teachings, one might also read Luther's statement at Leipzig as a comment on the problem of *coercion*. At stake in the Leipzig debate was whether the papal and conciliar inter-

---

[14] Peterson, "Correspondence," 341.
[15] *Sämtliche Schriften*, ed. Walch, XV.392.1207. Bainton's translation.

pretations could be *forced* upon the conscientious dissenter. Eck said yes; Luther said no.

Thus, one might well wonder why Peterson so mourned the loss of some means (either papal or civil) of enforcing church authority. While it is certainly true that Luther had a civil authority to rely upon, this does not mean that he necessarily had to do so – nor that he would have thought it wise to do so, had not his opponents been wielding some coercive power of their own. In fact, Luther seems to argue that neither sacred nor secular authority should seek to coerce the believer; one person's opinion could be weightier than that of the pope or a council, if it were grounded on a better reason (and that reason didn't need to be backed up by the secular authorities in order to be considered valid!). This is not to deny that one might have a better chance of physical survival if so protected; John Hus, for example, was not so fortunate. Nevertheless, Luther (not to mention many of the Radical Reformers) would surely have been nervous about the claim that authority is meaningful only if obedience can be compelled.

In his correspondence with Harnack, Peterson seemed to set up two possible paths: either the dogmatic authority of the Church must be guaranteed by enforcement, or else church pronouncements can have nothing more than the "non-binding character of a general moral exhortation."[16] And with the term *non-binding*, we can bring the issue into its sharpest focus: namely, the question of *how one gains adherence* to church teachings. If the coercive measures of the state are to be avoided at all costs, then some form of persuasion would seem to be necessary. Sometimes, this may have to take a form that appears very much like coercion (such as silencing or excommunication); but even these measures should be employed with the intention of persuading Christians to return to the Church. Luther was clearly uncomfortable with these practices, since they are so easily abused; and in the contemporary Western context, the fractured nature of Christendom often renders them ineffectual.[17] At any rate, such devices may only win an external, formal adherence to a dogma; conversion of the heart is something else altogether: "A man convinced against his will / Is of the same opinion still."[18]

---

[16] Peterson, "Correspondence," 334.

[17] There are exceptions, of course. In a context in which membership in a particular denomination is considered tantamount to membership in the Body of Christ, excommunication may make all the difference. For a positive assessment of the judicious use of excommunication (and other strong forms of "persuasion") in one such context, see Cavanaugh, *Torture and Eucharist.*

[18] Cited without reference in Newman, *Grammar of Assent*, 143.

The Peterson–Harnack correspondence suggests a need to rethink our understanding of authority. It is not primarily about compulsion, as both Peterson and Harnack seemed to think. But neither does this mean (as Harnack at least seemed to believe) that authority plays (or should play) no role in Christian practice. Indeed, although he eschewed the term *authority*, Harnack seemed to recognize that the practice of persuading has always been a characteristic of Christianity:

> *actual* religious community in the Christianity of all periods came into being exclusively through the "non-binding character of a moral exhortation," that is, through the experience and faith-witnessing of inspired persons which evoked resonance and light in other persons.[19]

And in his last letter, he expresses his belief that,

> by historical demonstration and ethical and philosophical consideration, the basic ideas of the gospel can be placed in a bright and convincing light.[20]

While Harnack probably would not have accepted the claim that this "practice of persuading" finds its form and its ultimate warrant in the doctrine of the Trinity, his comments here provide a useful account of how we might begin to describe the proper exercise of authority among Christians.

The authority of persuasion

During a rather large segment of the history of the Church – running roughly from the conversion of Constantine to the late Renaissance – theologians could expect the enforcement of certain beliefs and practices by various institutions (ecclesiastical or civil, though often there was little distinction between the two). Before and after this period, the structures of enforcement were (and now are) too diverse, diluted, or decentralized to expect them to be able to guarantee much uniformity. Interestingly, though, throughout the *whole* of Church history, Christians have often sought to persuade one other of certain forms of belief and practice, whether or not their positions could be enforced. In other words, Christianity has not typically relied solely on mechanisms of enforcement and compulsion in order to speak authoritatively, even when such mechanisms were available. Ultimately, the Church's

[19] Harnack, "Correspondence," 335.
[20] Harnack, "Correspondence," 338; the entire passage is italicized in the original.

authority has depended upon the degree to which it comes to be regarded as the truthful and credible *author* of a particular argument.

Different Christian confessions have attempted, in differing ways, to make their authority credible. According to one view, there can be no "office" that is authoritative in and of itself; rather, the authority of any particular teaching must be established, in each instance, by persuading people to accept it. These arguments may be based on interpretations of the Scripture, the claims of the Fathers or the councils, appeals to human experience, or a variety of other sources; but in each case, the success of the argument depends on whether a sufficiently persuasive appeal can be mounted. Simply referring to the fact that it "is taught" by the duly appointed officials is, by itself, insufficient.

According to another view, certain persons – simply by virtue of their office – can teach with authority. Here, the fact that a doctrine or practice is taught by the duly appointed official is considered sufficient to warrant the claim. On closer inspection, however, this view turns out to be a variant of the first position. In both cases, the authority of a doctrine is established by persuading the faithful to accept it; the cases differ only in that, in the second case, those who offer the argument become (by virtue of their office) *persuasive warrants* for that acceptance. Of course, one may still argue over who counts as an authoritative speaker, and whether that authority will survive if the holder of the office seems (in other respects) to be thoroughly untrustworthy. None of this changes the fact that persuasion often takes place, at least in part, by character. On account of their personal charisma, or their office, or the popular perception of their credibility, speakers or writers become "authoritative" for the reception of an argument.

The understanding of authority through the category of persuasion has a long history in Christian thought: it is very similar to the notion of a *sensus fidelium*, the sense of all faithful Christians, who must ultimately "consent" to doctrinal questions.[21] The view was affirmed in the Second Vatican Council, which proclaimed that "The body of the faithful as a whole, anointed as they are by the Holy One (John 2:20, 27) cannot err in matters of belief."[22] This notion had been largely lost in nineteenth and early twentieth century Roman Catholicism, with its celebration of hierarchical autonomy. But it was given new life by the attention that was eventually paid to thinkers such as John Henry Newman, who provided a number of historical examples to show that

[21] See the important essay by J.-M. R. Tillard, "Sensus Fidelium," *One in Christ* 11, no. 1 (1975): 2–29; for a brief summary of the history of this concept, see Robert Kinast, "When They Ask Your Opinion, Give It," *Emmanuel* 49 (Spring 1993): 402–7.
[22] *Lumen Gentium*, 12.

the body of faithful Christians often kept the truth alive, even when it was in danger of eclipse on the "official" levels of church teaching.[23] As Nicholas Lash observes, "Catholic theology has only recently begun to recover an awareness (lost during the eighteenth and nineteenth centuries) of the importance of the ancient doctrine of the consent of the church."[24]

Hence, the so-called "protestant" and "catholic" versions of authority are not as different from one another as some have assumed them to be. They both require that the authoritative teachings of the Church be promulgated in such a way that the faithful are persuaded to consent to them. They differ only in assigning different values to the persuasive power of the teaching office itself, as opposed to the other various means of persuasion.

Thus, in calling for the Christian exercise of authority to attend to the practice of persuading, I am not so much asking for change as I am calling for an acknowledgement that persuasion is always already taking place whenever authority is invoked. If we were to acknowledge this, we could focus on the real question at issue, which concerns the particular form that this persuasion should take. What are the advantages and disadvantages (for example) of treating a person (or office) as authoritative by virtue of the office itself? What must be assumed in order for the official's speech to be persuasive, and thus authoritative? When the faithful are not persuaded by the office alone, what happens next? Can a doctrine's loss of authority be reasserted in other ways? Attending to such questions would significantly reconfigure current debates about authority.

Moreover, if we agree that authority is primarily about the practice of persuading others, then we can also inquire into the degree that it reflects the persuasion that characterizes God's actions toward the world. This is a much better and more theologically appropriate way of assessing questions about authority than the contemporary penchant for attempting to model authority on particular forms of the nation-state or claims about human rights.[25] Such discourses are not necessarily attentive to the Christian doctrine of God, and they thus tend to transform the Church into some version of the nation-state (with all its attendant failures).

---

[23] *On Consulting the Faithful in Matters of Doctrine,* ed. with an Introduction by John Coulson (Kansas City, Mo.: Sheed and Ward, 1961)

[24] Lash, *Voices of Authority,* 47.

[25] As for example in Eugene C. Bianchi and Rosemary Radford Ruether, eds., *A Democratic Catholic Church: The Reconstruction of Roman Catholicism* (New York: Crossroad, 1993). For an insightful critique of this book in particular, see the review by William T. Cavanaugh in *Pro Ecclesia: A Journal of Catholic and Evangelical Theology* 4, no. 2 (Spring 1995): 238-41.

If the Christian understanding of authority were re-mapped with more attention to the practice of persuading (especially as it is modeled by God's Triunity), what might result? Do we have any examples of such an approach? Here, we have to deal with ideal types, since various instantiations of this model will vary greatly in their ability to conform to the ideal. But by attending to the trinitarian virtues, we might at least find some criteria for this approach to authority. First, it would need to allow multiple voices to be heard (polyphony). Secondly, the lives of those whose voices are considered authoritative would need to be woven into the lives of others. Here I am thinking of two different levels of participation: not only with those who are expected to be persuaded by the teaching, but also with other teachers (who might teach differently). Finally, such an approach to authority would need to recognize a space for particularity – a difference that is shaped by the mutual formation of Christians by one another.

This raises serious questions about forms of Christian authority that attempt to operate from "too far away" (where mutual participation is impossible), as well as those that fail to provide space for the different forms that Christianity will take in different contexts. On the other hand, it also suggests that authority cannot operate well if Christian communities become wholly discrete enclaves, unconcerned about whether or not their beliefs and practices can at least *resonate with* (even if they need not be identical to) the beliefs and practices of other Christians. Authority needs to be locally exercised, but also must be in conversation with the (equally local) exercise of authority in other Christian communities. I believe that the ancient and venerable office of the episcopate is probably the best way of insuring that the exercise of authority remains multiple (polyphonic), collegial (participative), and local (particular). The bishop needs to develop a participative relationship with the congregations in his or her jurisdictions, as well as with other bishops. However, the polyphony that is produced by the collegiality among the bishops cannot be merged into a single note through the authority of any one bishop. The notion of primacy does not seem warranted by an approach to authority that attends to the trinitarian virtues.

It should be noted, of course, that such an understanding of authority does not always, or even very often, result in homogeneity within or among congregations. But one of the advantages of speaking of "persuasion" is that it forces us to question how much of this desire for enforced unity comes from considerations internal to Christianity, and how much is a product of the modern search for permanent foundations. Is the desire to ground authority in some sort of "final court of appeal" simply one more manifestation of what

Richard Bernstein calls "the Cartesian Anxiety"? Bernstein names this anxiety after Descartes because his

> search for a foundation or Archimedean point is more than a device to solve metaphysical and epistemological problems. It is the quest for some fixed point, some stable rock upon which we can secure our lives against the vicissitudes that constantly threaten us.[26]

Bernstein argues that the modern era is marked by an anxiety-ridden search for fixed foundations. His hypothesis certainly seems active in modern Christian theology, given the rise of fundamentalism and assertions of authority that have so dramatically marked the last several centuries, and especially the most recent century, of Christian history in the West. We should thus not be surprised to find that this search – the search for a good example of the alternative conception of authority that I am advocating here – will lead us to look toward the East.

The authority of love

The problem of freedom and limit, the search for the final court of appeal, and the rhetorical transformation of authority – all these concerns are played out on the pages of a novel to which I have already referred: Dostoevsky's *The Brothers Karamazov*. One instance occurs early in the book, wherein, at a gathering of monks and family members, Ivan Karamazov summarizes an article he has written on the question of sacred and civil authority. Ivan's point seems to be that the Church wisely does not attempt to assert its authority coercively, as does the state, but instead by means of persuasion. The Elder Zosima agrees with Ivan's analysis: "Now the Church, having no active jurisdiction but merely the possibility of moral condemnation alone, withholds from actively punishing the criminal of its own accord. It does not excommunicate him, but simply does not leave him without paternal guidance."[27] Ivan's argument seems to be that the world would be a much better place if the state could learn to treat criminals as the Church does.

The other monks at the gathering echo these sentiments. One of the friends who has accompanied the Karamazovs to the gathering, Miüsov, thinks this is a disguised appeal to the vesting of all authority in a single office – a position

---

[26] Bernstein, *Beyond Objectivism and Relativism*, 17–18.
[27] Dostoevsky, *The Brothers Karamazov*, 64.

that had become known as "ultramontanism," since it looked "over the mountains" (to Rome) for that one source of authority. Miüsov sees this as a simple transformation of the Church into a state. But his view is challenged by another monk.

> "You have been pleased to understand it in a completely opposite sense," Father Paissy spoke sternly. "It is not the Church that turns into the state, you see. That is Rome and its dream. That is the third temptation of the devil! But, on the contrary, the state turns into the Church, it rises up to the Church and becomes the Church over all the earth, which is the complete opposite of Ultramontanism and of Rome, and of your interpretation, and is simply the great destiny of Orthodoxy on earth. This star will show forth from the East.[28]

Ivan's little article, and the discussion thereof, plays a small enough role in the novel as a whole. But it is, in some sense, a microcosm of that novel; for *The Brothers Karamazov* can be read as (among other things) Dostoevsky's description of how the Church might offer a form of moral guidance – without resorting to compulsion.

In Dostoevsky's view, the West had (quite unfortunately) embraced precisely the path of compulsion. It had attempted to insure its dominion through the media of miracle, mystery, and authority, and had enforced its judgments by fire: "In the splendid auto-da-fé / Evil heretics were burnt."[29] This tendency can be seen not only in Ivan's parable of the Grand Inquisitor, but also in Dostoevsky's own observations during his travels in Europe in the 1860s and 1870s. The author had become convinced that the Roman Church was all too willing to transform itself into an authority on the model of the state, rather than transforming the state on the model of the Church. According to George Panichas, the First Vatican Council served

> to impress on the minds of many in Europe the feeling that the Roman Catholic Church sought to fulfill its goals by *persuasion* if possible, but by *compulsion* if necessary, the latter being at times the case. And certainly Dostoevsky . . . could not have ignored the fact that increasing Papal power actually enshrined in the Church monarchical autocracy. He believed that in its ultimate connotation the great struggle between Russia and the West was in reality the conflict between the ascetical spirituality of the Holy Orthodox Church of the East and the ecclesiastical secularism of the Roman Catholic Church of the West.[30]

[28] Ibid., 66.
[29] A. I. Polezhayev, "Coriolanus" (1834), cited in an altered form in Dostoevsky, 248.
[30] George A. Panichas, "Fyodor Dostoevsky and Roman Catholicism," *Greek Orthodox Theological Review* 4 (Summer 1958): 16–34; here, 20.

Thus, Dostoevsky's characters try to find alternatives to the "legalism, regimentation, and edicts of external authority" which he saw as the downfall of Western Christianity.[31] Alyosha seeks to transform the world around him with acts of reverent love; Dmitri recognizes that he should accept punishment for a crime that (according to legal definitions, at least) he did not commit; and Ivan confesses to a murder from which he had hitherto considered himself wholly absolved. The clearest statement of this particular theme comes from the elder Zosima, whose dedication to acts of selfless love really constitute the true alternative to externally imposed compulsion. It is Zosima who says:

> One may stand perplexed before some thought, especially seeing men's sin, asking oneself: "Shall I take it by force, or by humble love?" Always resolve to take it by humble love. If you so resolve once and for all, you will be able to overcome the whole world. A loving humility is a terrible power, the most powerful of all, nothing compares with it. . . . There is only one salvation for you: take yourself up, and make yourself responsible for all the sins of men.[32]

Out of its literary context, Zosima's discourse can seem sentimental and unrealistic; and frequently it has been read as an inspirational moral exhortation that is – nevertheless – insufficiently "authoritative" as a means of assuring the believer's assent to the Church's teaching.

And yet Zosima *does* speak with a kind of authority, and does so despite the absence of miracles, magic shows, and coercive laws. The model for Zosima, of course, is Christ – not only the Christ of the Gospels, but even the Christ of the Grand Inquisitor legend, who appears, kisses his tormentor, and then passes on.

> In all His humility, He compels people to have intuitive faith in Him, not through external compulsion, but reverent love. Christ does not, in striking contrast to the Grand Inquisitor, dictate, command, judge, or condemn; He has no recourse to outside authority; He has come once again in human form to dwell among men, at a time when heretics were being burned in sixteenth century Seville. "The sun of love burns in his heart; light and power shine from his eyes; and their radiance, shed on the people, stirs their hearts with responsive love."[33]

Authority need not be compelled; indeed, its perfect exercise is that of the

[31] Ibid., 28.
[32] Dostoevsky, *The Brothers Karamazov*, 319–20.
[33] Panichas, "Fyodor Dostoevsky," 31–2.

teacher, the peacemaker, the obedient servant: "They were astounded at his teaching, for he taught them as one having authority, and not as the scribes" (Mark 1:22).

Although a thorough development of this theme would need to be much more specific about how God's persuasion might come to be mirrored in the Christian exercise of authority, we can begin to get a sense of what it might look like. If the Church is truly guided by the Holy Spirit, and if the Spirit is the continuation of Christ's work in the world, then the Church must operate by the same means as Christ: through the powerfully persuasive act of reverent love.

The Trinitarian Practice of Persuading

I want to close this chapter with two illustrations of how the approach to authority developed here might work itself out in concrete instances. I want to examine some teachings that have been officially promulgated by various Church communions, but which are not always received as "authoritative" by people who (nevertheless) consider themselves to be members of those communions. In each case, we will consider the kinds of "practices of persuading" that might help to "authorize" these doctrines.

Admission to communion

Most Christian communions teach that baptism is a necessary condition for the reception of the eucharist.[34] But in some communions, baptism is both a necessary *and a sufficient* condition for reception; that is, anyone who is baptized may receive, including infants and children. This is true for Eastern Orthodoxy and some provinces of the Anglican communion, as well as those denominations that practice "believer's baptism." For the majority of Christians, however, the sacraments of baptism and eucharist are separated; this is the practice in Roman Catholicism and in most Protestant churches. Children are routinely baptized very early (often very shortly after birth), but they are not allowed to receive communion until a later age (varying from approximately 7 to 16).

These varying practices raise an obvious question: why is the eucharist ever

---

[34] To offer but one example: in the US Episcopal Church, the official canon (title I, canon 17, section 7) states that "no unbaptized person shall be eligible to receive communion in this Church."

separated from baptism? Almost all Christian communions affirm the theological principle that one becomes a full member of the Body of Christ at baptism. Why are such "full members" excluded from communion? For at least a thousand years, these two sacraments were bound together very closely. The tendency of some denominations to deny communion to some of the baptized came about, as Robert Jenson notes,

> by sheer historical inadvertance. By all theological right, infant baptism must be accompanied by infant communion and was until the thirteenth century, when infant communion was incidentally terminated by the withdrawal of the cup from lay communicants. Infants had been given the cup, which they could always share one way or another, but not the bread, which the youngest could not swallow. When the cup was taken from the congregation, infants were left with nothing.[35]

Attempts to justify this practice theologically came later, and manifested an entirely *ad hoc* character – indeed, they had to do so, since the practice had come about without theological justification in the first place.

We will examine the theological warrants offered in defense of this practice in a moment. Our primary focus, however, is on the *authority* of these teachings. On the one hand, we might say that their authority seems to be respected in that there does not seem to be a large public outcry of protest against them. On the other hand, those baptized persons who are being denied communion are mostly children, who are routinely denied any voice in such matters. Thus, the number of protests lodged against a particular teaching is not necessarily a good indicator of whether its authority is being respected. A teaching is only authoritative if the faithful (a) know what it is, and (b) have at least a general sense of its theological justification.

There is obviously very little reliable information on just how many people are ignorant of, or do not understand the reasons for, or simply choose to ignore, their denomination's authoritative teaching on this subject (if any). I can testify, from personal experience, to the situation in the Episcopal Church in the United States, in which (as noted above) baptism is both a necessary and sufficient condition for receiving the eucharist.[36] Here, I have found that parish practice varies widely. Certainly, in many parishes, baptized children

---

[35] Jenson, *Visible Words*, 163.

[36] This became the official church teaching in 1988, after a period of trial usage in the 1970s and 1980s. The 1988 General Convention adopted a rubric for the *Book of Occasional Services* that clearly indicated that infants could receive communion as soon as they were baptized. A complete survey of the development of this teaching is provided in Leonel L. Mitchell,

of all ages are welcome to receive communion. But in some cases, children are taught to approach the altar with their arms folded across their chests, and to receive only a priestly blessing; if they ask to receive, their request is ignored or denied. In yet other cases, "all people" are invited to receive, whether they have been baptized or not.

Even in those Christian communions in which the teaching on this matter is well known (such as the Roman Catholic Church), its theological justification has not been made terribly clear. The new *Catechism of the Catholic Church,* for example, affirms other churches' inclusion of infants and younger children in the communion rite, but offers no justification for its own exclusion of them (§1244). Parents are often frustrated by their own inability, as well as that of the Church, to provide an answer to baptized children who wonder why they are excluded from this feast.[37] Customary answers, such as the designation of age seven as "the age of reason," are inadequate on a number of counts. For one thing, such arbitrary rules fail to differentiate among children who will grasp something of the meaning of the rite at vastly different ages. Perhaps more importantly, these restrictions attempt to describe the sacrament in rationalistic terms, as though understanding it made it effective. Not only is this contrary to the Church's theological claim (according to which the sacraments are made effective by God, not by the power of the minister or the merits of the recipient); it also renders us *all* unworthy recipients (for who can actually *comprehend* the mystery of the eucharist in any strong sense of the word?)

If we were to understand authority as involving the practice of *persuading,* two steps would be necessary to rectify the problems posed here. First, in order for an argument to be persuasive, it has to be communicated to its intended audience. If rules are simply generated and written secretly into obscure law-books, they cannot be "heard" by those who are expected to follow them. And secondly, the Church needs to offer compelling theological reasons for teaching as it does. This is not to deny that, for some Christians, the simple fact that a particular position is authoritatively taught may be, in itself, sufficient to persuade (this is a clear case of persuasion by *ēthos* – the character of the speaker). But on the other hand, those who are not persuaded by character alone ought not be rebuffed in their wholly legitimate request for some rationale for the teaching.

"The Communion of Infants and Little Children," *Anglican Theological Review* 71, no. 1 (Winter 1989): 63–78.

[37] See the poignant meditation by Peggy Ellsberg, "'Let the Little Children . . .'," *America* 168 (13 March 1993): 16.

What practical forms might this take? Denominational magazines and newsletters, which are so often filled only with human-interest stories and local news, might consider giving over a few pages each month to the clarification of Church teaching on various topics. Bishops, pastors, and other persons who constitute the "teaching authorities" of various denominations need to be well-informed about such teachings, and know whether the denomination actually has a position on the issue at stake. In the specific case of receiving communion, the following issues need to be communicated in persuasive ways: (1) why is baptism a *necessary* condition for participation in the eucharist? (2) must other conditions be met before a person can receive communion, and if so, what theological (and not merely cultural, social, or convenience-oriented) reasons require this? (3) Since the denial of access to the eucharist may be understood by some worshipers as an act of exclusion, what other community practices might help to insure that this exclusion does not extend beyond what is necessitated by issues 1 and 2 above? Without dismissing the differences among the answers that would necessarily be offered to these questions by different Christian communions, allow me to provide a few comments on each, to describe how certain practices might come to supplement the formal arguments advanced on behalf of each of these points (thereby helping to make them more persuasive).

1   The necessity of baptism for the believer's participation in the eucharist would be clearer if baptism were to become, once again, a more dramatic rite. In the ancient Church the rite often occurred only once a year, and was closely connected with the feast of Easter, in order to emphasize its life-and-death significance. The rite itself was "awe-inspiring," and perhaps even a bit "spine-chilling."[38] No one could fail to understand that this sacrament marked a fundamental change in the life of the believer. A number of steps can be taken to help restore this aspect of baptisms. For example, they might be performed only on high feast days, when a large congregation can be expected and when the rite's connection to the central narratives of the faith can be most easily accented. They could occur at night, perhaps illuminated only by candlelight (candles could be extinguished at the moment of the "baptism into Christ's death," and relit from the newly baptized person's baptismal candle). Alternatively, the service could take place in an unusual location, such as a river, or in a particularly expressive form; churches that have opted for sprinkling or pouring might reconsider how much more

---

[38] Edward Yarnold, S.J., *The Awe-Inspiring Rites of Initiation: The Origins of the RCIA*, 2nd edn (Collegeville, Minn.: Liturgical Press, 1994), ix.

thoroughly the life-and-death nature of this rite is accented by the act of immersion.[39]

2   The other conditions necessary for participation in the eucharist can only be articulated theologically, and here denominations have their work cut out for them, since there probably are no such reasons. I have already noted that in my own province (the US Episcopal Church), the basic theological principle is that baptism admits to communion. I have also noted that the distinction between these two rites came about by historical accident. It is now incumbent on all Christian denominations to review their own theological justification of any such separation, asking why certain customs have become so firmly entrenched, and whether they were theologically necessary or merely culturally convenient.

The problems surrounding the current practice of many denominations is well summarized by Robert Jenson:

> The separation of baptism and first communion lacks all justification, and can only be regarded as a catastrophic deprivation, both of the baptized children and of the communing congregation. Whatever arguments could disqualify persons of such-and-such age or attainments from the Supper would disqualify them also from baptism. Moreover, there can be no such arguments; for while there are indeed considerations that tell directly against infant baptism, in the nature of the case there can be nothing against infant communion. The one thing we do well at any age is to participate in fellowship by accepting nourishment.[40]

I do not deny that other arguments have been forwarded in favor of refusing communion to some baptized children, but this is not the place to respond to them. My larger point is that most denominations have not made these arguments well, and many have not made them at all. If authority is to be understood along the lines of persuasion, offering such arguments is a necessary feature of "teaching with authority."

3   Finally, with respect to inclusion and exclusion: it is true, I think, that the eucharist must exclude some in order to remain meaningful. In the ancient Church this was dramatically witnessed by the dismissal of the catechumens; that is, those who had not yet been baptized were not allowed even to view, let alone to participate in, the eucharistic rite. This itself helped underscore the

---

[39] See the helpful commentary as to why baptism should always resemble a *bath* in Jenson, *Visible Words*, 160–2.
[40] Ibid., 164.

cosmic significance of baptism, which was thus recognized as truly life-changing. But exclusion from the eucharist need not mean exclusion from the community; indeed, the very point of this exclusion is to encourage people to consider whether or not they *wish* to be included in such a community. To that end, Christians need to be especially welcoming of those who have not yet been baptized, and see to it that such persons can recognize the Christian community as one in which they might like to take part.

The practices that can most obviously achieve this end are those that embody the trinitarian virtues. The Christian community should embody a polyphonic response to the grace of God, so that outsiders can envision a place for themselves within this strange new world. It should encourage participation in one another's lives; and while this is demonstrated most dramatically through the eucharist, even those who cannot participate in that rite can be given a foretaste of it. This can be achieved through frequent table-fellowship, house-church gatherings, personal visits, and willing offers of assistance to those in need. Finally, the believing community needs to respect particularity – recognizing that each unbaptized person, just like each baptized person, will bring to every encounter with the Church an "active sediment" of experiences and relations, and that this ongoing process will shape and reshape each person's life in a different way. This means that Christians must be willing to meet the outsider where she or he is, listening carefully to the story that each has to tell, and carefully discerning both the resonances and the conflicts between those stories and the Christian narratives of the triune God

These practices, and others like them, can help us take the first steps toward re-imagining Christian authority through the category of persuasion.

Capital punishment

We now turn to a very different example of a teaching that is promulgated authoritatively but is often not received as such. Most Christian denominational bodies teach that capital punishment is wrong, and that Christians should do what they can to protest its use by the state. The positions against capital punishment vary, of course, ranging from absolute denunciations to restrictions of its use to very limited circumstances. The members of the denominations who have promulgated these teachings are often aware of it (though in the United States at least, it is rarely proclaimed with much fervor, perhaps because it is recognized to be singularly unpopular). Though occasionally buttressed with a generic claim about "human rights," official denominational statements about capital punishment are usually fairly clear in their theological rationale; the teachings of Jesus, the supreme authority of God as judge, and the provisional nature of all our knowledge are usually among the most salient features of such statements. Thus, church teachings about capital punishment are different from those about admission to communion, since most Christians are at least aware of the teaching and the rationale for it.[41]

Nevertheless, a large majority of Christians in the United States favor capital punishment; in fact, Christians appear to do so at a slightly higher rate than that of the general population.[42] They also tend to support extremely harsh sentences for offenders. Forgiveness of such persons, or any serious attempt to offer rehabilitation, is often considered out of the question.

What is missing here? Why are these teachings, which are usually encapsulated in carefully-drafted, intelligently-nuanced statements, so widely ignored by the faithful (and indeed by some leaders within the denominations, including priests and bishops)? Why is the culturally popular position, which emphasizes the need to return evil for evil, so much more successful than the Christian call to forgiveness? Here, I think, the answer is clear (and very painful): Christians have largely turned over their ethical formation to non-Christian institutions. For the most part, our ethical lives as Christians are shaped not by the Church, not by the narratives of Christ crucified and risen, not by a belief in the triune God, but by the prevailing winds of culture – and most importantly, by television, the media, and public education.

Let me make it clear, however, that I am not *blaming* these cultural forces for the effect that they have on Christians. They are not responsible to the Christian narrative; they are responsible to those who produce and pay for the products. (These persons may or may not be Christians, but in either case they rarely base their decisions primarily on the ethical teachings of Jesus and the doctrine of the Trinity.) The problem is not with these cultural institutions at all, but with the prevailing Christian attitudes toward them – an attitude that I would characterize as passive, naïve, and largely irresponsible to the Gospel.

Study after study shows that fear of crime, and therefore a willingness to advocate ever harsher measures against criminals, is inaccurately magnified by

[41] This is not to deny that denominational bodies could do more to translate these statements into "aggressive pastoral initiatives to educate clergy and membership on capital punishment," as Sister Helen Prejean argues in *Dead Man Walking* (New York: Random House, Vintage Books, 1993), 124.

[42] James Alan Fox, Michael L. Radalet, and Julie Bonstell, "Death Penalty Opinion in the Post-Furman Years," *New York University Review of Law and Social Change* 18 (1990–1): 499–525; here, table 1, 526–7.

news coverage of the crimes that do occur. This coverage panders to the public's desire for ever more sensational treatment of events, thus creating a vicious circle of escalation of fear and of calls for revenge. By age 18, the average TV-viewing child will often have witnessed many more acts of violence than will occur within a 50-mile radius of that child in his or her lifetime. And over and over again, the same message will be taught – namely, that the answer to this violence is more violence: kill the bad guys.

That the Christian churches have responded to this situation by simply standing by, largely in silence (or with only the occasional ineffective cry of protest), is a painful wounding of the Body of Christ. When the churches have spoken, it is usually against the cultural institution itself – calls for a reduction of violence on television, for example, or complaints about the way crime is covered in the newspapers. What the Church has failed to do is *to persuade its own members* to be formed in those virtues and practices that would resist and counteract the cultural messages that they are constantly being sent. Such practices need to help Christians recognize two important truths. First, the death of Christ puts an end of the cycle of revenge, thus calling into question any cooperation with a system that returns evil for evil (as discussed in chapter 7). Secondly, the criminal, the "other," is still a human being, still capable of repentance and reconciliation, still loved (and judged) by God in ways that we can scarcely imagine. What practices can persuade Christians of the authority of these claims?

These could include, first, some practices of resistance. We need to find real alternatives to the violent television programming that passes for "entertainment" today. The moral content of films needs to become, once again, the topic of Christian conversation (the so-called "rating" system having collapsed into a heap of sellouts to various commercial interests). Newspapers, especially local ones, need to be carefully chosen, and are probably best avoided altogether; after all, the newspaper that Karl Barth believed Christians should hold in one hand (while holding the Bible in the other) was not one in which the primary focus was local gossip, sensational reports of pathological crime, and fashion advertisements. It is simply naïve to expect Christians to be persuaded by the authority of the two or three hours that they devote, each week, to the Christian narrative, while they watch 20 hours of television and 5 hours of film each week, as well as devoting most of their reading energy to the local newspaper and a few magazines. We need to admit that we have often allowed the Christian story to be overshadowed by the maelstrom of cultural voices that point us in fundamentally non-Christian directions. As was the case in our discussion of the reckoning of time in chapter 8, we need to make sure that the Christian perspective on violence, forgiveness, and reconciliation is at least given a hearing *alongside* culturally-dominant voices. This, at least, is a place to start.

But there are also some positive persuasive practices to be mentioned here, and they should take pride of place; for if they were practiced more regularly, there would simply not be enough time for Christians to be shaped by the prevailing winds of network programming. One of the most important of these practices, for the current topic, is the practice of communicating with or visiting those who are in prison. We tend to be more frivolous with the lives of those whom we do not know; thus, one of the best ways to humanize our attitudes toward those who are incarcerated is to get to know them. This is a good example of putting the virtue of *participation* into practice; by sitting down to eat, or at least to talk, with those who are in prison, we begin to recognize the degree to which we are bound together, formed in the image of the triune God.

Another practice is that of prayer. Christian prayer often includes petitions for the forgiveness of sins – both for ourselves and for others as well. Unfortunately these prayers are probably not given adequate content; the petition in the Lord's Prayer, for example, in which we ask God to "forgive us our sins as we forgive those who sin against us," can often become an abstract formula, without concrete shape. But such formulaic prayers can be given specificity through the judicious use of narratives that describe acts of forgiveness.[43]

Consider, for example, the case of Lloyd LeBlanc, whose son David was murdered in Louisiana in 1977. His story is told by Sister Helen Prejean in *Dead Man Walking*. (Reading this book should be added to the list of formative Christian practices on this subject. You saw the film? Fine. But read the book too.) Lloyd LeBlanc tells Sister Helen that

> when he arrived with sheriff's deputies there in the cane field to identify his son, he had knelt by his boy – "laying down there with his two little eyes sticking out like bullets" – and prayed the Our Father. And when he came to the words: "Forgive us our trespasses as we forgive those who trespass against us," he had not halted or equivocated, and he said, "Whoever did this, I forgive them."[44]

How can the petition of a prayer translate into this depth of mercy, this beautiful but almost unimaginable act of forgiveness? It surely will not do so unless we allow these words (as Wittgenstein says) to "make a difference at

---

[43] An important resource here is Jones, *Embodying Forgiveness*.
[44] Prejean, *Dead Man Walking*, 244.

various points in our lives." Only our formation in various practices of forgiveness could possibly prepare us to react as Lloyd LeBlanc reacted. And yet, only if we *are* so formed can we give meaning to the Lord's Prayer, to Jesus' teaching to "love your enemies," and to the Creed's description of our belief in "the forgiveness of sins."

The simple act of putting a concrete narrative together with the prayer itself may go a long way toward forming us in these practices. Since I read that passage in *Dead Man Walking*, I have been unable to say the Lord's Prayer without seeing in my mind the image of this man, kneeling by his dead son, and forgiving those who murdered him. I try to imagine myself doing the same thing with my own children. It is difficult even to imagine. But my own difficulties in praying this prayer are nothing compared to the struggles faced by Lloyd LeBlanc.

> He acknowledges that it's a struggle to overcome the feelings of bitterness and revenge that well up, especially as he remembers David's birthday year by year and loses him all over again: David at twenty, David at twenty-five, David getting married, David standing at the back door with his little ones clustered around his knees, grown-up David, a man like himself, whom he will never know. Forgiveness is never going to be easy. Each day it must be prayed for and struggled for and won.[45]

The Authority of the Crown

To suggest that authority is primarily about persuasion is part of a larger methodological claim – namely, that theology cannot aspire to final, definitive pronouncements. Its authority depends upon its ability to make its case to the faithful. This, of course, makes some people very nervous; for them, the Church has always been an institution that is able to settle those matters about which the world seemed decidedly unsettled. And because postmodern culture has bequeathed to us so very many unsettled matters, there will always be some desire for structures that can declare some "absolutes."

For centuries, such absolutes were delivered by kings and other rulers, and in the modern era by the nation-state. Christians have become accustomed to relying on the "authority of the crown," expecting that matters will be classified as right or wrong, good or bad, with a level of final authority that cannot be questioned (or that has its own internal structures to determine

---

[45] Ibid., 244–5.

precisely when all questioning must stop). As I have noted throughout this chapter, the model of Christian authority in the West has been to a great extent dependent upon this "authority of the crown."

And yet, such structures may not adequately reflect the shape of the Christian vision. At its center is the triune God, the God who is always going forth, giving up everything, risking all for the sake of the Other. This eternal procession is internal to God and defines God's very being; but it is also external, in that God also goes forth into the world. God is born into it, suffers it, dies at its hands – a truth revealed to us in the resurrection of Jesus, this glorious raising up of God by God. And this loving, giving, risk-laden act of "producing the world" is continued through the pouring out of the Living Water on all flesh. A God so willing to put everything at risk for the sake of the Other gains authority from just this willingness; such a God does not need mechanisms of enforcement or the power of violent compulsion to win souls. We see these acts of love and care, and we are already persuaded.

In an article that I have already cited in this chapter, Robert Murray suggests that we should think about the authority of God, and thus of the Church, not on the model of the coercive power of the nation-state, but on the model of the medical profession.[46] We often accept the authority of doctors, even though they have no power to enforce their injunctions by coercion. Rather, we believe that they have the knowledge and the wisdom to make the right decision. Doctors have expressed their personal concern about our well-being by means of an oath. Moreover (at least in the ideal case), we come to know our doctors fairly well, so that a relationship of trust develops over time.

The model is imperfect, of course; doctors are concerned with other matters in addition to our well-being, and some of them may be corrupt or incompetent or worse. But their authority is marked by the practice of persuading, in that – by their character, their words, their gestures, and their specific appeals to their patients – they move us to particular beliefs and practices. And this is how the authority of the Church should operate, for it is also how the authority of God operates. Murray admits the model's imperfections; but he believes that it is a vast improvement over models of authority based on the nation-state. In the closing lines of his article,[47] he remarks that, at the very least, the model of the doctor "has the advantage that Jesus acted as a healer, whereas he never acted as a ruler, though once he wore a crown of a sort."

---

[46] Murray, "Authority in the New Testament," 38.
[47] Ibid.

Epilogue

PROVISIONALITY

Not only in the last chapter, but throughout this book, I have often called into question our desire to find absolute, final, risk-free solutions to the theological problems that we face. In the first part of this book, I challenged some of the time-honored language and assumptions surrounding the doctrine of the Trinity, and urged that it be made more intelligible and persuasive – even if this required an approach (the *vestigia* tradition) that has sometimes threatened to get out of control. In part two, the trinitarian virtues of polyphony, participation, and particularity all implied the importance of some degree of uncertainty and instability: admitting no single dominant melody in music, accepting no notion of an isolated individual who can ultimately be "in charge" of a particular sphere of influence. And in part three, the practices of peacemaking, pluralizing, and persuading tend to call into question any attempt to remain in complete control of circumstances, leading us instead toward perspectives of vulnerability and risk.

The connections among these aspects of the book are not accidental. In my view, the appeal to an absolute, "totalizing" discourse – though it has often characterized Christianity – is ultimately incompatible with the doctrine of the triune God. According to that doctrine, God is always going forth from God, placing the divine essence at risk, loving and seeking the good of the Other in a constant process of abundant mutual donation. And God is always going forth from God, into the world, creating and redeeming and sustaining it – without any assurance that the creatures upon whom these gifts are lavished will offer the slightest bit of gratitude, let alone heartfelt praise and worship, to the One, the Three, who gave these gifts. Can this risk-taking, other-seeking, ultimately *vulnerable* God be used, in any authentic way, as a warrant for theological absolutes?

Many people have often assumed that Christian theology seeks to provide the foundations for such absolutes. That we feel compelled to seek these rock-solid foundations is understandable; life is difficult, the horizon is constantly receding, and we are not sure where to put our feet. This creates anxiety – but it also reminds us that we are gifted with freedom, with hope, with joy. Nietzsche made the point well, with a metaphor that acknowledged both elements at once: "perhaps there has never yet been such an 'open sea'."[1] As Nicholas Lash wisely remarks:

> The search for security, for firm ground under our feet, is indeed a constituent feature of our quest for knowledge . . . [yet] if we would not succumb to illusion, then we cannot afford to lose sight of the fact that the assurance characteristic of living faith in the mystery of God, and of [our] future in God, is quite compatible with the uncertainty, tentativeness, and provisionality that necessarily and painfully mark all forms of the human quest for truth.[2]

And in the end, the "uncertainty, tentativeness, and provisionality" that mark the theological task have something to do with our understanding of God, in whom these Three are One.

This does not mean that theologians can have nothing to say. We can, of course, develop criteria; we can speak of methods, sources, and norms; we can postulate standards and work according to reasonable assumptions. We can point to the biblical narratives, the historic creeds, and the writings of theologians through the ages. The sea in which we are afloat is not a sea of relativism. But theological claims and references do not yield absolute and unrevisable answers to our questions. Our rock, our certainty, is God – not the shifting sands of theological formulation. We may occasionally be led to some provisional and tentative answers; but these answers will, in all likelihood, be swept away by a future generation of interpreters who are more wise and intelligent (and better grounded in trinitarian virtues and practices) than are we. Moreover, *most* of our theological investigations do not even lead to *tentative* answers. Mostly, they lead to more questions.

I once believed that this was merely a feature of our creaturely state; that, when we "see face to face," all the provisionality and tentativeness would fall away. And perhaps it will. But the more I think about the mystery of the triune God – the dynamic activity of procession and convergence, the vulnerability and the risk, the eternal process of profound self-giving and abundant love – the more I wonder. After all, Paul's claim that we will see God "face to face,"

---

[1] Friedrich Nietzsche, *The Gay Science*, trans. Walter Kaufmann (New York: Random House, Vintage Books, 1974), 280 [ET of: *Die fröhliche Wissenschaft* (Leipzig: E. W. Fritzsch, 1887), sect. 343].

[2] Lash, *Voices of Authority*, 100.

while certainly a very intimate image, implies not the slightest evacuation of the risk, tentativity, and love that have marked every face-to-face encounter that we have experienced thus far. Even the most intimate encounters, and perhaps especially these, are filled with tentativity, and provisionality, and risk. If the "beatific vision" (which is said to mark our ultimate experience of the presence of God) means being somehow joined to God, does this necessarily mean that all uncertainties will vanish? Or might it not mean that the provisionality that we experience today, in human terms, will continue to be experienced – but now in divine terms? That we will know something of what it might mean, not only to put our merely *human* selves at risk, but to put the divine self at risk? That we might know, in addition to the painful uncertainty of our limited range of human loves, the extravagant uncertainty of extravagant Love?

I hope so. For despite the praise that has been sung, throughout the history of Christian thought, to the certainty, the absolute knowledge, and the final rest that transpire in the beatific vision, it does sometimes sound just a trifle *boring*. It would be rather disappointing to discover that, having finally arrived at one's proper destination, one had nothing left to risk.

Appendix I

RECENT WORKS IN TRINITARIAN THEOLOGY

Making selections for a bibliography such as this is difficult. Keeping in mind that it is mainly intended to guide students and other non-specialists to recent work in the field, I have restricted it to works that meet the following criteria:

- They were written in (or have been translated into) English.
- They were written within the last thirty years.
- They cover the doctrine broadly (this listing omits studies of any one very specialized point within trinitarian theology).
- In the case of a collection of articles, all (or almost all) the articles focus on trinitarian doctrine.

Of the books that meet these criteria, *some* are listed below.

Each text is placed into one of three categories. "Introductory" (I) describes those works that can serve as a student's first introduction to the subject. "Advanced" (A) assumes some knowledge of the doctrine, but is still reasonably accessible to students. "Technical" (T) requires a fairly deep grounding in the technical aspects of trinitarian doctrine, and is mainly intended for advanced graduate students and scholars. The "border-regions" between these categories are noted by the designations I/A and A/T.

Leonardo Boff, *Trinity and Society*, trans. Paul Burns (Tunbridge Wells: Burnes and Oates; Maryknoll, NY: Orbis Books, 1988) [ET of: *A Trinidade, a Sociedade e a Libertação*, 3rd edn (Petrópolis: Editora Vozes, 1987)]

> *A comprehensive account of the doctrine, with special attention to its potential for the liberation of the poor and the oppressed. (I/A)*

David Brown, *The Divine Trinity* (LaSalle, Ill.: Open Court Publishing, 1985)

An attempt to ground trinitarian doctrine in anglo-American analytic philosophy. (T)

Mary Ann Fatula, O.P., *The Triune God of Christian Faith*, Zacchaeus Studies: Theology, ed. Monika K. Hellwig (Collegeville, Minn.: Liturgical Press, Michael Glazier Books, 1990)

A very basic introduction from a Roman Catholic perspective. (I)

Colin Gunton, *The Promise of Trinitarian Theology* (Edinburgh: T. & T. Clark, 1990)

A series of individual studies rather than a unified argument, advocating a trinitarian perspective but highly critical of certain strands in its development (especially the contributions of Augustine). (A)

Colin Gunton, *The One, the Three and the Many: God, Creation and the Culture of Modernity* (Cambridge: Cambridge University Press, 1993)

A description of the relationships between trinitarian doctrine and the wider sweep of intellectual history. (A)

William J. Hill, O.P., *The Three-Personed God: The Trinity and a Mystery of Salvation* (Washington, D.C.: Catholic University of America Press, 1982)

A technical account of the doctrine, with attention to the history of its development (especially in St Thomas Aquinas) but also heavily influenced by existentialism and process thought. (T)

Robert W. Jenson, *The Triune Identity: God According to the Gospel* (Philadelphia: Fortress Press, 1982)

A philosophically rigorous inquiry into the traditional doctrine and an account of some of its little-explored implications. (T)

Elizabeth A. Johnson, *She Who Is: The Mystery of God in Feminist Theological Discourse* (New York: Crossroad, 1992)

An examination of some of the classical claims of the doctrine with attention to feminist claims and hermeneutical strategies. (A)

Eberhard Jüngel, *The Doctrine of the Trinity: God's Being is in Becoming*, trans. Horton Harris (Edinburgh: Scottish Academic Press, Ltd., 1976) [ET of: *Gottes sein ist im Werden*, 2e. Aufl. (Tübingen: J. C. B. Mohr, Paul Siebeck, 1966)]

A "paraphrase" of Karl Barth's trinitarian doctrine by means of a thorough reading of the Church Dogmatics. (T)

Eberhard Jüngel, *God as the Mystery of the World*, trans. Darrell L. Guder (Grand Rapids, Mich.: William B. Eerdmans, 1983) [ET of: *Gott als Geheimnis der Welt*, 3e. Aufl. (Tübingen: J. C. B. Mohr, Paul Siebeck, 1977)]

Jüngel's own trinitarian perspective, taking seriously the effects of Enlightenment assumptions about God on the historical sojourn of the doctrine. (T)

Walter Kasper, *The God of Jesus Christ*, trans. Matthew J. O'Connell (London: SCM Press, 1983) [ET of: *Der Gott Jesu Christi* (Mainz: Matthias Grünewald Verlag, 1982)]

> *A thorough exploration of the doctrine, which (like Jüngel) pays close attention to the ongoing effects of modern atheism, but from an ecumenically-oriented Roman Catholic perspective. (A/T)*

Catherine Mowry LaCugna, *God For Us: The Trinity and Christian Life* (San Francisco: Harper/Collins, 1991)

> *A recapitulation of the historical development of the doctrine, with an appreciation for its grounding in salvation history and a sharp polemic against speculative accounts of the interior life of God. The second half of the book offers some initial observations on the doctrine's practical ramifications. (A)*

Nicholas Lash, *Believing Three Ways In One God: A Reading of the Apostles' Creed* (Notre Dame, Ind.: University of Notre Dame Press, 1992)

> *Not (strictly speaking) a theology of the Trinity, but rather an explication of the Creed that gives considerable attention to trinitarian questions. The book requires no detailed theological background, but its author assumes a readership with a reasonably high level of general education. (I)*

James P. Mackey, *The Christian Experience of God as Trinity* (London: SCM Press, 1983)

> *A somewhat idiosyncratic interpretation, ultimately questioning the need for anything like a doctrine of the Trinity as it is classically conceived. (A)*

Thomas Marsh, *The Triune God: a Biblical, Historical, and Theological Study* (Dublin: Columba Press; Mystic, Conn.: Twenty-Third Publications, 1994)

> *A general introduction to the doctrine from a broad Roman Catholic perspective. The author is aware of questions of gender and language and is open to new and creative solutions. (I)*

Alister E. McGrath, *Understanding the Trinity* (Grand Rapids, Mich.: Zondervan Publishing House, Academie Books, 1988)

> *A very basic introduction from an Evangelical perspective. (I)*

Jürgen Moltmann, *History and the Triune God: Contributions to Trinitarian Theology*, trans. John Bowden (New York: Crossroad, 1992) [ET of: *In der Geschichte des dreieinigen Gottes. Beiträge zur trinitarischen Theologie* (München: Christian Kaiser Verlag, 1991)]

> *A collection of essays on various themes of current interest, including several on matters of gender and politics. Can be read independently of Moltmann's major work on the Trinity (see next entry). (A)*

Jürgen Moltmann, *The Trinity and the Kingdom: The Doctrine of God*, trans. Margaret Kohl (New York: Harper and Row, 1981) [ET of: *Trinität und Reich Gottes* (München: Christian Kaiser Verlag, 1980)]

> *Slightly more accessible than Jüngel and Kasper, but still providing a fairly thorough overview*

of trinitarian doctrine. The book attempts to unpack Moltmann's claim (in The Crucified God*) that trinitarian doctrine has important practical implications for political life. (A/T)*

Ted Peters, *GOD as Trinity: Relationality and Temporality in Divine Life* (Louisville: Westminster/John Knox Press, 1993)

A general introduction to the central issues, an author-by-author account of current contributions, and a final section on some specific technical issues. (I/A)

Karl Rahner, *The Trinity*, trans. Joseph Donceel (New York: Herder and Herder, 1970) [ET of: "Der dreifaltige Gott als transzendenter Urgrund der Heilsgeschichte," chapter in *Mysterium Salutis: Grundriss heilsgeschichtlicher Dogmatik*, ed. Johannes Feiner and Magnus Löhrer, vol. 2, *Die Heilsgeschichte vor Christus* (Einsiedeln: Benziger Verlag, 1967), 317-404.]

An important but technical inquiry into the relevance of the doctrine for modern theology from a philosophically-sophisticated and ecumenically-open Roman Catholic perspective. (T)

Christoph Schwöbel, ed., *Trinitarian Theology Today: Essays on Divine Being and Act* (Edinburgh: T. & T. Clark, 1995)

A series of essays by several important trinitarian theologians, some of them expounding ideas developed elsewhere but offered here in a more condensed form. (A/T)

Alan J. Torrance, *Persons in Communion: Trinitarian Description and Human Participation* (Edinburgh: T. & T. Clark, 1996)

A more specific inquiry, defending the suitability of the word person *to describe the Three, relying very heavily on the work of Karl Barth. (T)*

Thomas F. Torrance, *The Christian Doctrine of God: One Being Three Persons* (Edinburgh: T. & T. Clark, 1995)

An introduction to the patristic roots of the doctrine, assuming no prior theological knowledge – but not conversant with the current conversation, and not written in a very user-friendly style. (I/A)

Thomas G. Weinandy, O.F.M.Cap., *The Father's Spirit of Sonship: Reconceiving the Trinity* (Edinburgh: T. & T. Clark, 1994)

A specific inquiry into the relation of the Spirit to the other Two of the Three, which attempts to work through the problems surrounding the filioque *controversy, but without much attention to the processions and relations from which trinitarian theology developed. (T)*

Appendix II

GLOSSARY OF FOREIGN WORDS AND PHRASES

Each entry begins with a page number (on which the word first appears), followed by the word, a transliteration, and the most common English translation(s) of the word. I then offer a brief description of the problems of these common translations.

5: יהוה, *YHWH*, Yahweh or the Lord or God. The etymology in the text of Exodus 3:14 suggests something like "I am who (or what) I am" or "I will be what I will be"; the general sense seems to accent divine freedom and sovereignty. Most modern translations show the appearance of this word by printing "the LORD" in small capitals. The four Hebrew letters took on an aura of mystery and reverence, such that the name was not usually pronounced in readings of the Torah. Leaving the letters untransliterated seems the best way to preserve all these elements.

25: οὐσία, *ousia*, being or substance. This word traditionally described that of which there was only one in God. At the time it was already a very equivocal term; later questions about substantialist metaphysics have made its resonances unclear.

27: τρόπος ὑπάρξεως, *tropos hyparxeōs*, mode of existence. The word *mode* makes this description of the Three sound modalist, but the original Greek doesn't seem to have this tendency. I suggest a focus on the rhetorical reference of the word *tropos* as a figure of speech, and translate "figures of speech for specifying the orientation of activity" in God. See chapter 6 for a thorough discussion.

27: ὑπόστασις, *hypostasis*, person or hypostasis. The word is more or less untranslatable into English, which is why I simply refer to "the Three" instead of "three hypostases" or "persons." See the discussion in chapter 1.

71: πατήρ, *patēr*, father. The New Testament records this word as a name for God and/or for one of the Three, namely the one usually referred to in this book as "the Source." The word attempts to translate a traditional Aramaic word that Jesus apparently used in prayer and other references to God, but the lines of translation are muddled. The current English translation is enormously complicated by the masculine associations of the word *father*, as well as the deep-seated patriarchal symbolism of much Christian art and language. See the discussion in chapter 2, and my article "On Translating the Divine Name"; see also Duck, *Gender and the Name of God;* Geitz, *Gender and the Nicene Creed;* and Johnson, *She Who Is.*

78: πνεῦμα, *pneuma,* Spirit or wind or breath. This Greek word, as well as its Hebrew counterpart (רוּחַ), opened up a wide range of figurative connections between breath and the divine. It is very evocative language, and I continue to employ it; my primary reason for employing "Living Water" to designate the "Holy Spirit" is its coherence with the water-related imagery of "Source" and "Wellspring."

81: υἱός, *huios,* son. In addition to the general points about the patriarchal associations of the language (see under πατήρ, above), this word is additionally complicated by the fact that Jesus was in fact a male human being, and so the connection of the word *Son* to him in particular tends to reinforce the strongly masculine associations that the word evokes, thereby attributing gender to God.

115: περιχώρησις, *perichōrēsis,* coinherence or interpenetration. See the extended discussion in chapter 5.

117: ἦθος, *ēthos,* character; λόγος, *logos,* word; πάθος, *pathos,* emotion. These signified the three "means of persuasion" in Aristotle's *Rhetoric.*

141: אֱלֹהִים, *elohim,* God. The Hebrew word is a plural, which is masked by the usual translation; moreover, since the word *God* is used to translate a variety of different Hebrew words, it tends to mask the variety of divine names in the Old Testament.

141: רוּחַ, *ruach,* spirit. See the comments under πνεῦμα, above.

142: אָדָם, *adam,* man or Adam. The Hebrew word can mean human beings of either sex, whereas the English *man* is now much more commonly restricted to males, and *Adam* is a given name for males. While original Hebrew-speaking readers undoubtedly understood the first human creature described in Genesis 2 as male, their language allowed them to see a difference between this creature and the specifically male and female creatures that God makes in Genesis 2:21–22.

142: אִישׁ, *ish,* man; אִשָּׁה, *ishshah,* woman. These two words denote sexual differentiation, and are different from the word used to describe the solitary, undifferentiated creature of Genesis 2:7–21.

145: νόμος, *nomos*, law; תּוֹרָה, *Torah*, law. The contemporary connotations of the word *law*, which almost always involve rule and restriction, fail to evoke the gift-oriented associations of the Torah for the Hebrew people. See the discussion in chapter 4.

168: ἐκκλησία, *ekklēsia*, church. The Greek root clearly suggests a "calling out" or "setting apart" of a particular group, indicating some sort of distinction between the members of the Church and the wider culture. This distinction is often lost today, given various established churches and the co-optation of the Church for political purposes. Matters are further complicated by the use of the same word to mean the people, the building, the worship service, and the bureaucracy of the churches.

182: κοινωνία, *koinōnia*, fellowship. See the discussion in chapter 6.

211: אֵל שַׁדַּי, *El Shaddai*, and אֵל, *El*, both usually translated God. See the comments under אֱלֹהִים, above.

212: ὁ υἱὸς τοῦ ἀνθρώπου, *ho huios tou anthrōpou*, the Son of Man or the Human One. The last word is a Greek word for all human beings, male and female, and its continuing translation as English *man*, both in this phrase and in other contexts, provides a wholly unwarranted increase in the patriarchal associations of the texts. This phrase in particular is described as Jesus' self-reference, and may have had messianic overtones, depending on one's interpretation of Daniel 7 and various rabbinic writings. For a thorough treatment see Barnabas Lindars, *Jesus – Son of Man* (London: SPCK, 1983).

212: παράκλητος, *paraklētos*, paraclete or advocate. A verbal name given to the Living Water (Holy Spirit), which in itself offered something of an appropriation of a particular activity (advocacy, pleading a person's case to another) to this particular one of the Three.

212: מָשִׁיחַ, *messiah*, messiah, and Χριστός, *Christos*, Christ or messiah. The main point here is that the word *Christ* would have had, for Jewish audiences, strong resonances to the (highly contested) notion of a messiah – somewhat obscured by our use of the words "Jesus Christ" as a name.

213: בְּנִי, *ben*, son. While Hebrew culture would have put greater stock in the birth of a son than in a daughter, current sensibilities do not usually reflect this bias; thus the exclusive translation of the word as a male reference may obscure the point being made by the interpretation of the passage.

216: ἀγέννητος, *agennētos*, unbegotten. The Late Arian controversy, especially in the work of Eunomius, attempted to offer this Greek word as the one and only name for God. Against this position, the Cappadocians and others argued that God has many names, and that if this word is to be attributed to God it applies only to one of the Three, namely the Source.

216:   ἰδιότης, *idiotēs*, particularity. See the discussion in chapter 6.

239:   שָׁלוֹם, *shalom*, and εἰρήνη, *eirēnē*, both translated "peace." See the discussion in chapter 7.

Appendix III

LITURGICAL RESOURCES

At a number of points in this book, I have introduced new language for some of the standard elements of Trinitarian discourse. *Some* of this language may be usable in *some* aspects of Christian worship. I here offer a brief compilation of some of this material. I offer it without comment; the justification for much of the language offered here is developed at length in the book as a whole, and should not be examined in isolation from that justification.

Words that appear in [square brackets] may be useful as transitional language, to be added (at least temporarily) by those communities that choose to adopt new language and want to incorporate certain elements of the worship texts with which they are more familiar.

The Nicene Creed

We believe in one God
[The Father,] The Source, the all-powerful,
Creator of heaven and earth,
Of all that is, seen and unseen.

We believe in one Lord, Jesus Christ,
the [only Son and] sole Wellspring of God,
eternally brought forth by [the Father,] the Source,
God from God, Light from Light,
true God from true God,
brought forth by birth, not merely made;
of one being with the Source,
and through whom all things were made.
Who, for us and for our salvation
Came down from heaven,
And became incarnate
by the Holy Spirit and the virgin Mary
and was born a human being.

For our sake he was crucified under Pontius Pilate,
he suffered death and was buried.
On the third day, he rose again
in accordance with the Scriptures;
he ascended into heaven
And is accorded the place of honor, equal to that of the Source.
Christ will come again in glory to judge the living and the dead
and God's Reign will have no end.

We believe in the [Holy Spirit,] Living Water,
the Lord and Giver of Life,
emerging from the Source,★
who with the Source and the Wellspring is worshipped and glorified,
who has spoken through the prophets.
We believe in one, holy, catholic, and apostolic Church;
We acknowledge one baptism for the forgiveness of sins;
We look for the resurrection of the dead
And the life of the world to come.

★ If the *filioque* clause is to be retained, the words "and the Wellspring" can be added here.

PRAYER OVER THE WATER AT BAPTISM

We thank you, Almighty God, for the gift of water. Over water the Holy Spirit moved in the beginning of creation. Through water you led the children of Israel out of their bondage in Egypt into the land of promise. In water your Son Jesus received the baptism of John and was anointed by the Holy Spirit as the Messiah, the Christ, to lead us, through his death and resurrection, from the bondage of sin into everlasting life.

Born into this word to deliver us from sin, you indwelt in the waters of Mary's womb; walking upon the earth, you did signs and wonders with the water that became wine, and with the waters of the deep; dying on the Cross you poured forth water with your blood.

We thank you, [Father and] Source of All, for the water of Baptism. In water we are buried with Jesus Christ in death. By water we share in his resurrection. Through water we are reborn by the Holy Spirit.

Therefore in joyful obedience to Jesus Christ our Lord we bring into your fellowship those who come to you in faith, baptizing them in the name of [the Father, the Son, and the Holy Spirit:] the Source, the Wellspring, and the Living Water.

HYMN

Three And One

Tune: BARRETT 8.7.8.7
Copyright ©1997 by David S. Cunningham

Words copyright ©1997 by
David S. Cunningham

1. God the Source of all a - round us,
2. Je - sus Christ, the son of Ma - ry,
3. Ho - ly Spir - it, Liv - ing Wa - ter,
4. Source and Well - spring Liv - ing Wa - ter,

Earth, and seas, and stars a - bove:
Well - spring of the one true Source:
Bear - rer of all earth - ly care:
Three in One and One in Three:

Grant us grace that we may hon - or
From your moth - er's womb you loved us,
Teach us how to love each oth - er,
With your love, en - fold, in - dwell us,

All you give in per - fect love.
From the cross your mer - cy pours.
Make our lives a con - stant pray'r.
Mend our hearts and set us free.

This hymn may be photocopied for use by a congregation without permission or fees.

INDEX OF NAMES

Note: This index includes many biblical names as well as ancient and modern authors and translators. It also includes many of the more frequently-referenced names for God; Greek and Hebrew are transliterated for purposes of alphabetization. Boldface references indicate relatively sustained discussions of an author or name. An asterisk (*) indicates that the author's recent work on trinitarian theology appears in Appendix I.

INDEX OF SCRIPTURAL CITATIONS

INDEX OF SUBJECTS

Note: Most foreign words and phrases appear under several possible translations, cross-referenced to one another (see Appendix II for a partial listing). Page numbers followed by *n* refer to a footnote; if followed by +*n*, the subject is discussed both in a note and in the text (but these are often omitted in references across several pages). Citations to the Index of Names and Index of Scriptural Citations are abbreviated ION and IOSC, respectively. N.B.: Names, *including names for God*, are listed only in the Index of Names.